Say I Love You. volume 14 is a work of fiction. Names, characters, places, and incidents are the products of the author's imagination or are used fictitiously. Any resemblance to actual events, locales, or persons, living or dead, is entirely coincidental.

A Kodansha Comics Trade Paperback Original
Say I Love You. volume 14 copyright © 2015 Kanae Hazuki
English translation copyright © 2016 Kanae Hazuki

Published in the United States by Kodansha Comics, an imprint of Kodansha USA Publishing, LLC, New York.

Publication rights for this English edition arranged through Kodansha Ltd, Tokyo.

First published in Japan in 2015 by Kodansha Ltd., Tokyo as *Sukitte iinayo.* volume 14.

ISBN 978-1-63236-268-1

Printed in the United States of America.

www.kodanshacomics.com

9 8 7 6 5 4 3 2 1
Translation: Alethea and Athena Nibley
Lettering: Jennifer Skarupa
Editing: Ajani Oloye
Kodansha Comics Edition Cover Design: Phil Balsman

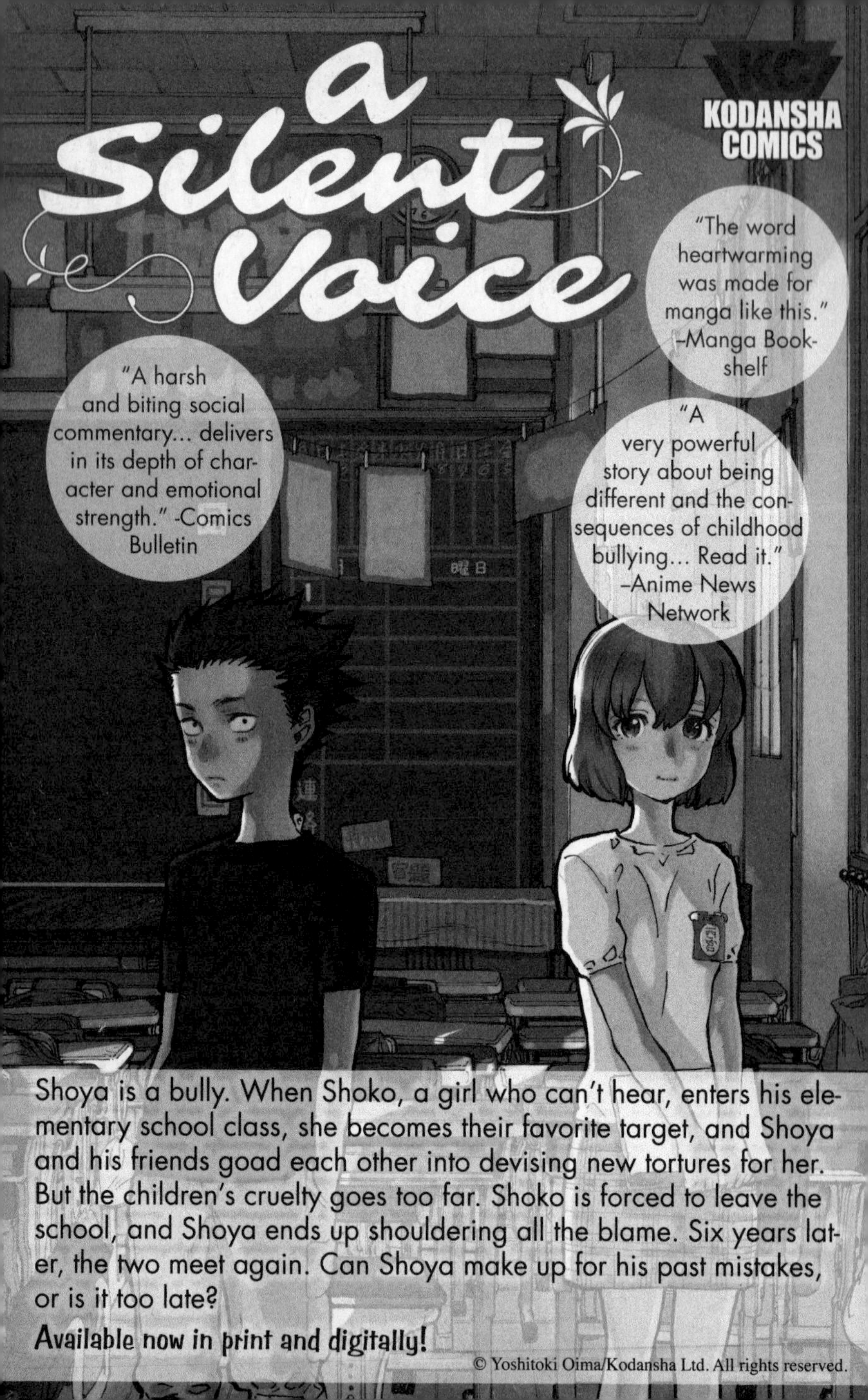
a Silent Voice
KODANSHA COMICS
"The word heartwarming was made for manga like this." –Manga Bookshelf
"A harsh and biting social commentary... delivers in its depth of character and emotional strength." -Comics Bulletin
"A very powerful story about being different and the consequences of childhood bullying... Read it." –Anime News Network
Shoya is a bully. When Shoko, a girl who can't hear, enters his elementary school class, she becomes their favorite target, and Shoya and his friends goad each other into devising new tortures for her. But the children's cruelty goes too far. Shoko is forced to leave the school, and Shoya ends up shouldering all the blame. Six years later, the two meet again. Can Shoya make up for his past mistakes, or is it too late?
Available now in print and digitally!
© Yoshitoki Oima/Kodansha Ltd. All rights reserved.

Say I Love You.

by
Kanae
Hazuki

14

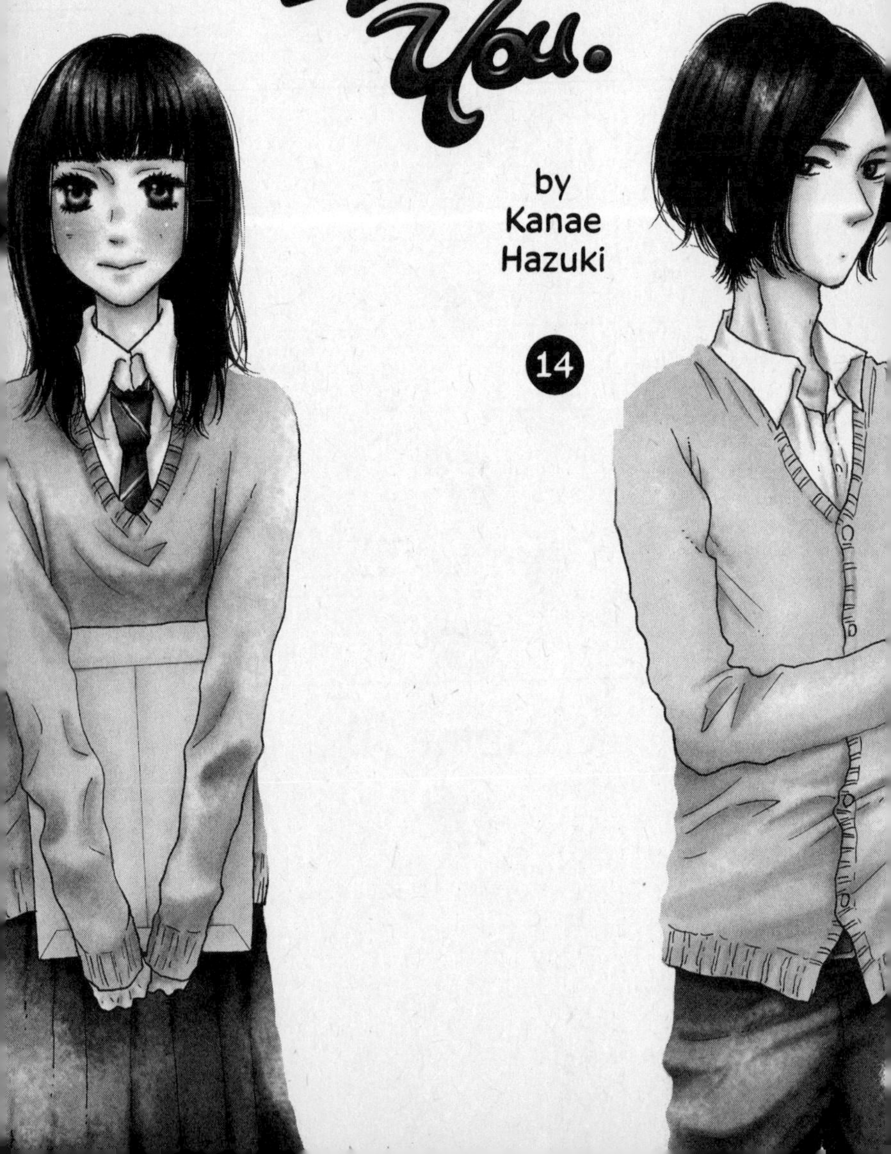

Kanae Hazuki
presents

Chapter 53

Chapter 54

Chapter 55

Chapter 56

CHARACTER

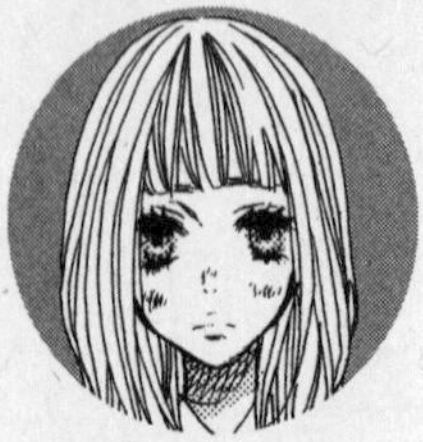

Mei Tachibana

A girl who hasn't had a single friend, let alone a boyfriend, in sixteen years, and has lived her life trusting no one. She finds herself attracted to Yamato, who, for some reason, just won't leave her alone, and they start dating.

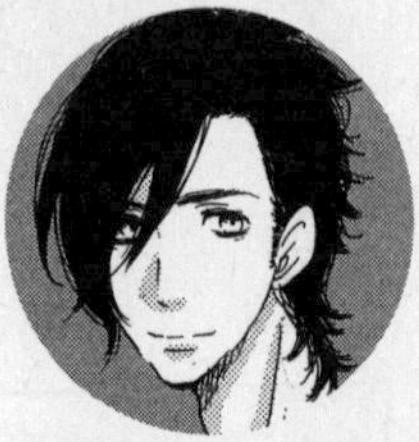

Yamato Kurosawa

The most popular boy at Mei's school. He has the love of many girls, yet for some reason, he is obsessed with Mei, the brooding weirdo girl from another class. ♡

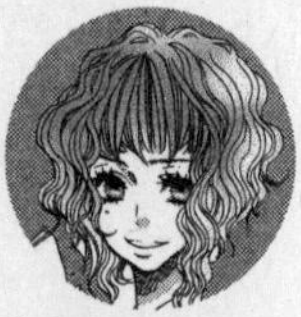

Megumi

A popular amateur model. She had her sights set on Yamato, but he rejected her. She has set off on her own for Paris to advance her modeling career.

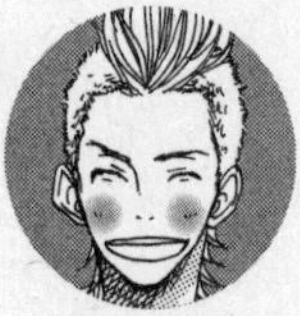

Kai

Yamato's classmate from middle school who had been the victim of bullying. For his own reasons, he started high school a year late. He likes Mei and told her so, but...?

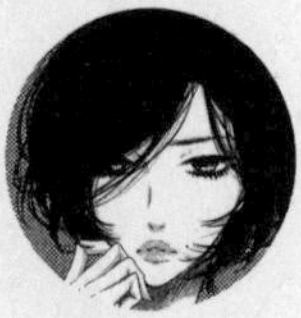

Rin Aoi

A first-year student at Mei's school, who is currently modeling under the name RIN. She fell in love with Kai at first sight, and told him how she feels. Now they are dating, but...?

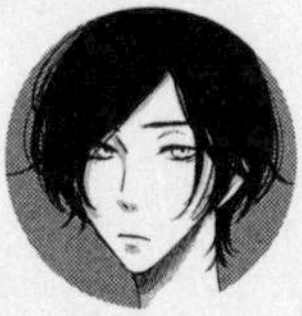

Ren Aoi

Rin's twin brother. The complete opposite of his social sister, he is rather unfriendly, but has a kind side. He introduced Mei to a preschool where she could volunteer.

STORY

Mei Tachibana spent sixteen years without a single friend or boyfriend, but now she's starting the third year of her relationship with Yamato Kurosawa, the most popular boy in her school. Now third-year high school students, the two struggle to decide what to do with their futures, and Mei takes an interest in working in childcare, while Yamato decides to pursue photography. New students, the twins Rin and Ren, become a part of their circle, and Rin starts officially dating Kai after going on to Land on a date with him. Meanwhile, Megumi takes advantage of her summer vacation to go to Paris. She struggles to find an agency in France, but she encounters a certain photographer and...?!

Say "I love you".

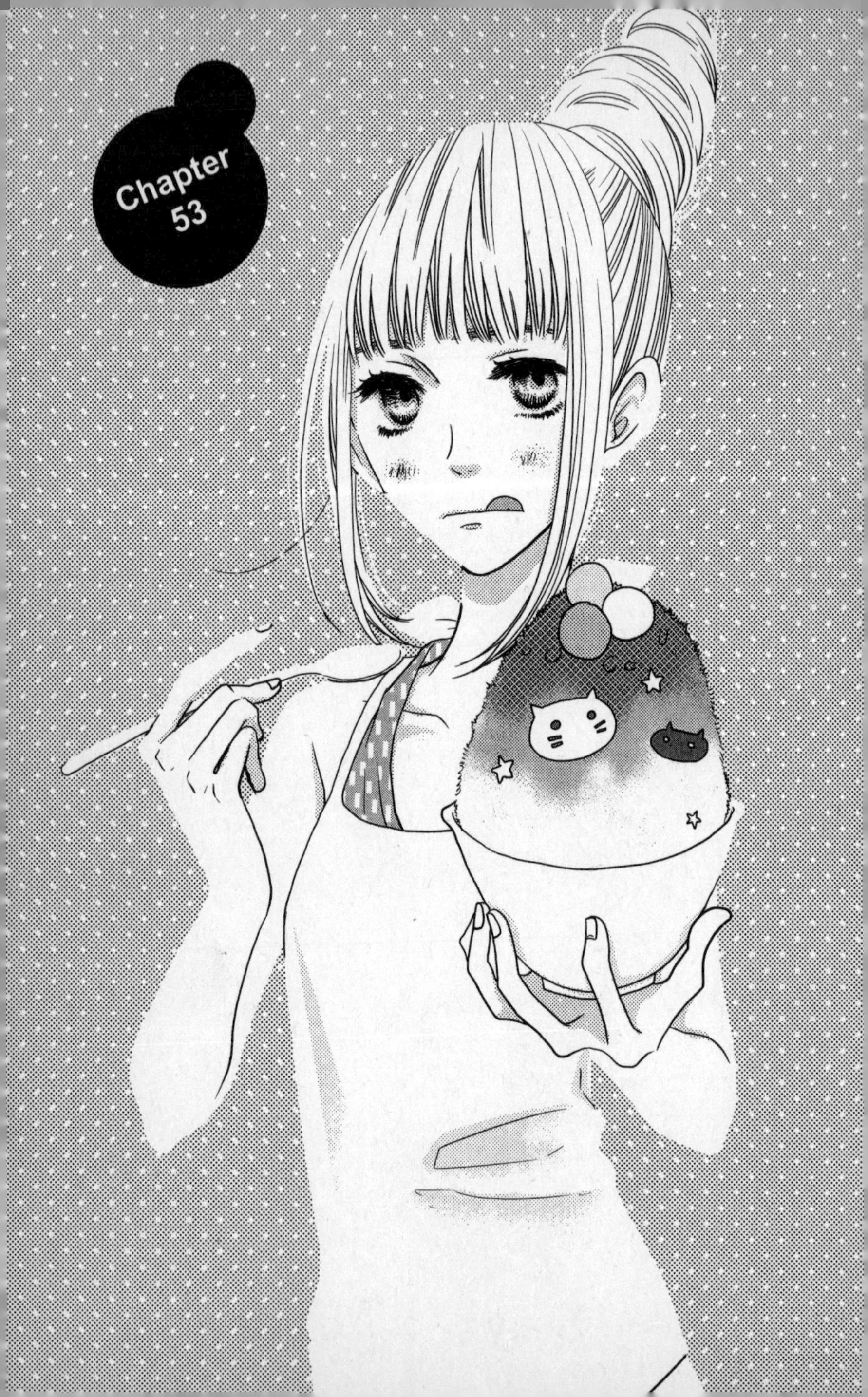
Chapter
53

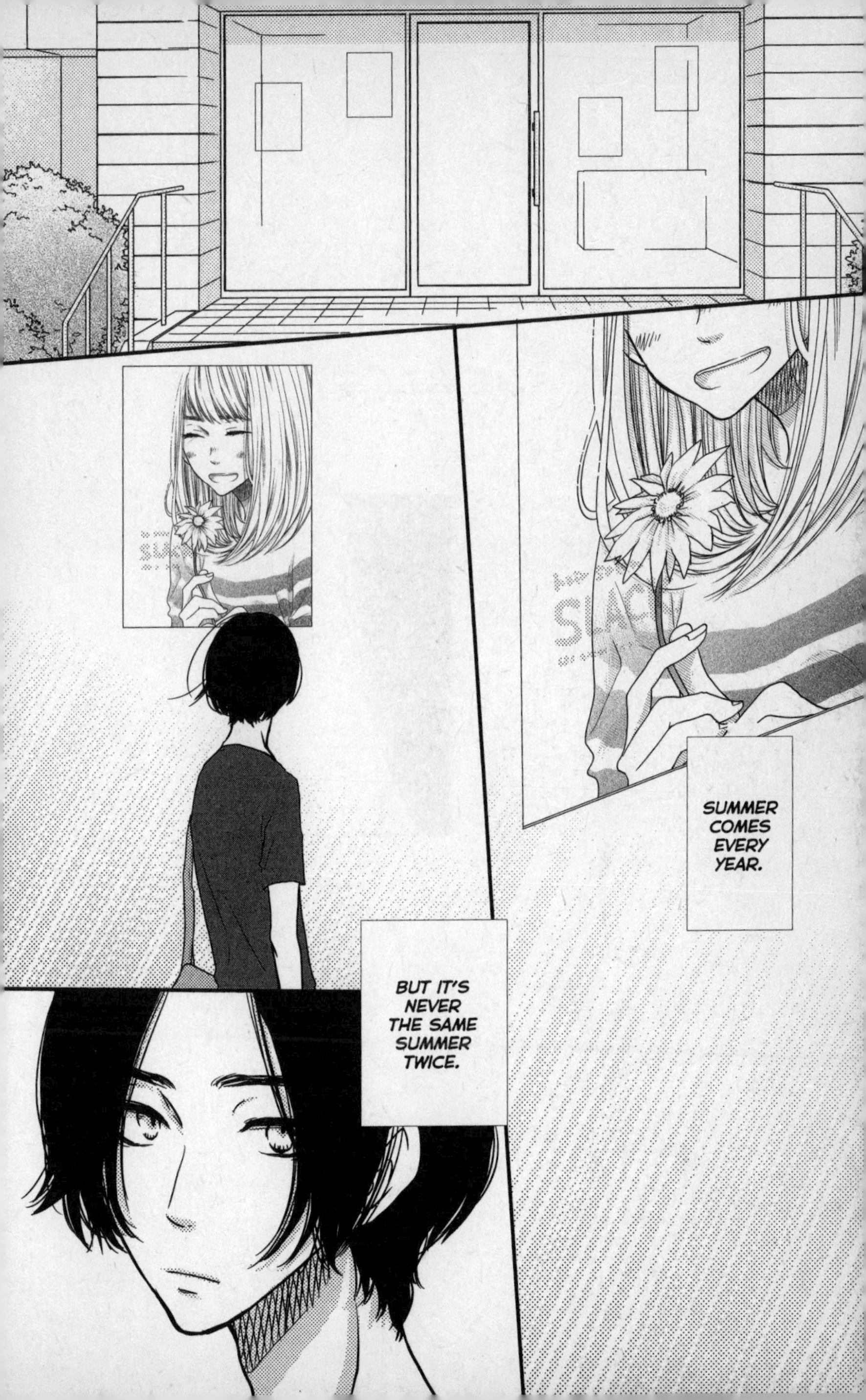
SUMMER COMES EVERY YEAR.
BUT IT'S NEVER THE SAME SUMMER TWICE.

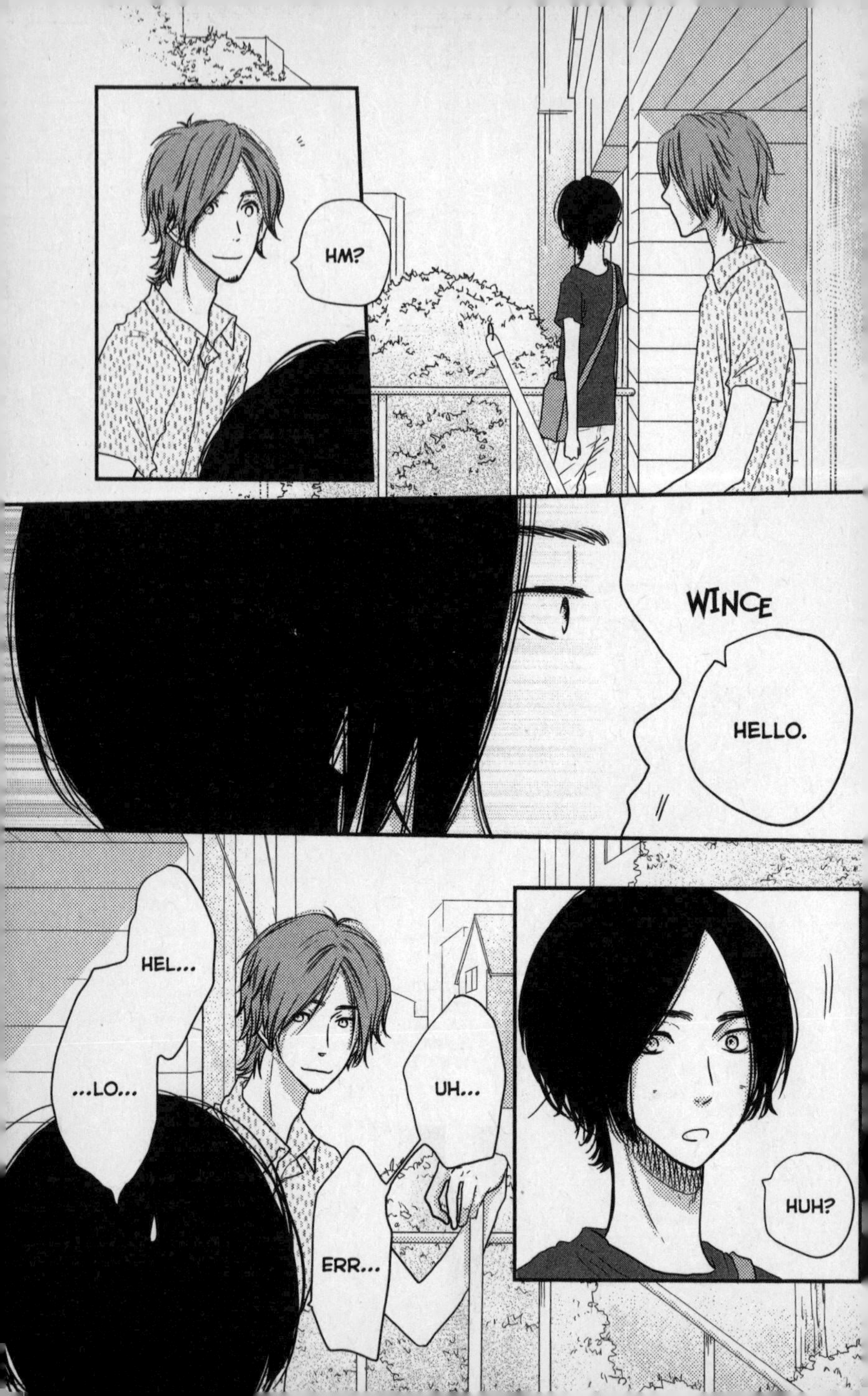
HM?
WINCE
HELLO.
HUH?
HEL...
...LO...
UH...
ERR...

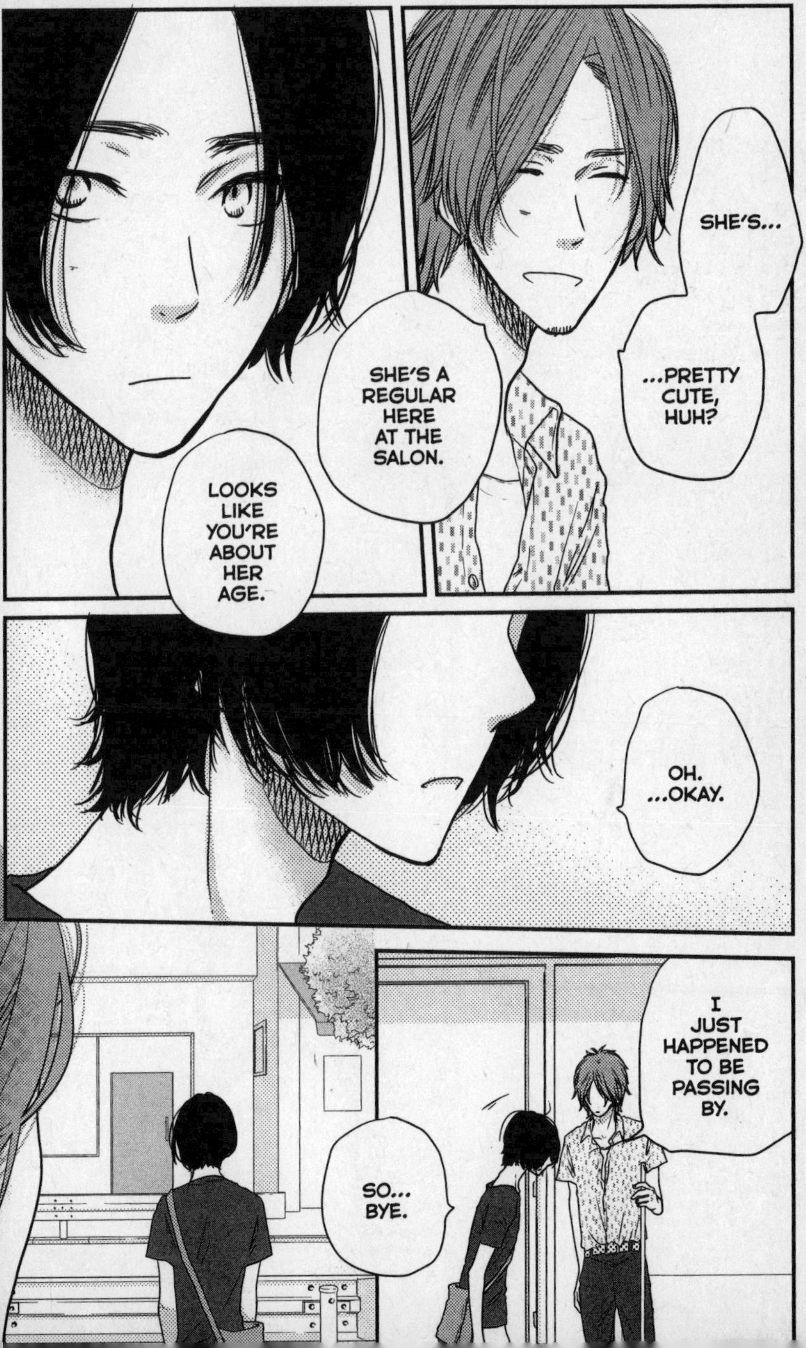
SHE'S...
...PRETTY CUTE, HUH?
SHE'S A REGULAR HERE AT THE SALON.
LOOKS LIKE YOU'RE ABOUT HER AGE.
OH. ...OKAY.
I JUST HAPPENED TO BE PASSING BY.
SO... BYE.

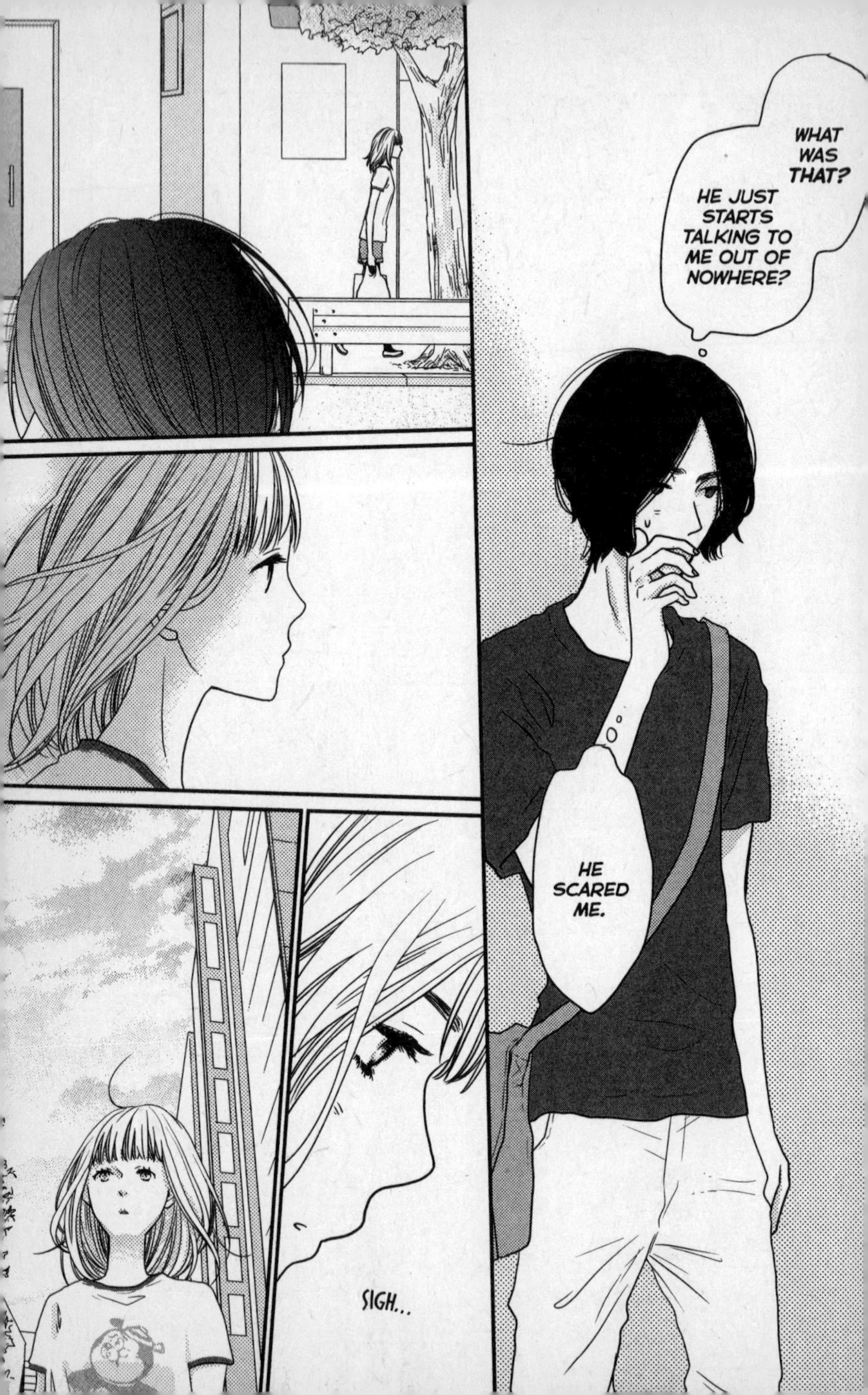
WHAT WAS THAT?
HE JUST STARTS TALKING TO ME OUT OF NOWHERE?
HE SCARED ME.
SIGH...

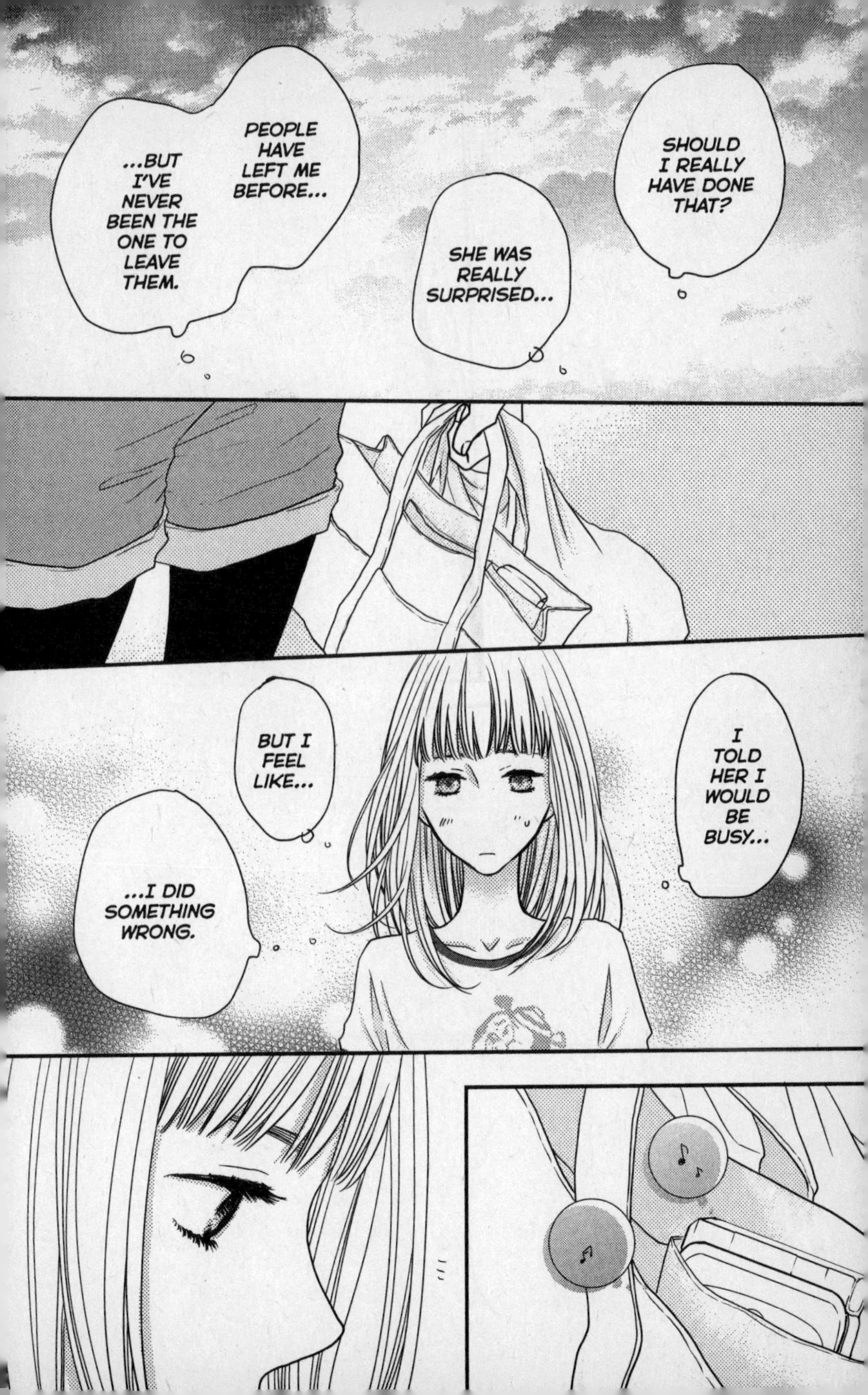
SHOULD I REALLY HAVE DONE THAT?
SHE WAS REALLY SURPRISED...
PEOPLE HAVE LEFT ME BEFORE...
...BUT I'VE NEVER BEEN THE ONE TO LEAVE THEM.
I TOLD HER I WOULD BE BUSY...
BUT I FEEL LIKE...
...I DID SOMETHING WRONG.

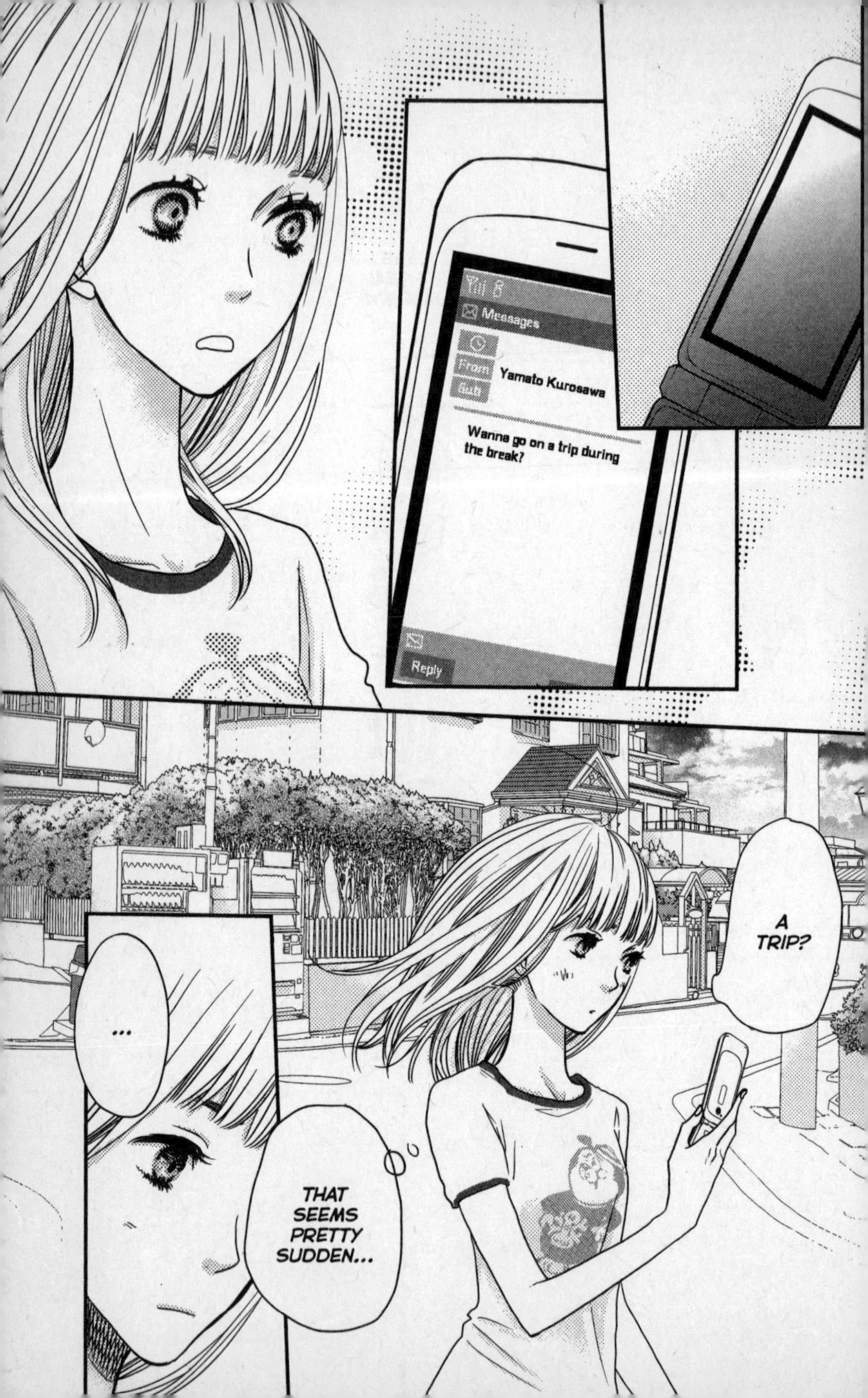

Messages
From
Sub
Yamato Kurosawa
Wanna go on a trip during the break?
Reply
A TRIP?
...
THAT SEEMS PRETTY SUDDEN...

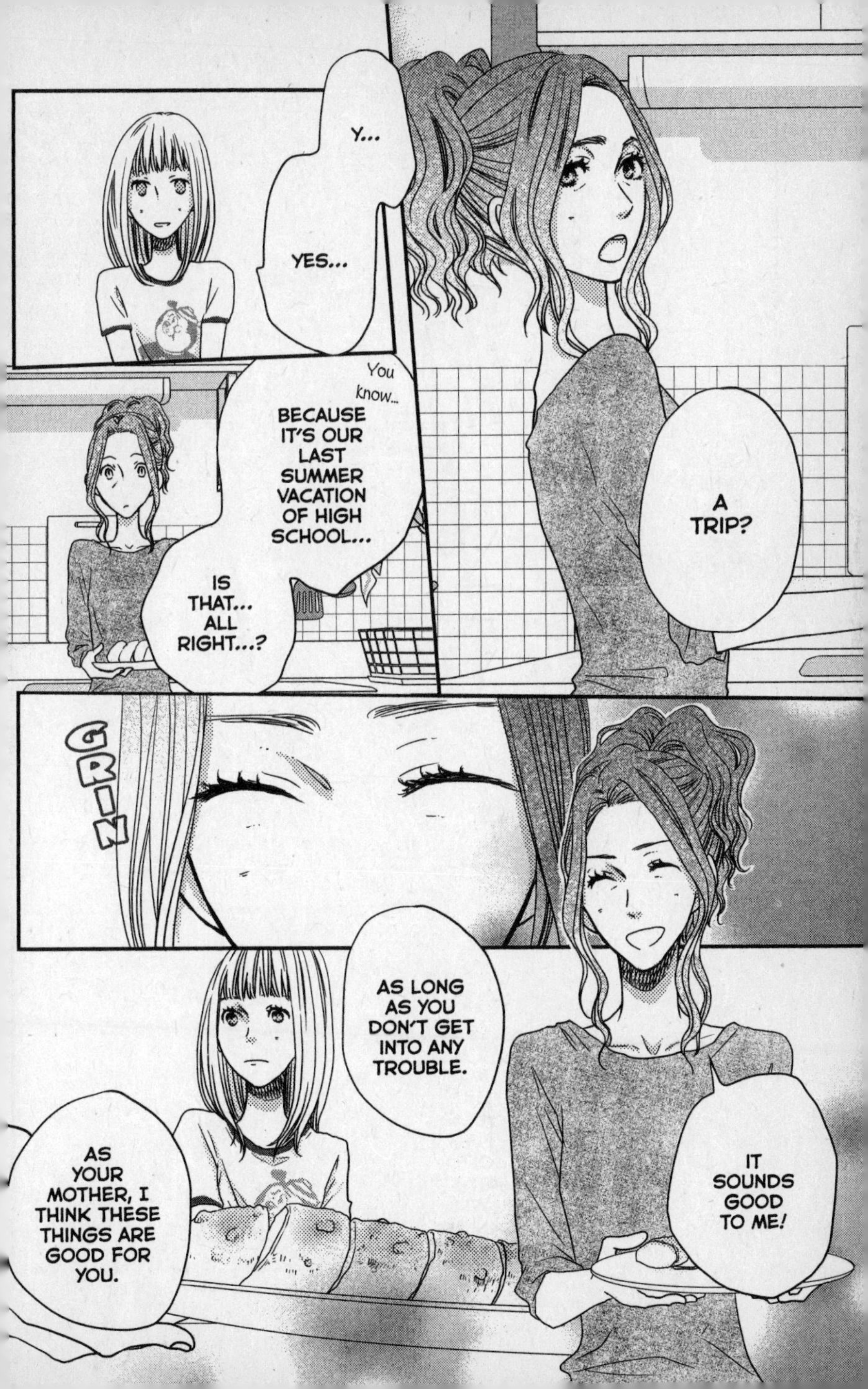
A TRIP?
Y...
YES...
You know...
BECAUSE IT'S OUR LAST SUMMER VACATION OF HIGH SCHOOL...
IS THAT... ALL RIGHT...?
GRIN
IT SOUNDS GOOD TO ME!
AS LONG AS YOU DON'T GET INTO ANY TROUBLE.
AS YOUR MOTHER, I THINK THESE THINGS ARE GOOD FOR YOU.

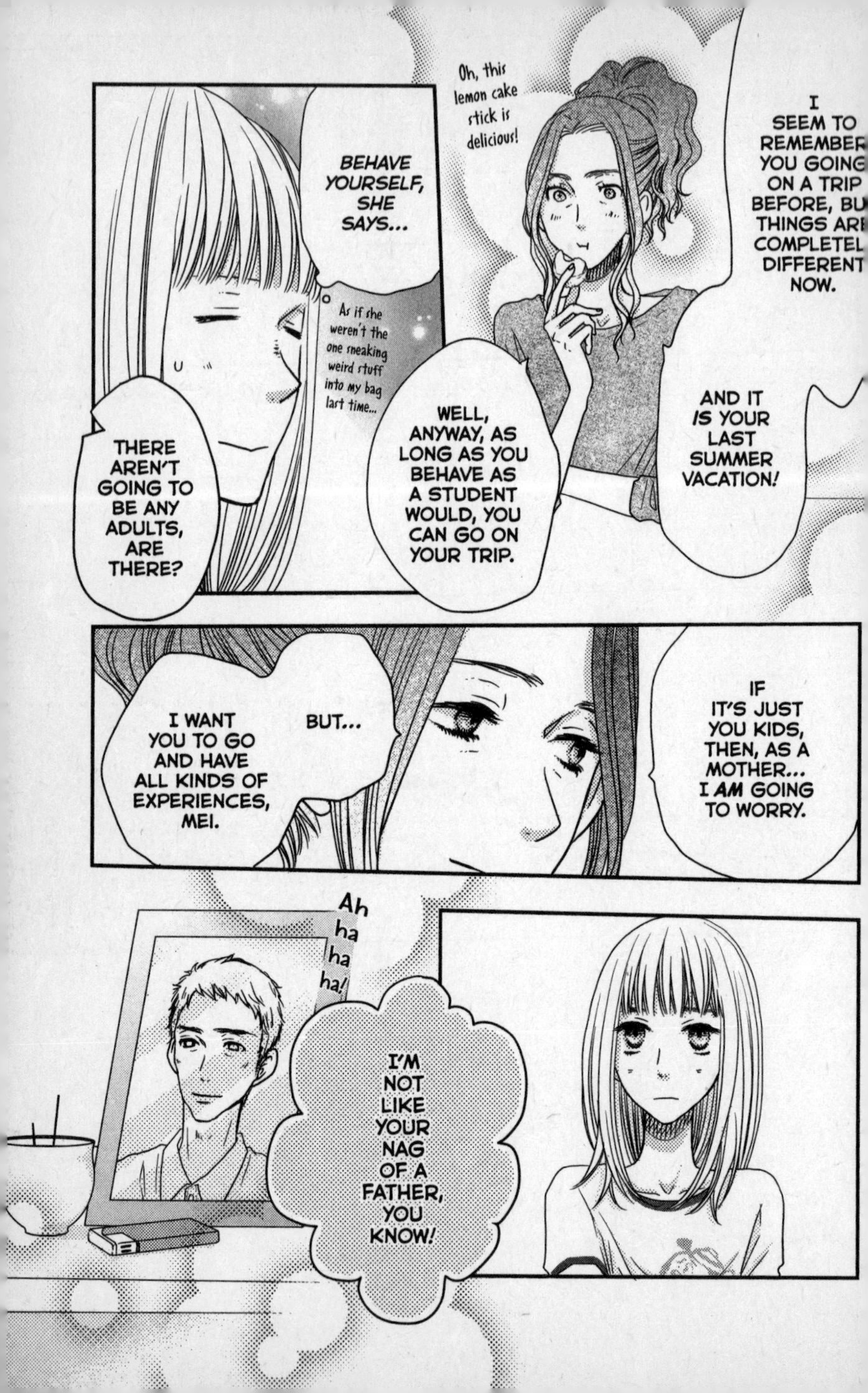

I SEEM TO REMEMBER YOU GOING ON A TRIP BEFORE, BU THINGS ARE COMPLETEL DIFFERENT NOW.
Oh, this lemon cake stick is delicious!
AND IT IS YOUR LAST SUMMER VACATION!
WELL, ANYWAY, AS LONG AS YOU BEHAVE AS A STUDENT WOULD, YOU CAN GO ON YOUR TRIP.
BEHAVE YOURSELF, SHE SAYS...
As if she weren't the one sneaking weird stuff into my bag last time...
THERE AREN'T GOING TO BE ANY ADULTS, ARE THERE?
IF IT'S JUST YOU KIDS, THEN, AS A MOTHER... I AM GOING TO WORRY.
BUT...
I WANT YOU TO GO AND HAVE ALL KINDS OF EXPERIENCES, MEI.
Ah ha ha ha!
I'M NOT LIKE YOUR NAG OF A FATHER, YOU KNOW!

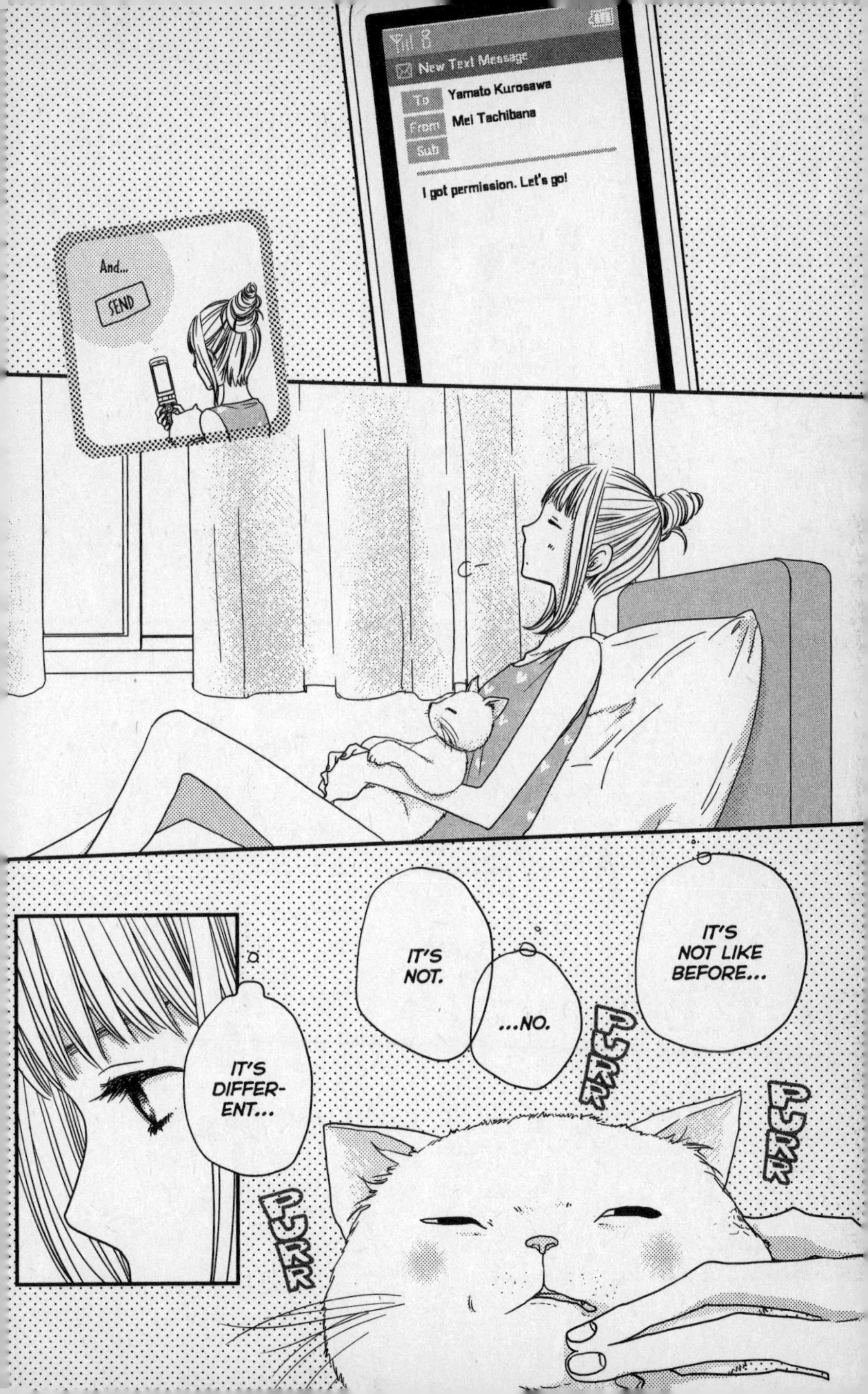
New Text Message
To Yamato Kurosawa
From Mei Tachibana
Sub
I got permission. Let's go!
And...
SEND
IT'S NOT LIKE BEFORE...
...NO.
IT'S NOT.
IT'S DIFFERENT...

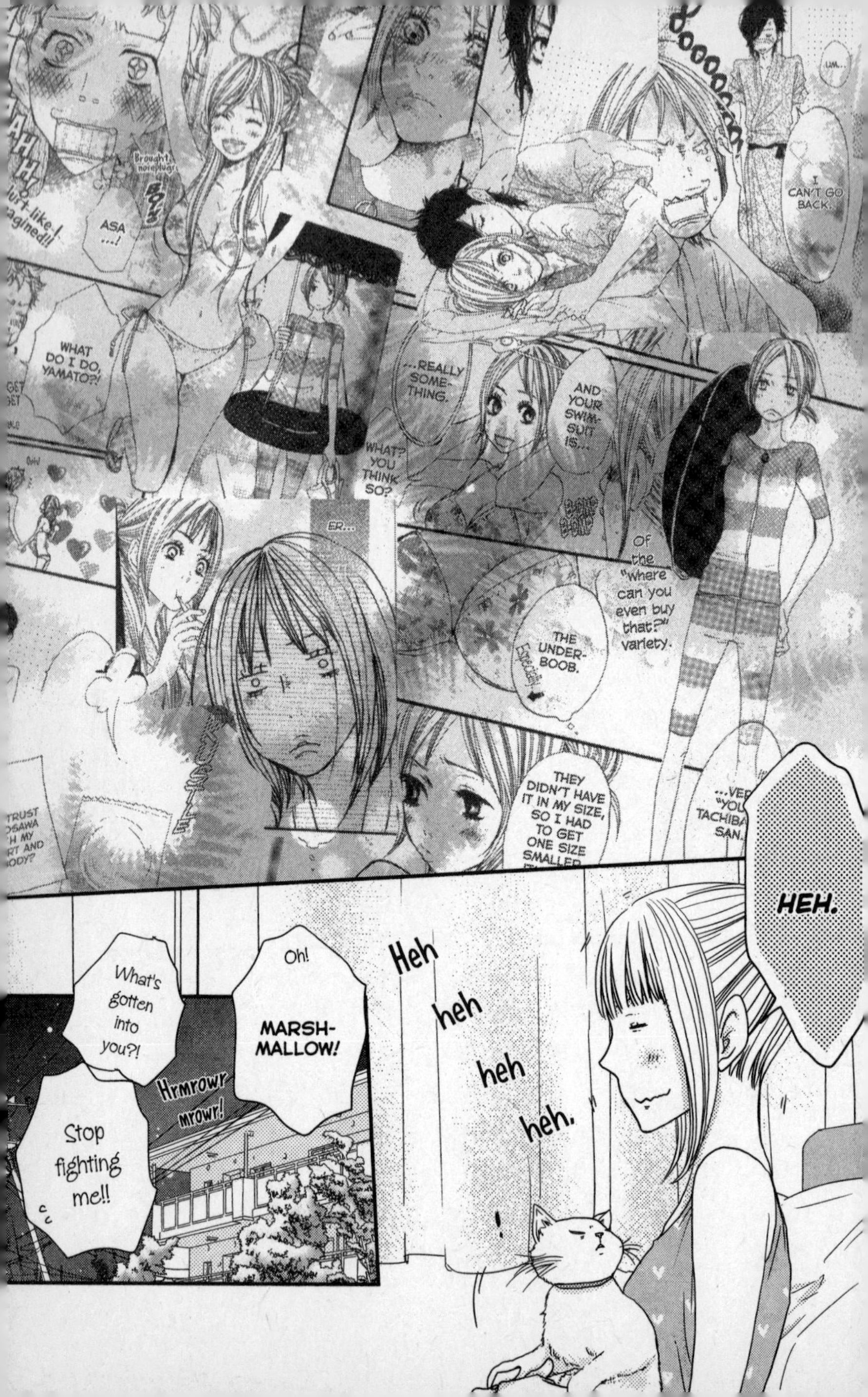
UM...
I CAN'T GO BACK.
ASA ...!
WHAT DO I DO, YAMATO?!
AND YOUR SWIM-SUIT IS...
...REALLY SOME-THING.
WHAT? YOU THINK SO?
Of the "where can you even buy that?" variety.
THE UNDER-BOOB.
Especially
ER...
THEY DIDN'T HAVE IT IN MY SIZE, SO I HAD TO GET ONE SIZE SMALLER
HEH.
Heh heh heh heh.
Oh! MARSH-MALLOW!
What's gotten into you?!
Hrmrowr mrowr!
Stop fighting me!!

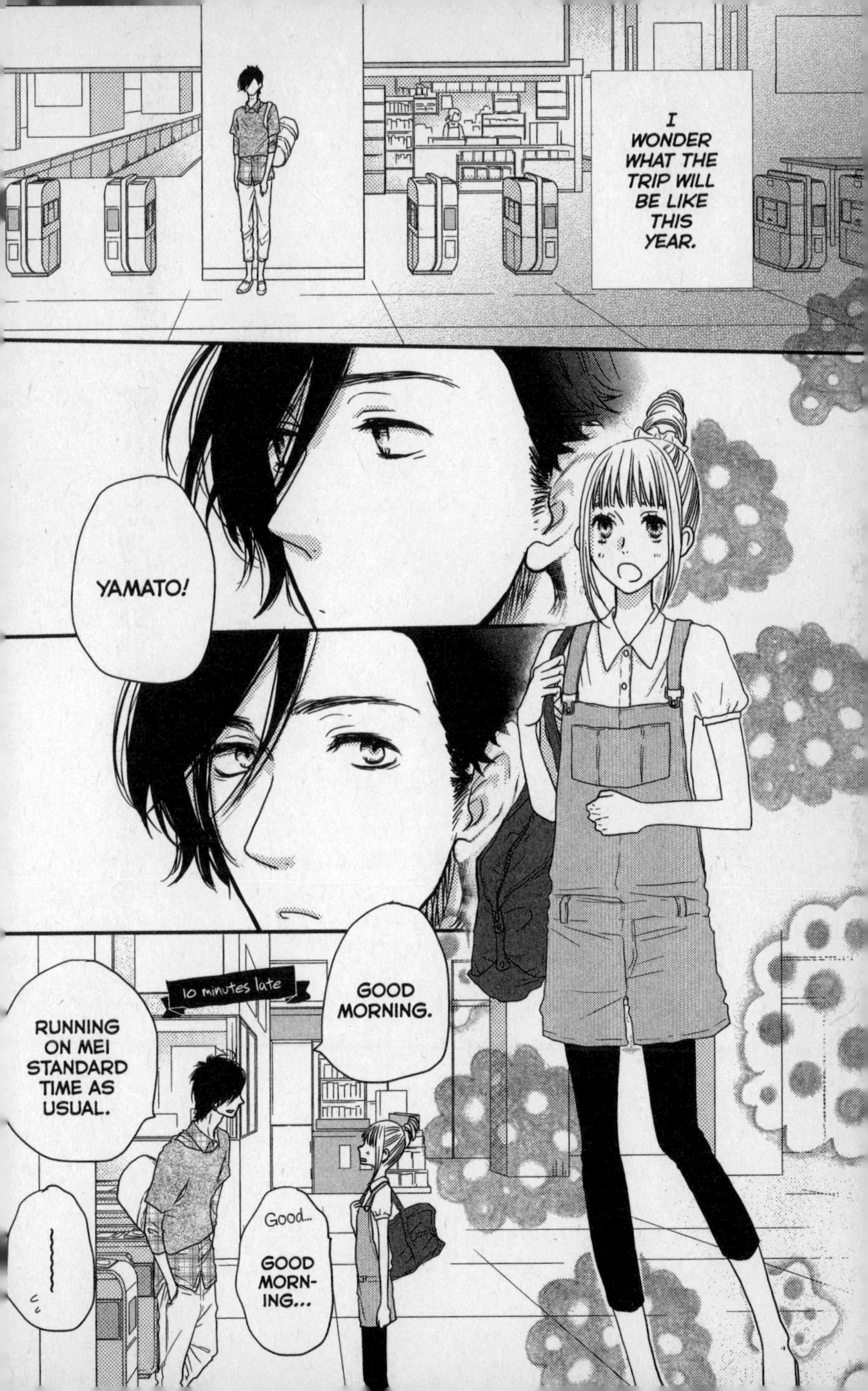
I WONDER WHAT THE TRIP WILL BE LIKE THIS YEAR.
YAMATO!
GOOD MORNING.
10 minutes late
RUNNING ON MEI STANDARD TIME AS USUAL.
Good...
GOOD MORNING...

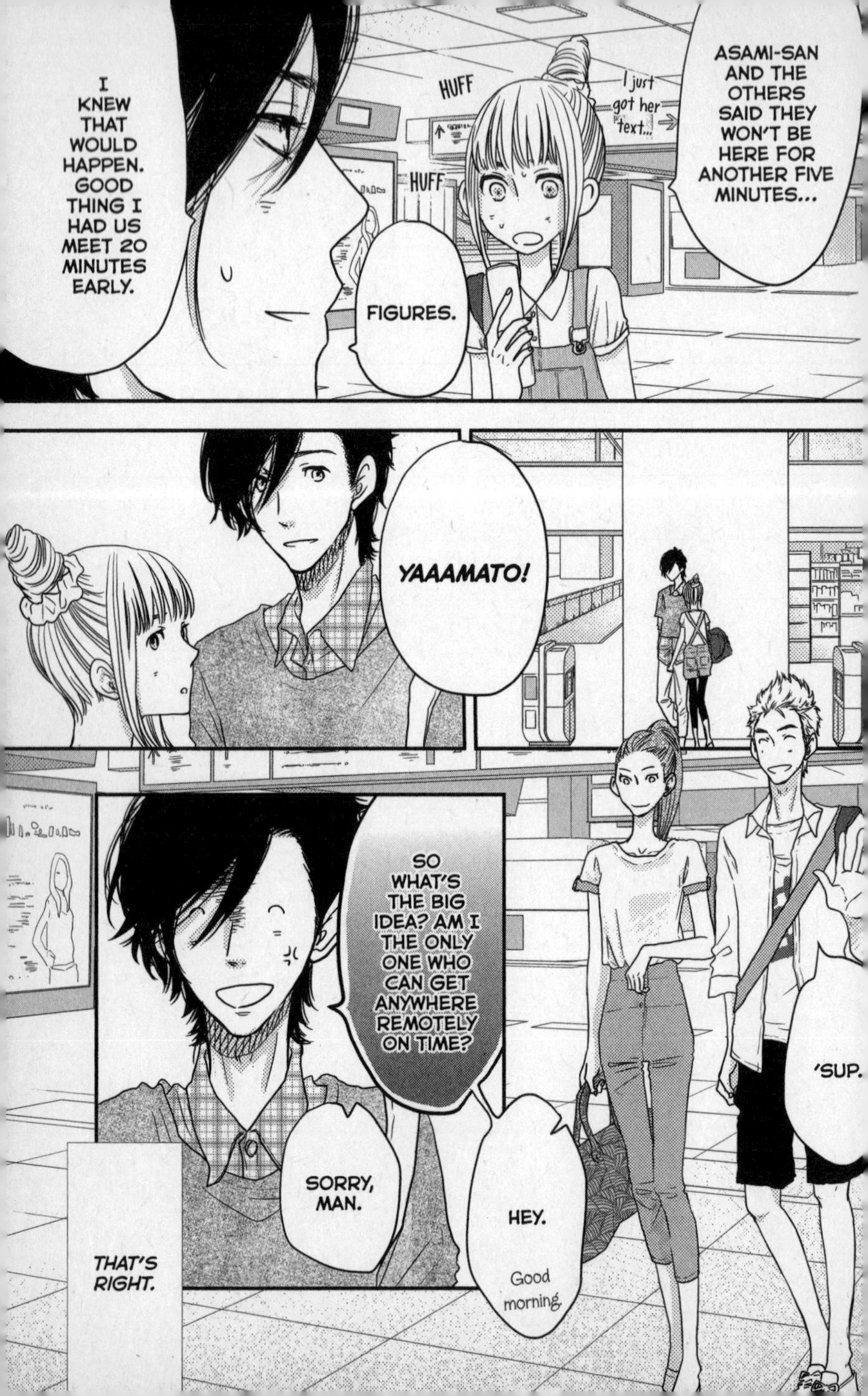
ASAMI-SAN AND THE OTHERS SAID THEY WON'T BE HERE FOR ANOTHER FIVE MINUTES...
I just got her text...
HUFF
HUFF
FIGURES.
I KNEW THAT WOULD HAPPEN. GOOD THING I HAD US MEET 20 MINUTES EARLY.
YAAAMATO!
'SUP.
SO WHAT'S THE BIG IDEA? AM I THE ONLY ONE WHO CAN GET ANYWHERE REMOTELY ON TIME?
HEY.
Good morning.
SORRY, MAN.
THAT'S RIGHT.

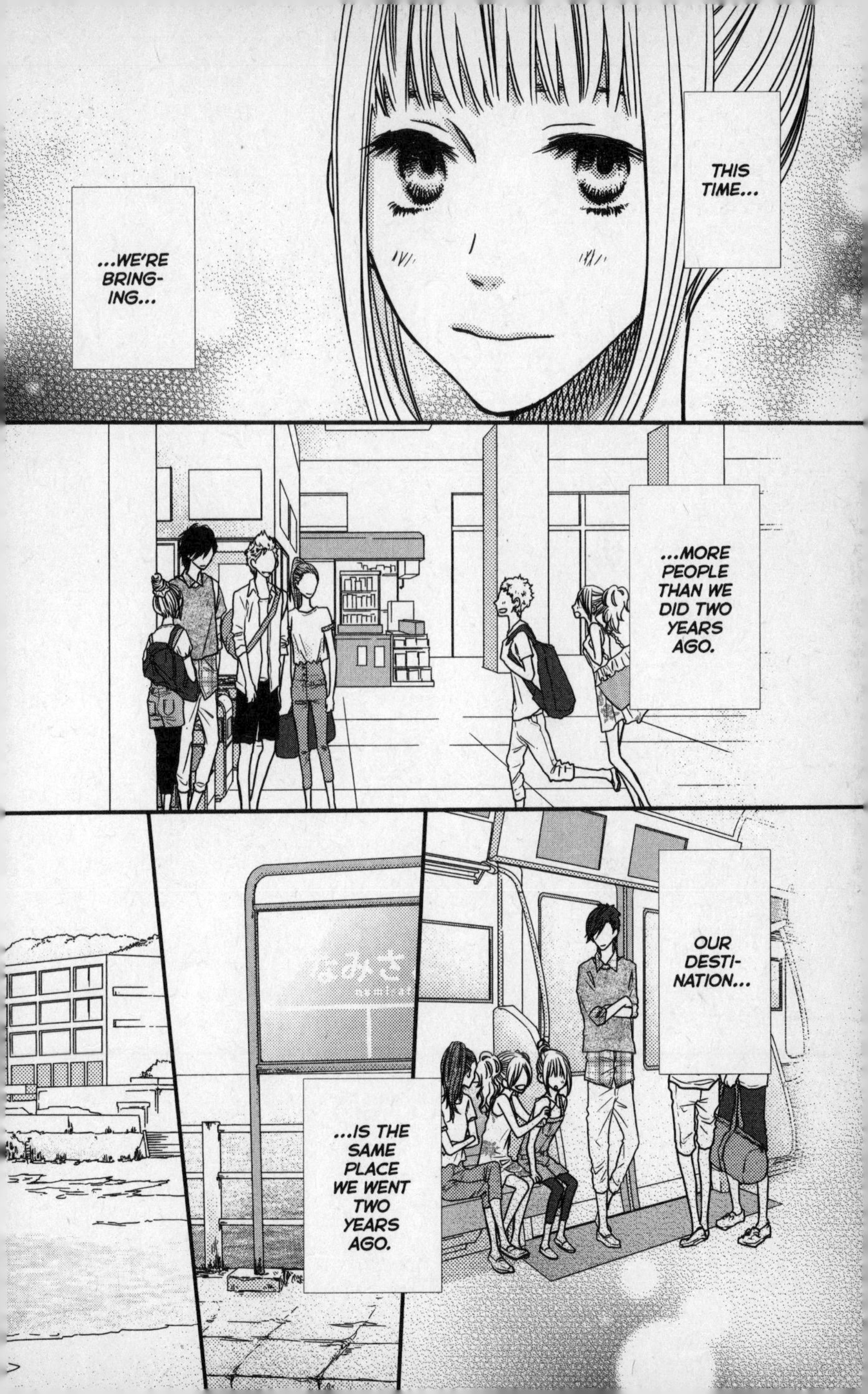
THIS TIME...
...WE'RE BRING-ING...
...MORE PEOPLE THAN WE DID TWO YEARS AGO.
OUR DESTI-NATION...
...IS THE SAME PLACE WE WENT TWO YEARS AGO.

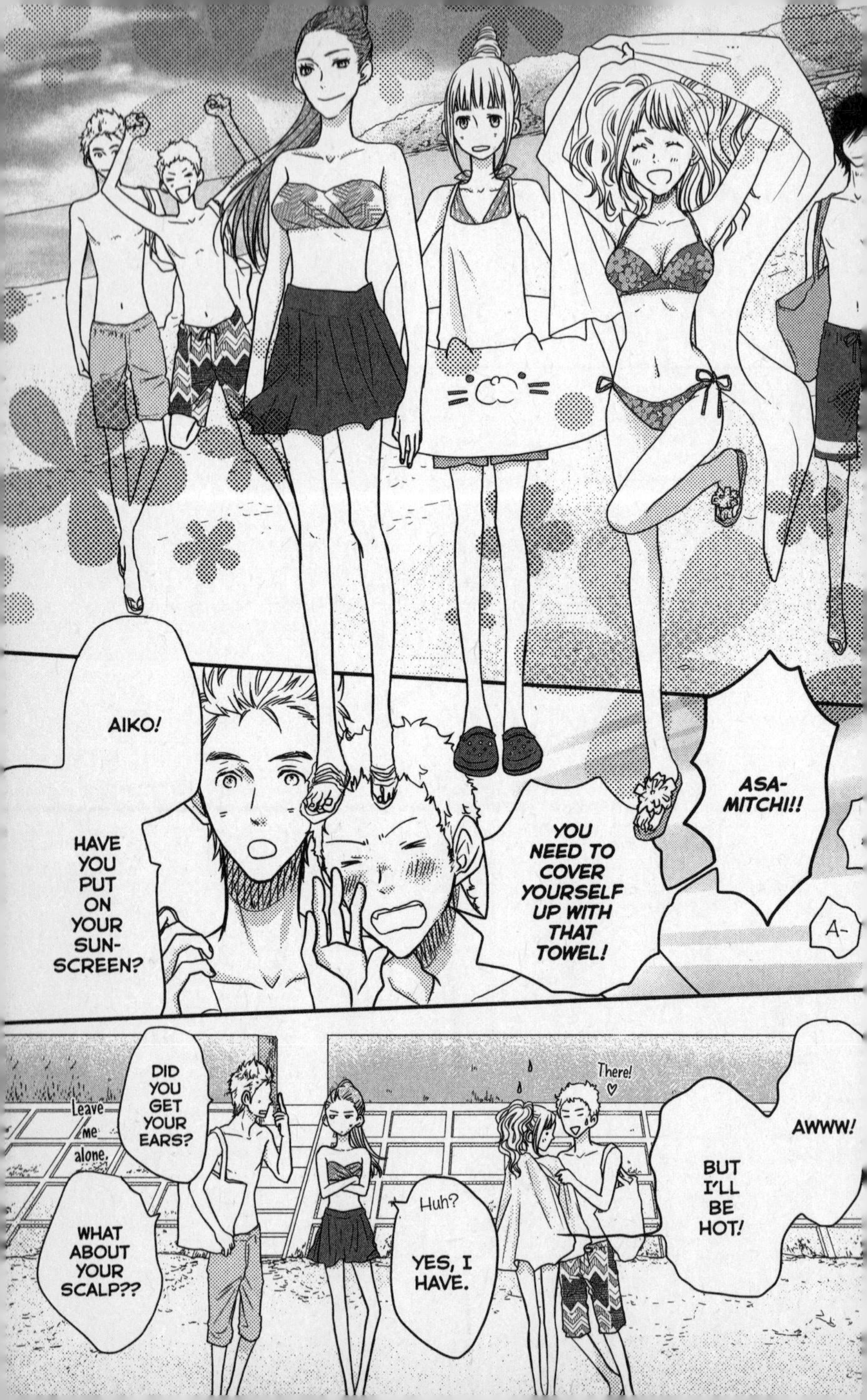
ASA-MITCHI!!
A-
YOU NEED TO COVER YOURSELF UP WITH THAT TOWEL!
AIKO!
HAVE YOU PUT ON YOUR SUN-SCREEN?
AWWW!
BUT I'LL BE HOT!
There!
YES, I HAVE.
DID YOU GET YOUR EARS?
Huh?
WHAT ABOUT YOUR SCALP??
Leave me alone.

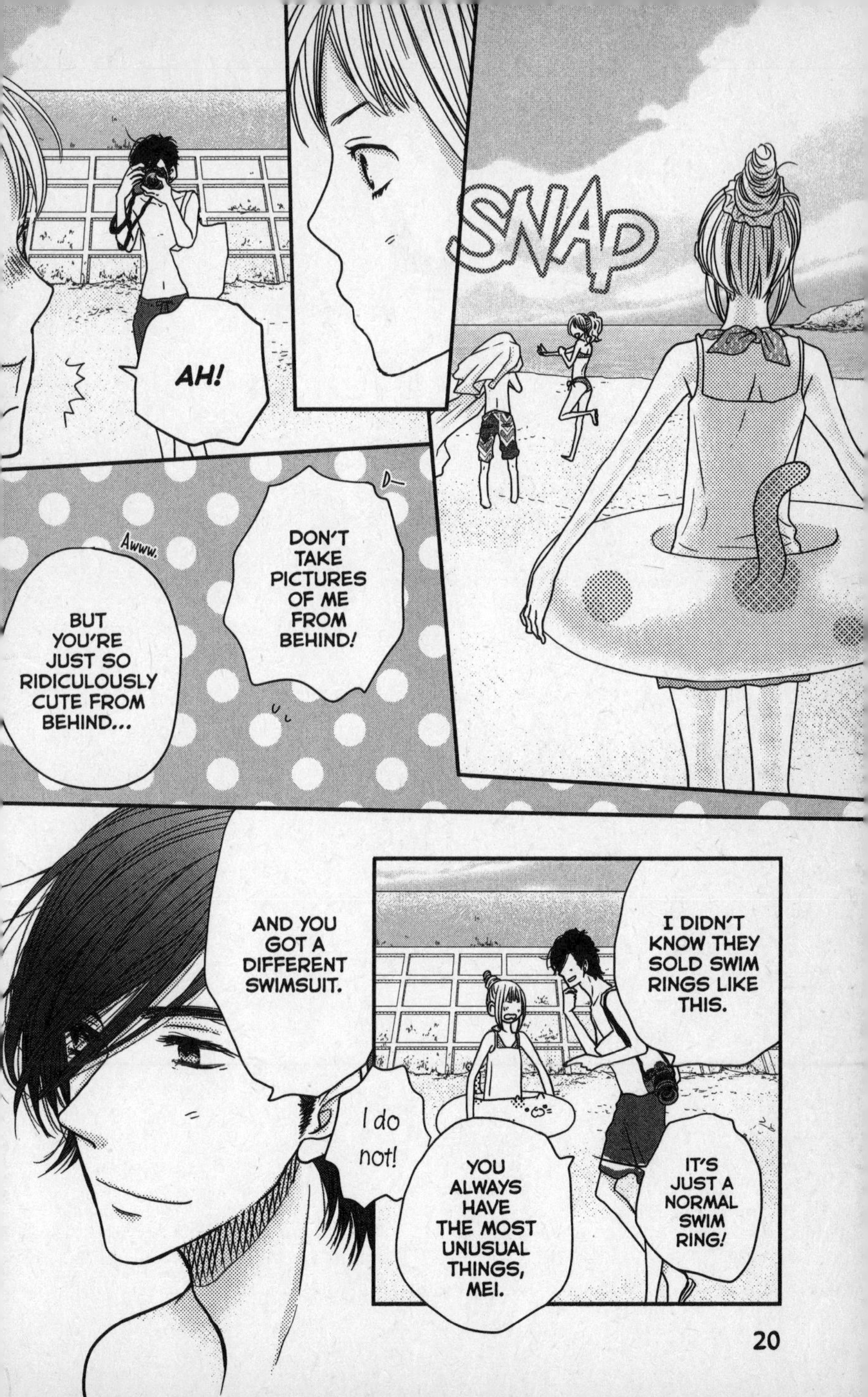
SNAP
AH!
D—
DON'T TAKE PICTURES OF ME FROM BEHIND!
Awww.
BUT YOU'RE JUST SO RIDICULOUSLY CUTE FROM BEHIND...
I DIDN'T KNOW THEY SOLD SWIM RINGS LIKE THIS.
IT'S JUST A NORMAL SWIM RING!
YOU ALWAYS HAVE THE MOST UNUSUAL THINGS, MEI.
I do not!
AND YOU GOT A DIFFERENT SWIMSUIT.

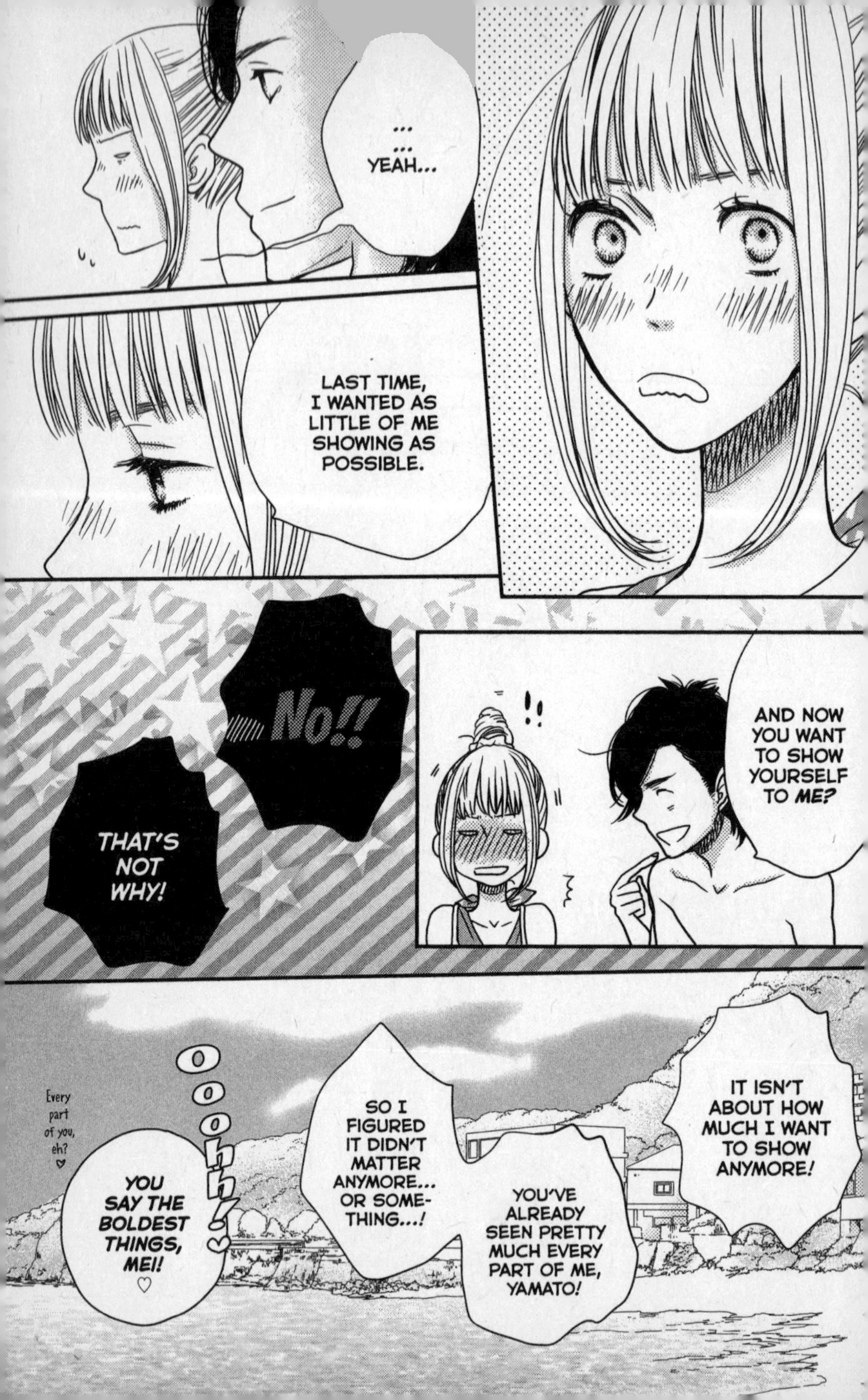
... ... YEAH...
LAST TIME, I WANTED AS LITTLE OF ME SHOWING AS POSSIBLE.
AND NOW YOU WANT TO SHOW YOURSELF TO ME?
!!
No!!
THAT'S NOT WHY!
IT ISN'T ABOUT HOW MUCH I WANT TO SHOW ANYMORE!
YOU'VE ALREADY SEEN PRETTY MUCH EVERY PART OF ME, YAMATO!
SO I FIGURED IT DIDN'T MATTER ANYMORE... OR SOME-THING...!
Ooooh!♡
YOU SAY THE BOLDEST THINGS, MEI! ♡
Every part of you, eh? ♡

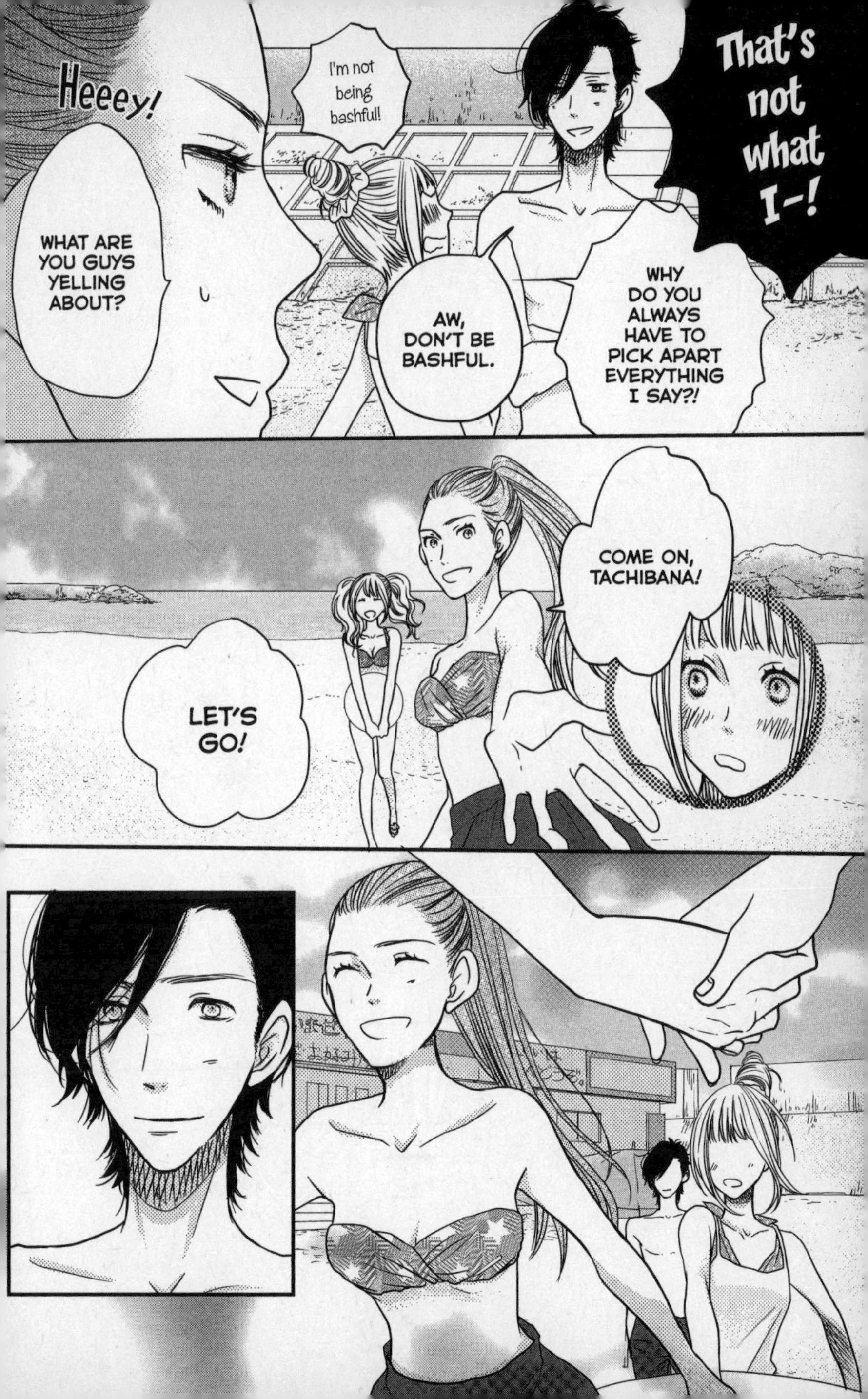
That's not what I-!
WHY DO YOU ALWAYS HAVE TO PICK APART EVERYTHING I SAY?!
AW, DON'T BE BASHFUL.
I'm not being bashful!
Heeey!
WHAT ARE YOU GUYS YELLING ABOUT?
COME ON, TACHIBANA!
LET'S GO!

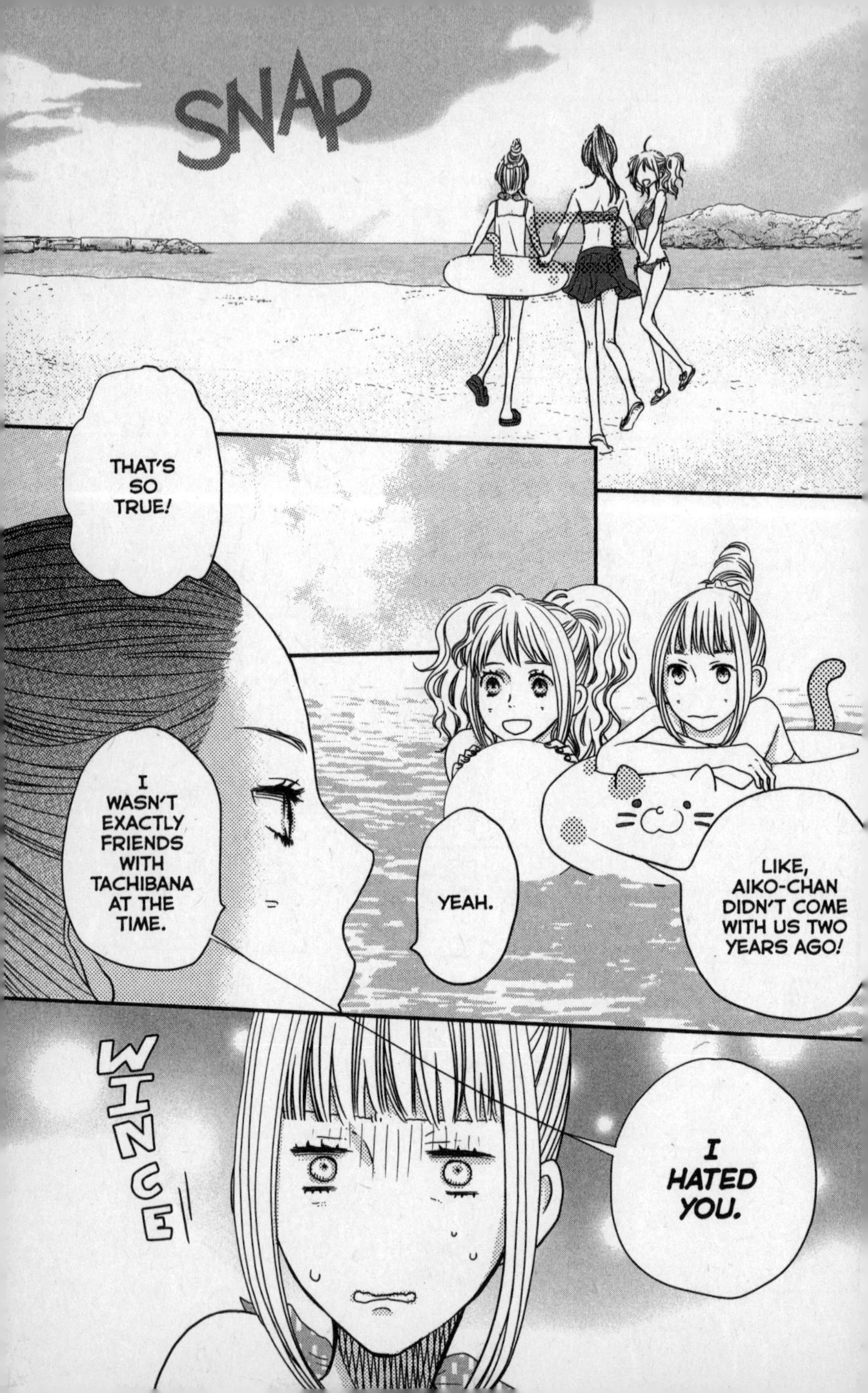
SNAP
LIKE, AIKO-CHAN DIDN'T COME WITH US TWO YEARS AGO!
YEAH.
THAT'S SO TRUE!
I WASN'T EXACTLY FRIENDS WITH TACHIBANA AT THE TIME.
I HATED YOU.
WINCE

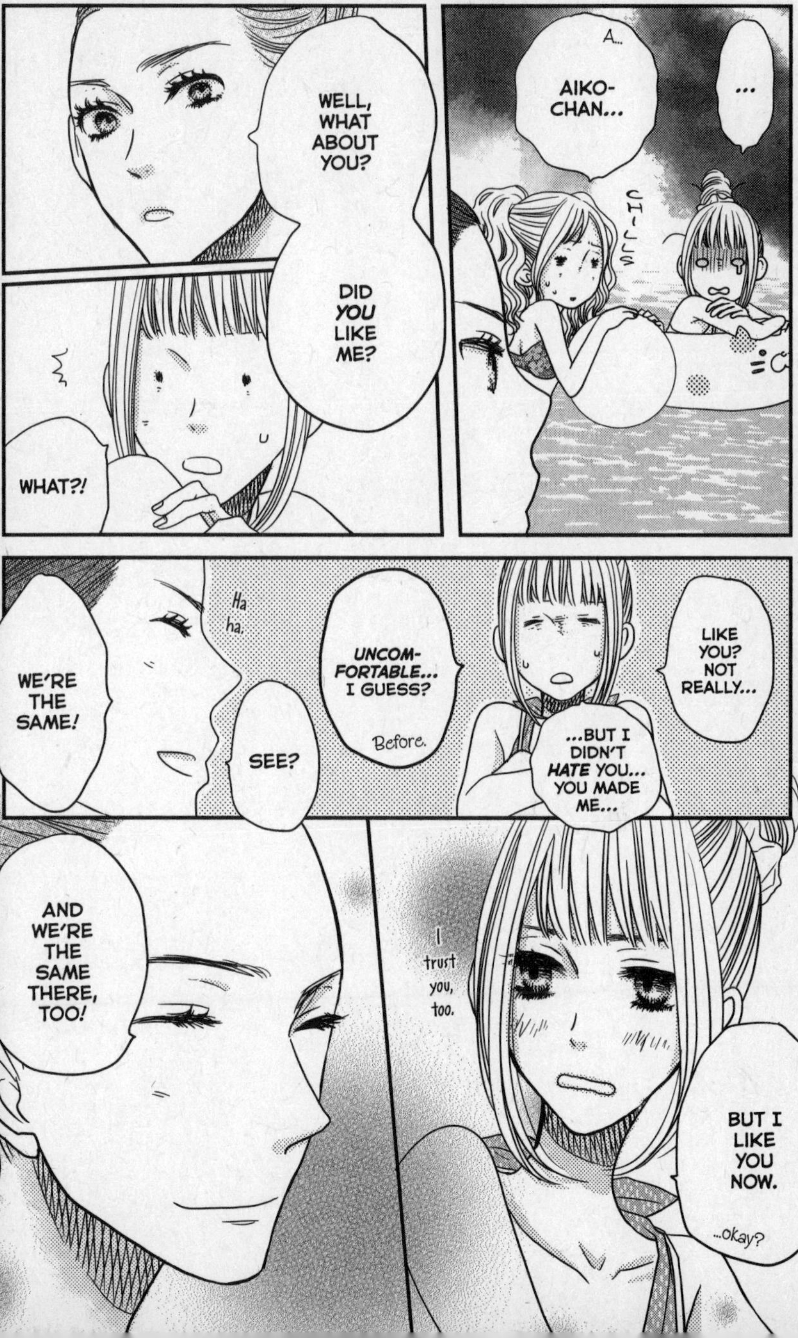
...
A...
AIKO-CHAN...
WELL, WHAT ABOUT YOU?
DID YOU LIKE ME?
WHAT?!
LIKE YOU? NOT REALLY...
...BUT I DIDN'T HATE YOU... YOU MADE ME...
UNCOMFORTABLE... I GUESS?
Before.
Ha ha.
SEE?
WE'RE THE SAME!
BUT I LIKE YOU NOW.
...okay?
I trust you, too.
AND WE'RE THE SAME THERE, TOO!

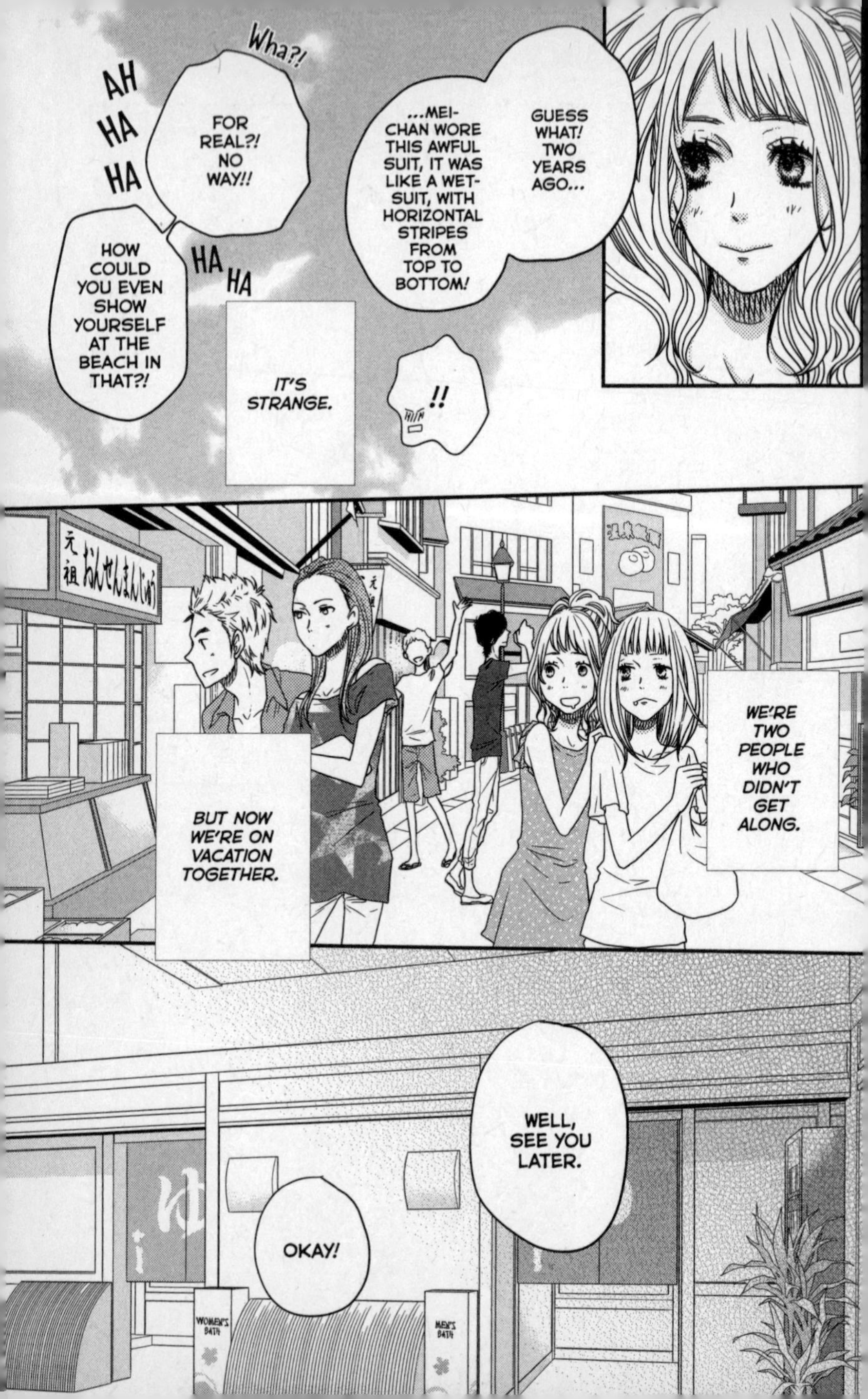

GUESS WHAT! TWO YEARS AGO...
...MEI-CHAN WORE THIS AWFUL SUIT, IT WAS LIKE A WET-SUIT, WITH HORIZONTAL STRIPES FROM TOP TO BOTTOM!
Wha?!
FOR REAL?! NO WAY!!
AH HA HA
!!
HOW COULD YOU EVEN SHOW YOURSELF AT THE BEACH IN THAT?!
HA HA
IT'S STRANGE.
WE'RE TWO PEOPLE WHO DIDN'T GET ALONG.
BUT NOW WE'RE ON VACATION TOGETHER.
元祖 おんせんまんじゅう
WELL, SEE YOU LATER.
OKAY!
MEN'S BATH
WOMEN'S BATH

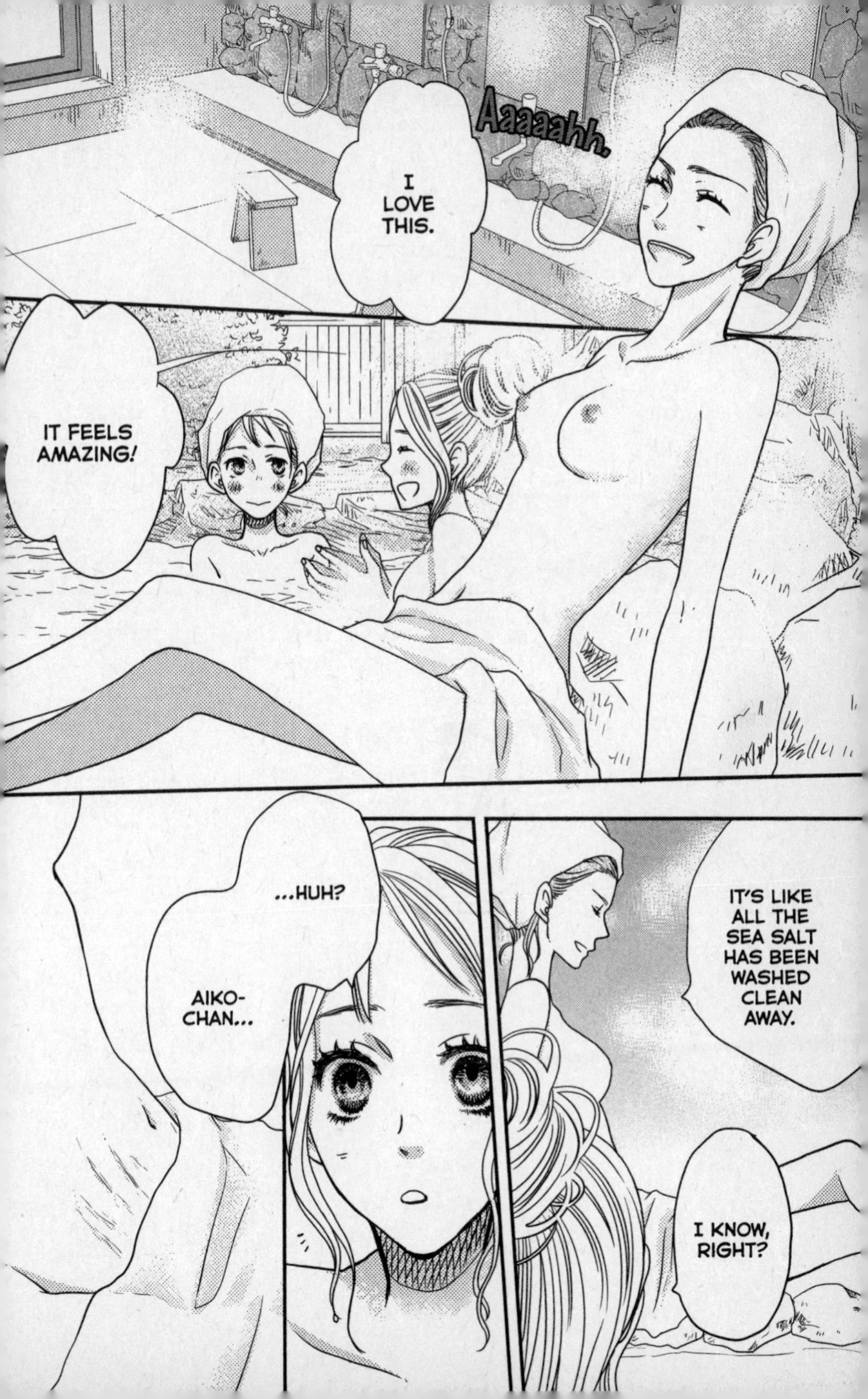
Aaaaahh.
I LOVE THIS.
IT FEELS AMAZING!
IT'S LIKE ALL THE SEA SALT HAS BEEN WASHED CLEAN AWAY.
I KNOW, RIGHT?
...HUH?
AIKO-CHAN...

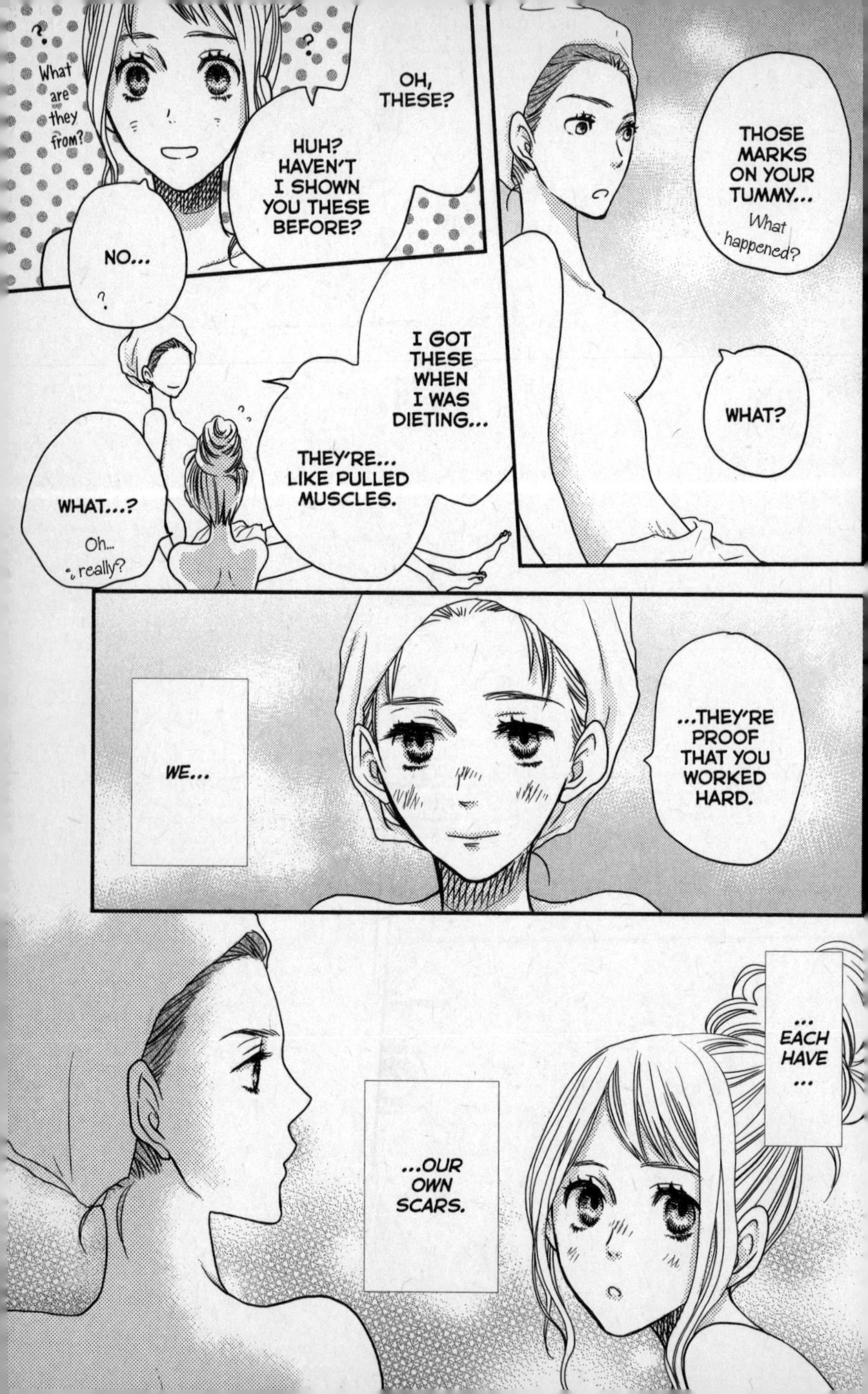
THOSE MARKS ON YOUR TUMMY...
What happened?
WHAT?
OH, THESE?
HUH? HAVEN'T I SHOWN YOU THESE BEFORE?
What are they from?
NO...
?
I GOT THESE WHEN I WAS DIETING...
THEY'RE... LIKE PULLED MUSCLES.
WHAT...?
Oh... really?
...THEY'RE PROOF THAT YOU WORKED HARD.
WE...
...EACH HAVE...
...OUR OWN SCARS.

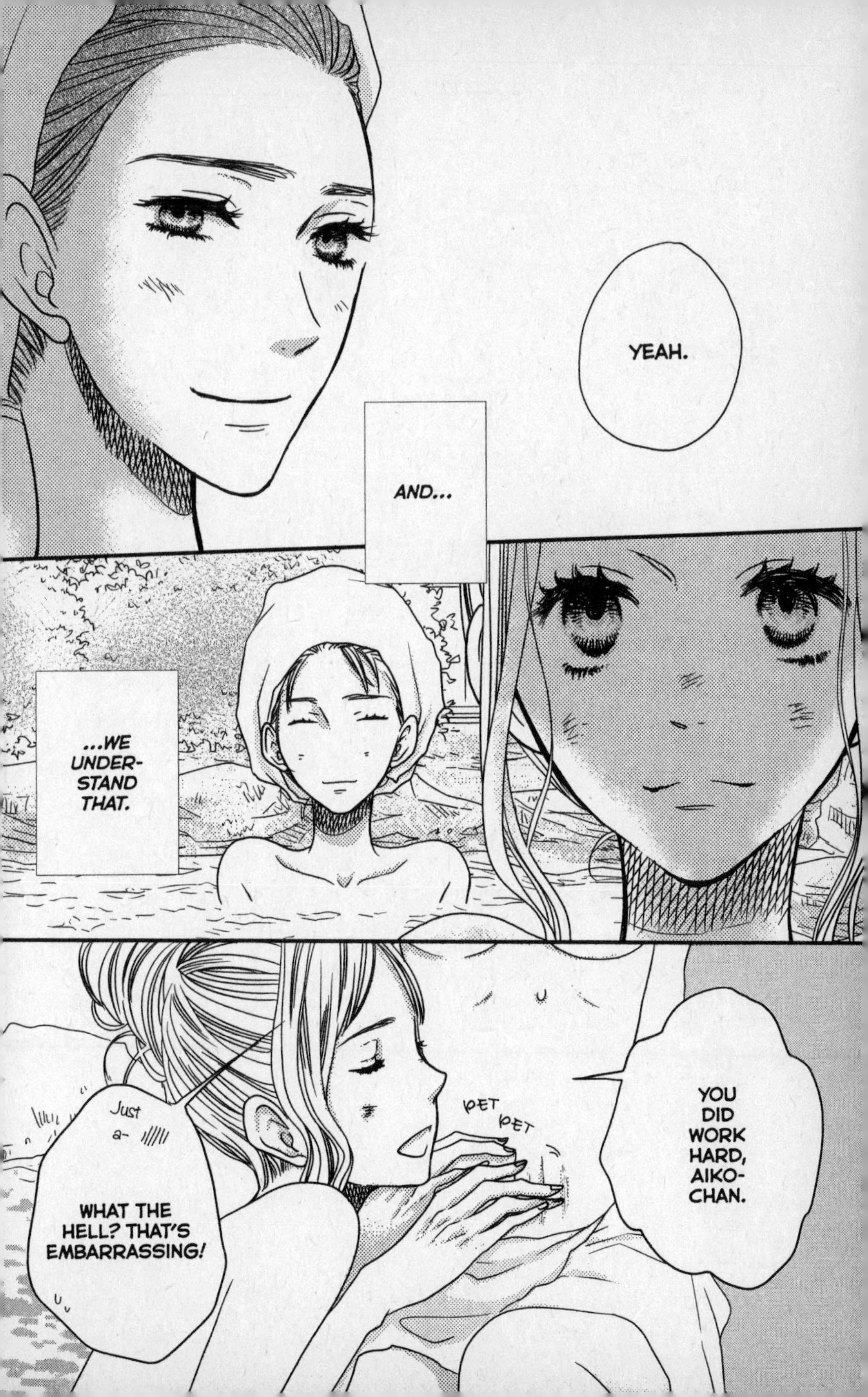
YEAH.
AND...
...WE UNDERSTAND THAT.
YOU DID WORK HARD, AIKO-CHAN.
PET PET
Just a-
WHAT THE HELL? THAT'S EMBARRASSING!

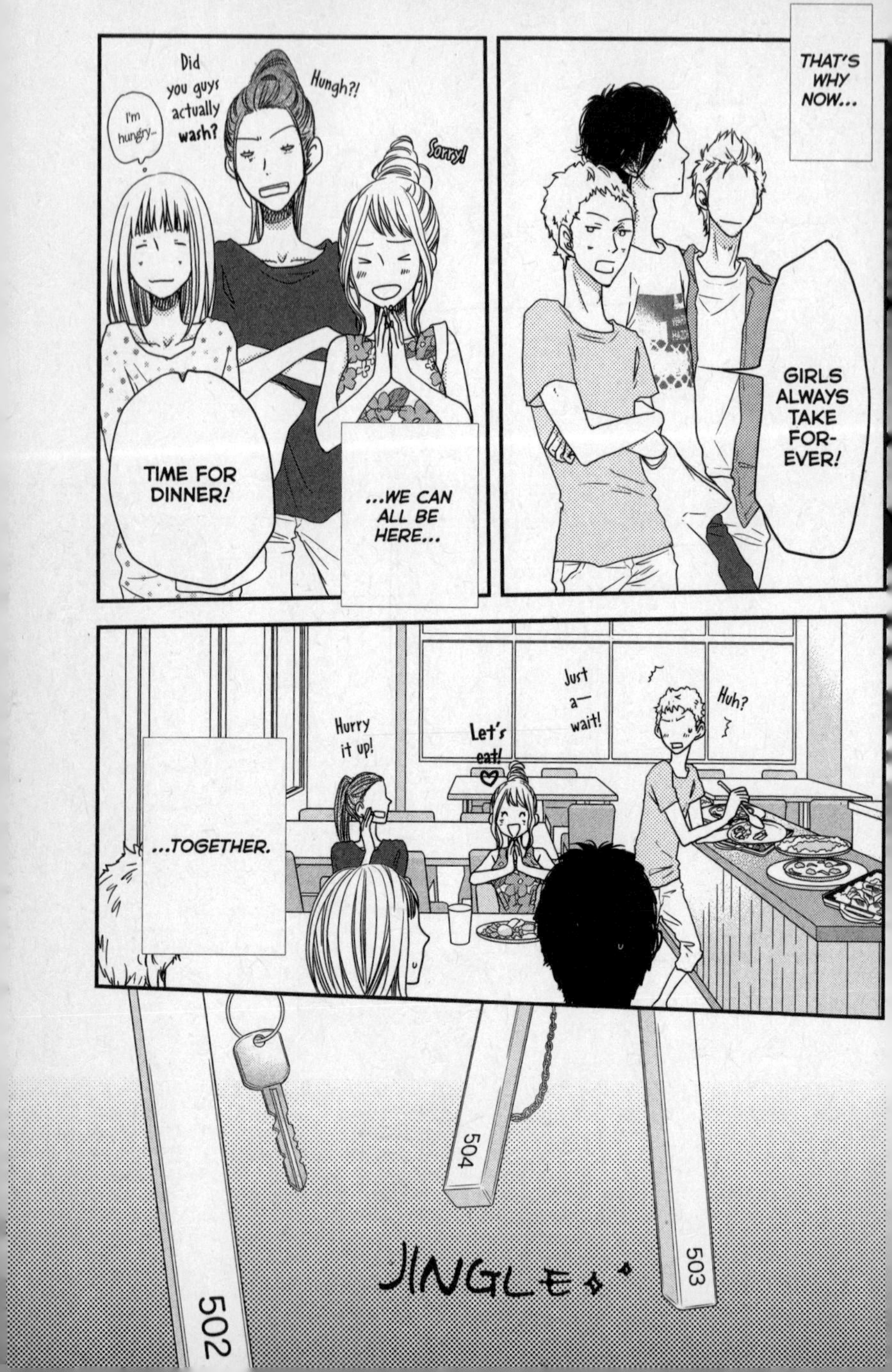
THAT'S WHY NOW...
GIRLS ALWAYS TAKE FOR-EVER!
...WE CAN ALL BE HERE...
Sorry!
Hungh?!
Did you guys actually wash?
I'm hungry...
TIME FOR DINNER!
Huh?
Just a— wait!
Let's eat!
Hurry it up!
...TOGETHER.
504
503
JINGLE
502

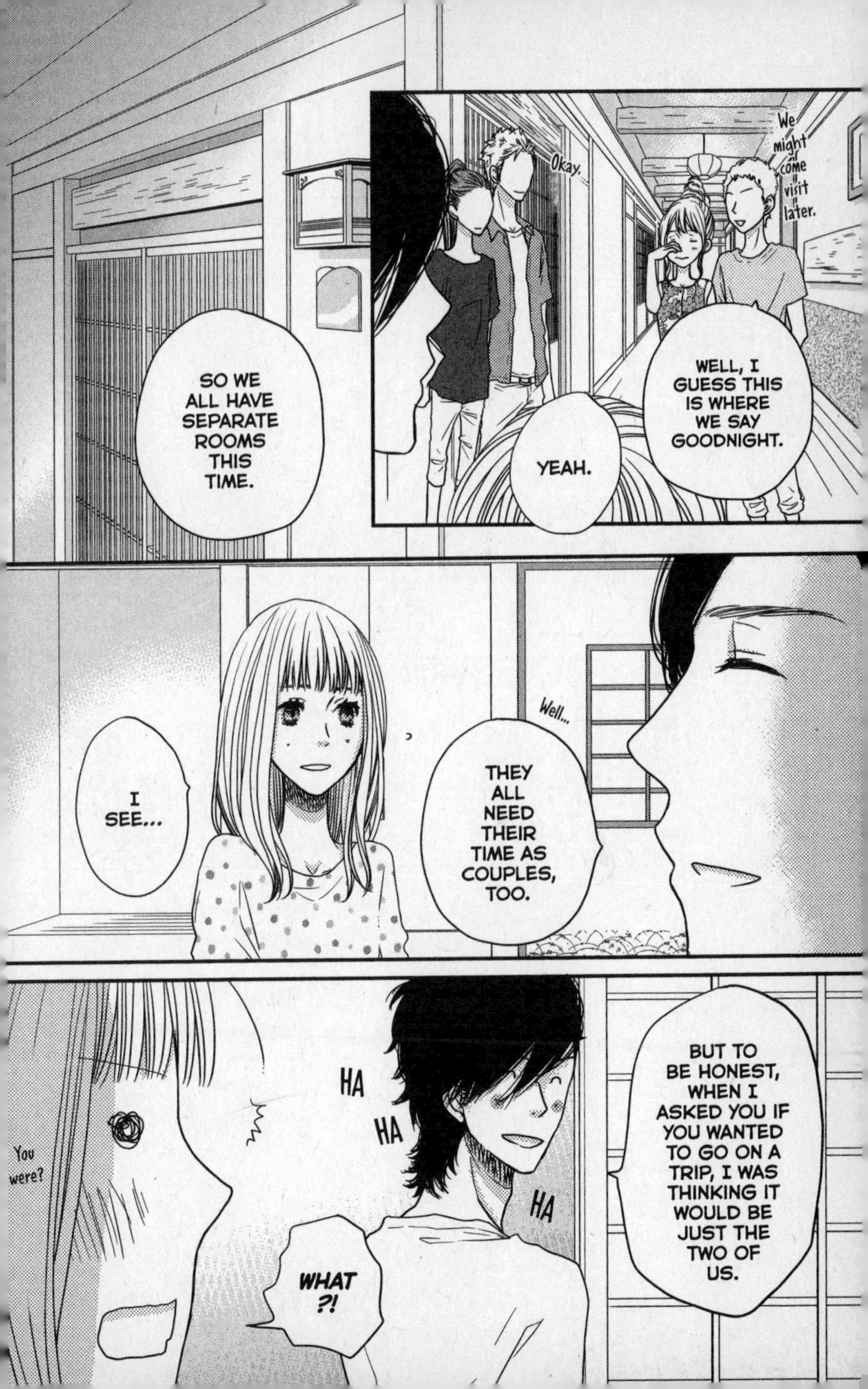
We might come visit later.
Okay.
WELL, I GUESS THIS IS WHERE WE SAY GOODNIGHT.
YEAH.
SO WE ALL HAVE SEPARATE ROOMS THIS TIME.
Well...
THEY ALL NEED THEIR TIME AS COUPLES, TOO.
I SEE...
BUT TO BE HONEST, WHEN I ASKED YOU IF YOU WANTED TO GO ON A TRIP, I WAS THINKING IT WOULD BE JUST THE TWO OF US.
HA
HA
HA
WHAT ?!
You were?

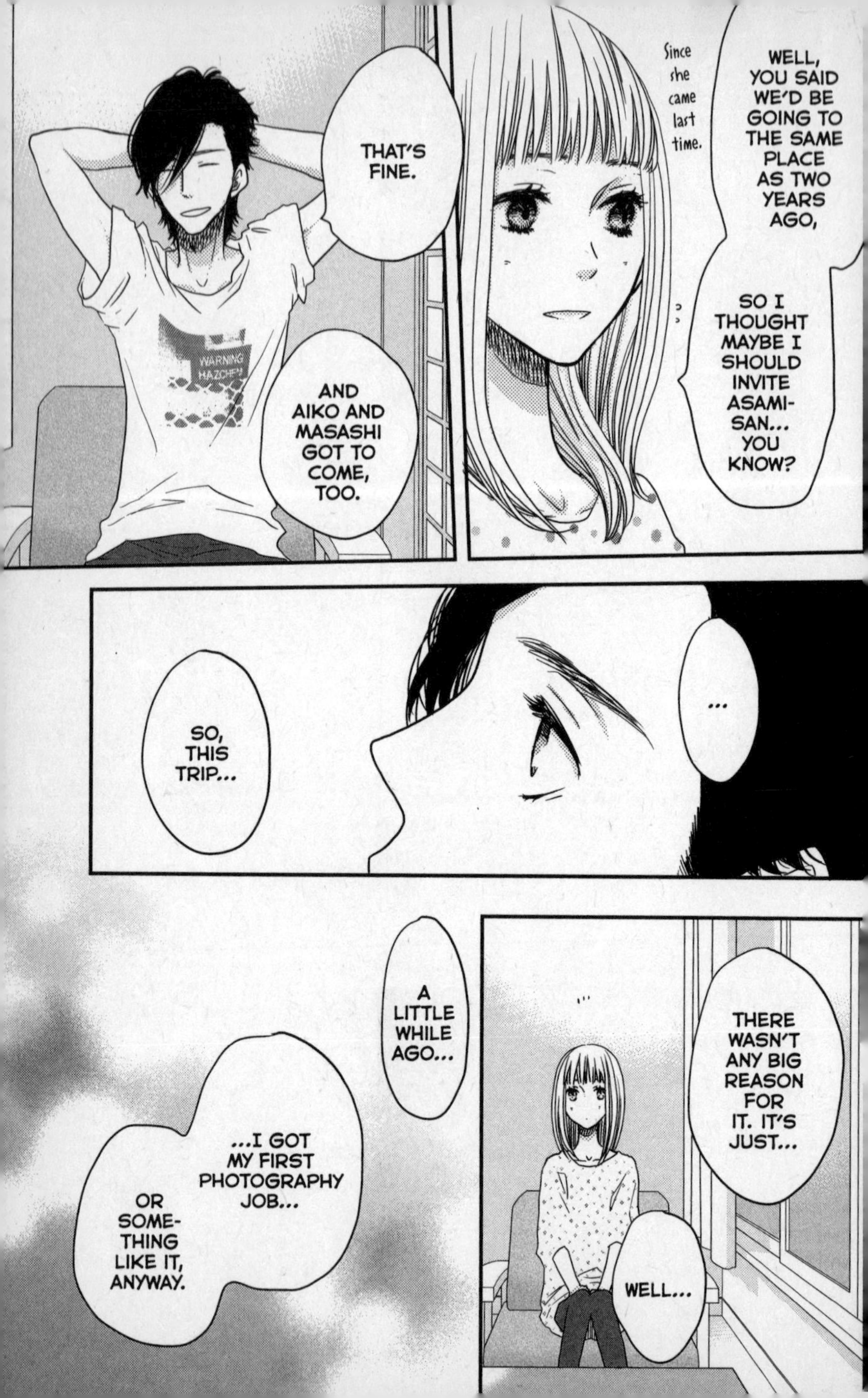
WELL, YOU SAID WE'D BE GOING TO THE SAME PLACE AS TWO YEARS AGO,
Since she came last time.
SO I THOUGHT MAYBE I SHOULD INVITE ASAMI-SAN... YOU KNOW?
THAT'S FINE.
AND AIKO AND MASASHI GOT TO COME, TOO.
...
SO, THIS TRIP...
THERE WASN'T ANY BIG REASON FOR IT. IT'S JUST...
...
WELL...
A LITTLE WHILE AGO...
...I GOT MY FIRST PHOTOGRAPHY JOB...
OR SOMETHING LIKE IT, ANYWAY.

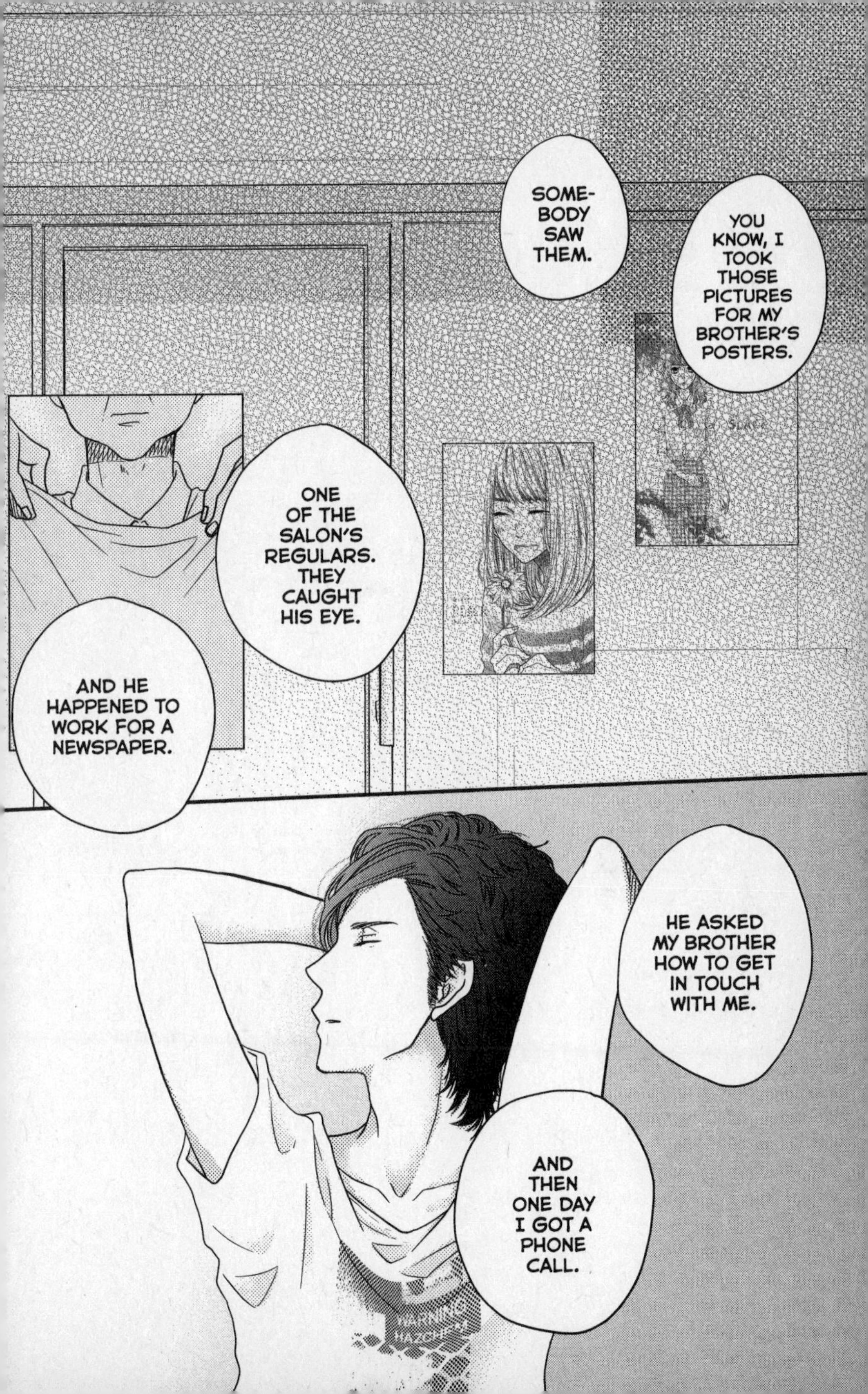
YOU KNOW, I TOOK THOSE PICTURES FOR MY BROTHER'S POSTERS.
SOME-BODY SAW THEM.
ONE OF THE SALON'S REGULARS. THEY CAUGHT HIS EYE.
AND HE HAPPENED TO WORK FOR A NEWSPAPER.
HE ASKED MY BROTHER HOW TO GET IN TOUCH WITH ME.
AND THEN ONE DAY I GOT A PHONE CALL.

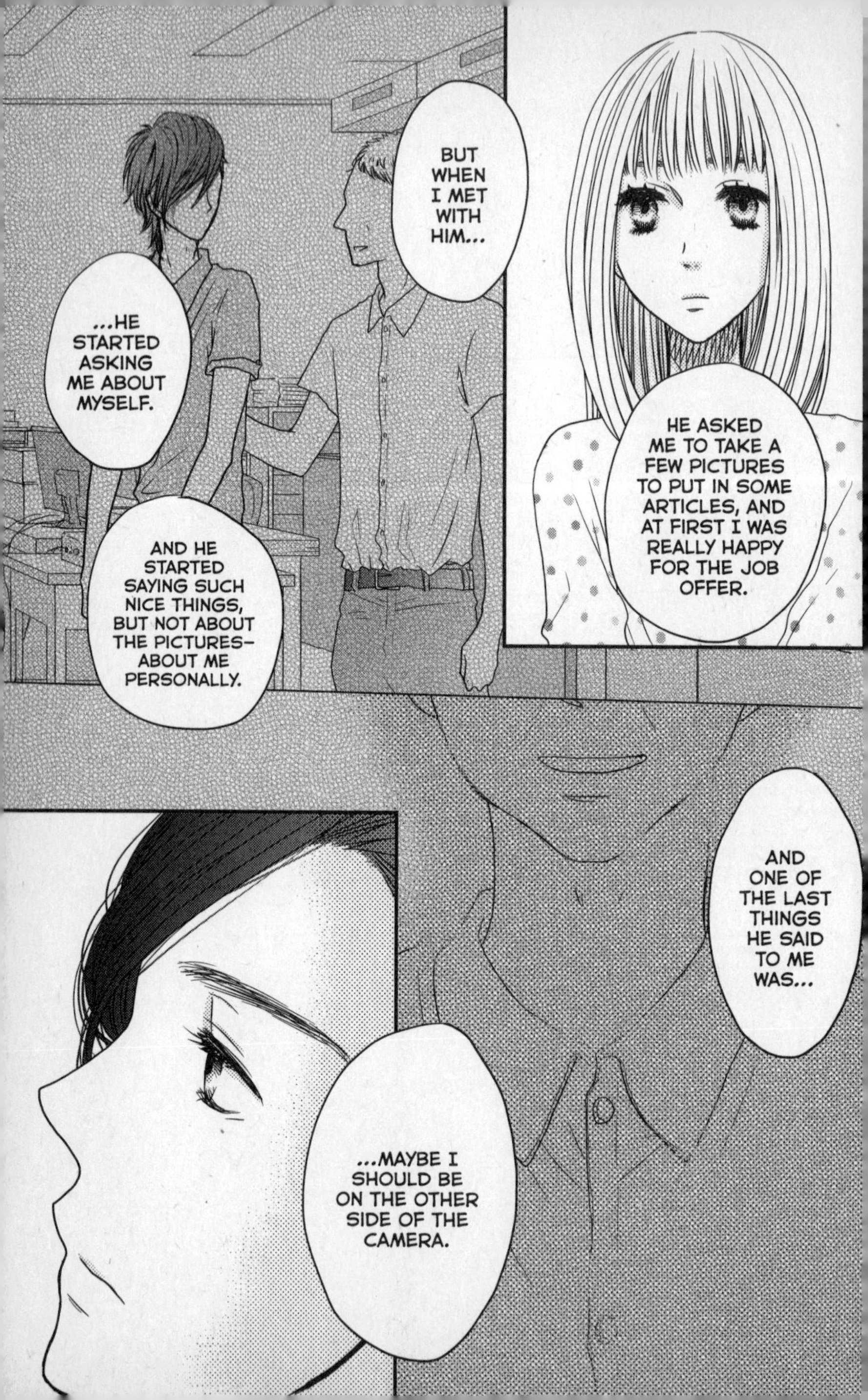
HE ASKED ME TO TAKE A FEW PICTURES TO PUT IN SOME ARTICLES, AND AT FIRST I WAS REALLY HAPPY FOR THE JOB OFFER.
BUT WHEN I MET WITH HIM...
...HE STARTED ASKING ME ABOUT MYSELF.
AND HE STARTED SAYING SUCH NICE THINGS, BUT NOT ABOUT THE PICTURES–ABOUT ME PERSONALLY.
AND ONE OF THE LAST THINGS HE SAID TO ME WAS...
...MAYBE I SHOULD BE ON THE OTHER SIDE OF THE CAMERA.

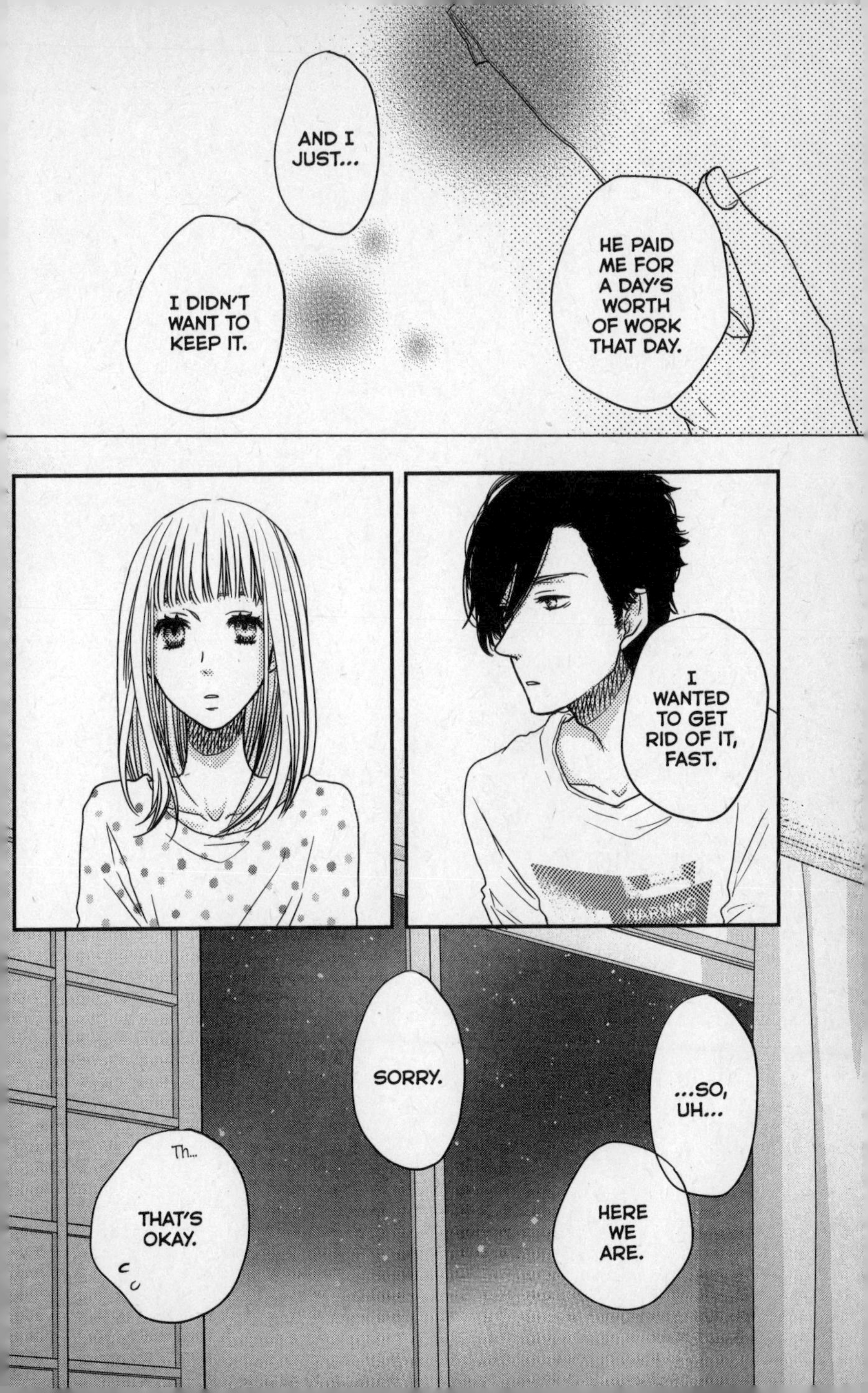
HE PAID ME FOR A DAY'S WORTH OF WORK THAT DAY.
AND I JUST...
I DIDN'T WANT TO KEEP IT.
I WANTED TO GET RID OF IT, FAST.
WARNING
...SO, UH...
HERE WE ARE.
SORRY.
Th...
THAT'S OKAY.

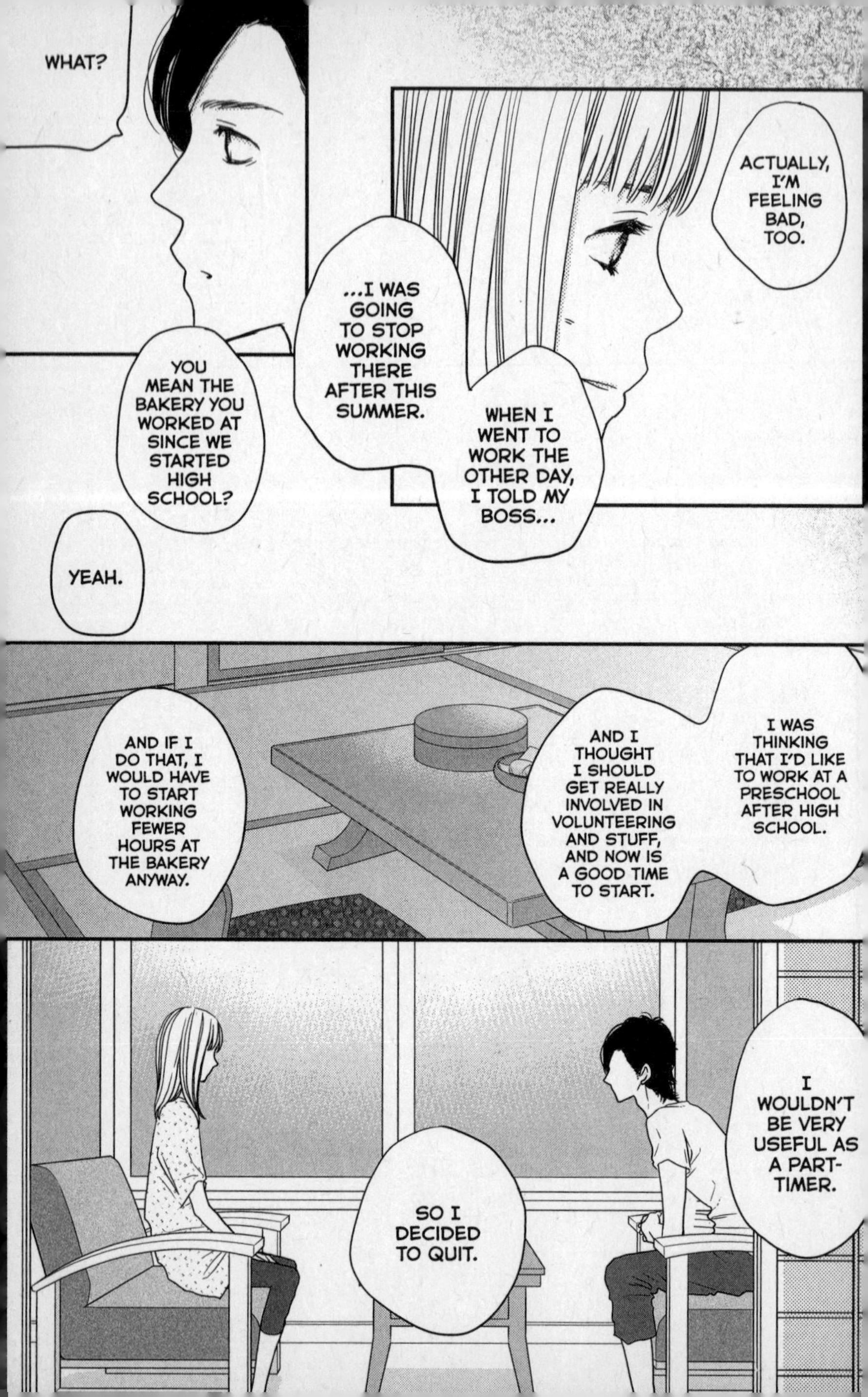
ACTUALLY, I'M FEELING BAD, TOO.
WHEN I WENT TO WORK THE OTHER DAY, I TOLD MY BOSS...
...I WAS GOING TO STOP WORKING THERE AFTER THIS SUMMER.
WHAT?
YOU MEAN THE BAKERY YOU WORKED AT SINCE WE STARTED HIGH SCHOOL?
YEAH.
I WAS THINKING THAT I'D LIKE TO WORK AT A PRESCHOOL AFTER HIGH SCHOOL.
AND I THOUGHT I SHOULD GET REALLY INVOLVED IN VOLUNTEERING AND STUFF, AND NOW IS A GOOD TIME TO START.
AND IF I DO THAT, I WOULD HAVE TO START WORKING FEWER HOURS AT THE BAKERY ANYWAY.
I WOULDN'T BE VERY USEFUL AS A PART-TIMER.
SO I DECIDED TO QUIT.

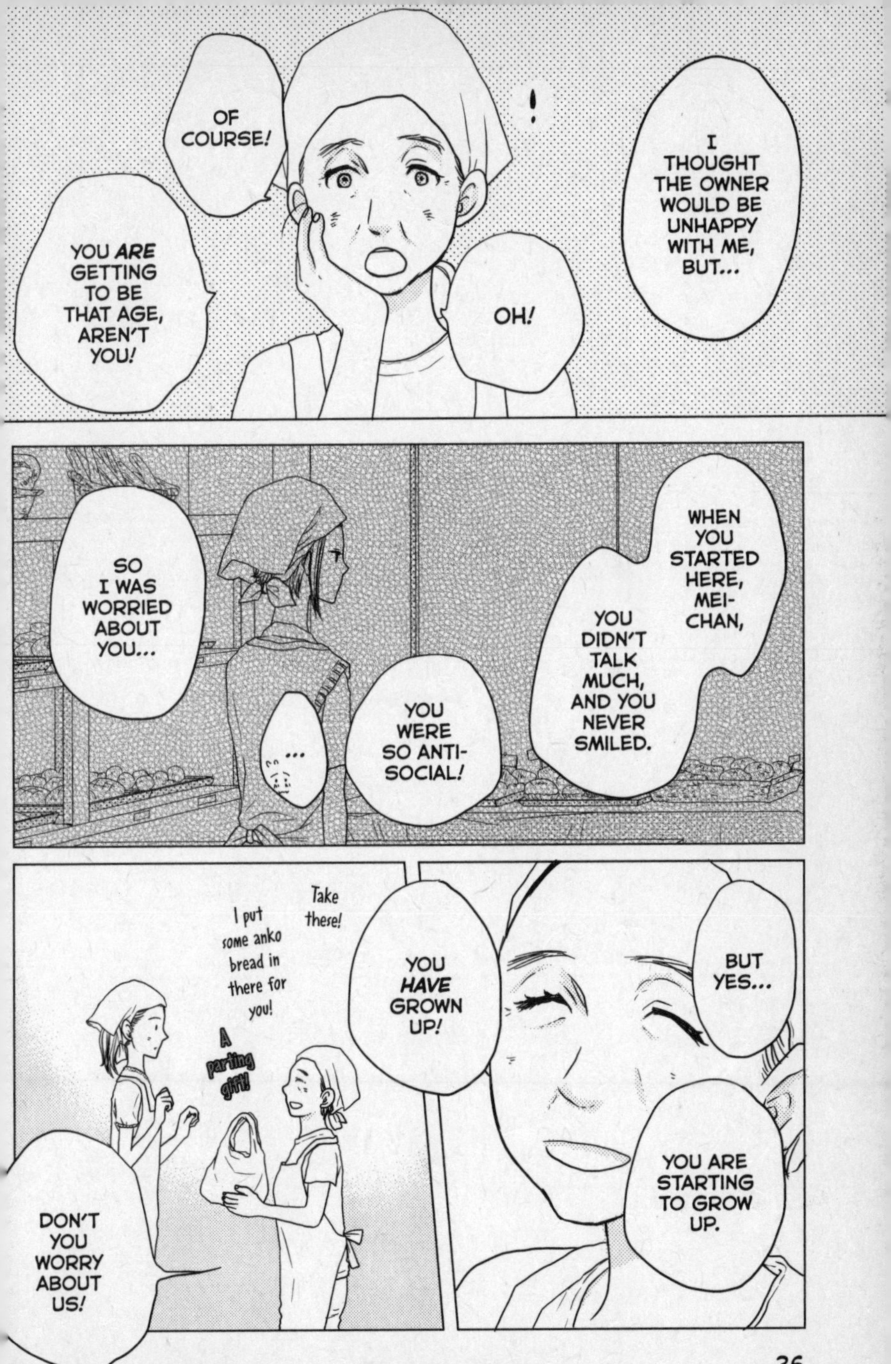
I THOUGHT THE OWNER WOULD BE UNHAPPY WITH ME, BUT...
!
OH!
OF COURSE!
YOU ARE GETTING TO BE THAT AGE, AREN'T YOU!
WHEN YOU STARTED HERE, MEI-CHAN,
YOU DIDN'T TALK MUCH, AND YOU NEVER SMILED.
YOU WERE SO ANTI-SOCIAL!
...
SO I WAS WORRIED ABOUT YOU...
BUT YES...
YOU ARE STARTING TO GROW UP.
YOU HAVE GROWN UP!
Take these!
I put some anko bread in there for you!
A parting gift!
DON'T YOU WORRY ABOUT US!

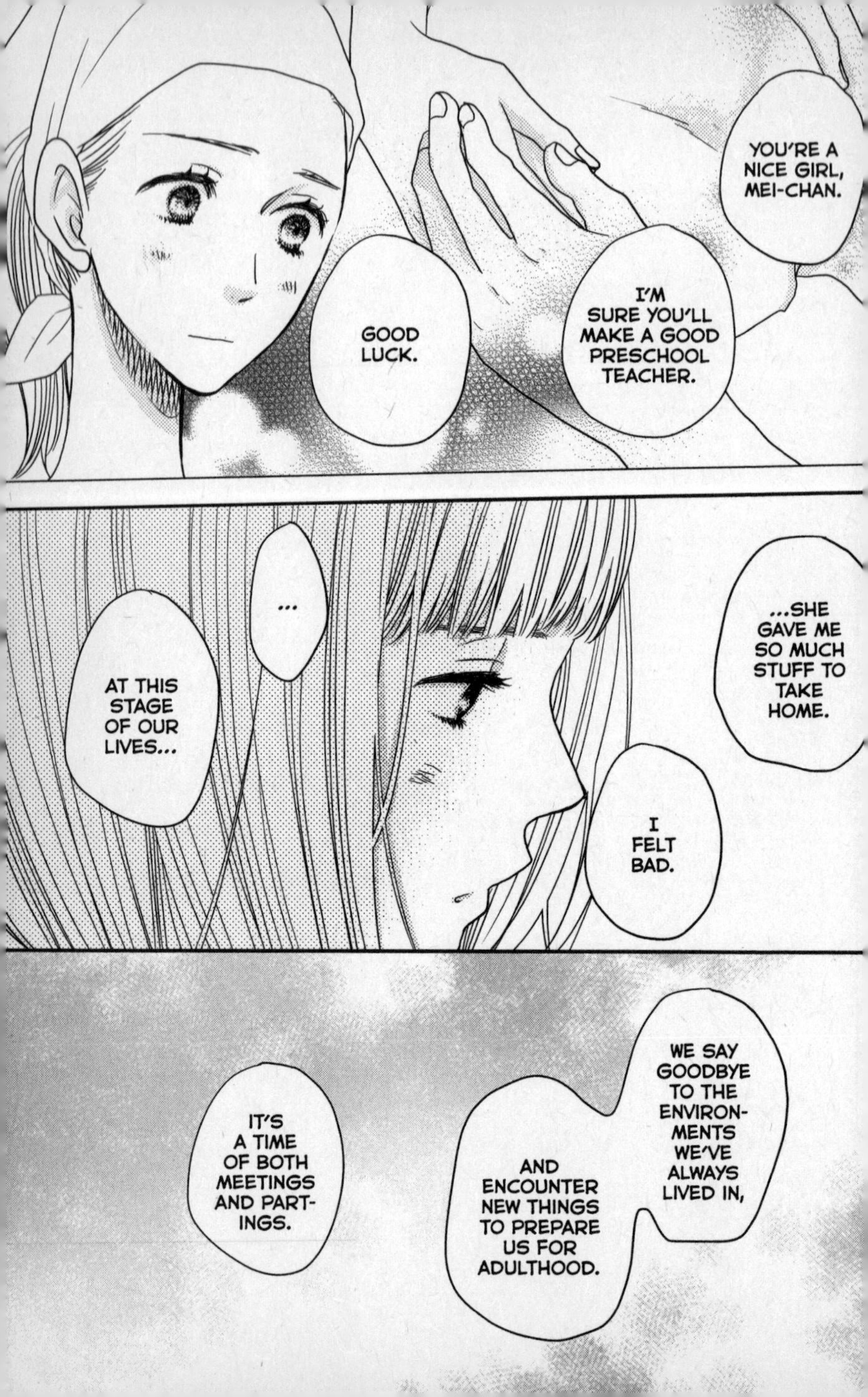
YOU'RE A NICE GIRL, MEI-CHAN.
I'M SURE YOU'LL MAKE A GOOD PRESCHOOL TEACHER.
GOOD LUCK.
...SHE GAVE ME SO MUCH STUFF TO TAKE HOME.
I FELT BAD.
...
AT THIS STAGE OF OUR LIVES...
WE SAY GOODBYE TO THE ENVIRON-MENTS WE'VE ALWAYS LIVED IN,
AND ENCOUNTER NEW THINGS TO PREPARE US FOR ADULTHOOD.
IT'S A TIME OF BOTH MEETINGS AND PART-INGS.

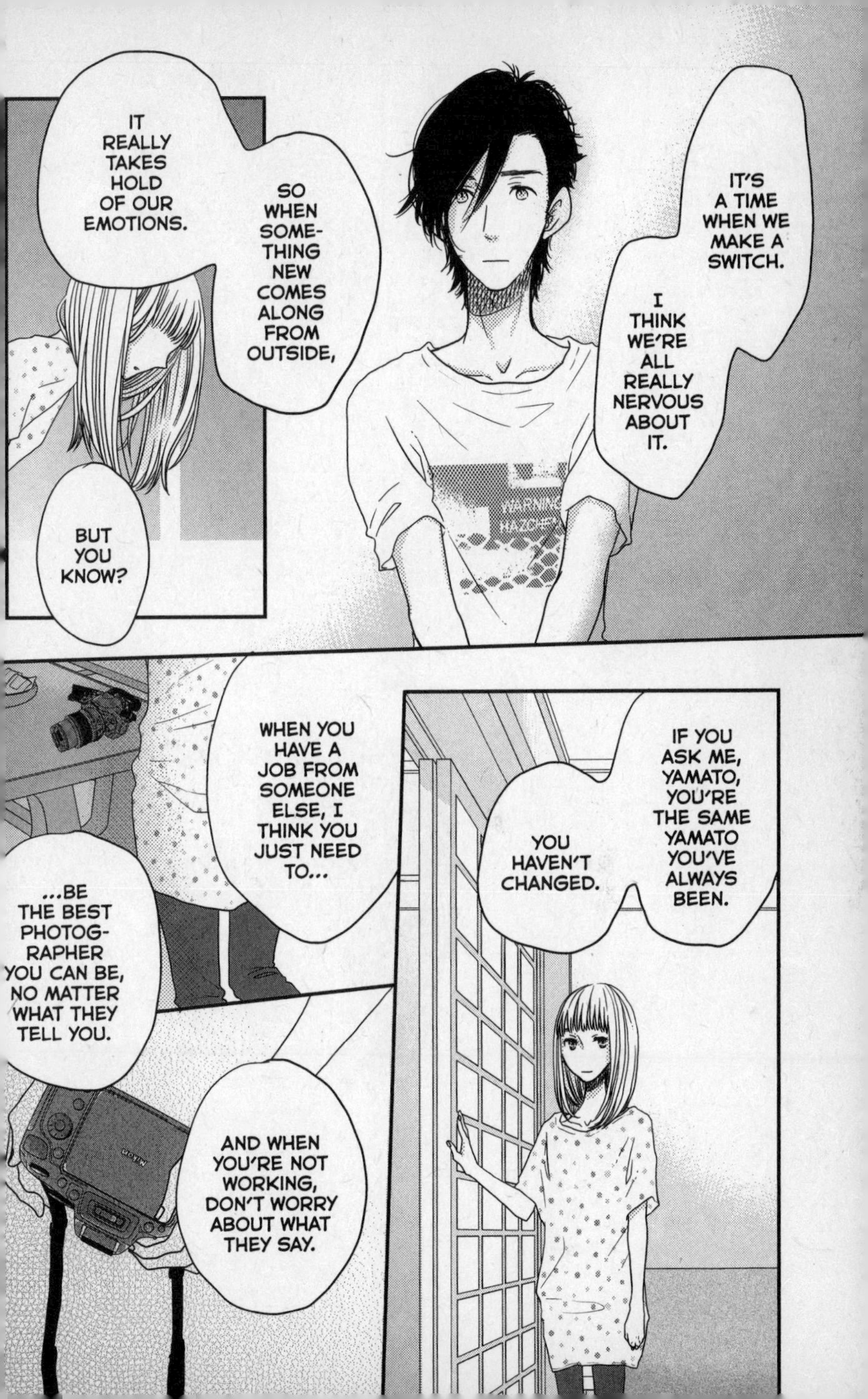
IT'S A TIME WHEN WE MAKE A SWITCH.
I THINK WE'RE ALL REALLY NERVOUS ABOUT IT.
SO WHEN SOME-THING NEW COMES ALONG FROM OUTSIDE,
IT REALLY TAKES HOLD OF OUR EMOTIONS.
BUT YOU KNOW?
IF YOU ASK ME, YAMATO, YOU'RE THE SAME YAMATO YOU'VE ALWAYS BEEN.
YOU HAVEN'T CHANGED.
WHEN YOU HAVE A JOB FROM SOMEONE ELSE, I THINK YOU JUST NEED TO...
...BE THE BEST PHOTOG-RAPHER YOU CAN BE, NO MATTER WHAT THEY TELL YOU.
AND WHEN YOU'RE NOT WORKING, DON'T WORRY ABOUT WHAT THEY SAY.

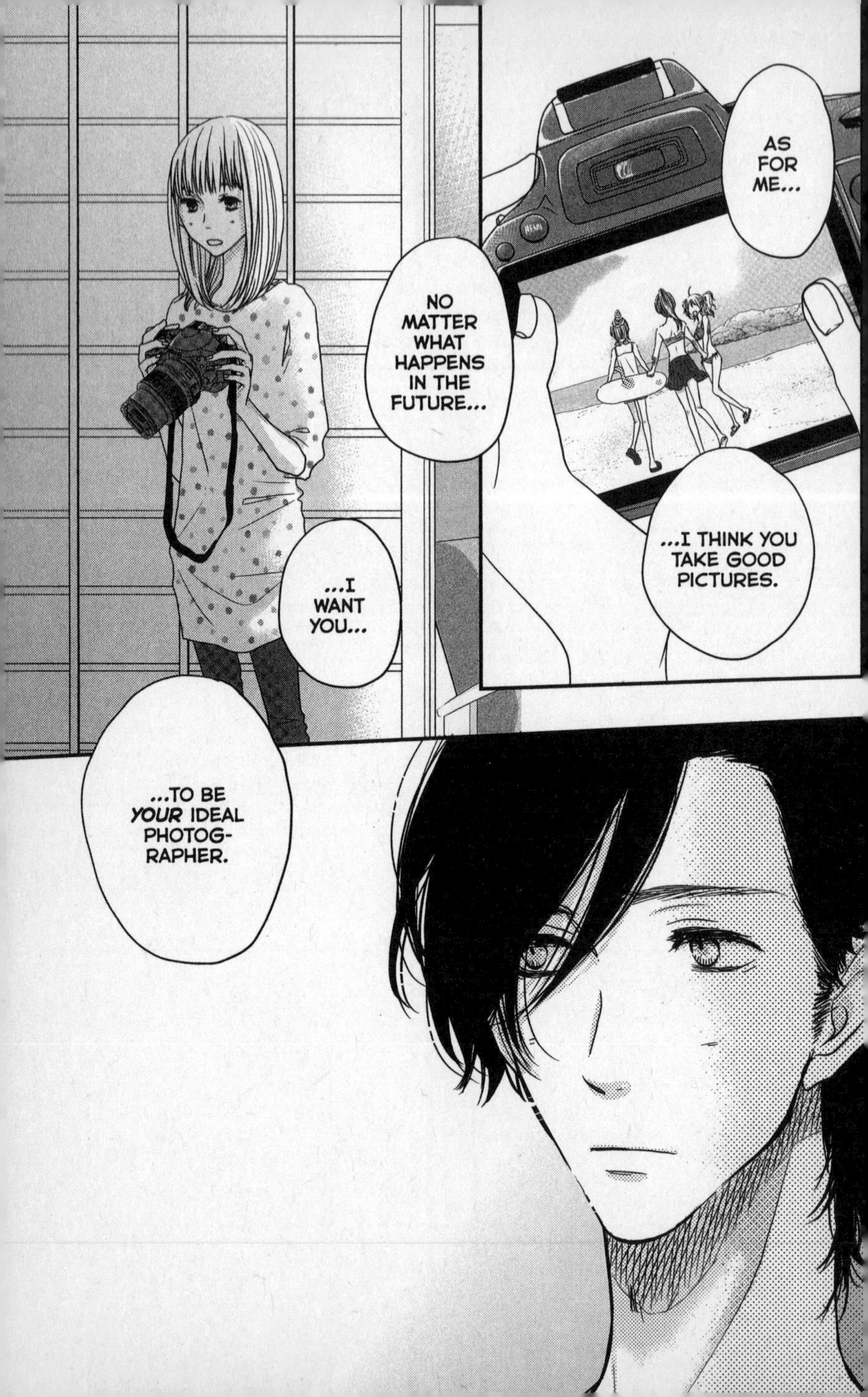
AS FOR ME...
...I THINK YOU TAKE GOOD PICTURES.
NO MATTER WHAT HAPPENS IN THE FUTURE...
...I WANT YOU...
...TO BE *YOUR* IDEAL PHOTOG-RAPHER.

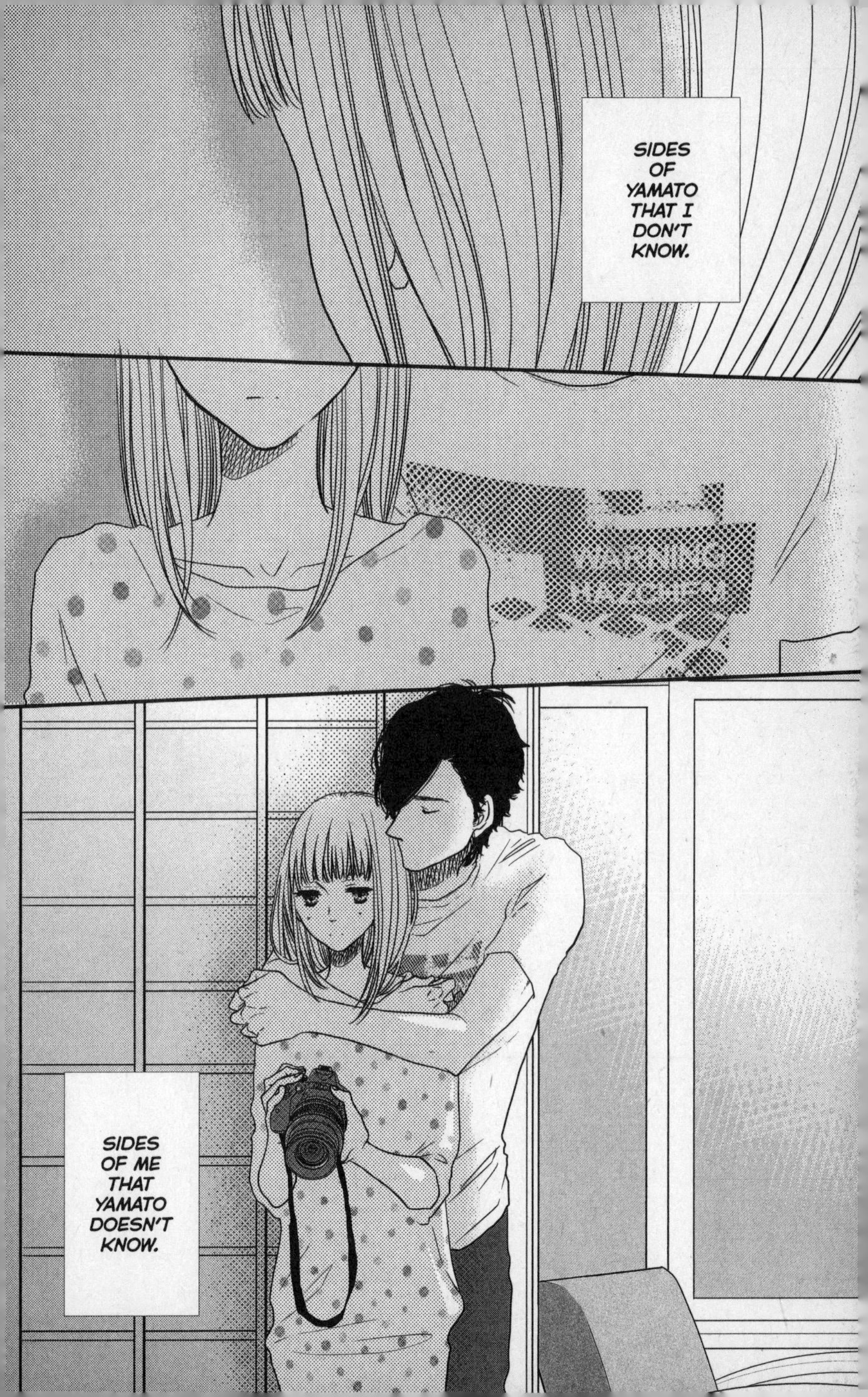
SIDES OF YAMATO THAT I DON'T KNOW.
SIDES OF ME THAT YAMATO DOESN'T KNOW.

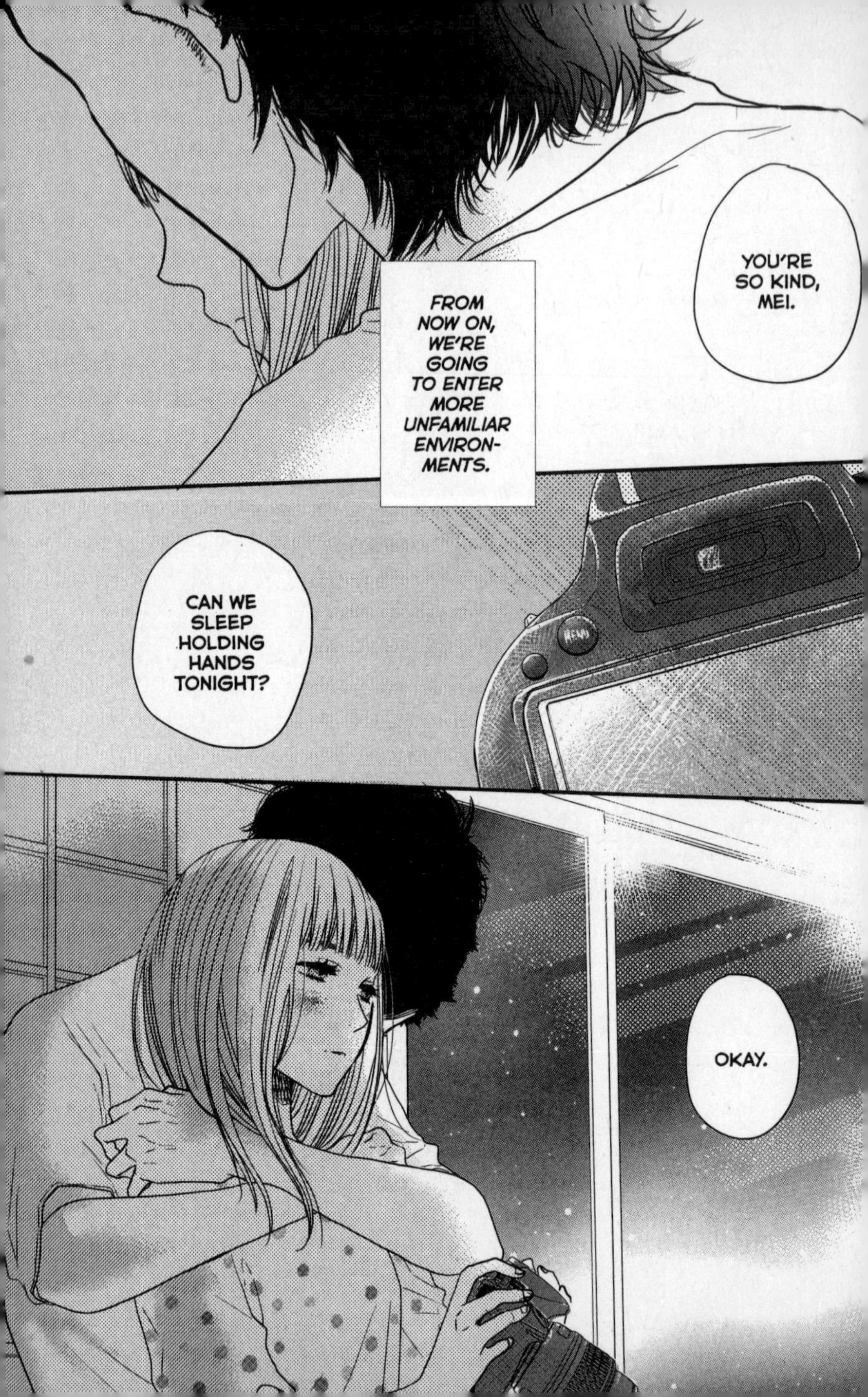
YOU'RE SO KIND, MEI.
FROM NOW ON, WE'RE GOING TO ENTER MORE UNFAMILIAR ENVIRON-MENTS.
CAN WE SLEEP HOLDING HANDS TONIGHT?
OKAY.

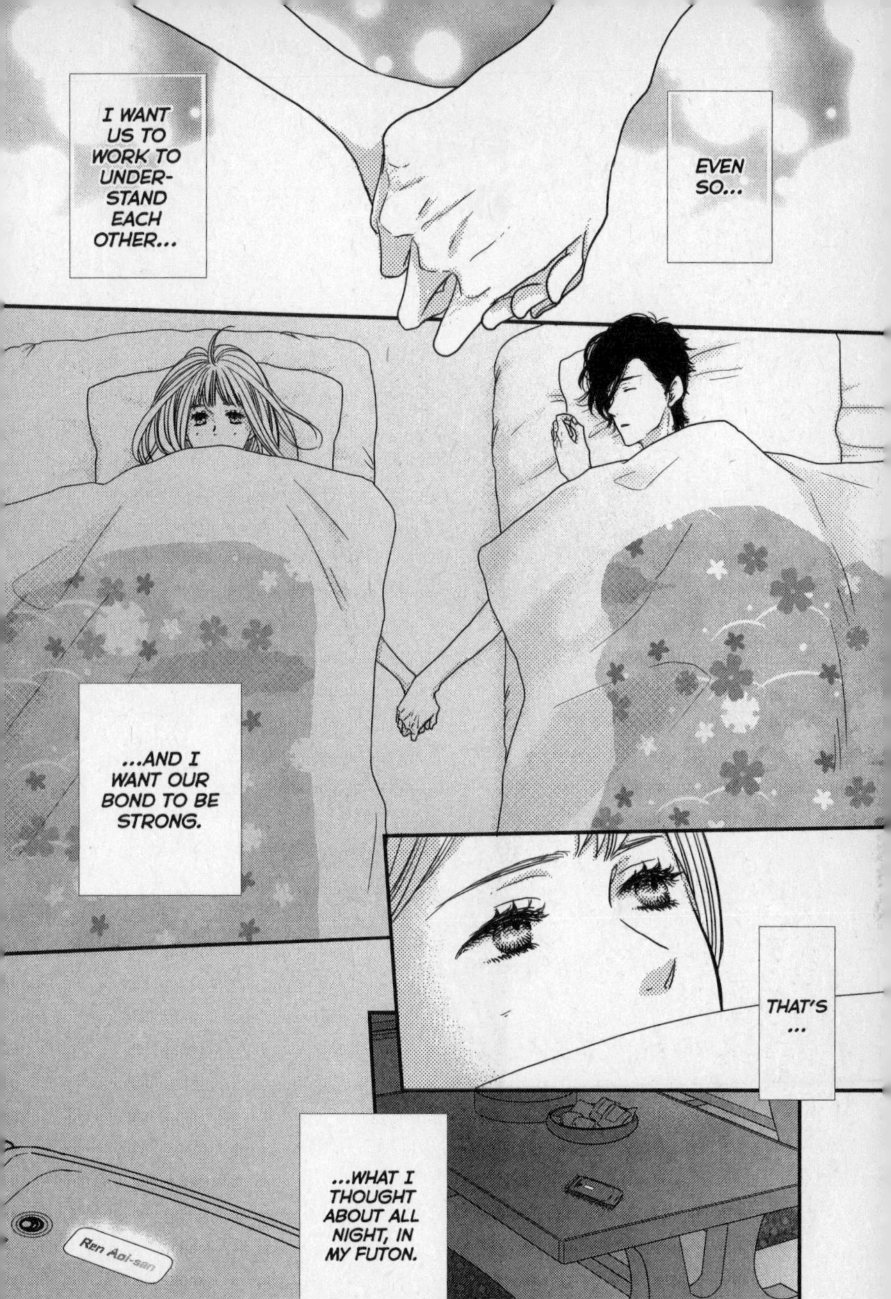
EVEN SO...
I WANT US TO WORK TO UNDERSTAND EACH OTHER...
...AND I WANT OUR BOND TO BE STRONG.
THAT'S ...
...WHAT I THOUGHT ABOUT ALL NIGHT, IN MY FUTON.
Ren Aoi-san

Chapter 53 / end

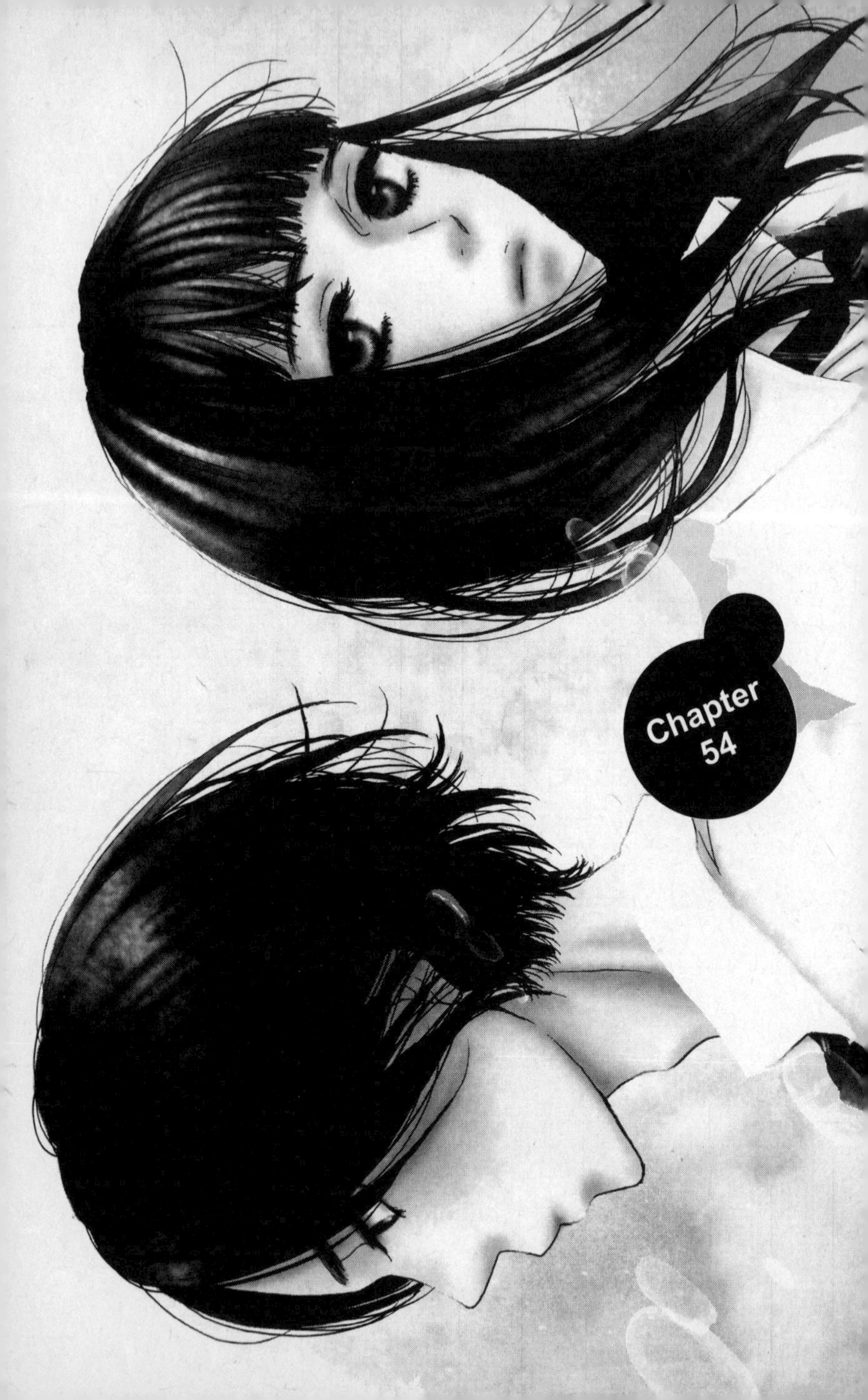
Chapter
54

Say "I love you".

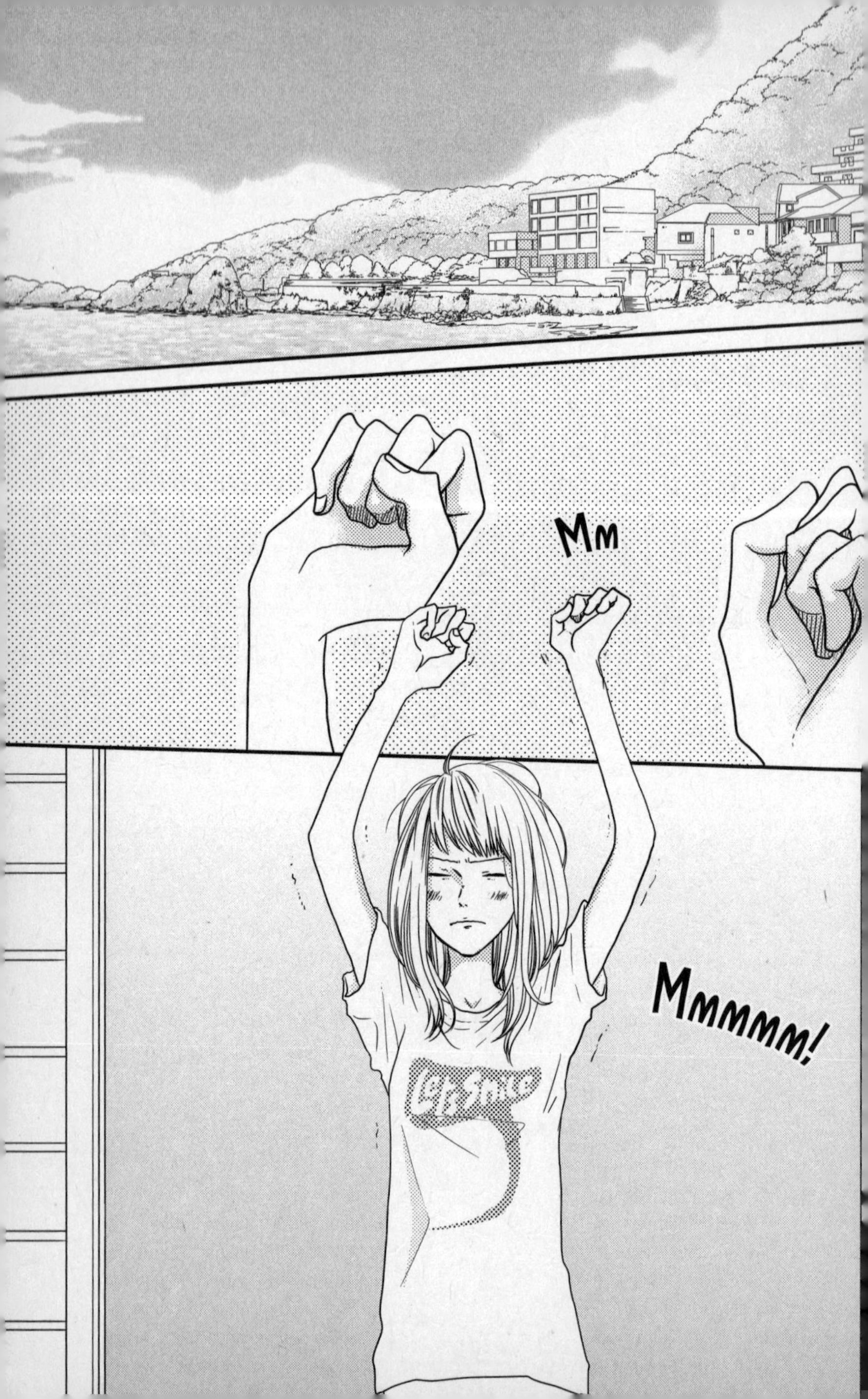
Mm
Mmmmm!

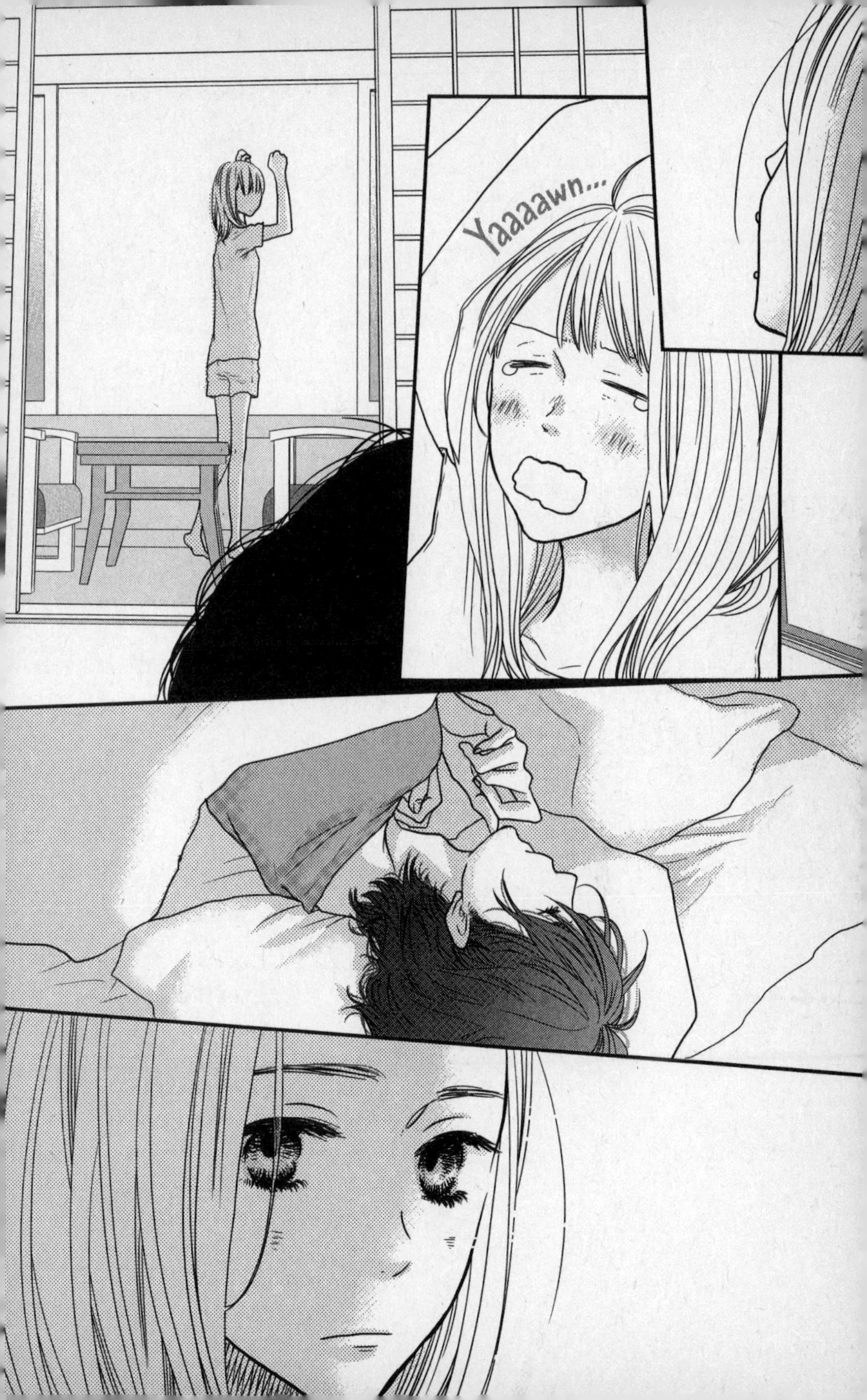
Yaaaawn...

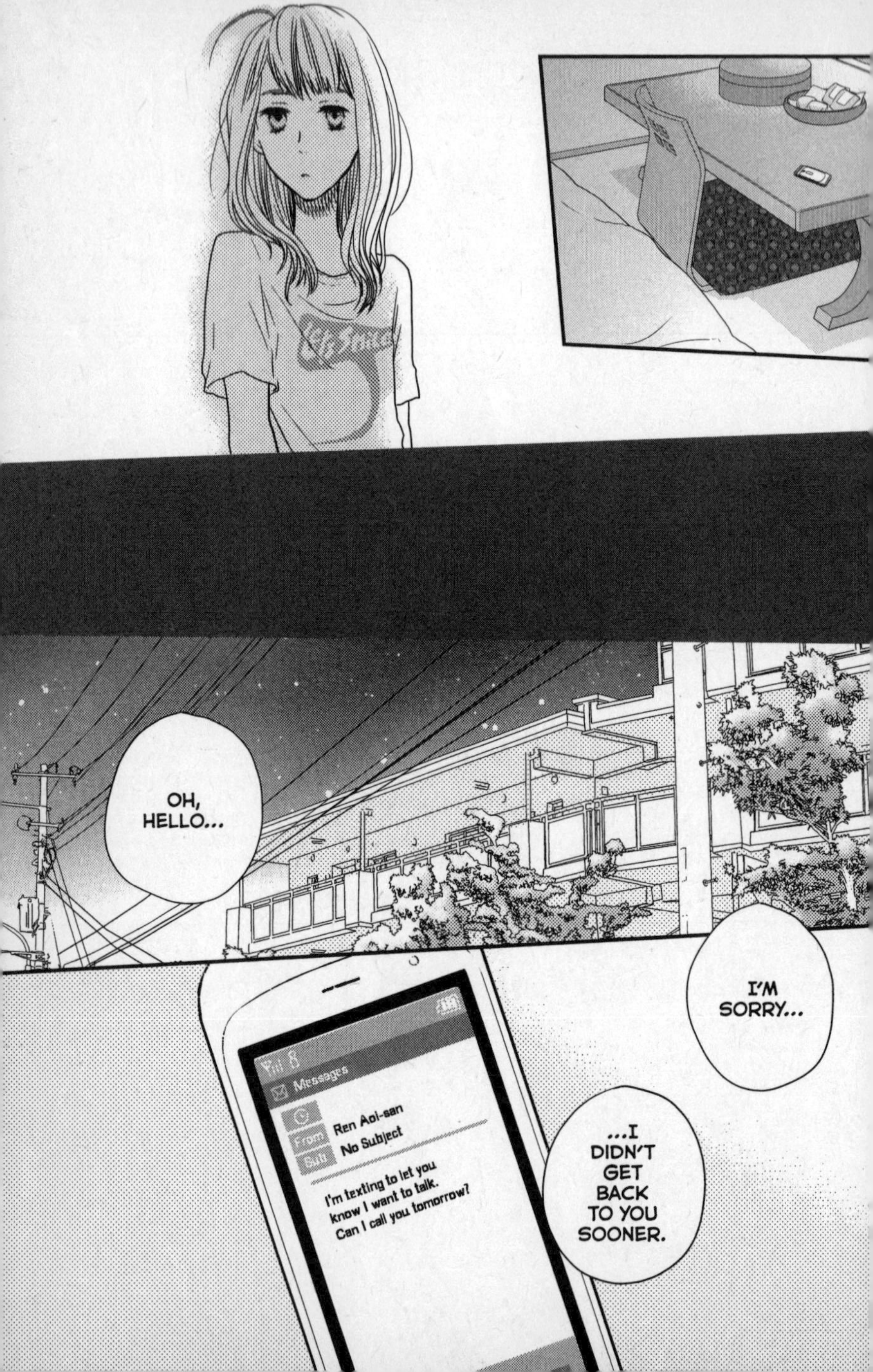
OH, HELLO...
I'M SORRY...
...I DIDN'T GET BACK TO YOU SOONER.
Messages
From Ren Aoi-san
Sub No Subject
I'm texting to let you know I want to talk. Can I call you tomorrow?

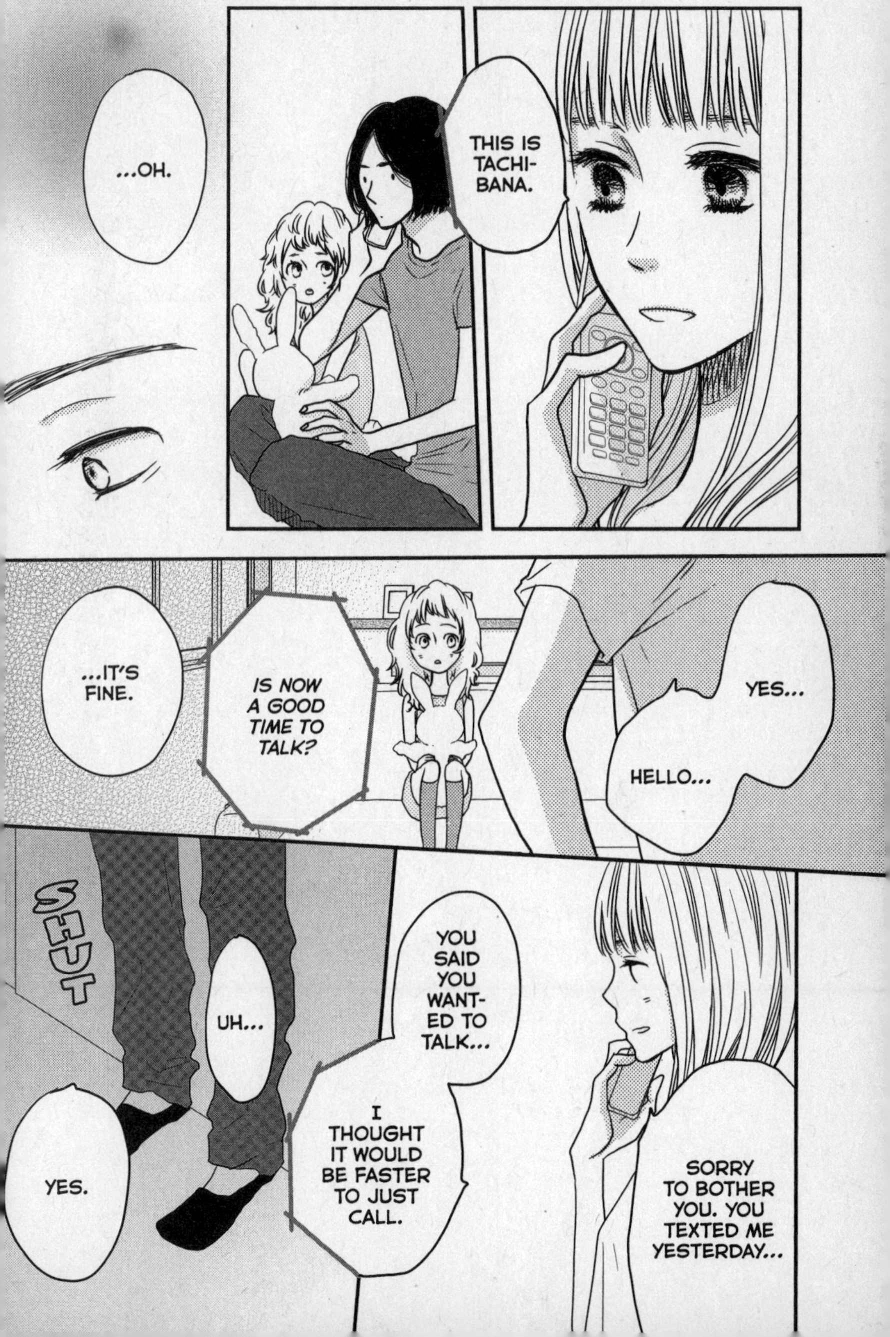
THIS IS TACHIBANA.
...OH.
YES...
HELLO...
IS NOW A GOOD TIME TO TALK?
...IT'S FINE.
SORRY TO BOTHER YOU. YOU TEXTED ME YESTERDAY...
YOU SAID YOU WANTED TO TALK...
I THOUGHT IT WOULD BE FASTER TO JUST CALL.
SHUT
UH...
YES.

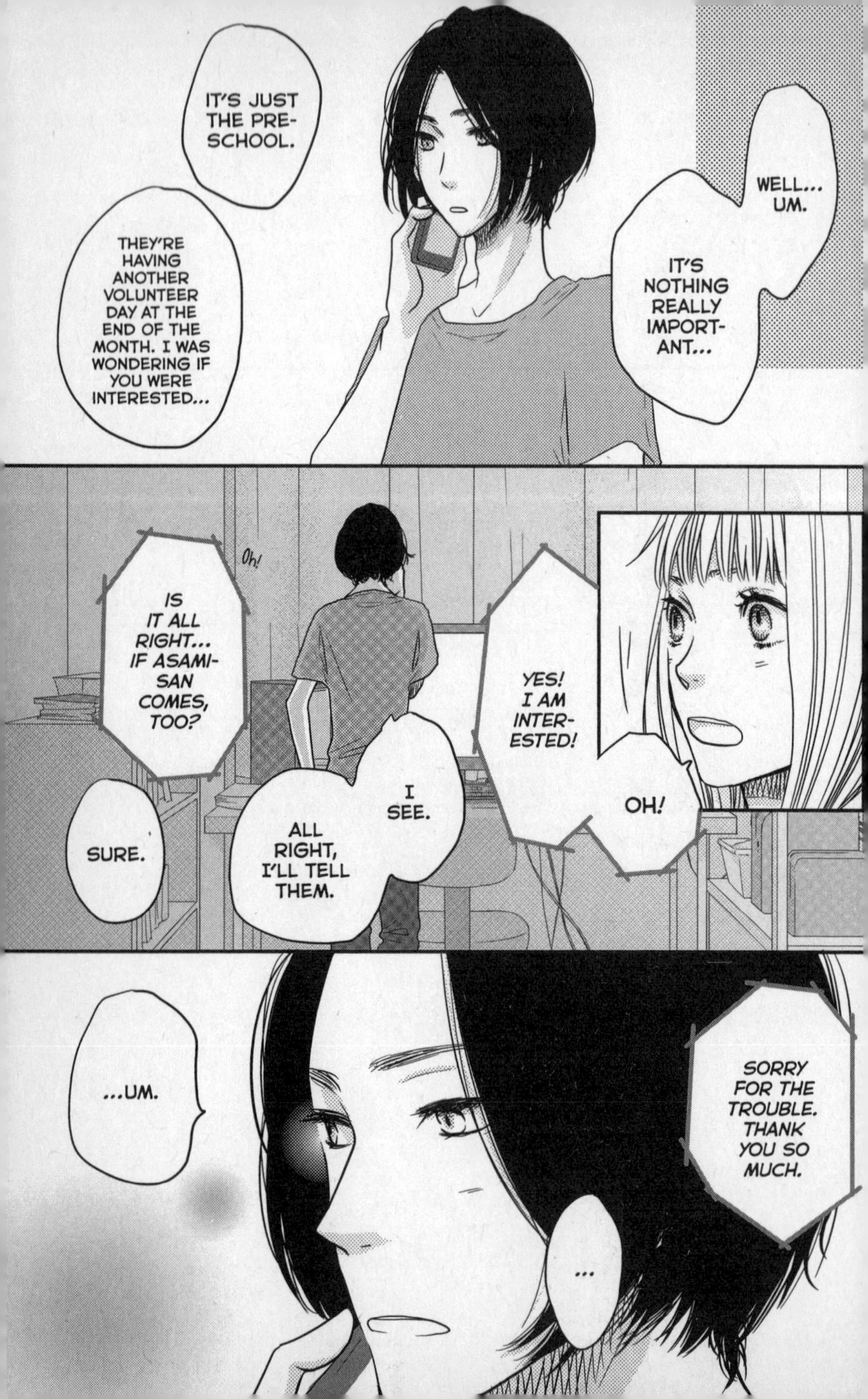
WELL... UM.
IT'S NOTHING REALLY IMPORT-ANT...
IT'S JUST THE PRE-SCHOOL.
THEY'RE HAVING ANOTHER VOLUNTEER DAY AT THE END OF THE MONTH. I WAS WONDERING IF YOU WERE INTERESTED...
OH!
YES! I AM INTER-ESTED!
I SEE.
ALL RIGHT, I'LL TELL THEM.
Oh!
IS IT ALL RIGHT... IF ASAMI-SAN COMES, TOO?
SURE.
SORRY FOR THE TROUBLE. THANK YOU SO MUCH.
...
...UM.

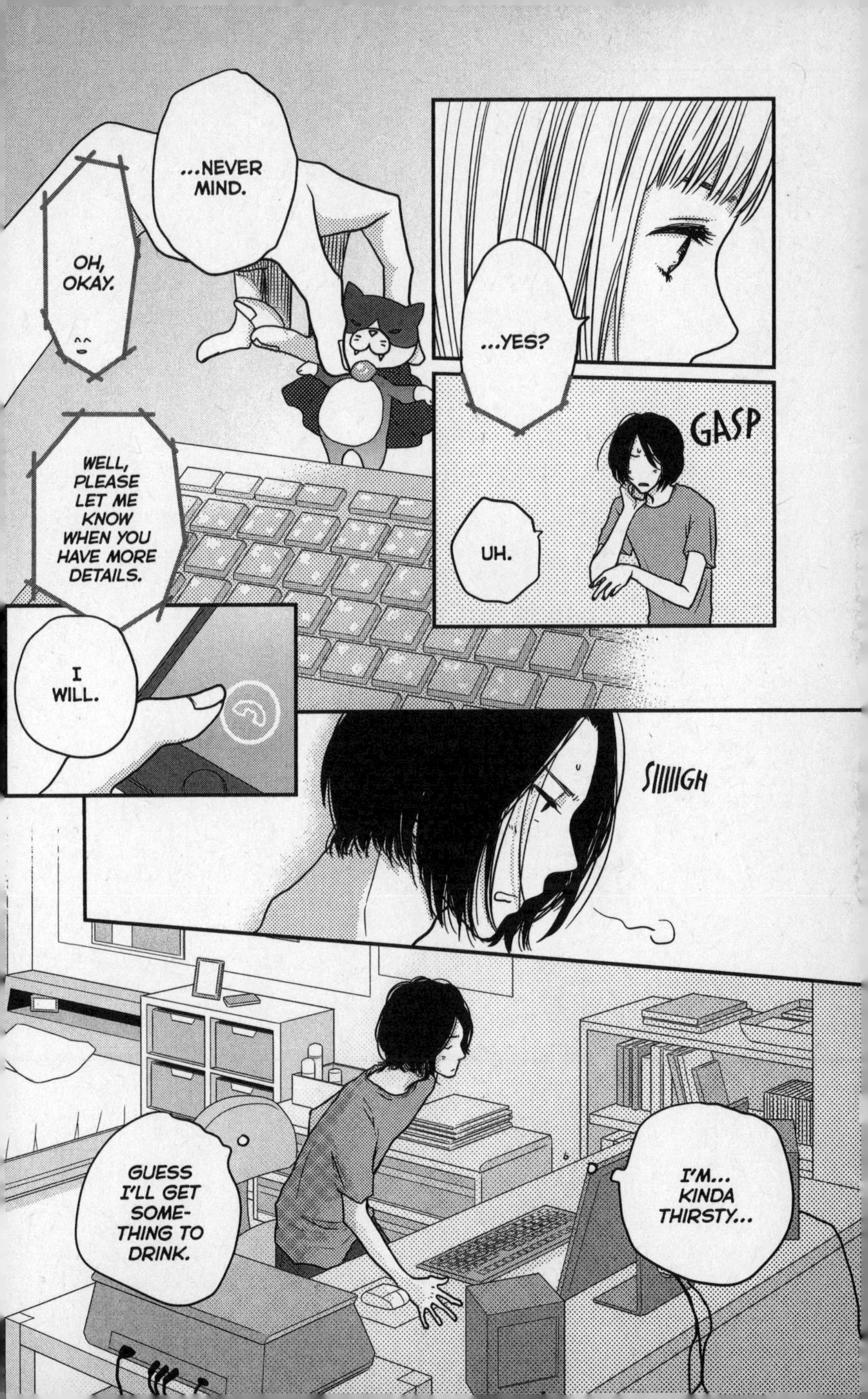

...YES?
GASP
UH.
...NEVER MIND.
OH, OKAY.
WELL, PLEASE LET ME KNOW WHEN YOU HAVE MORE DETAILS.
I WILL.
SIIIIGH
I'M... KINDA THIRSTY...
GUESS I'LL GET SOME-THING TO DRINK.

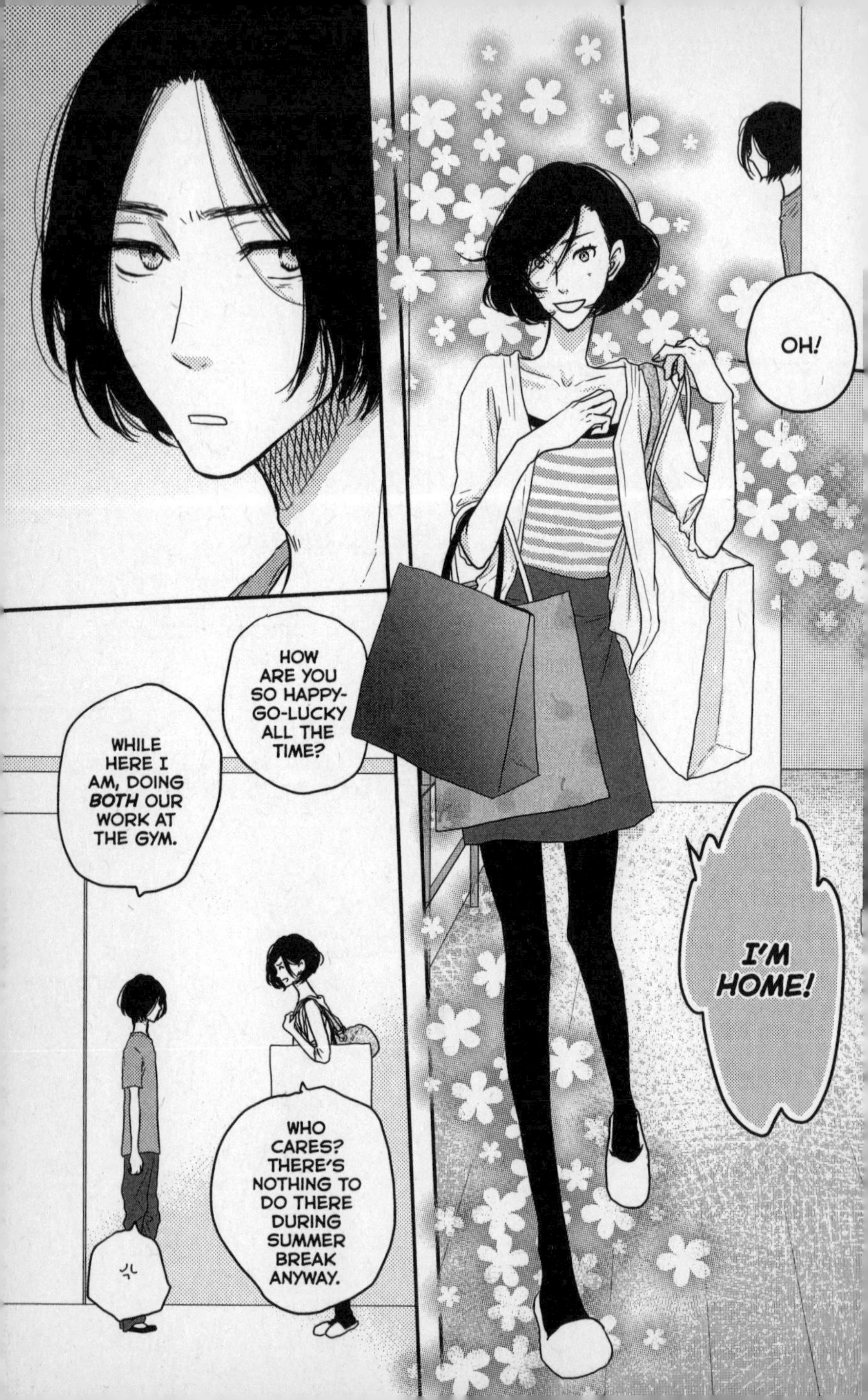
OH!
I'M HOME!
HOW ARE YOU SO HAPPY-GO-LUCKY ALL THE TIME?
WHILE HERE I AM, DOING *BOTH* OUR WORK AT THE GYM.
WHO CARES? THERE'S NOTHING TO DO THERE DURING SUMMER BREAK ANYWAY.

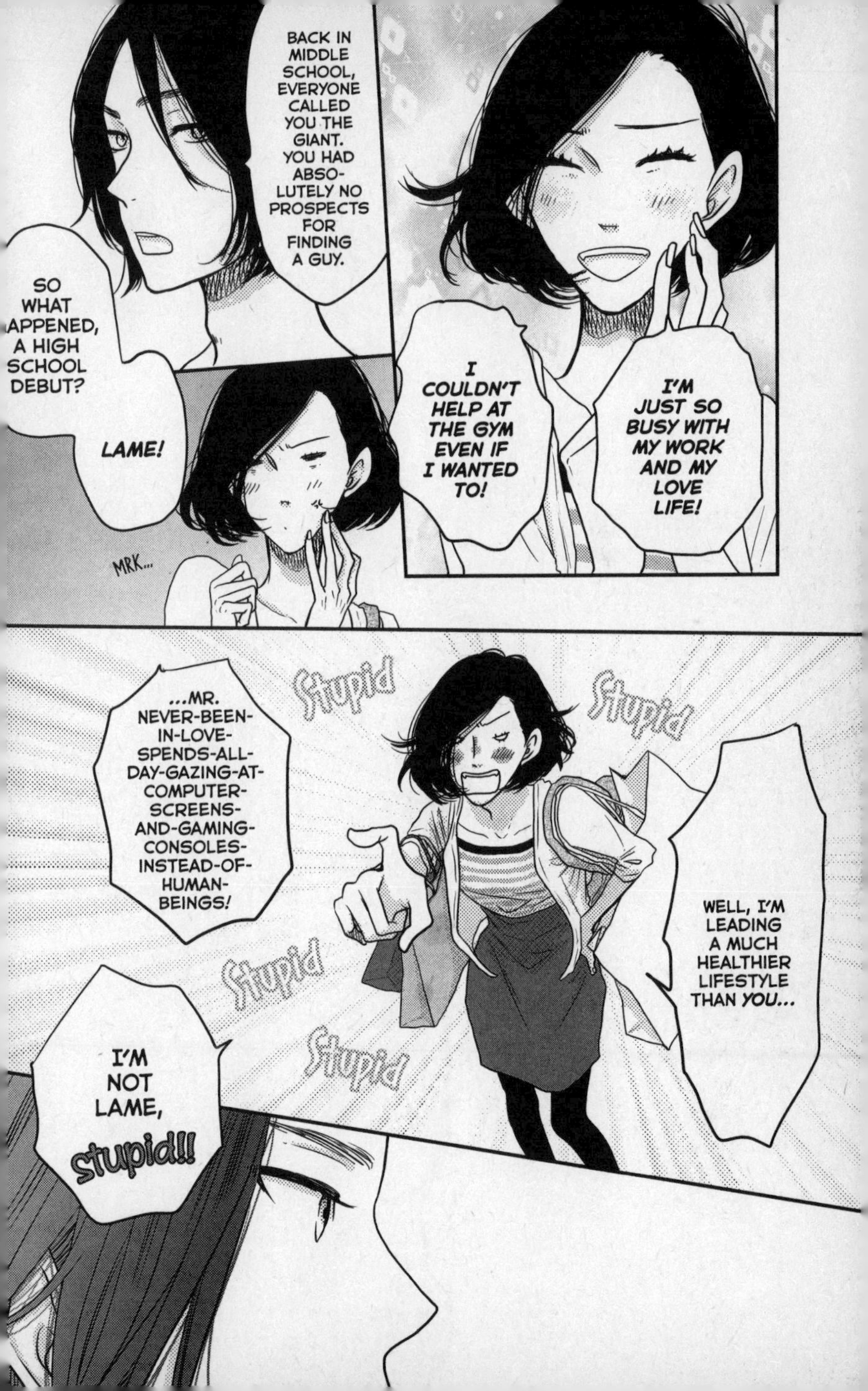
I'M JUST SO BUSY WITH MY WORK AND MY LOVE LIFE!
I COULDN'T HELP AT THE GYM EVEN IF I WANTED TO!
BACK IN MIDDLE SCHOOL, EVERYONE CALLED YOU THE GIANT. YOU HAD ABSO-LUTELY NO PROSPECTS FOR FINDING A GUY.
SO WHAT APPENED, A HIGH SCHOOL DEBUT?
LAME!
MRK...
WELL, I'M LEADING A MUCH HEALTHIER LIFESTYLE THAN YOU...
...MR. NEVER-BEEN-IN-LOVE-SPENDS-ALL-DAY-GAZING-AT-COMPUTER-SCREENS-AND-GAMING-CONSOLES-INSTEAD-OF-HUMAN-BEINGS!
Stupid
Stupid
Stupid
Stupid
I'M NOT LAME, stupid!!

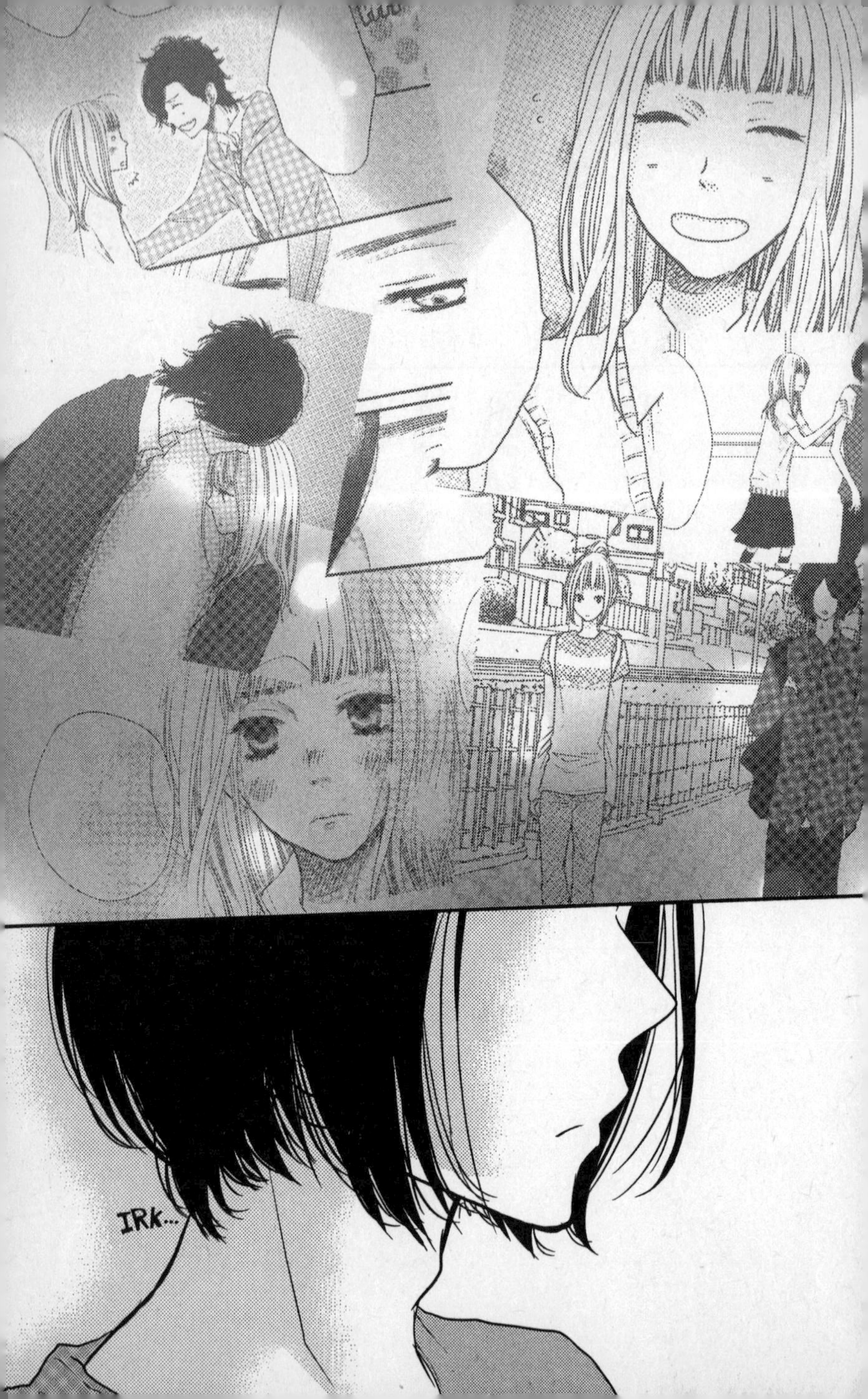
IRK...

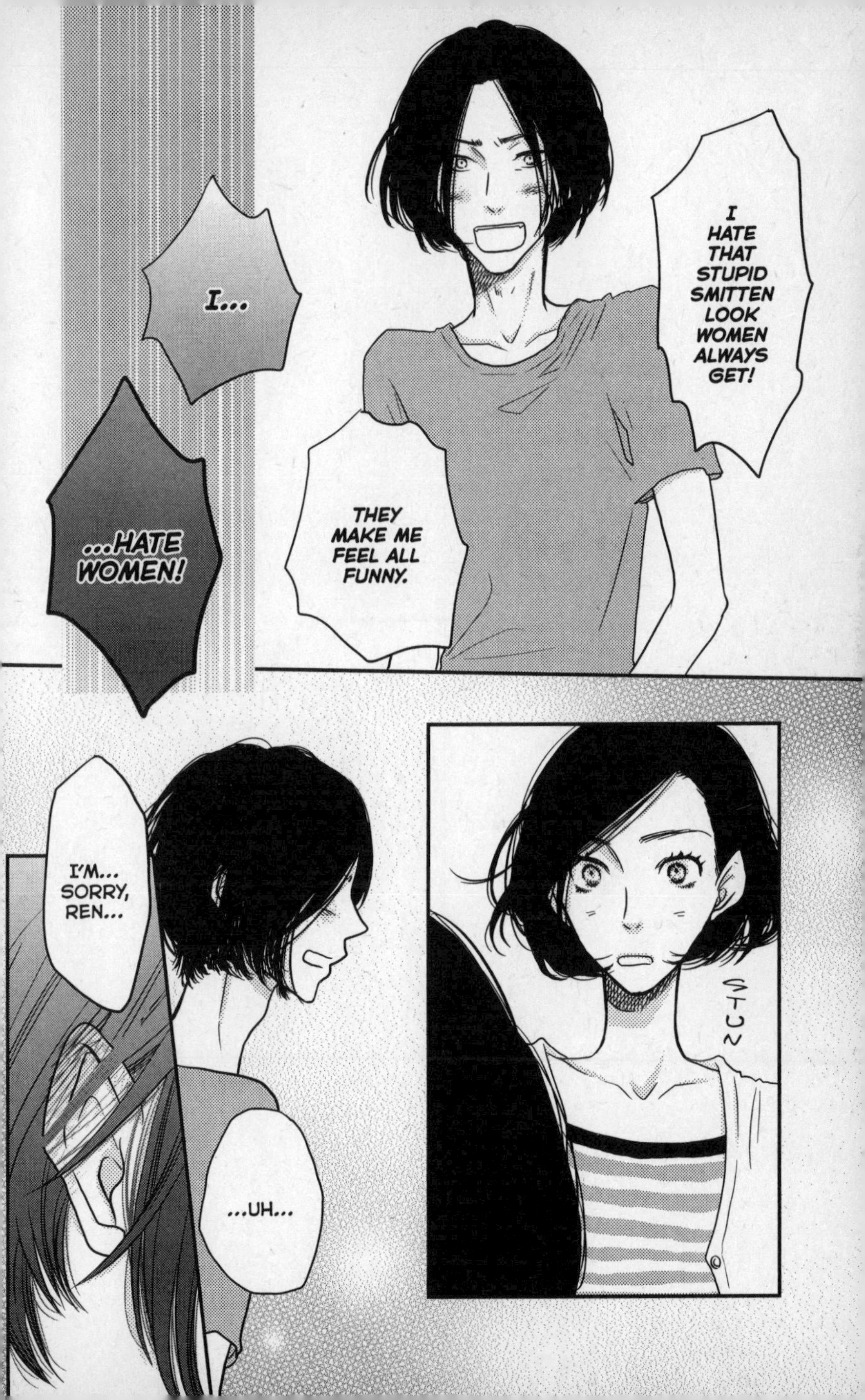
I HATE THAT STUPID SMITTEN LOOK WOMEN ALWAYS GET!
THEY MAKE ME FEEL ALL FUNNY.
I...
...HATE WOMEN!
STUN
I'M... SORRY, REN...
...UH...

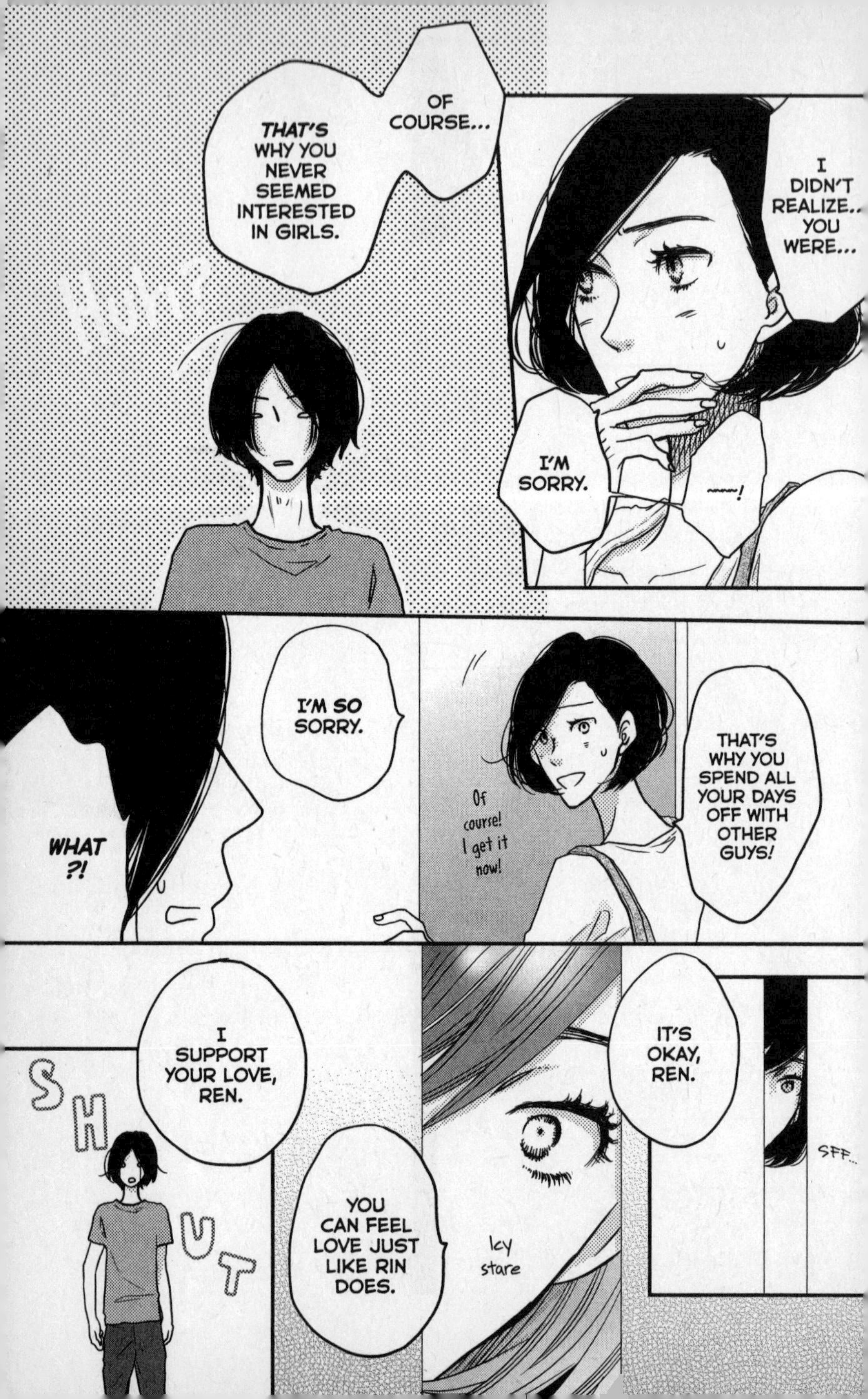
I DIDN'T REALIZE.. YOU WERE...
I'M SORRY.
~~~!
OF COURSE...
THAT'S WHY YOU NEVER SEEMED INTERESTED IN GIRLS.
Huh
THAT'S WHY YOU SPEND ALL YOUR DAYS OFF WITH OTHER GUYS!
Of course! I get it now!
I'M SO SORRY.
WHAT?!
IT'S OKAY, REN.
SFF...
Icy stare
YOU CAN FEEL LOVE JUST LIKE RIN DOES.
I SUPPORT YOUR LOVE, REN.
SHUT
~~~

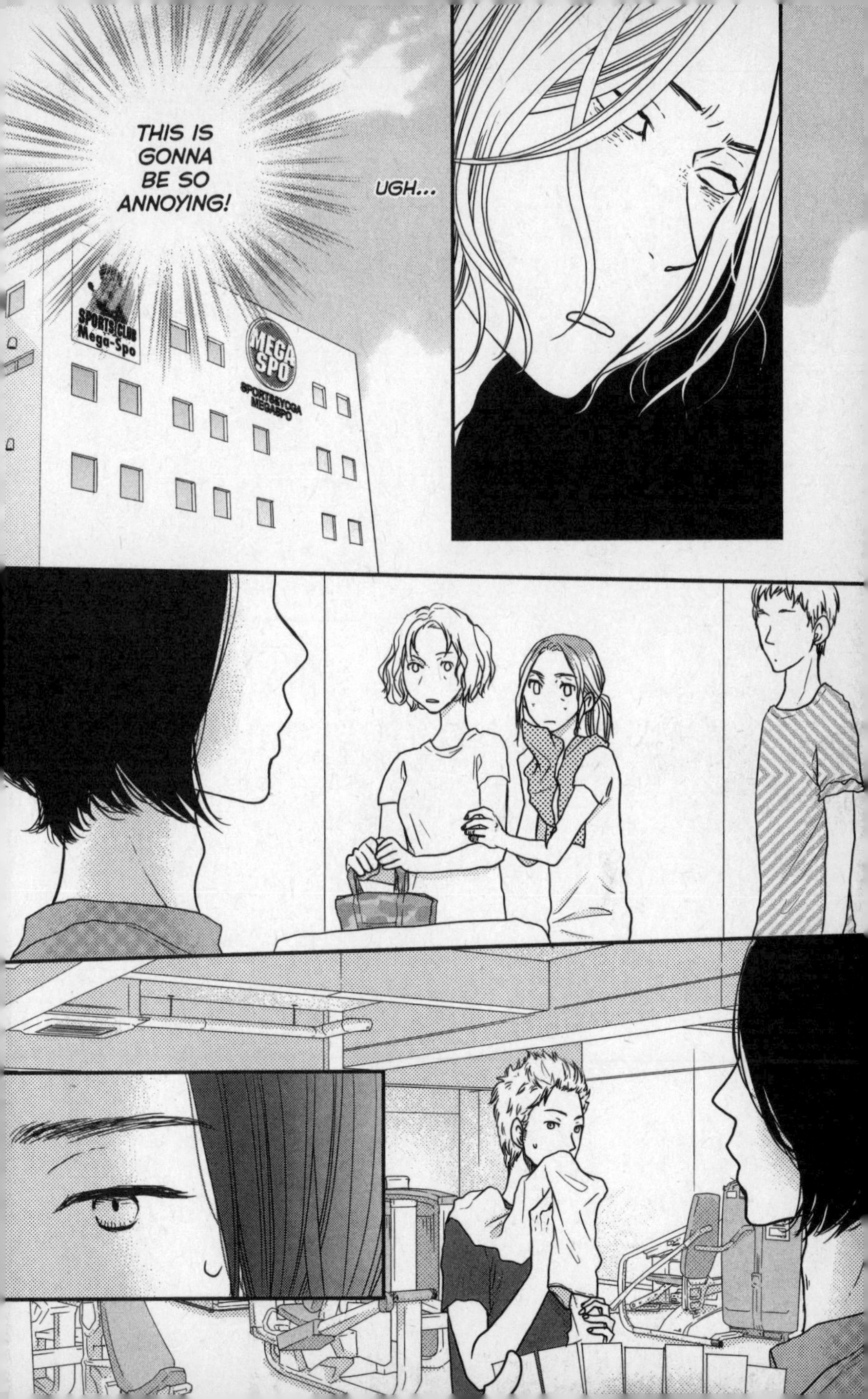
UGH...
THIS IS GONNA BE SO ANNOYING!
SPORTS CLUB Mega-Spo
MEGA SPO
SPORTS&YOGA MEGASPO

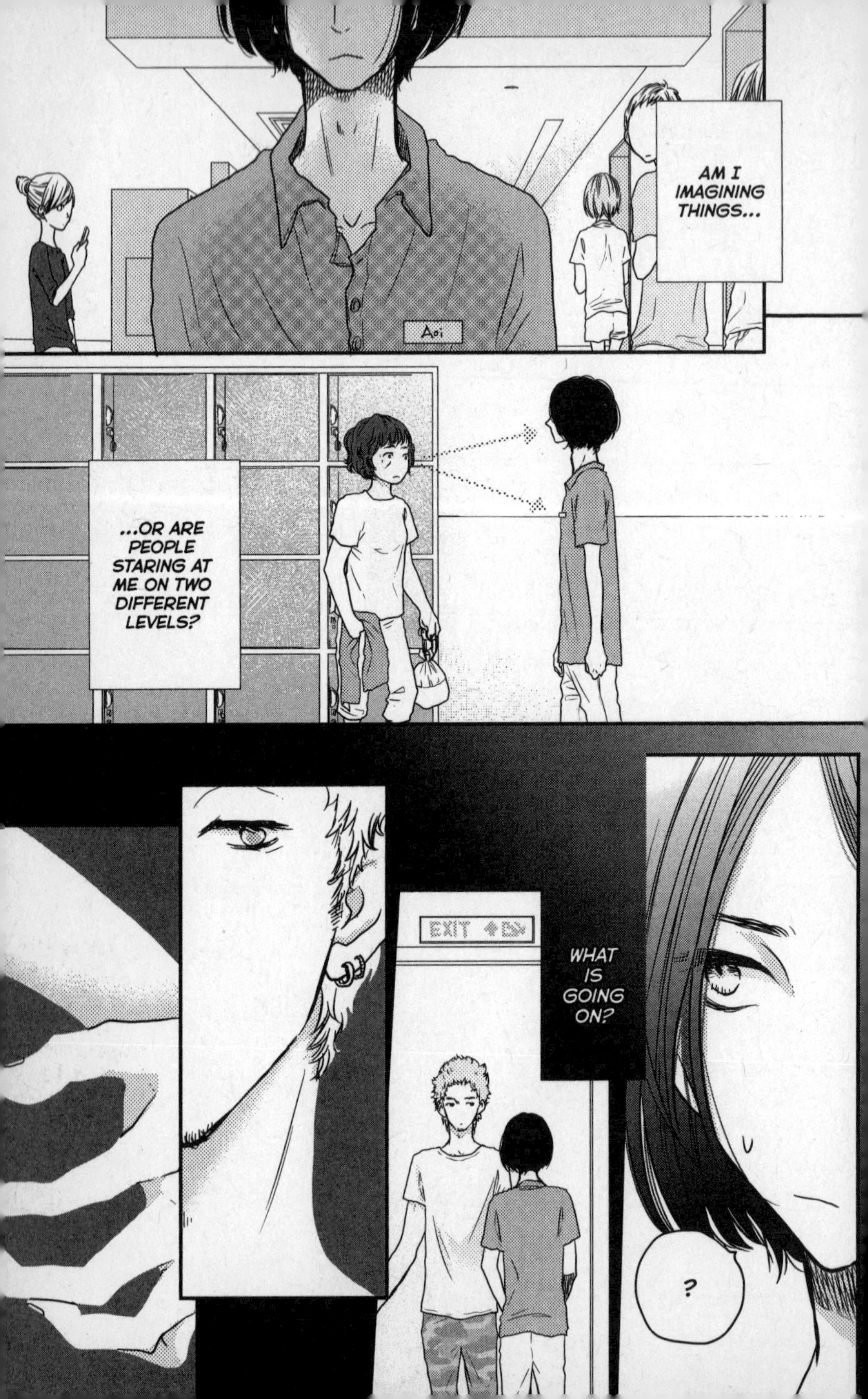
AM I IMAGINING THINGS...
Aoi
...OR ARE PEOPLE STARING AT ME ON TWO DIFFERENT LEVELS?
?
WHAT IS GOING ON?
EXIT

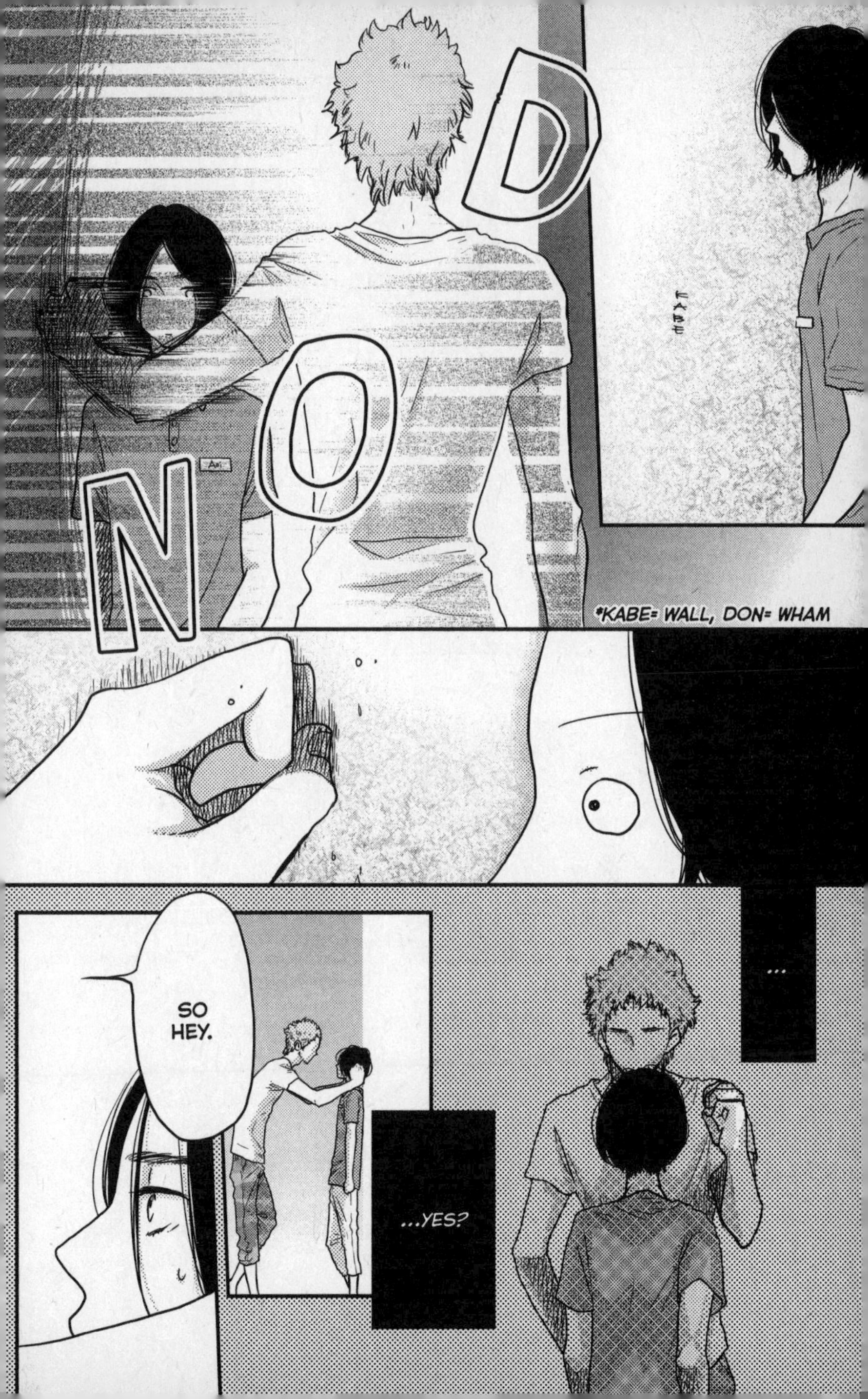
KABE
*KABE= WALL, DON= WHAM
DON
...
SO HEY.
...YES?

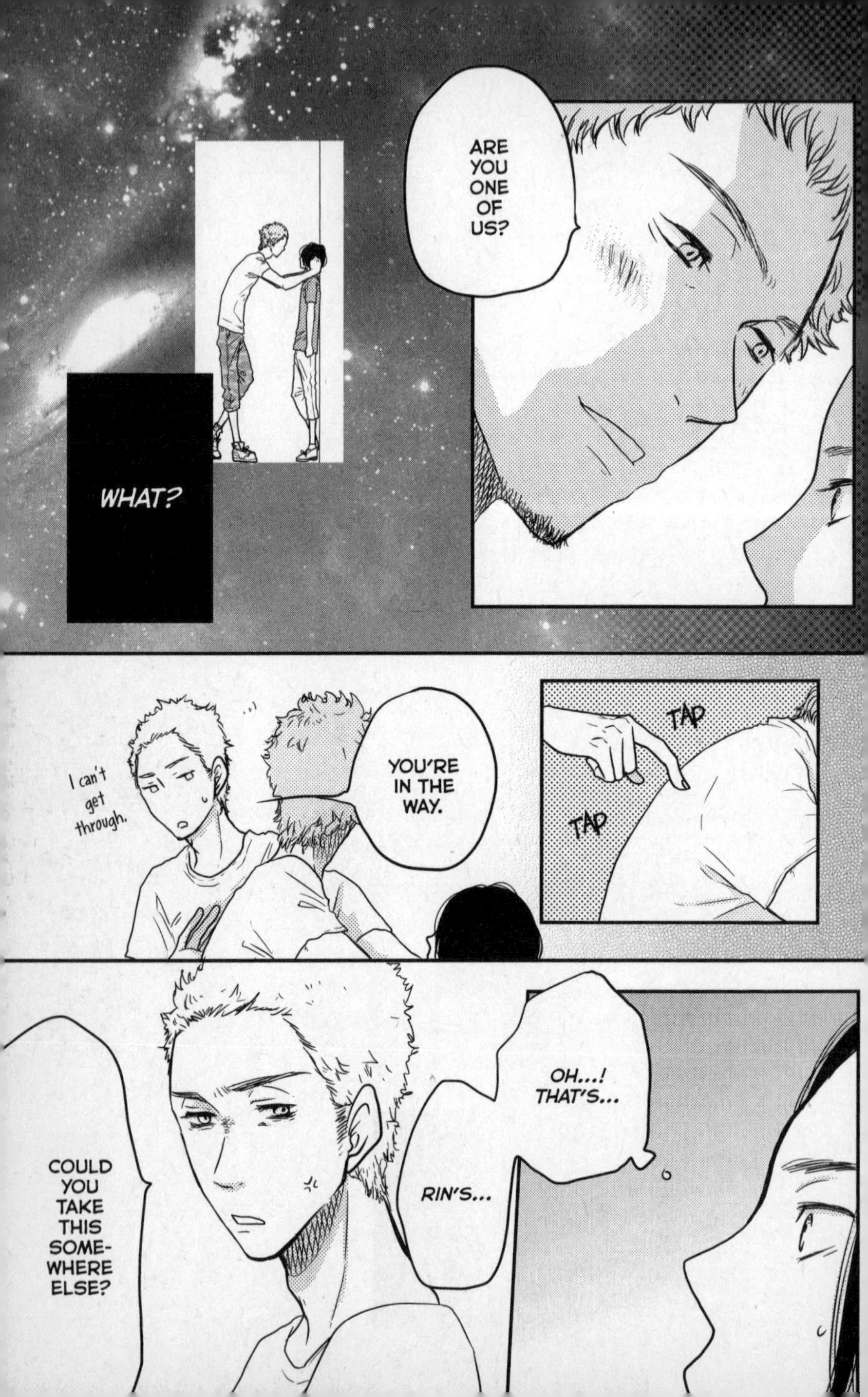
ARE YOU ONE OF US?
WHAT?
TAP
TAP
YOU'RE IN THE WAY.
I can't get through.
OH...! THAT'S...
RIN'S...
COULD YOU TAKE THIS SOME-WHERE ELSE?

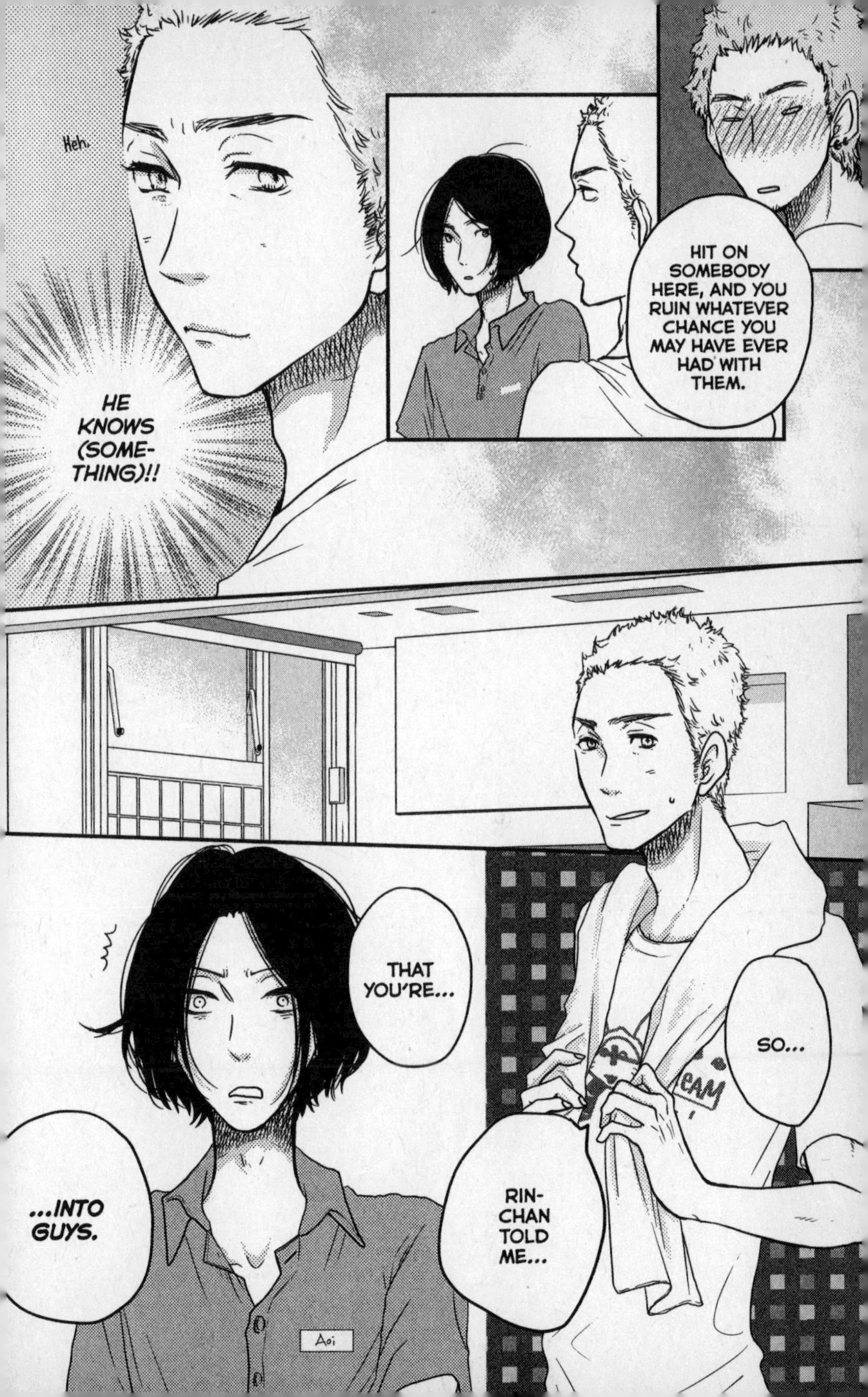
HIT ON SOMEBODY HERE, AND YOU RUIN WHATEVER CHANCE YOU MAY HAVE EVER HAD WITH THEM.
Heh.
HE KNOWS (SOMETHING)!!
SO...
RIN-CHAN TOLD ME...
THAT YOU'RE...
...INTO GUYS.
Aoi

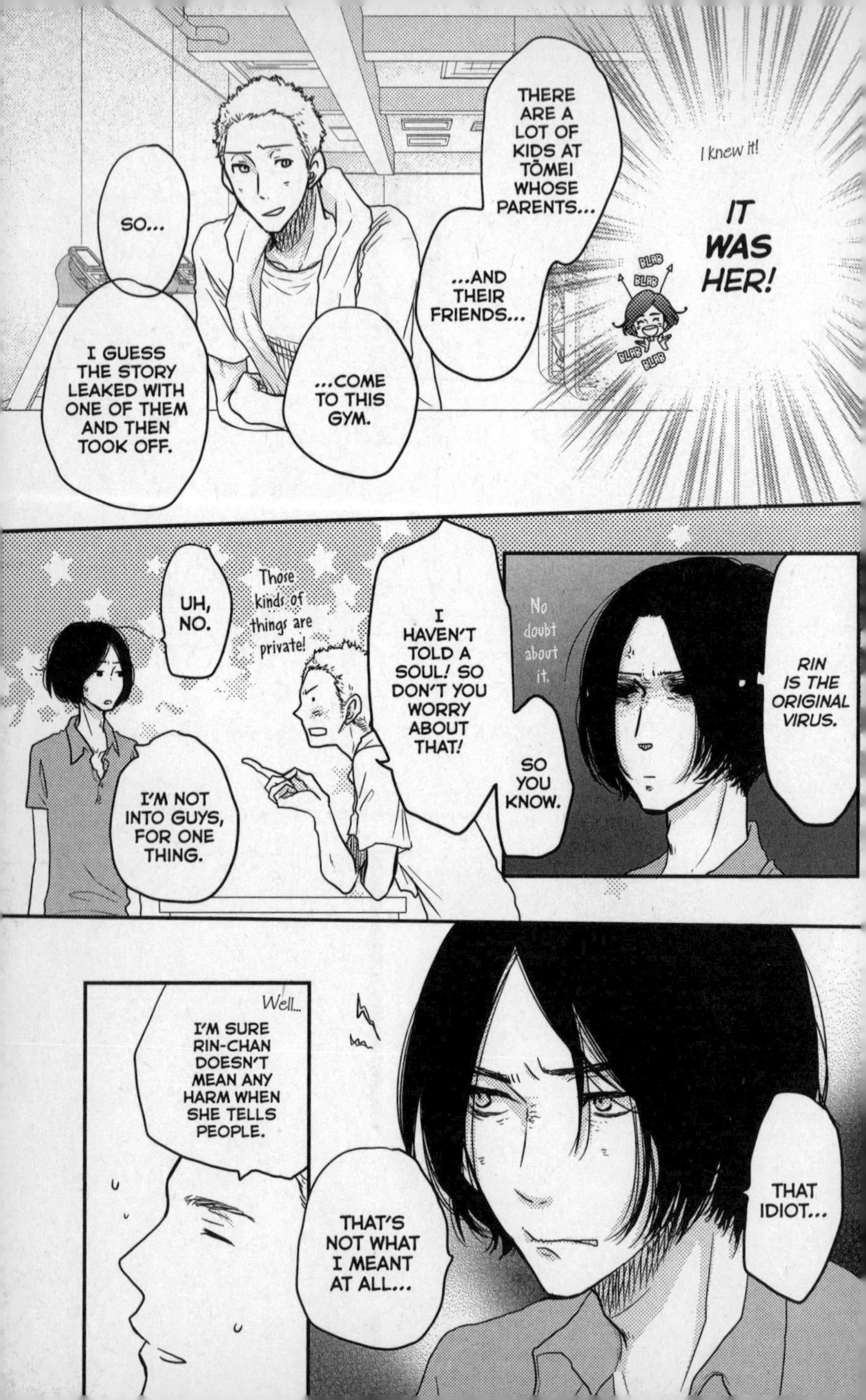
I knew it!
IT WAS HER!
BLAB BLAB BLAB BLAB
THERE ARE A LOT OF KIDS AT TŌMEI WHOSE PARENTS...
...AND THEIR FRIENDS...
...COME TO THIS GYM.
SO...
I GUESS THE STORY LEAKED WITH ONE OF THEM AND THEN TOOK OFF.
RIN IS THE ORIGINAL VIRUS.
No doubt about it.
SO YOU KNOW.
I HAVEN'T TOLD A SOUL! SO DON'T YOU WORRY ABOUT THAT!
Those kinds of things are private!
UH, NO.
I'M NOT INTO GUYS, FOR ONE THING.
THAT IDIOT...
Well...
I'M SURE RIN-CHAN DOESN'T MEAN ANY HARM WHEN SHE TELLS PEOPLE.
THAT'S NOT WHAT I MEANT AT ALL...

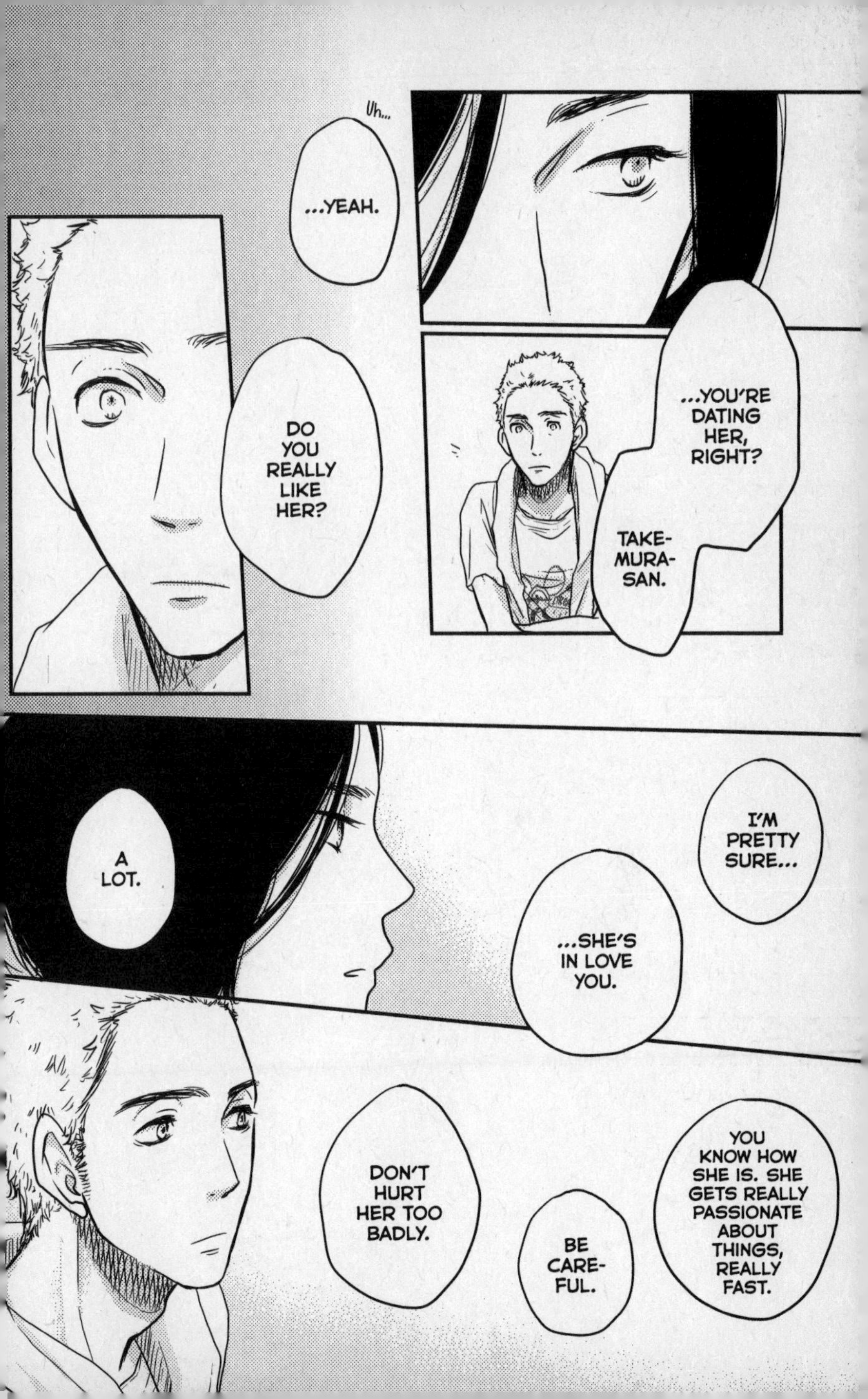

...YOU'RE DATING HER, RIGHT?
TAKE-MURA-SAN.
Uh...
...YEAH.
DO YOU REALLY LIKE HER?
I'M PRETTY SURE...
...SHE'S IN LOVE YOU.
A LOT.
YOU KNOW HOW SHE IS. SHE GETS REALLY PASSIONATE ABOUT THINGS, REALLY FAST.
BE CARE-FUL.
DON'T HURT HER TOO BADLY.

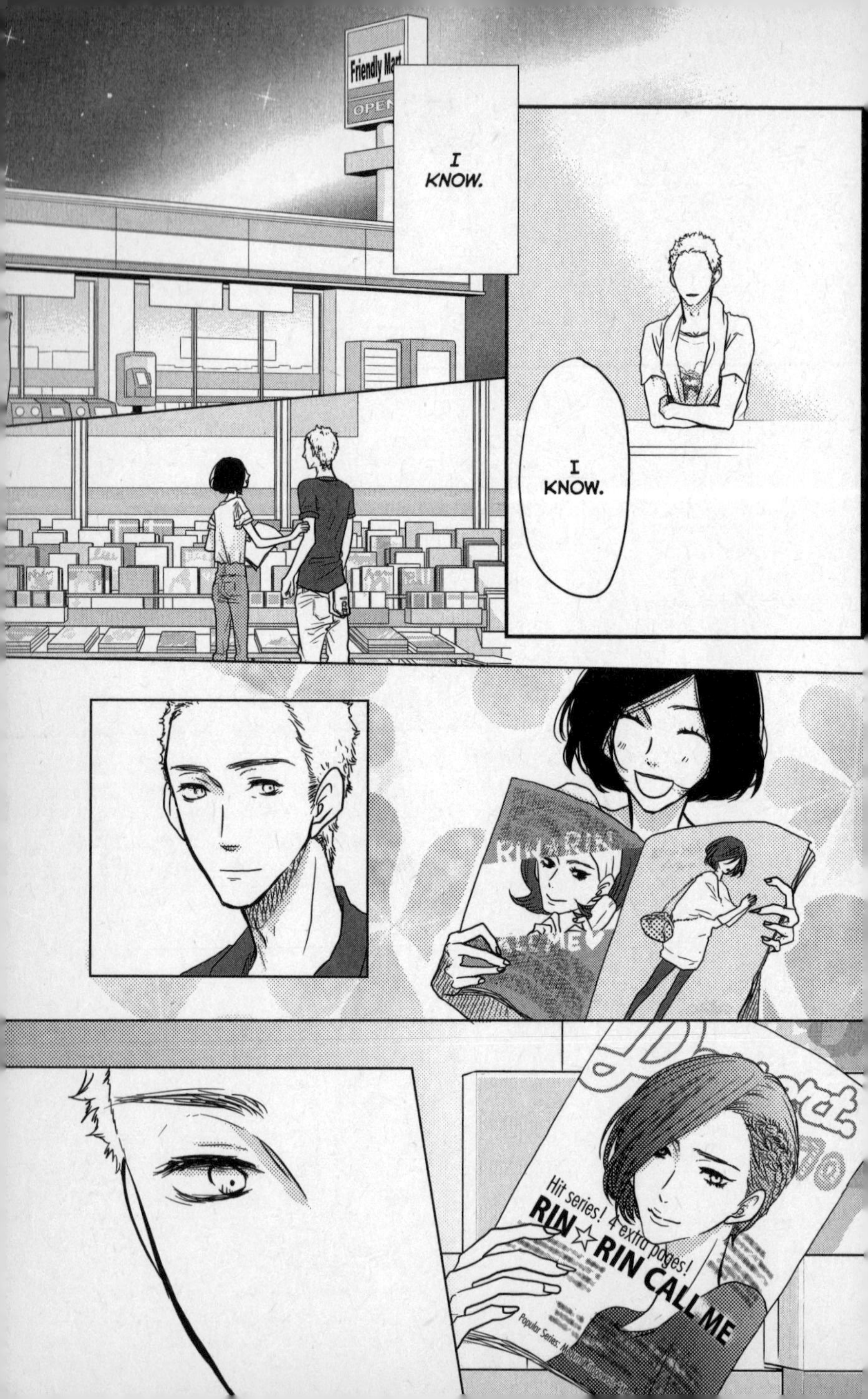
I KNOW.
I KNOW.
Friendly Mart
OPEN
Hit series! 4 extra pages!
RIN☆RIN CALL ME

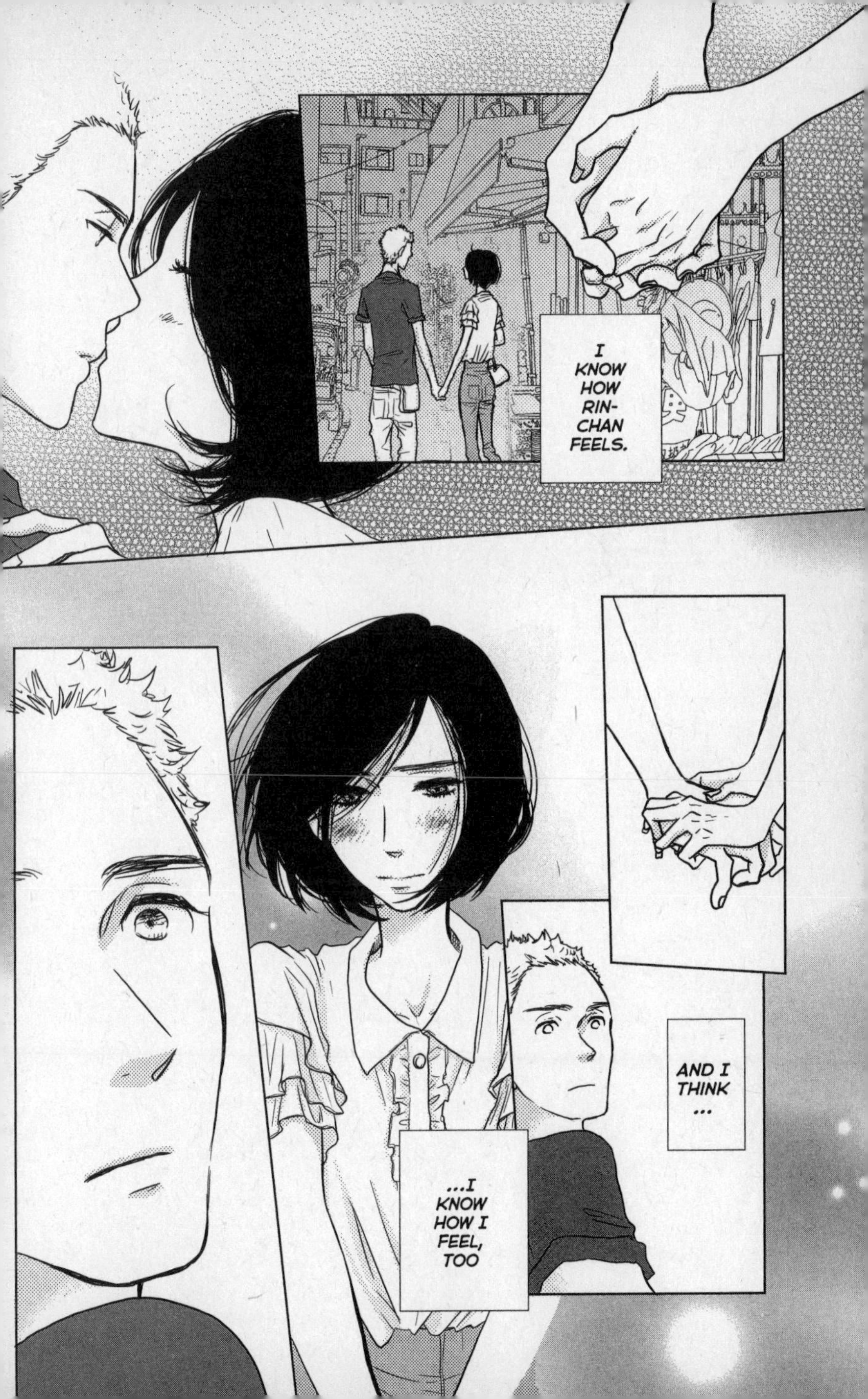
I KNOW HOW RIN-CHAN FEELS.
AND I THINK ...
...I KNOW HOW I FEEL, TOO

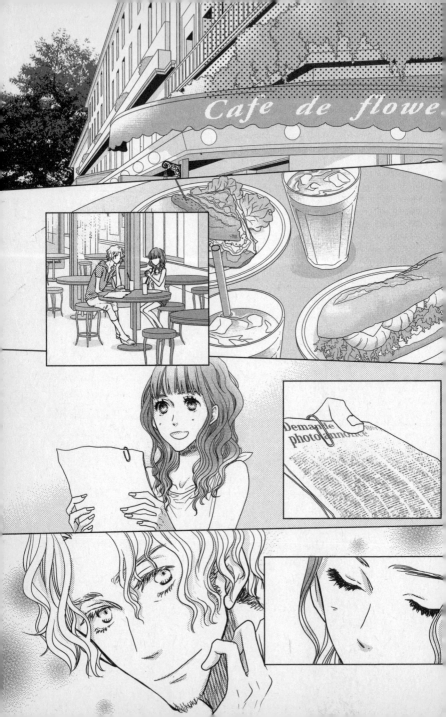

Cafe de flowe

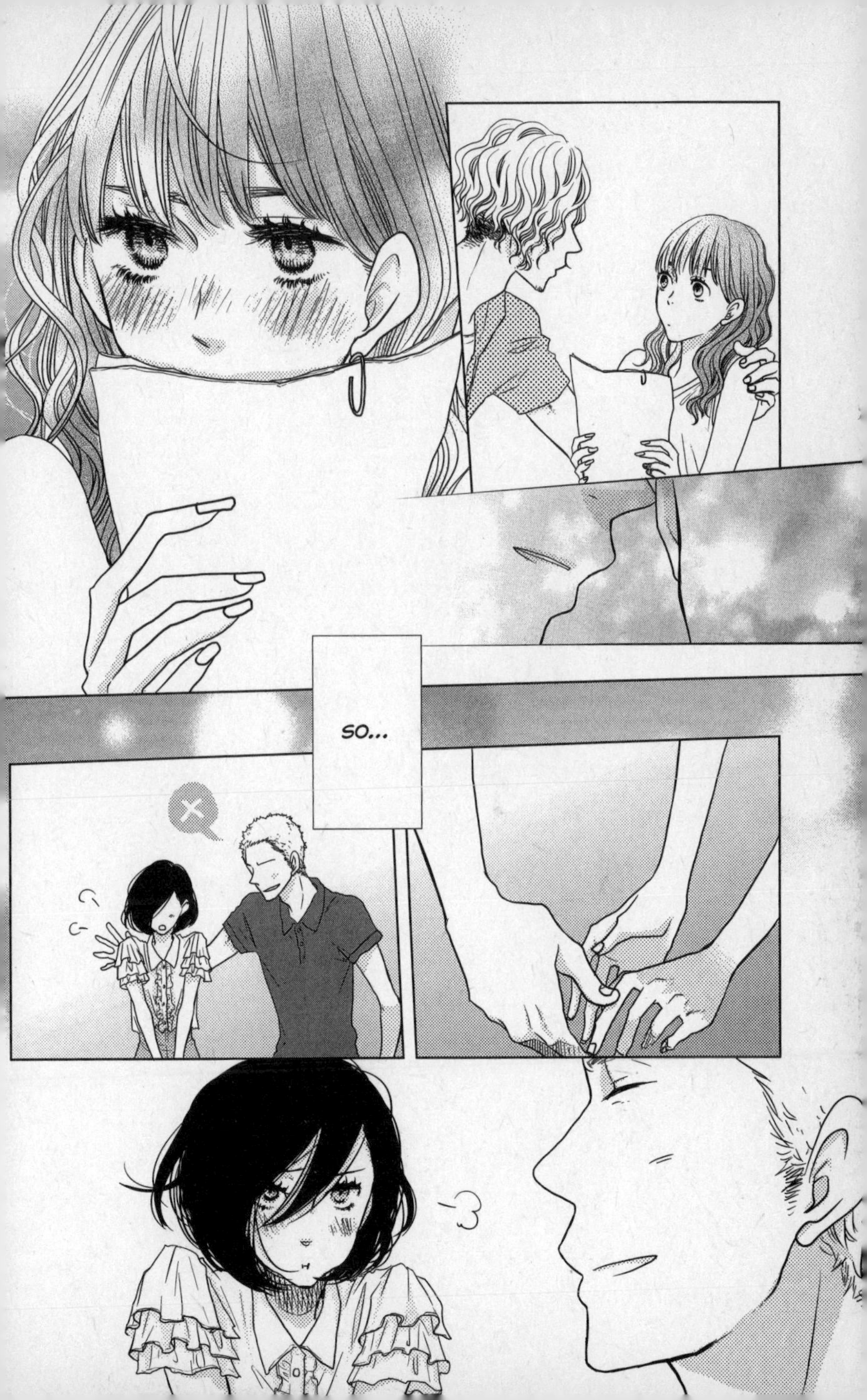
SO...

IF I DON'T WANT TO RUIN HER SMILE...
...I HAVE TO BE VERY CAREFUL...
...ABOUT HOW I MOVE FORWARD.
Hey, Rin! You told everyone I'm into guys, didn't you?
You've got to be kidding me!
I do not like guys!
RIN♡
What? Really? But you said you hate women, so I was sure you liked men!
RIN♡
SORRY
SORRY
IRK
Die.
Die.
Die.
PLEASE TELL ME THEY HAVE NOT HEARD ABOUT THIS!

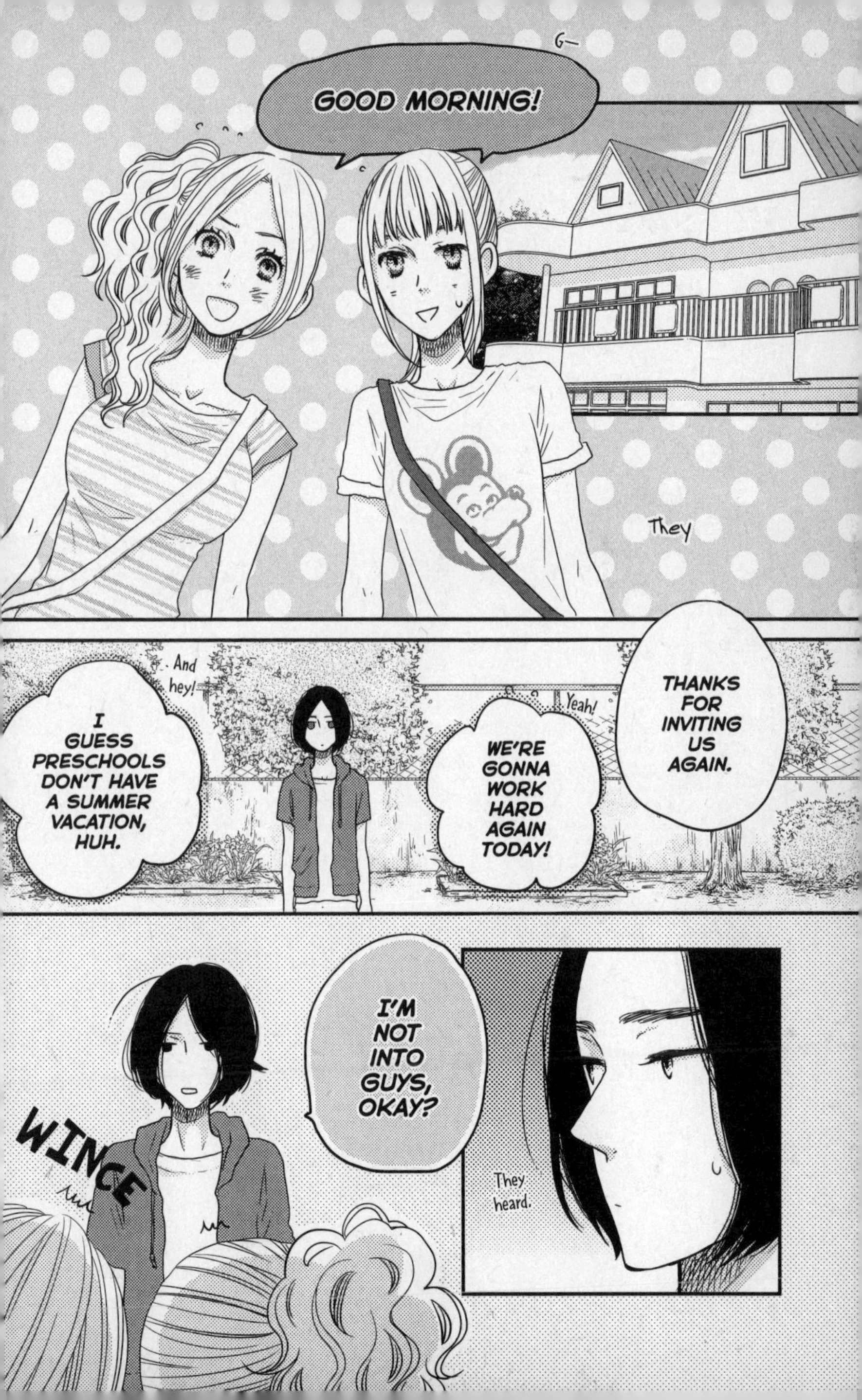
G—
GOOD MORNING!
They
THANKS FOR INVITING US AGAIN.
Yeah!
WE'RE GONNA WORK HARD AGAIN TODAY!
And hey!
I GUESS PRESCHOOLS DON'T HAVE A SUMMER VACATION, HUH.
They heard.
I'M NOT INTO GUYS, OKAY?
WINCE

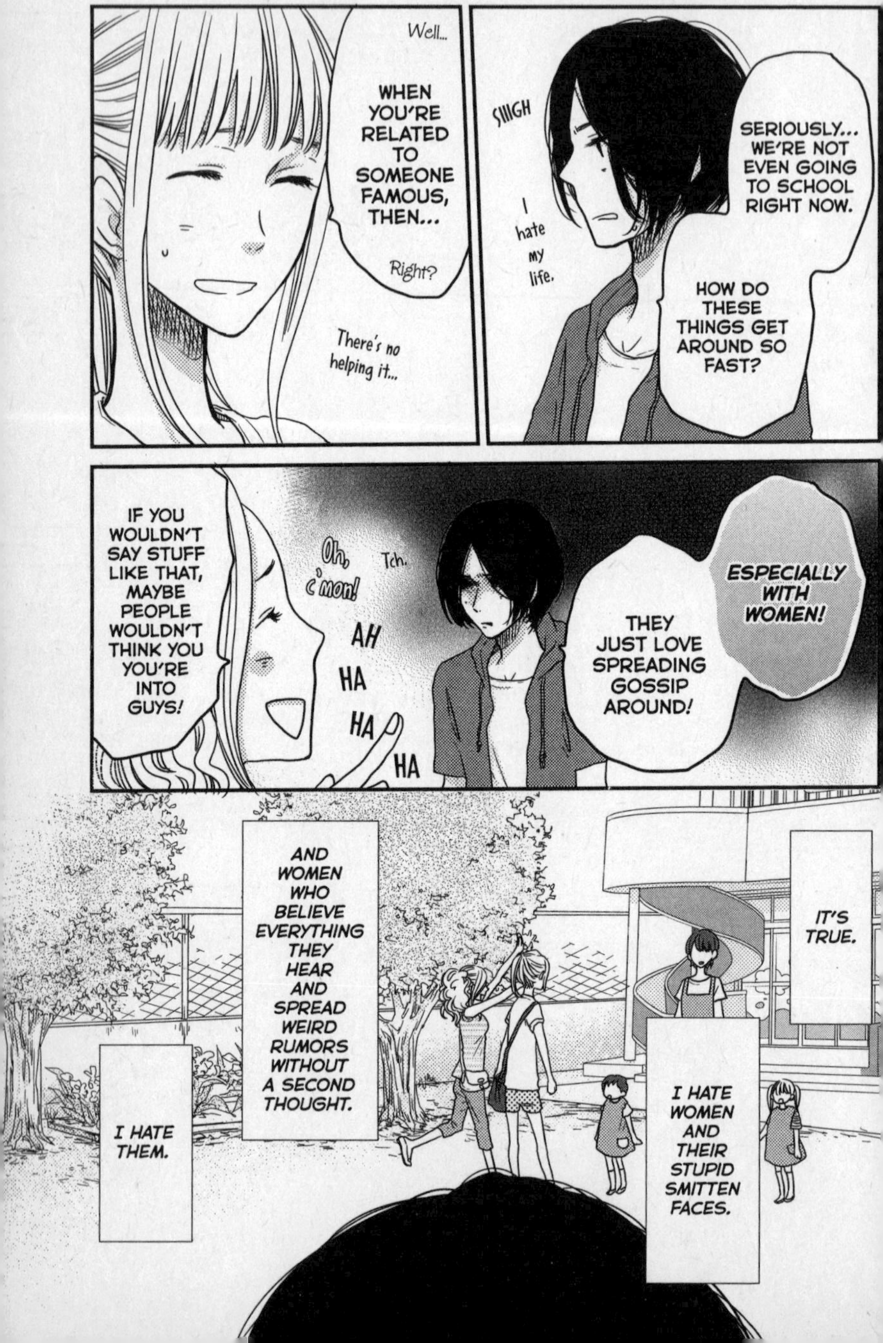
SERIOUSLY... WE'RE NOT EVEN GOING TO SCHOOL RIGHT NOW.
HOW DO THESE THINGS GET AROUND SO FAST?
SIIIGH
I hate my life.
Well...
WHEN YOU'RE RELATED TO SOMEONE FAMOUS, THEN...
Right?
There's no helping it...
ESPECIALLY WITH WOMEN!
THEY JUST LOVE SPREADING GOSSIP AROUND!
Tch.
Oh, c'mon!
AH HA HA HA
IF YOU WOULDN'T SAY STUFF LIKE THAT, MAYBE PEOPLE WOULDN'T THINK YOU YOU'RE INTO GUYS!
IT'S TRUE.
I HATE WOMEN AND THEIR STUPID SMITTEN FACES.
AND WOMEN WHO BELIEVE EVERYTHING THEY HEAR AND SPREAD WEIRD RUMORS WITHOUT A SECOND THOUGHT.
I HATE THEM.

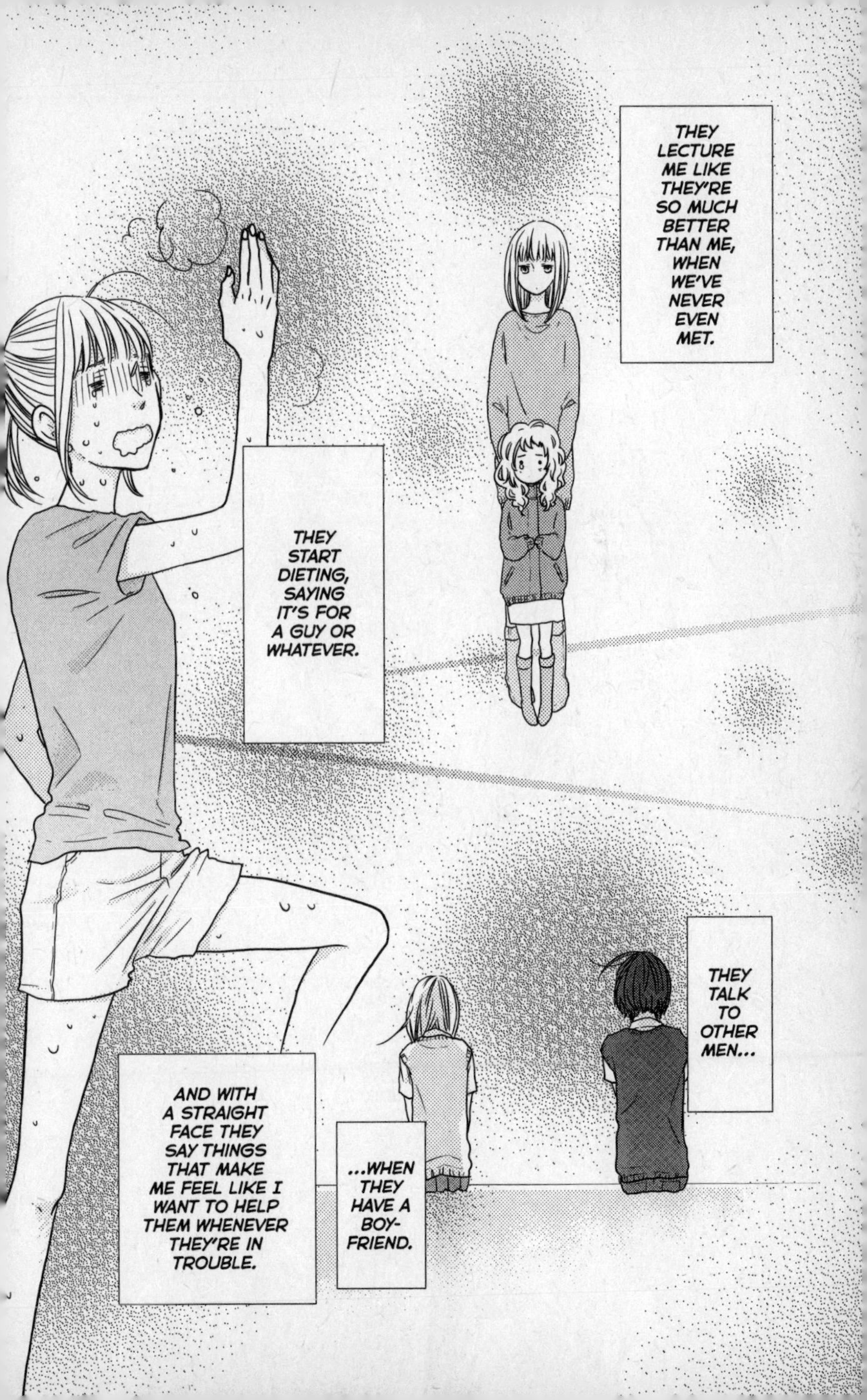
THEY LECTURE ME LIKE THEY'RE SO MUCH BETTER THAN ME, WHEN WE'VE NEVER EVEN MET.
THEY START DIETING, SAYING IT'S FOR A GUY OR WHATEVER.
THEY TALK TO OTHER MEN...
...WHEN THEY HAVE A BOY-FRIEND.
AND WITH A STRAIGHT FACE THEY SAY THINGS THAT MAKE ME FEEL LIKE I WANT TO HELP THEM WHENEVER THEY'RE IN TROUBLE.

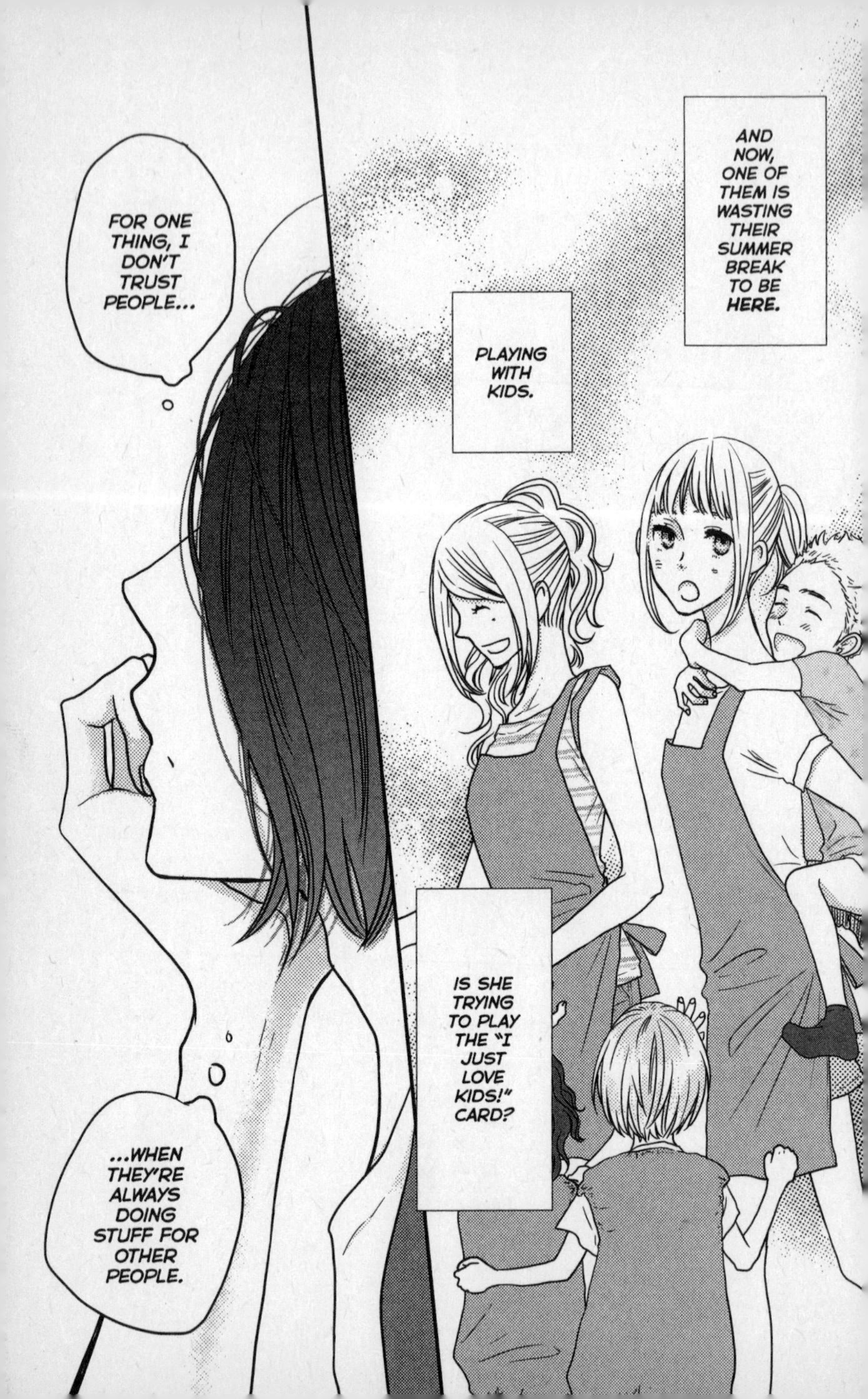
AND NOW, ONE OF THEM IS WASTING THEIR SUMMER BREAK TO BE HERE.
PLAYING WITH KIDS.
IS SHE TRYING TO PLAY THE "I JUST LOVE KIDS!" CARD?
FOR ONE THING, I DON'T TRUST PEOPLE...
...WHEN THEY'RE ALWAYS DOING STUFF FOR OTHER PEOPLE.

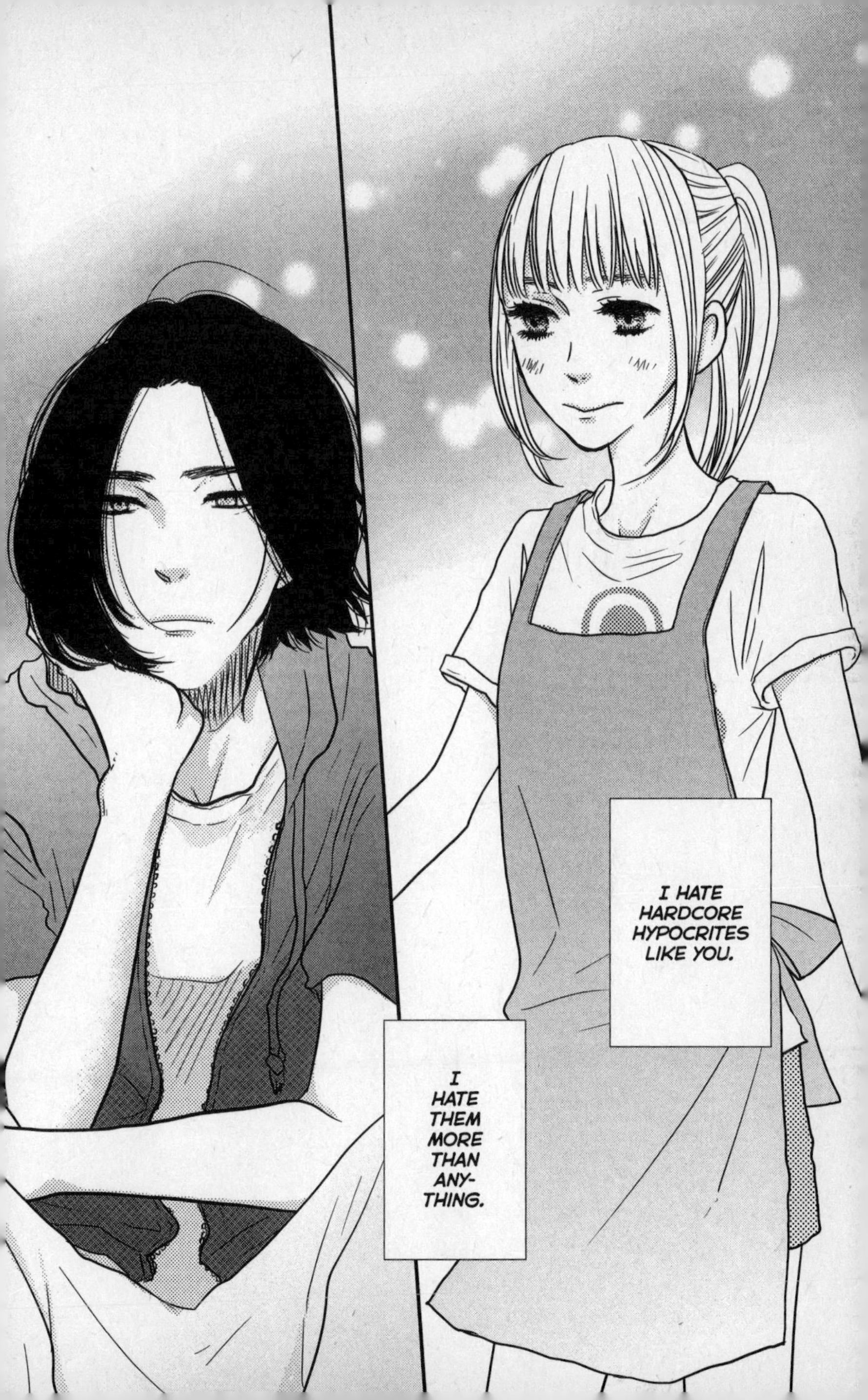
I HATE HARDCORE HYPOCRITES LIKE YOU.
I HATE THEM MORE THAN ANY-THING.

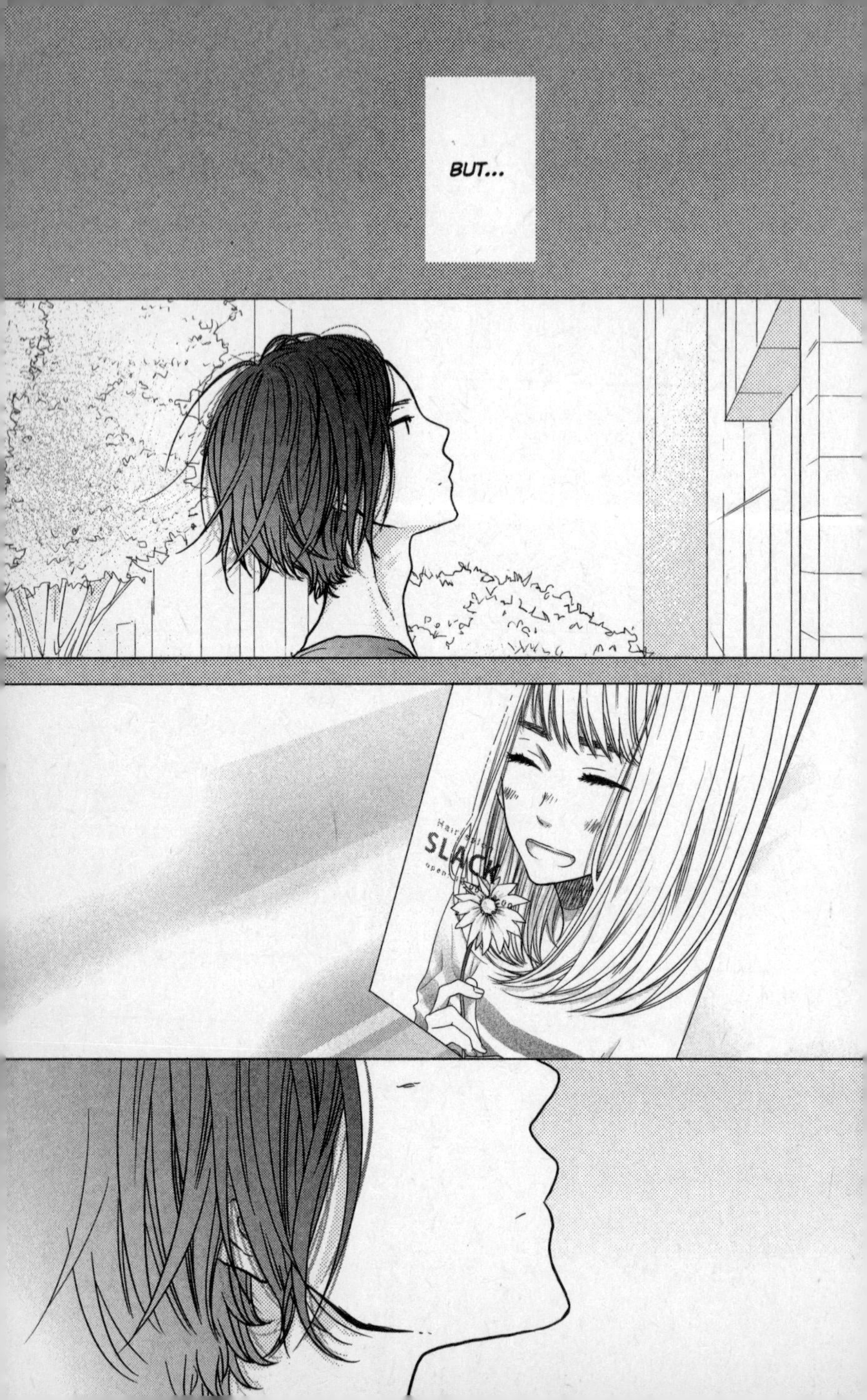
BUT...
SLACK

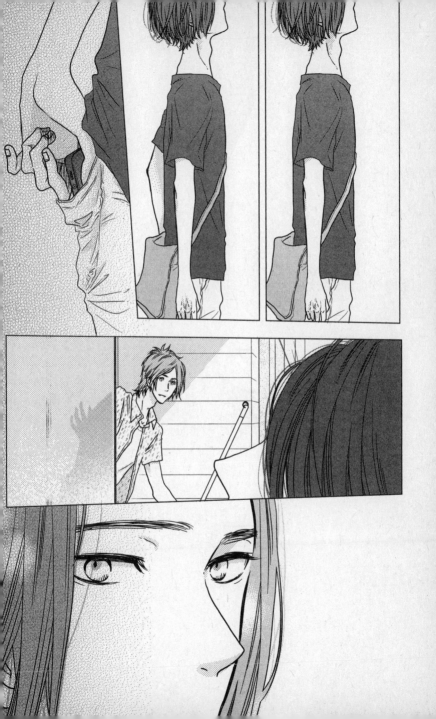

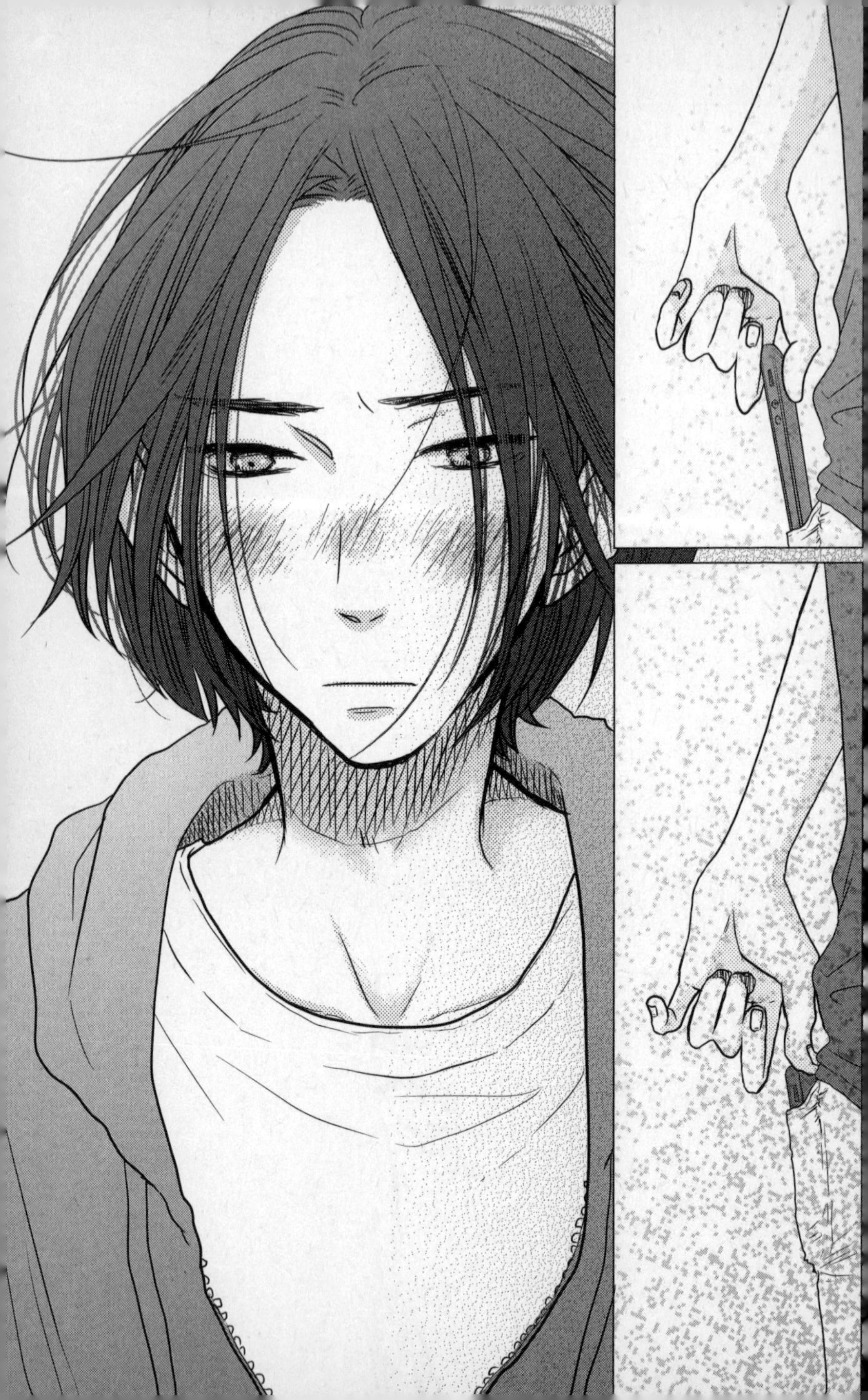

WHAT I HATE EVEN MORE THAN THAT...

...IS THE GUY WHO SEES THE BAD IN EVERYTHING...

...AND WON'T ADMIT HOW HE REALLY FEELS.

AND THAT GUY IS ME.

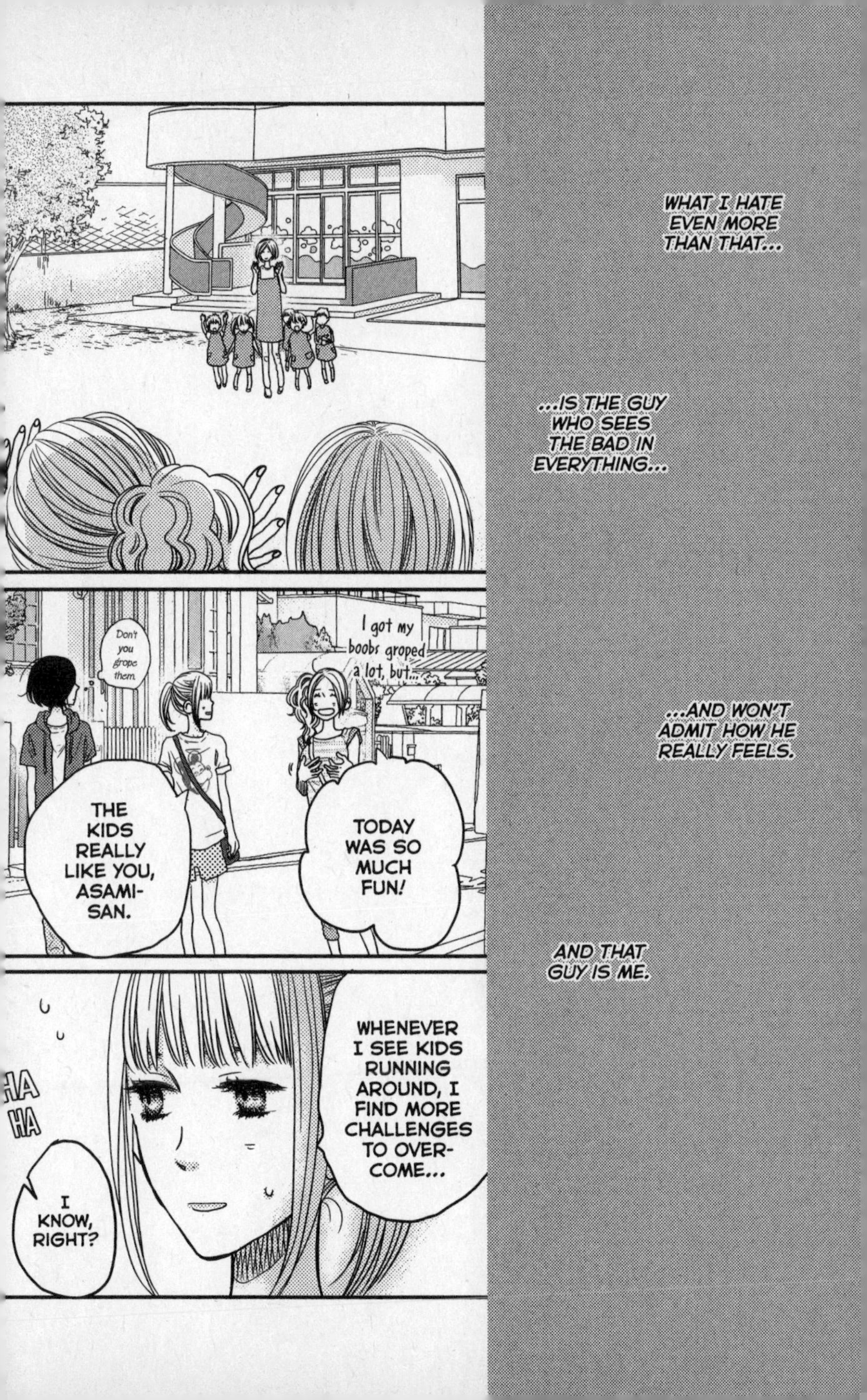
I got my boobs groped a lot, but...
Don't you grope them.
TODAY WAS SO MUCH FUN!
THE KIDS REALLY LIKE YOU, ASAMI-SAN.
WHENEVER I SEE KIDS RUNNING AROUND, I FIND MORE CHALLENGES TO OVER-COME...
HA HA
I KNOW, RIGHT?

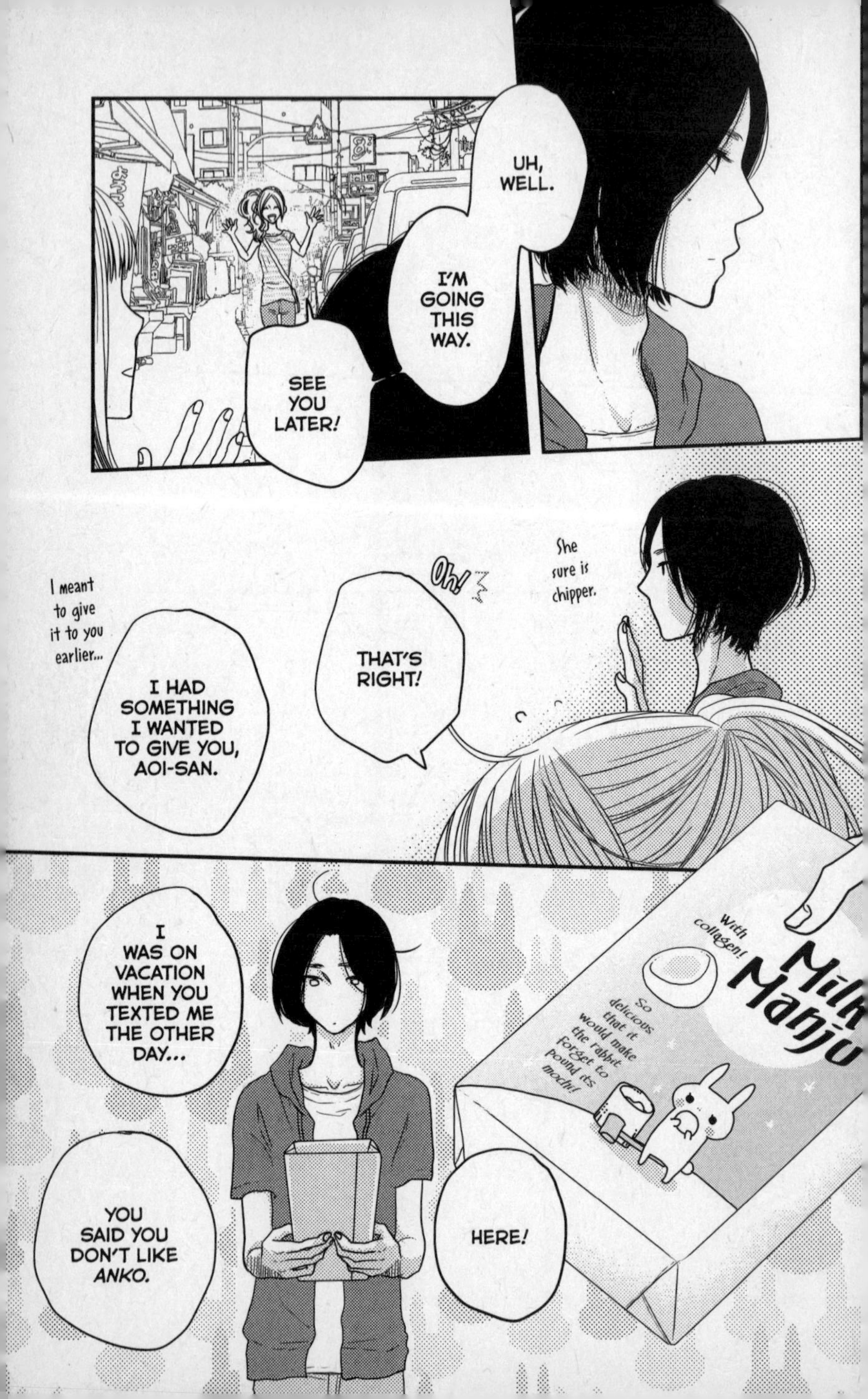
UH, WELL.
I'M GOING THIS WAY.
SEE YOU LATER!
She sure is chipper.
Oh!
THAT'S RIGHT!
I meant to give it to you earlier...
I HAD SOMETHING I WANTED TO GIVE YOU, AOI-SAN.
With collagen!
Milk Manju
So delicious that it would make the rabbit forget to pound its mochi!
HERE!
I WAS ON VACATION WHEN YOU TEXTED ME THE OTHER DAY...
YOU SAID YOU DON'T LIKE ANKO.

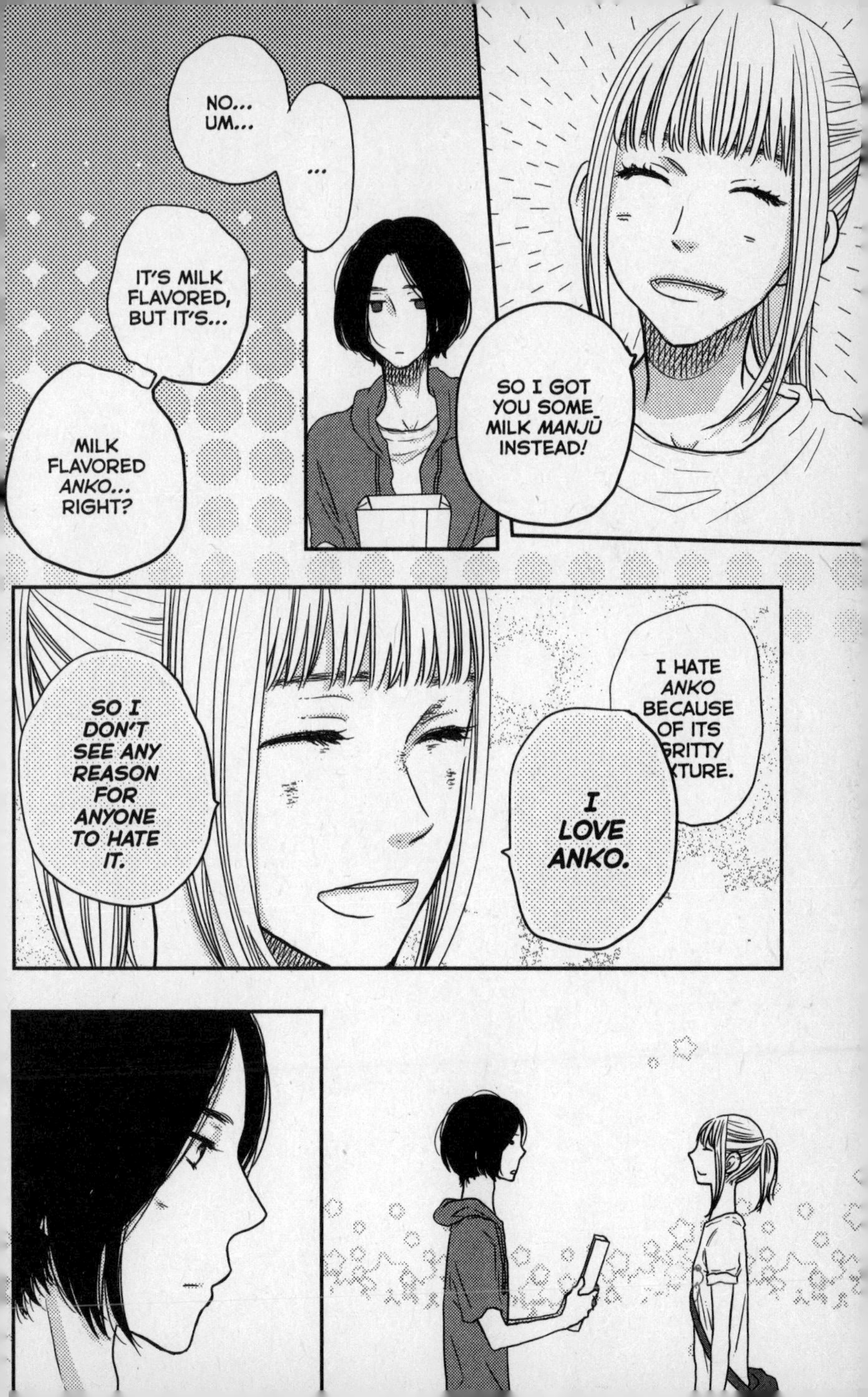
SO I GOT YOU SOME MILK MANJŪ INSTEAD!
...
NO... UM...
IT'S MILK FLAVORED, BUT IT'S...
MILK FLAVORED ANKO... RIGHT?
I HATE ANKO BECAUSE OF ITS GRITTY XTURE.
I LOVE ANKO.
SO I DON'T SEE ANY REASON FOR ANYONE TO HATE IT.

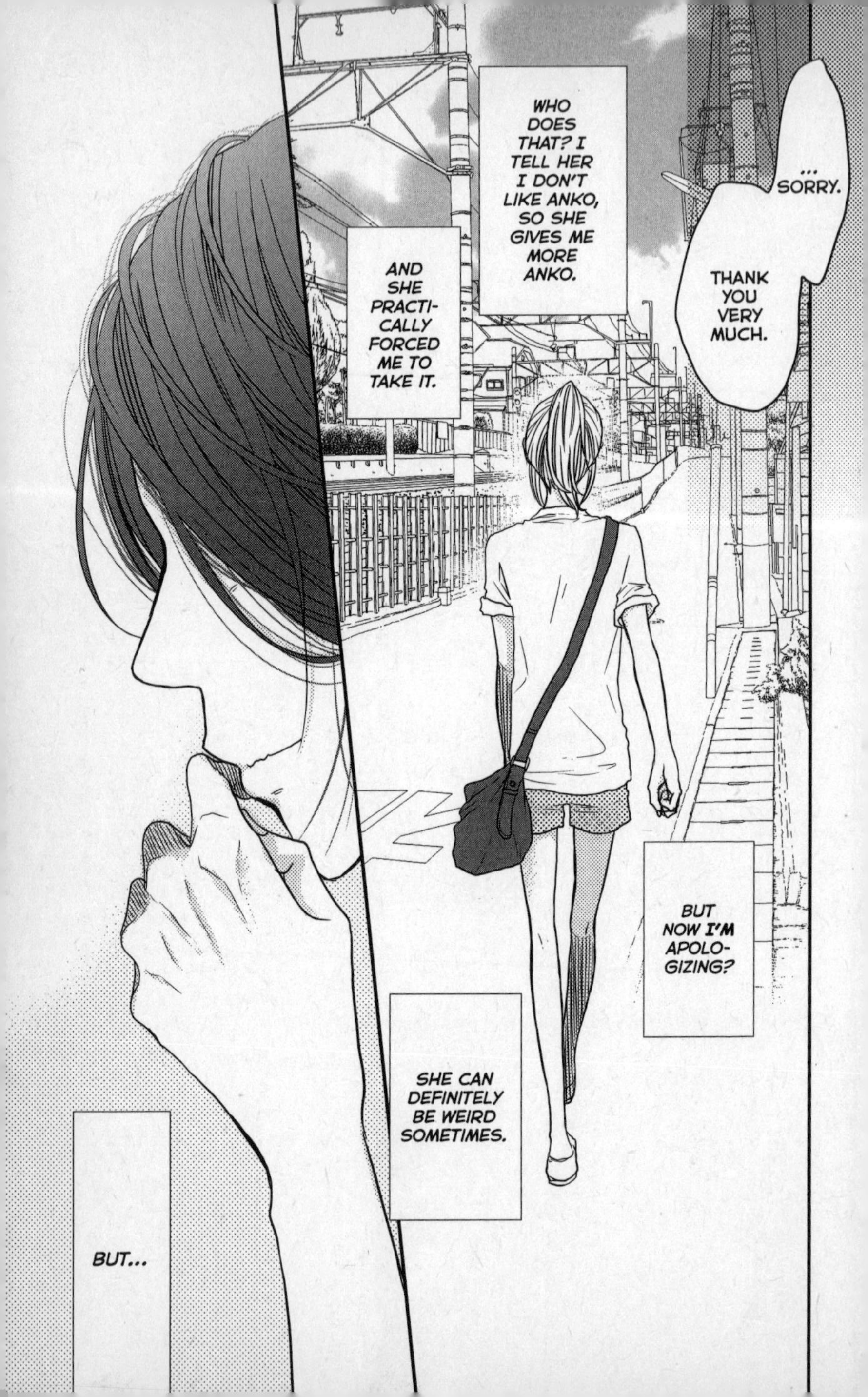
...SORRY.
THANK YOU VERY MUCH.
WHO DOES THAT? I TELL HER I DON'T LIKE ANKO, SO SHE GIVES ME MORE ANKO.
AND SHE PRACTICALLY FORCED ME TO TAKE IT.
BUT NOW I'M APOLOGIZING?
SHE CAN DEFINITELY BE WEIRD SOMETIMES.
BUT...

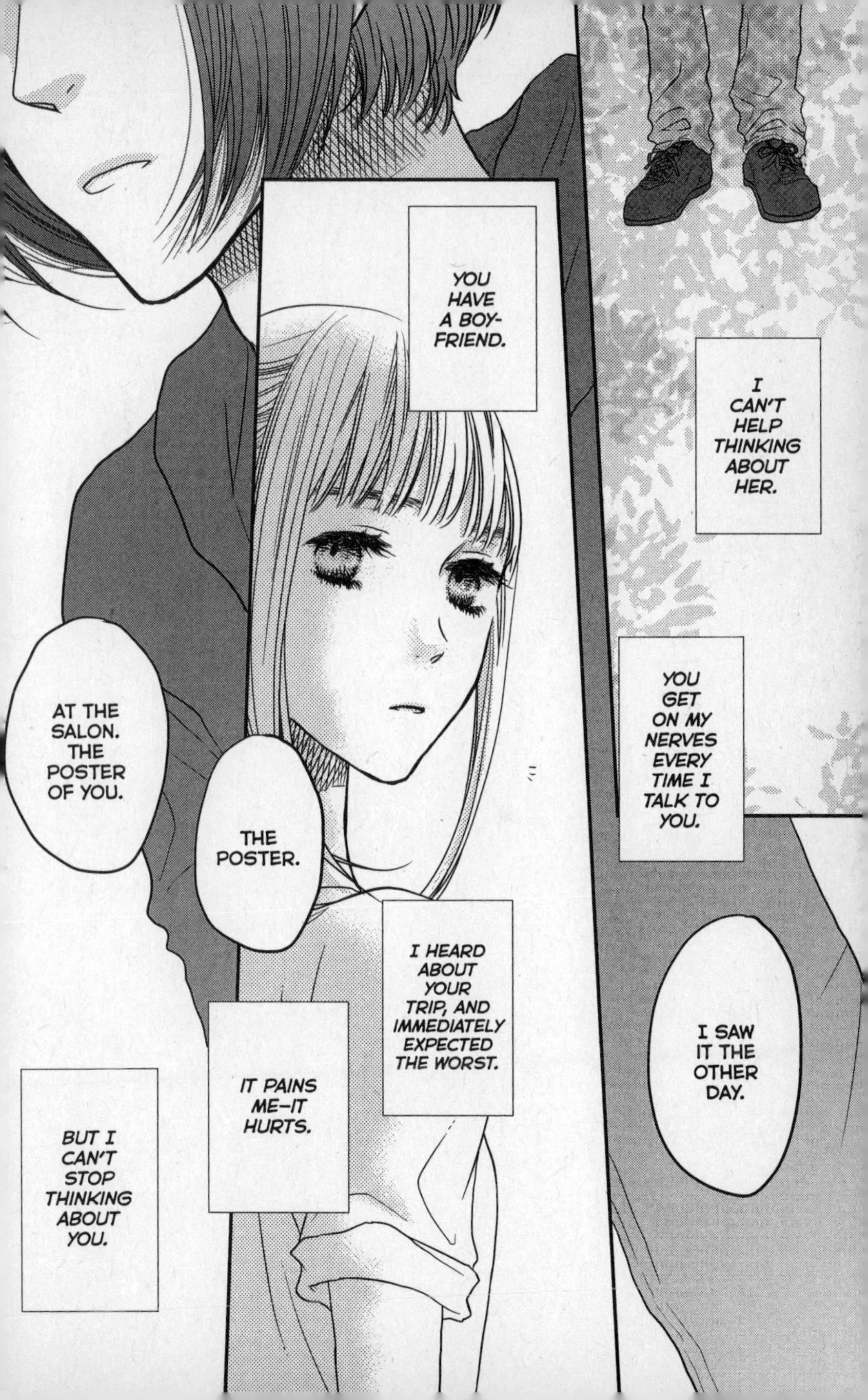
I CAN'T HELP THINKING ABOUT HER.
YOU GET ON MY NERVES EVERY TIME I TALK TO YOU.
YOU HAVE A BOY-FRIEND.
I SAW IT THE OTHER DAY.
THE POSTER.
AT THE SALON. THE POSTER OF YOU.
I HEARD ABOUT YOUR TRIP, AND IMMEDIATELY EXPECTED THE WORST.
IT PAINS ME—IT HURTS.
BUT I CAN'T STOP THINKING ABOUT YOU.

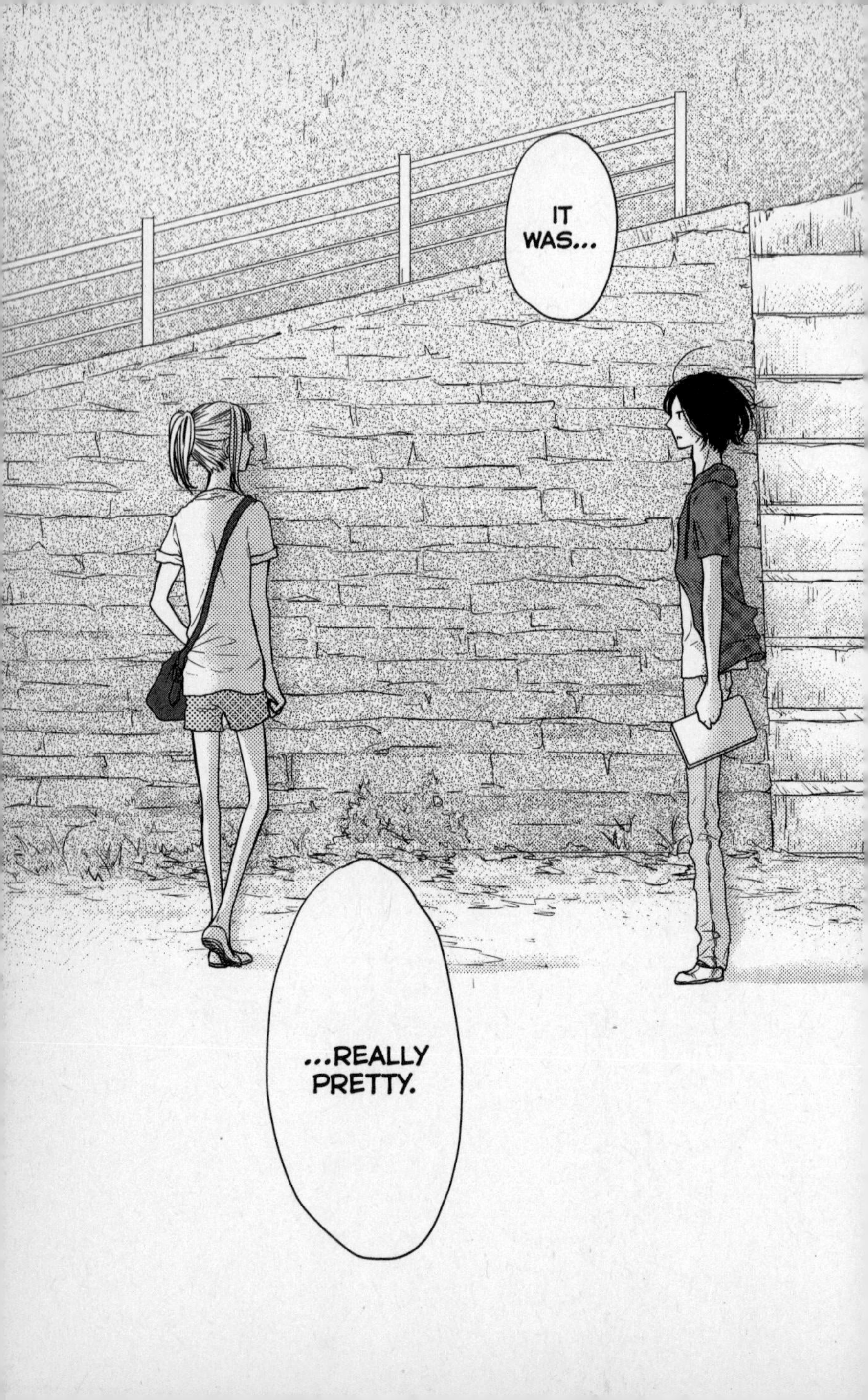
IT WAS...
...REALLY PRETTY.

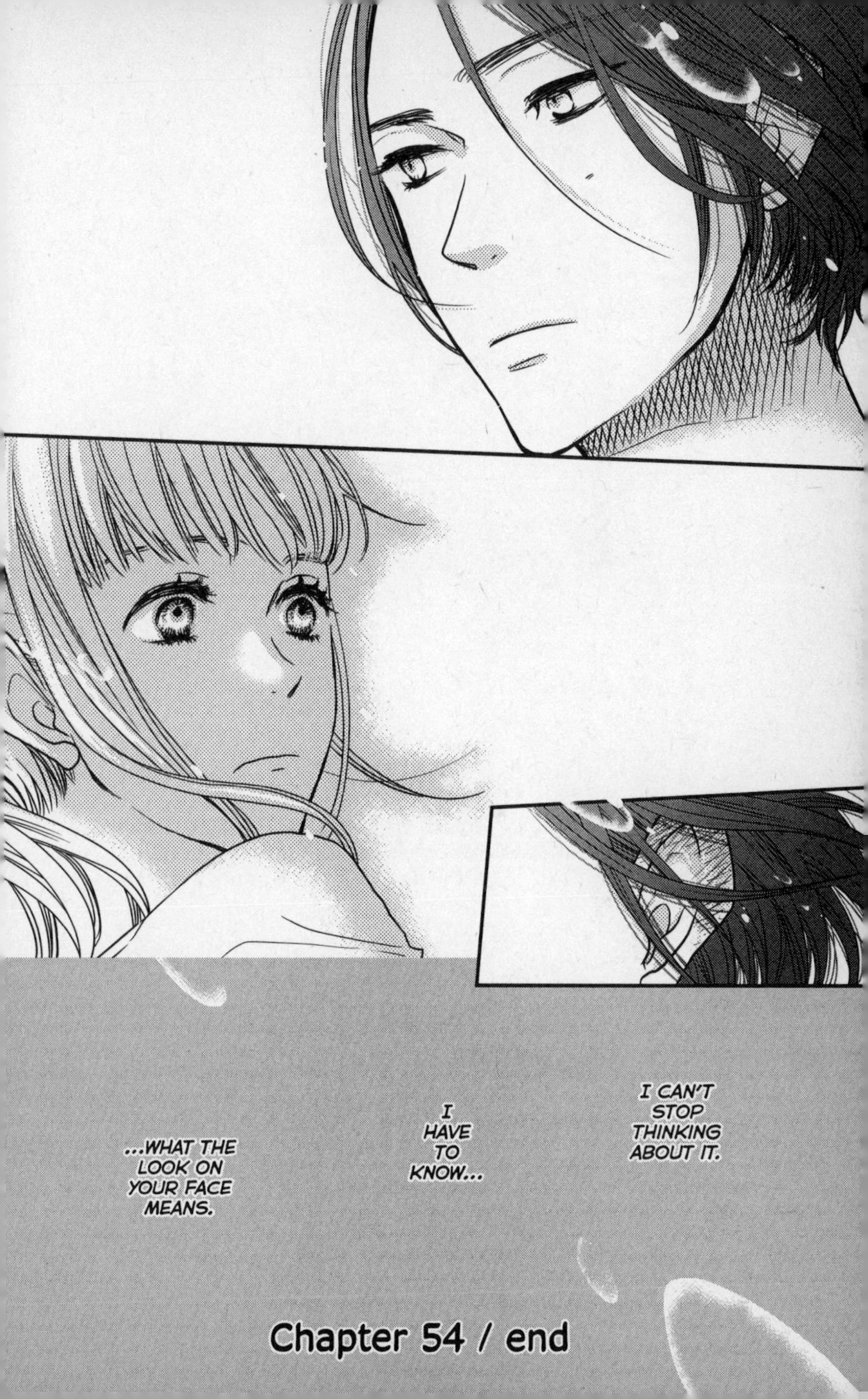
I CAN'T STOP THINKING ABOUT IT.
I HAVE TO KNOW...
...WHAT THE LOOK ON YOUR FACE MEANS.
Chapter 54 / end

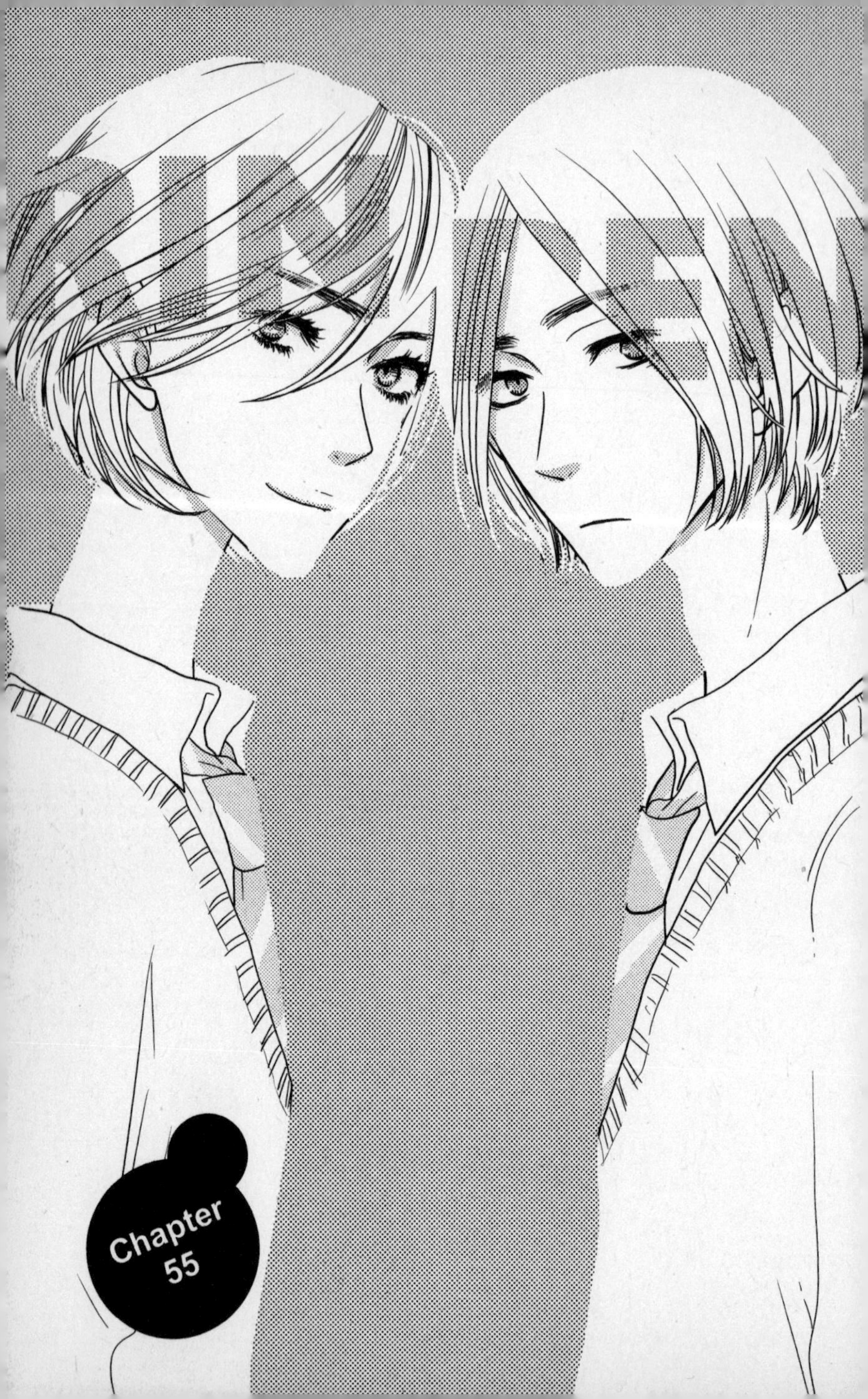
Chapter
55

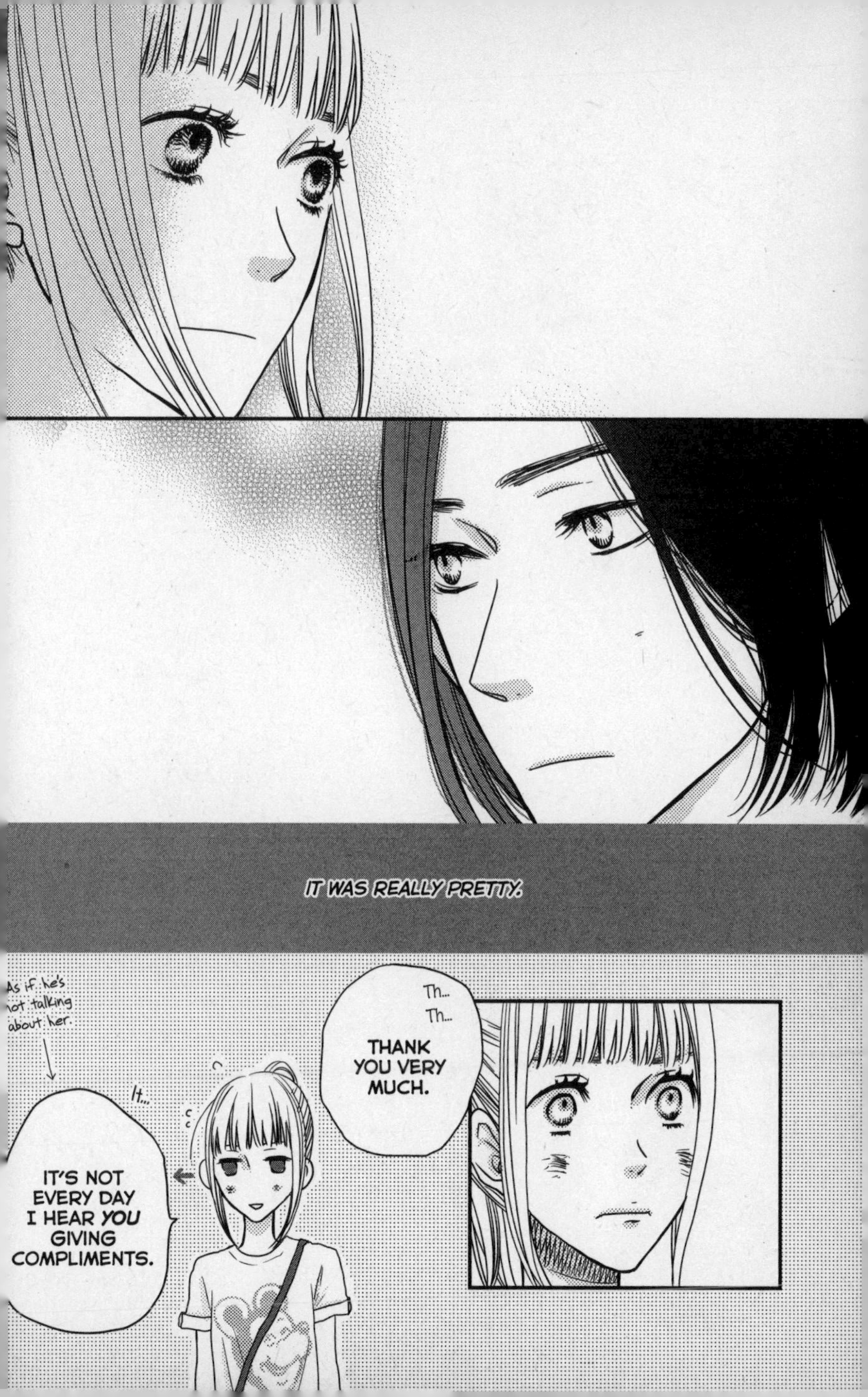
IT WAS REALLY PRETTY.
Th... Th...
THANK YOU VERY MUCH.
It...
IT'S NOT EVERY DAY I HEAR *YOU* GIVING COMPLIMENTS.
As if he's not talking about her.

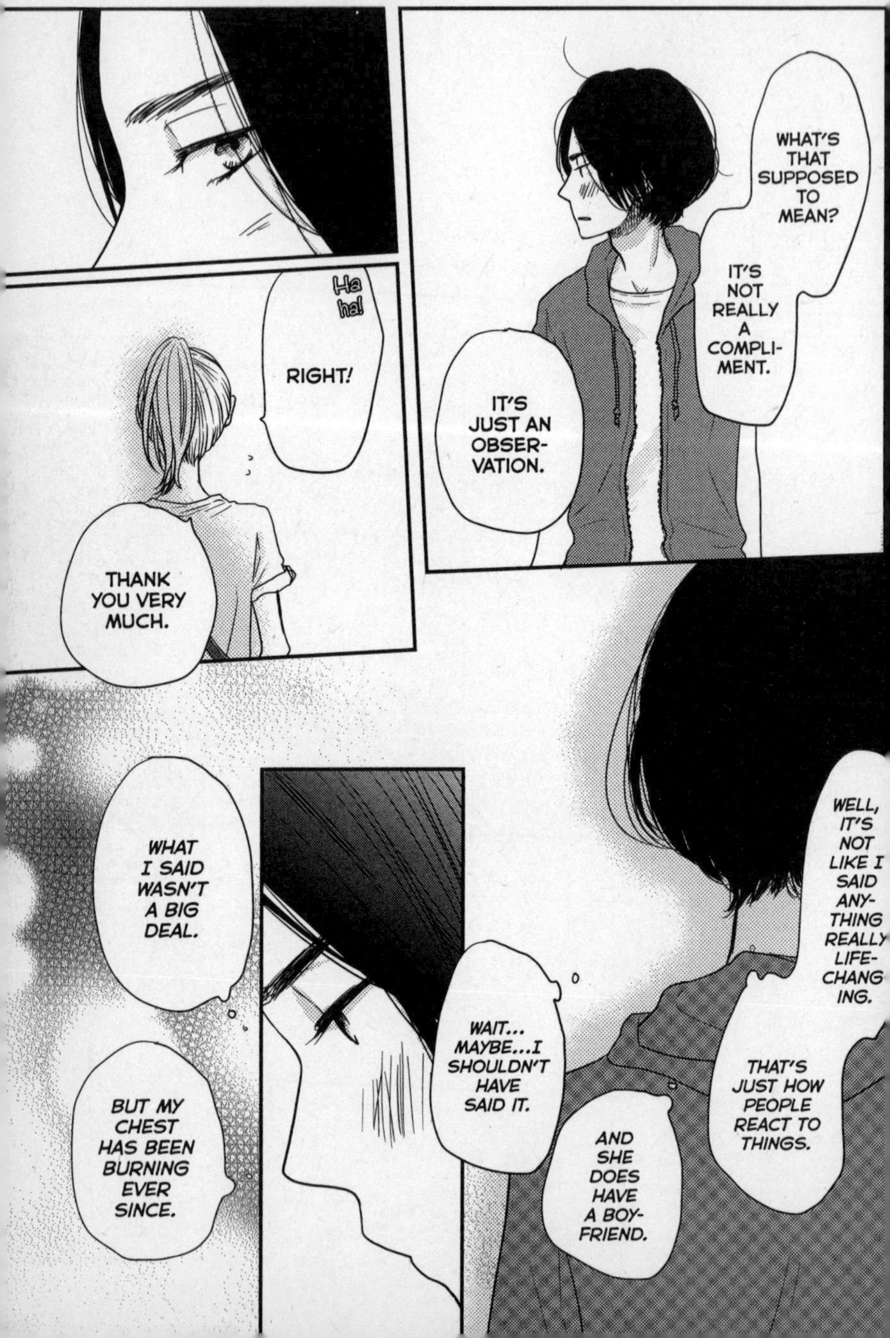

WHAT'S THAT SUPPOSED TO MEAN?
IT'S NOT REALLY A COMPLIMENT.
IT'S JUST AN OBSERVATION.
Ha ha!
RIGHT!
THANK YOU VERY MUCH.
WELL, IT'S NOT LIKE I SAID ANYTHING REALLY LIFE-CHANGING.
THAT'S JUST HOW PEOPLE REACT TO THINGS.
AND SHE DOES HAVE A BOY-FRIEND.
WAIT... MAYBE...I SHOULDN'T HAVE SAID IT.
WHAT I SAID WASN'T A BIG DEAL.
BUT MY CHEST HAS BEEN BURNING EVER SINCE.

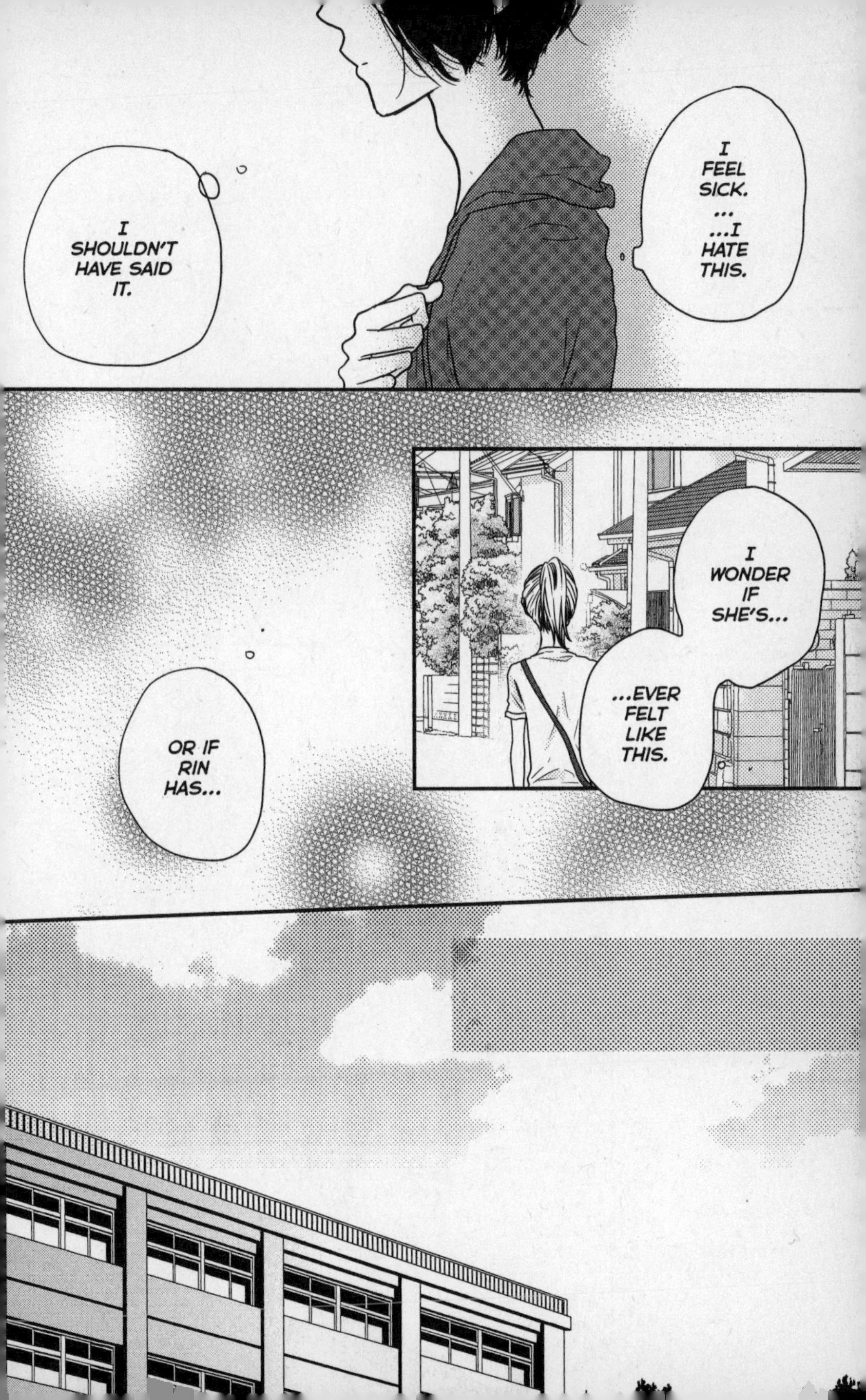
I FEEL SICK. ... ...I HATE THIS.
I SHOULDN'T HAVE SAID IT.
I WONDER IF SHE'S...
...EVER FELT LIKE THIS.
OR IF RIN HAS...

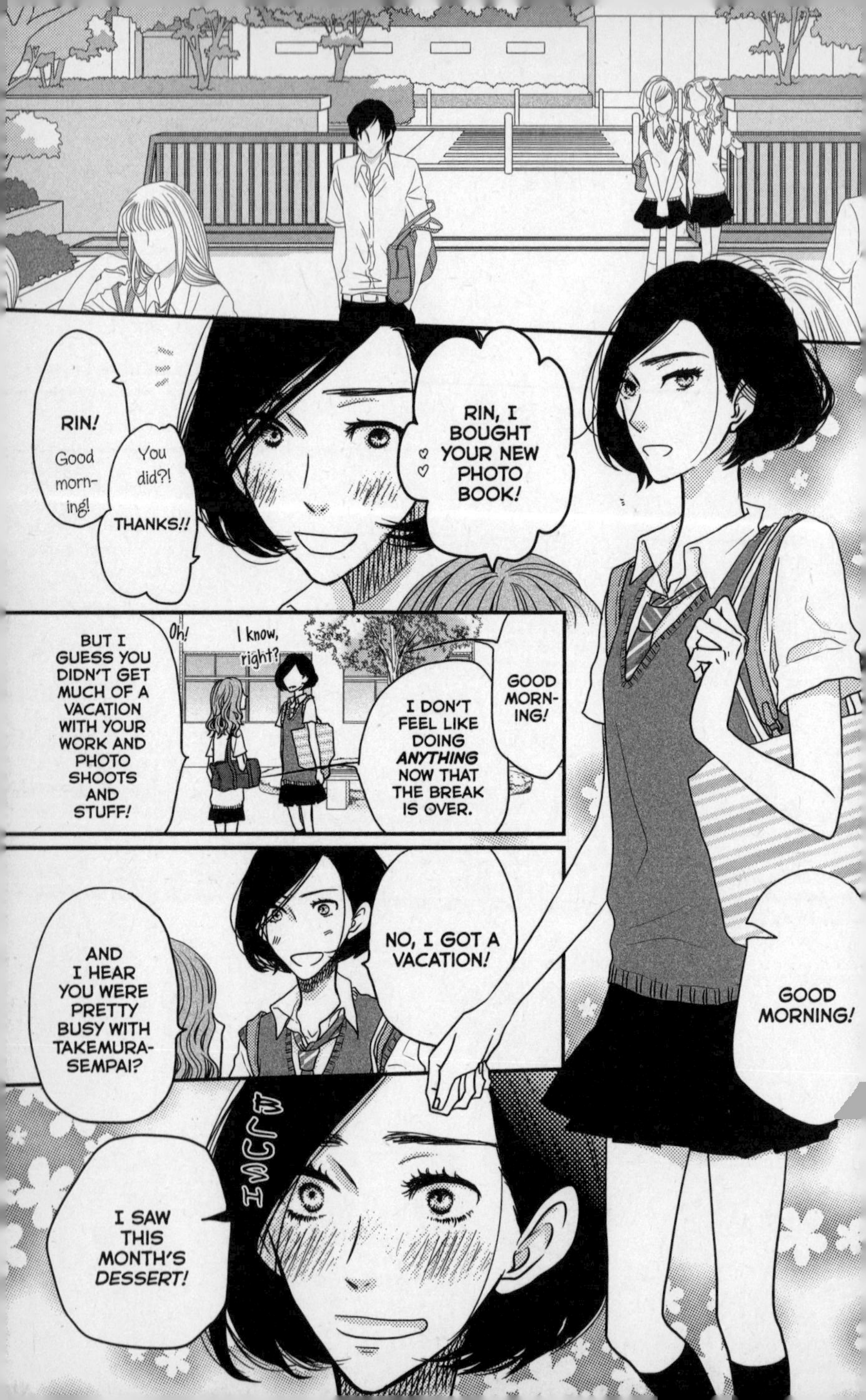
GOOD MORNING!
RIN, I BOUGHT YOUR NEW PHOTO BOOK!
RIN! Good morning!
You did?! THANKS!!
GOOD MORNING!
I DON'T FEEL LIKE DOING *ANYTHING* NOW THAT THE BREAK IS OVER.
I know, right?
Oh!
BUT I GUESS YOU DIDN'T GET MUCH OF A VACATION WITH YOUR WORK AND PHOTO SHOOTS AND STUFF!
NO, I GOT A VACATION!
AND I HEAR YOU WERE PRETTY BUSY WITH TAKEMURA-SEMPAI?
I SAW THIS MONTH'S *DESSERT*!

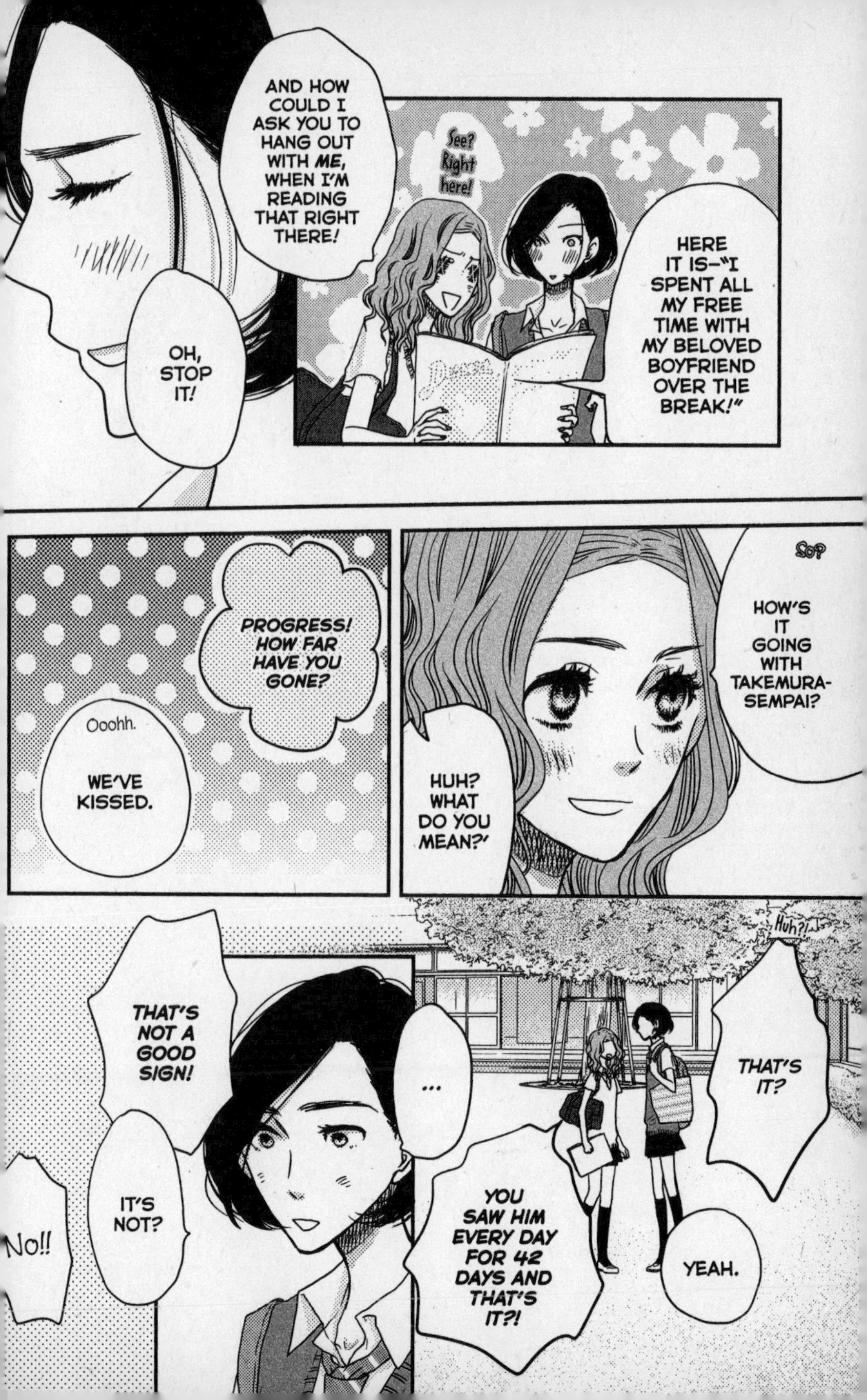
HERE IT IS—"I SPENT ALL MY FREE TIME WITH MY BELOVED BOYFRIEND OVER THE BREAK!"
See? Right here!
AND HOW COULD I ASK YOU TO HANG OUT WITH ME, WHEN I'M READING THAT RIGHT THERE!
OH, STOP IT!
So?
HOW'S IT GOING WITH TAKEMURA-SEMPAI?
HUH? WHAT DO YOU MEAN?'
PROGRESS! HOW FAR HAVE YOU GONE?
Ooohh.
WE'VE KISSED.
Huh?!
THAT'S IT?
YEAH.
YOU SAW HIM EVERY DAY FOR 42 DAYS AND THAT'S IT?!
...
THAT'S NOT A GOOD SIGN!
IT'S NOT?
No!!

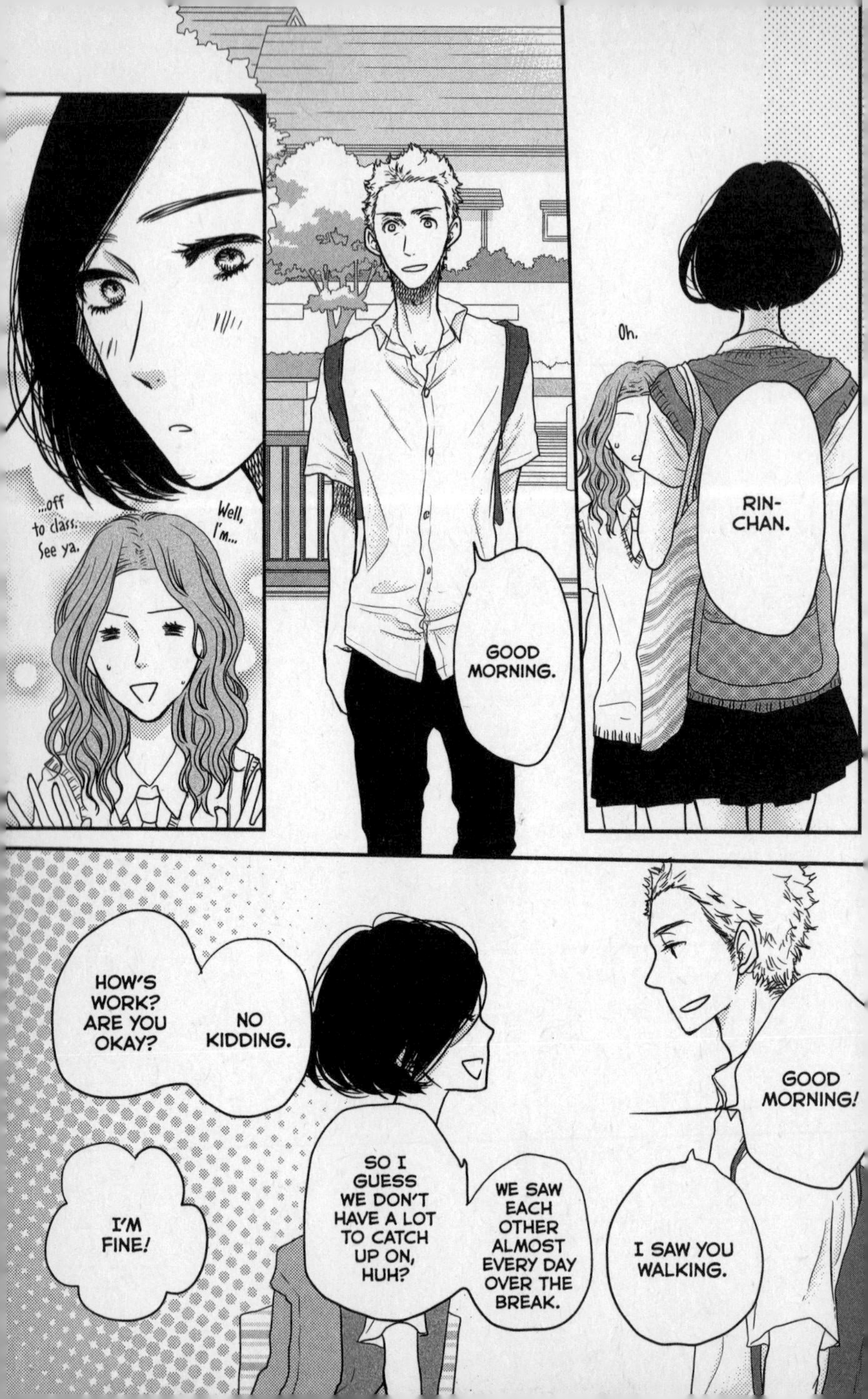
RIN-CHAN.
Oh.
GOOD MORNING.
Well, I'm...
...off to class. See ya.
GOOD MORNING!
I SAW YOU WALKING.
WE SAW EACH OTHER ALMOST EVERY DAY OVER THE BREAK.
SO I GUESS WE DON'T HAVE A LOT TO CATCH UP ON, HUH?
NO KIDDING.
HOW'S WORK? ARE YOU OKAY?
I'M FINE!

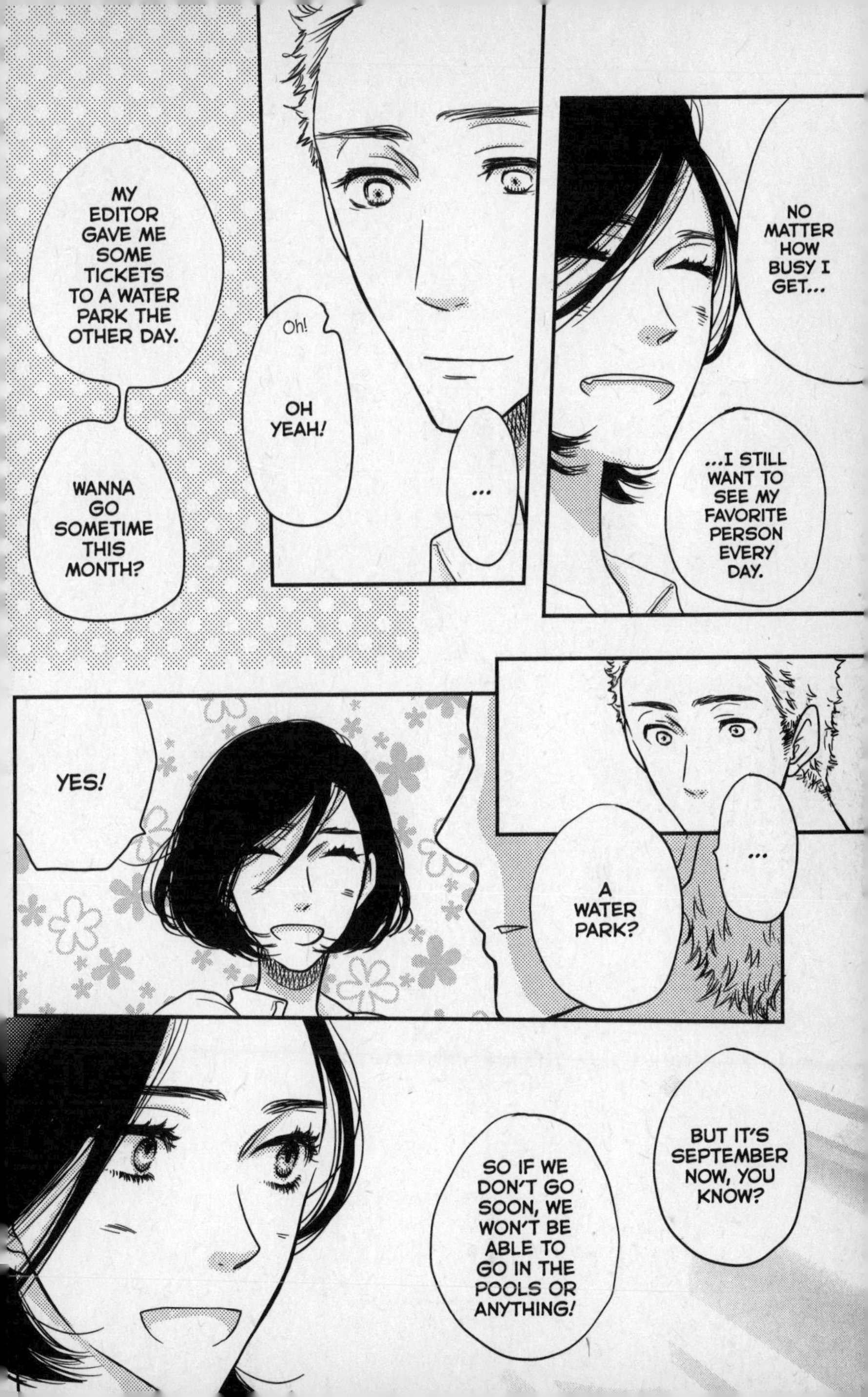
NO MATTER HOW BUSY I GET...
...I STILL WANT TO SEE MY FAVORITE PERSON EVERY DAY.
...
Oh!
OH YEAH!
MY EDITOR GAVE ME SOME TICKETS TO A WATER PARK THE OTHER DAY.
WANNA GO SOMETIME THIS MONTH?
...
A WATER PARK?
YES!
BUT IT'S SEPTEMBER NOW, YOU KNOW?
SO IF WE DON'T GO SOON, WE WON'T BE ABLE TO GO IN THE POOLS OR ANYTHING!

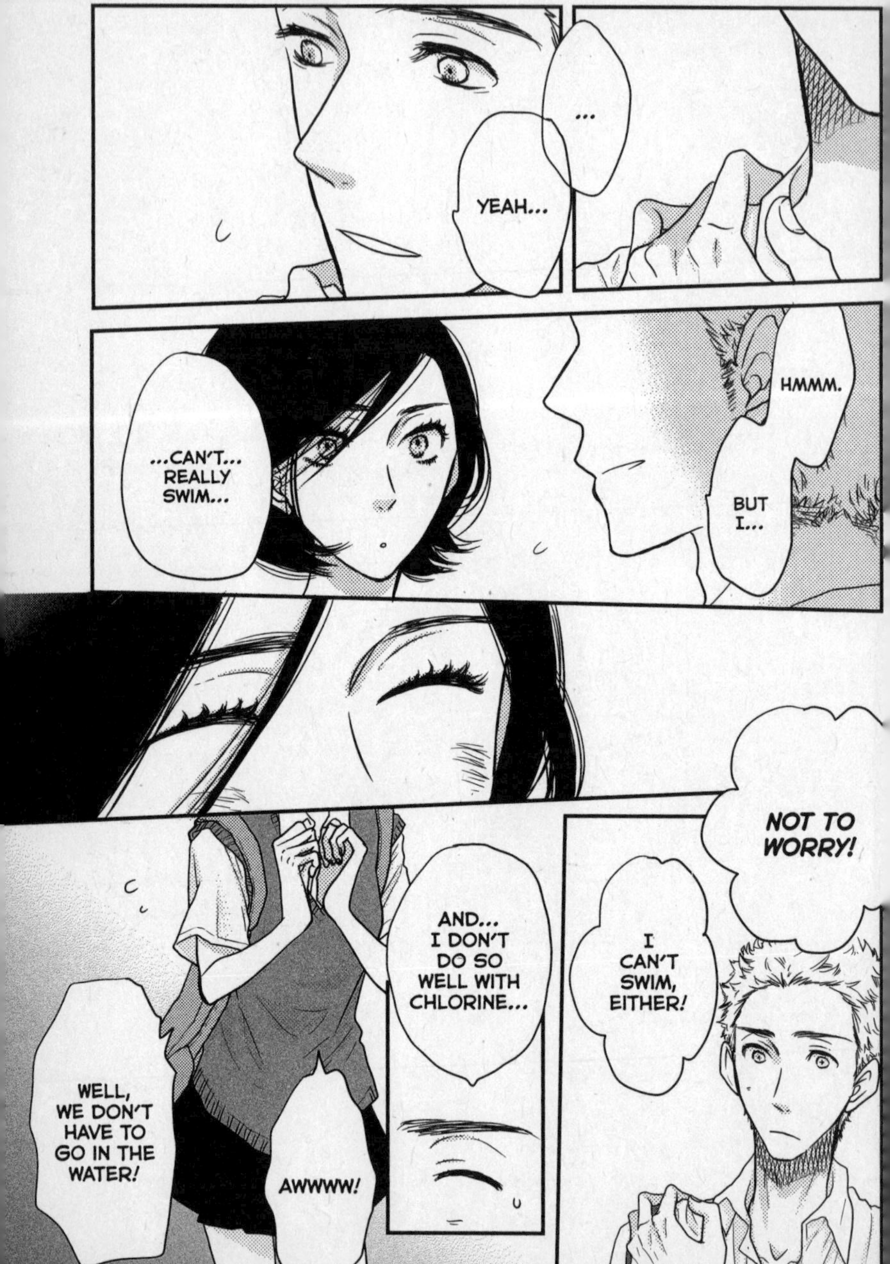
...
YEAH...
HMMM.
BUT I...
...CAN'T... REALLY SWIM...
NOT TO WORRY!
I CAN'T SWIM, EITHER!
AND... I DON'T DO SO WELL WITH CHLORINE...
AWWWW!
WELL, WE DON'T HAVE TO GO IN THE WATER!

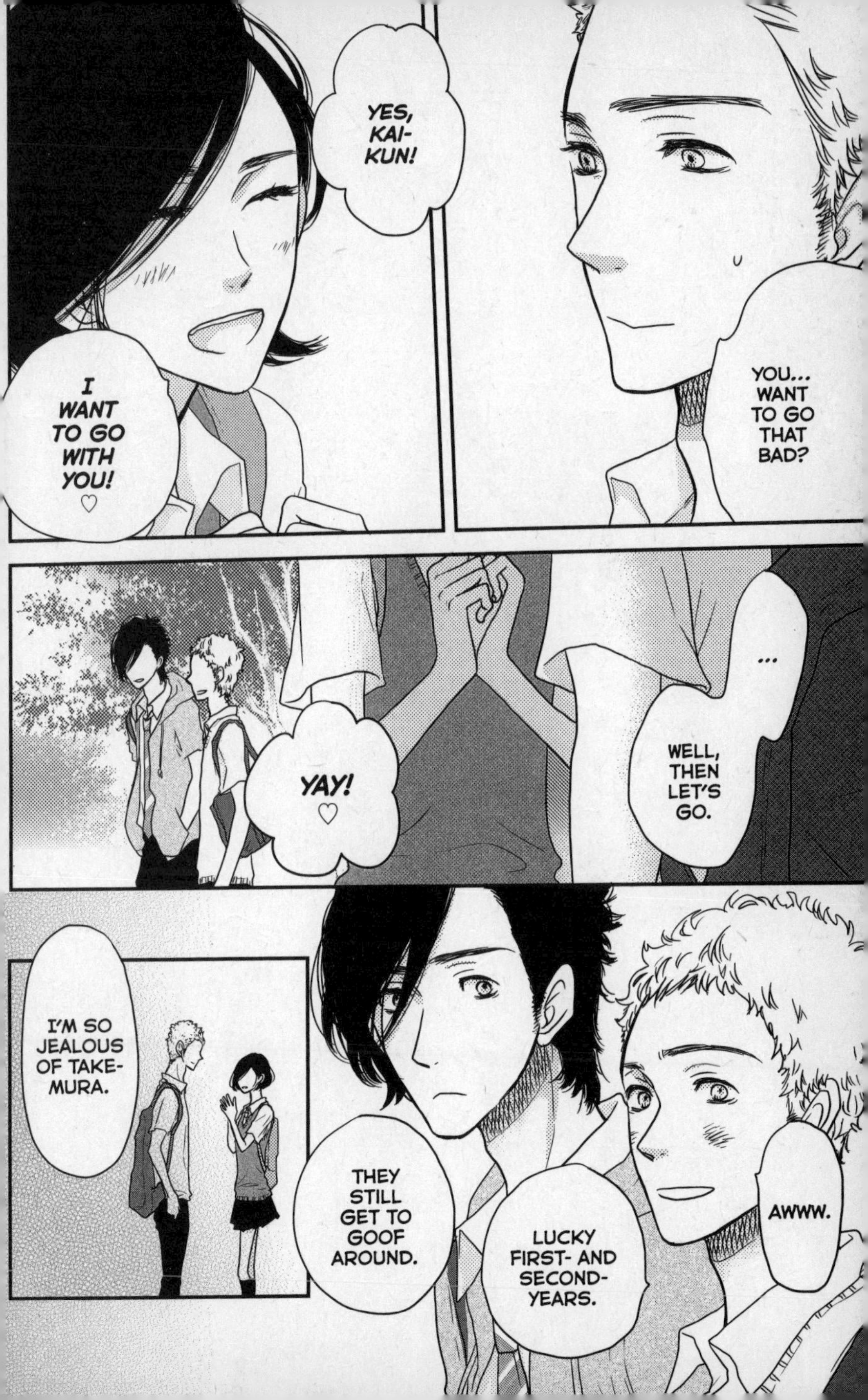
YOU... WANT TO GO THAT BAD?
YES, KAI-KUN!
I WANT TO GO WITH YOU! ♡
...
WELL, THEN LET'S GO.
YAY! ♡
AWWW.
LUCKY FIRST- AND SECOND-YEARS.
THEY STILL GET TO GOOF AROUND.
I'M SO JEALOUS OF TAKE-MURA.

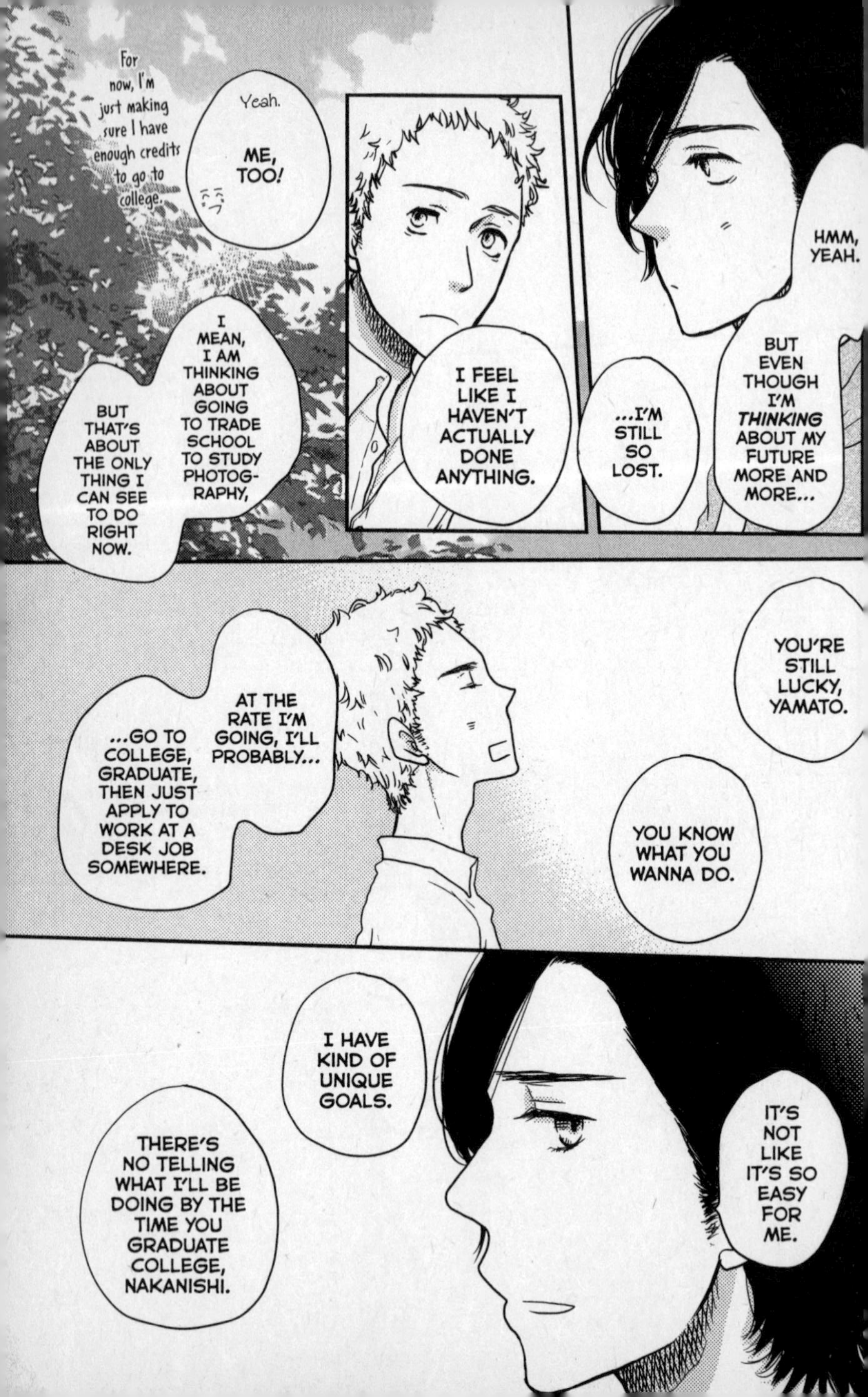
HMM, YEAH.
BUT EVEN THOUGH I'M *THINKING* ABOUT MY FUTURE MORE AND MORE...
...I'M STILL SO LOST.
I FEEL LIKE I HAVEN'T ACTUALLY DONE ANYTHING.
Yeah.
ME, TOO!
For now, I'm just making sure I have enough credits to go to college.
I MEAN, I AM THINKING ABOUT GOING TO TRADE SCHOOL TO STUDY PHOTOGRAPHY,
BUT THAT'S ABOUT THE ONLY THING I CAN SEE TO DO RIGHT NOW.
YOU'RE STILL LUCKY, YAMATO.
YOU KNOW WHAT YOU WANNA DO.
AT THE RATE I'M GOING, I'LL PROBABLY...
...GO TO COLLEGE, GRADUATE, THEN JUST APPLY TO WORK AT A DESK JOB SOMEWHERE.
IT'S NOT LIKE IT'S SO EASY FOR ME.
I HAVE KIND OF UNIQUE GOALS.
THERE'S NO TELLING WHAT I'LL BE DOING BY THE TIME YOU GRADUATE COLLEGE, NAKANISHI.

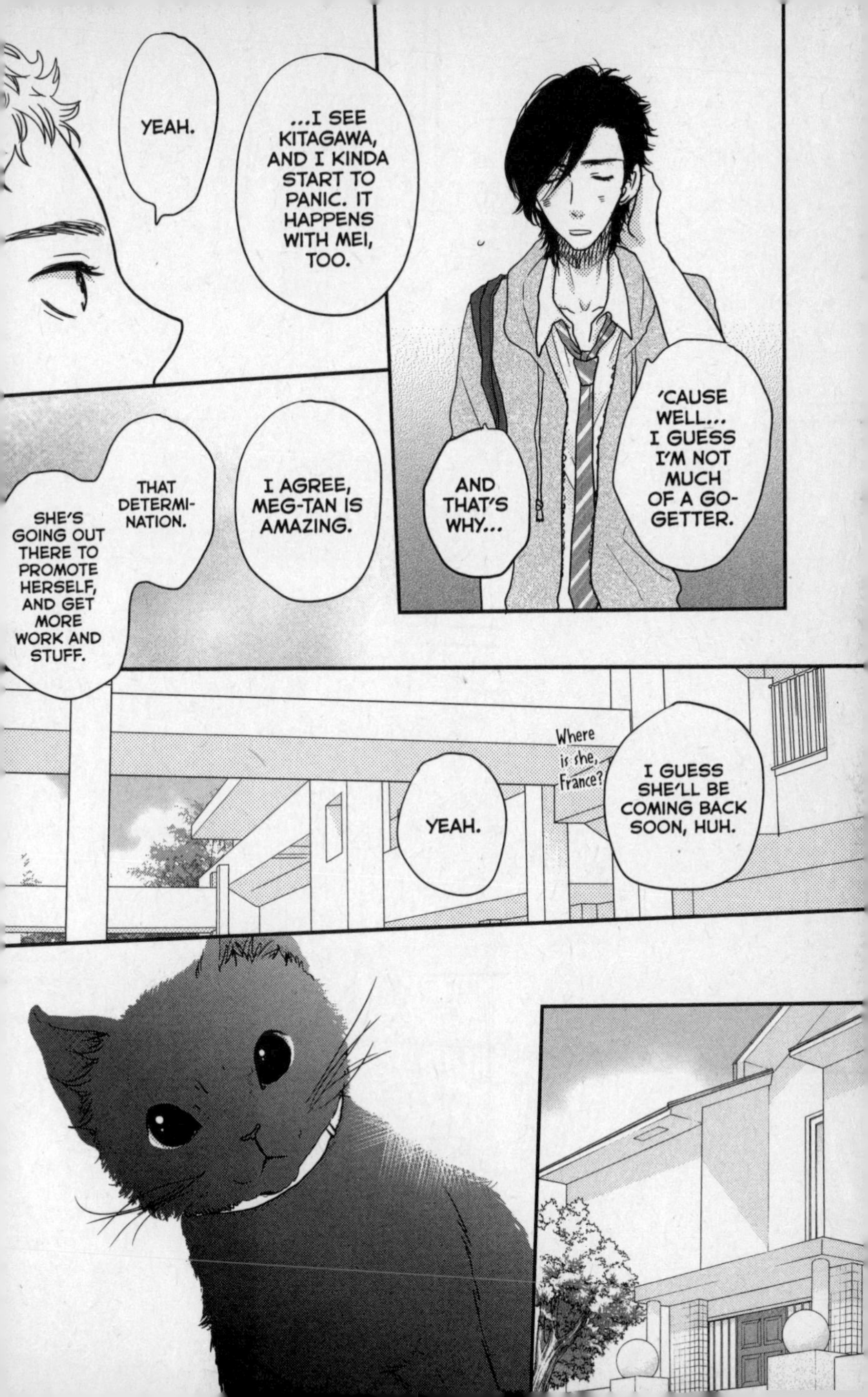
'CAUSE WELL... I GUESS I'M NOT MUCH OF A GO-GETTER.
AND THAT'S WHY...
...I SEE KITAGAWA, AND I KINDA START TO PANIC. IT HAPPENS WITH MEI, TOO.
YEAH.
I AGREE, MEG-TAN IS AMAZING.
THAT DETERMINATION.
SHE'S GOING OUT THERE TO PROMOTE HERSELF, AND GET MORE WORK AND STUFF.
I GUESS SHE'LL BE COMING BACK SOON, HUH.
Where is she, France?
YEAH.

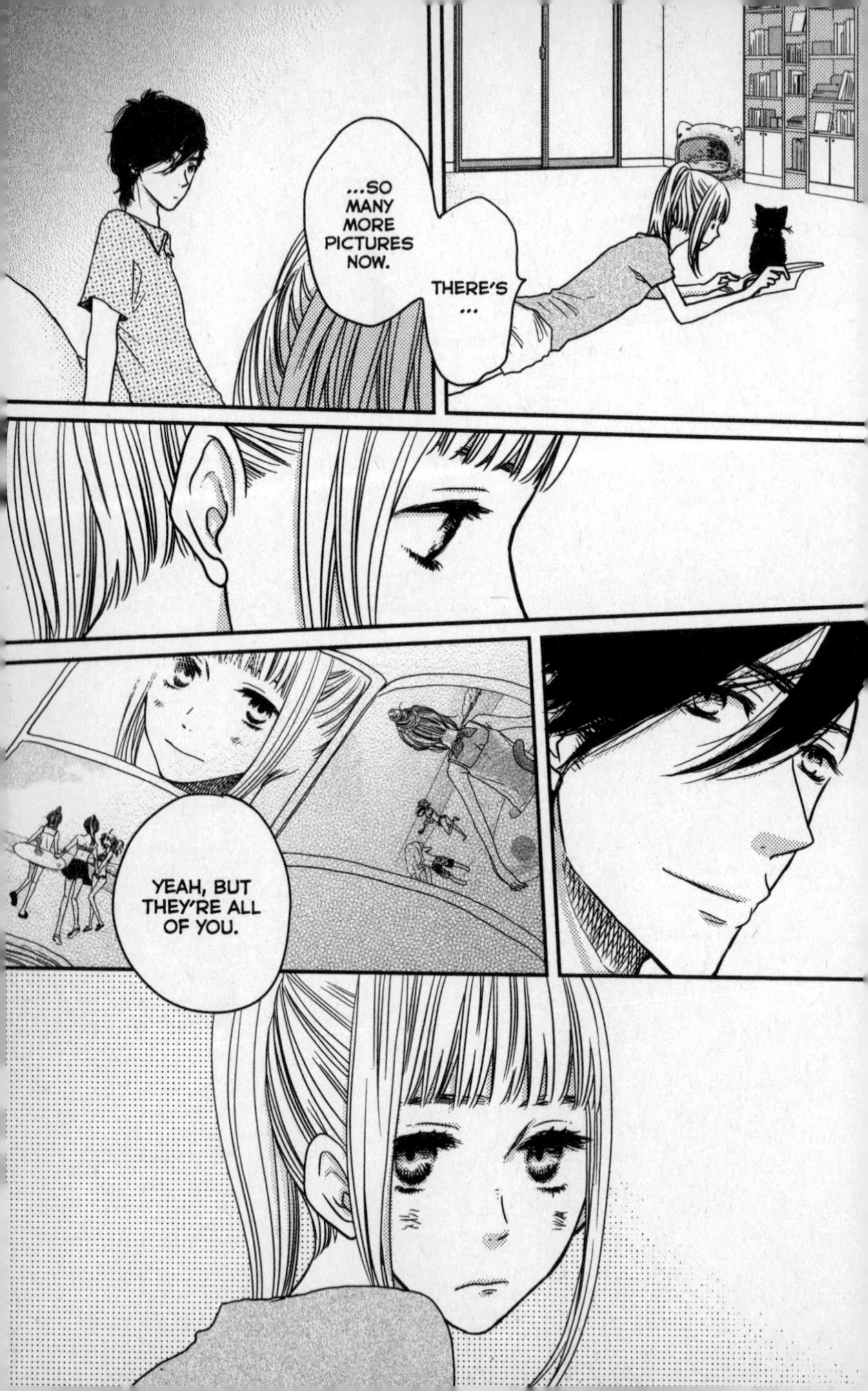
THERE'S ...
...SO MANY MORE PICTURES NOW.
YEAH, BUT THEY'RE ALL OF YOU.

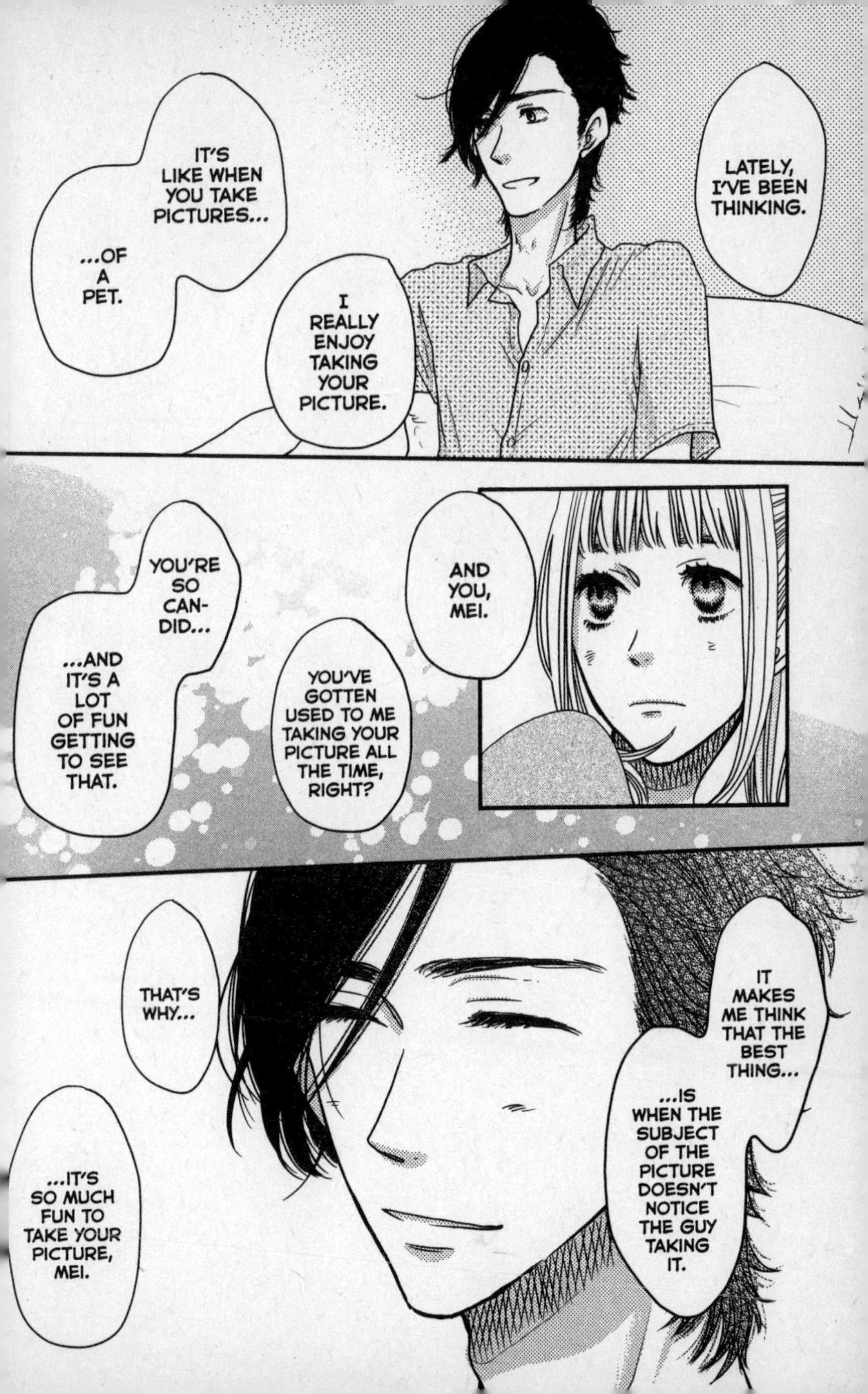
LATELY, I'VE BEEN THINKING.
I REALLY ENJOY TAKING YOUR PICTURE.
IT'S LIKE WHEN YOU TAKE PICTURES...
...OF A PET.
AND YOU, MEI.
YOU'VE GOTTEN USED TO ME TAKING YOUR PICTURE ALL THE TIME, RIGHT?
YOU'RE SO CAN-DID...
...AND IT'S A LOT OF FUN GETTING TO SEE THAT.
IT MAKES ME THINK THAT THE BEST THING...
...IS WHEN THE SUBJECT OF THE PICTURE DOESN'T NOTICE THE GUY TAKING IT.
THAT'S WHY...
...IT'S SO MUCH FUN TO TAKE YOUR PICTURE, MEI.

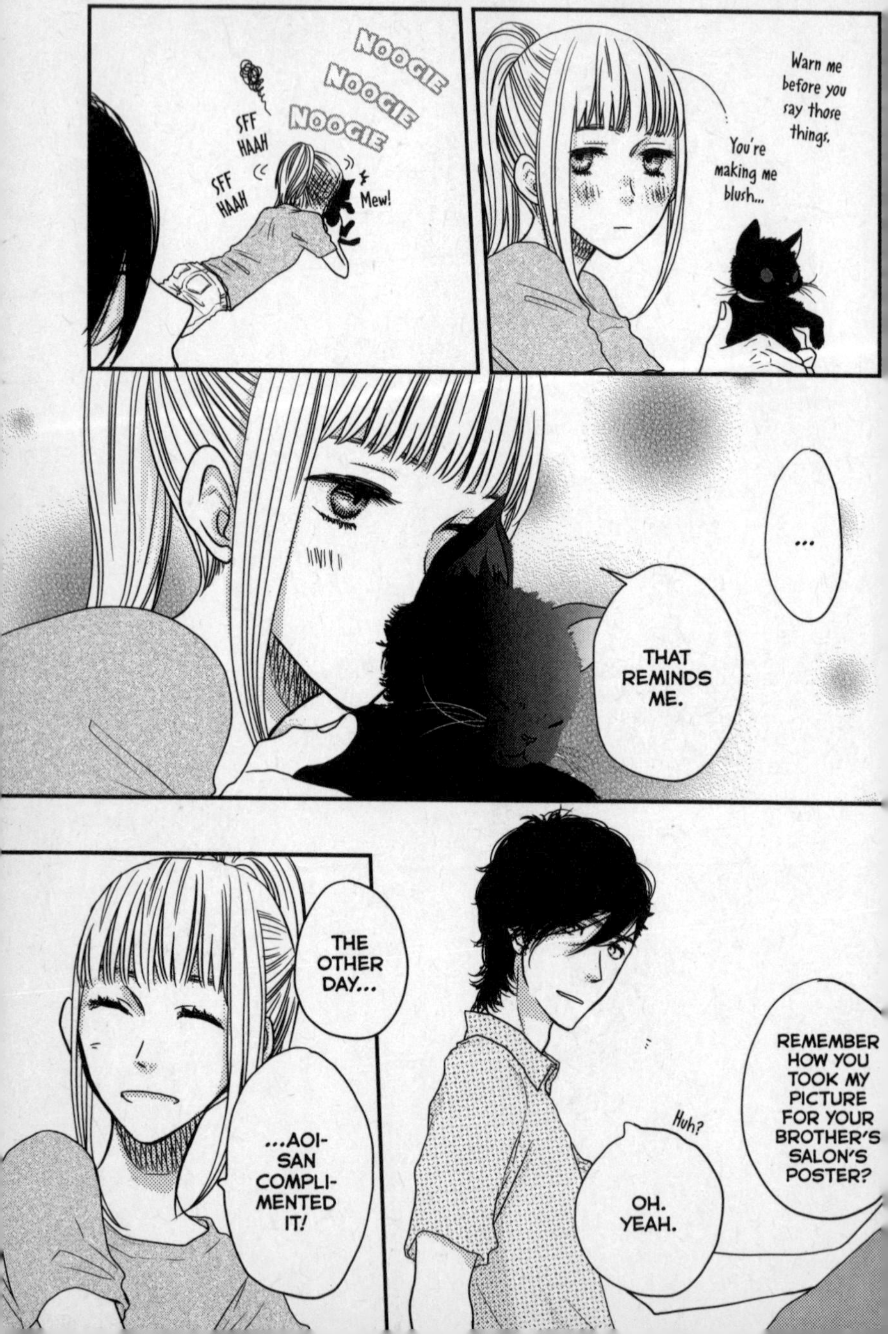
Warn me before you say those things.
You're making me blush...
NOOGIE
NOOGIE
NOOGIE
SFF HAAH
SFF HAAH
Mew!
...
THAT REMINDS ME.
REMEMBER HOW YOU TOOK MY PICTURE FOR YOUR BROTHER'S SALON'S POSTER?
Huh?
OH. YEAH.
THE OTHER DAY...
...AOI-SAN COMPLIMENTED IT!

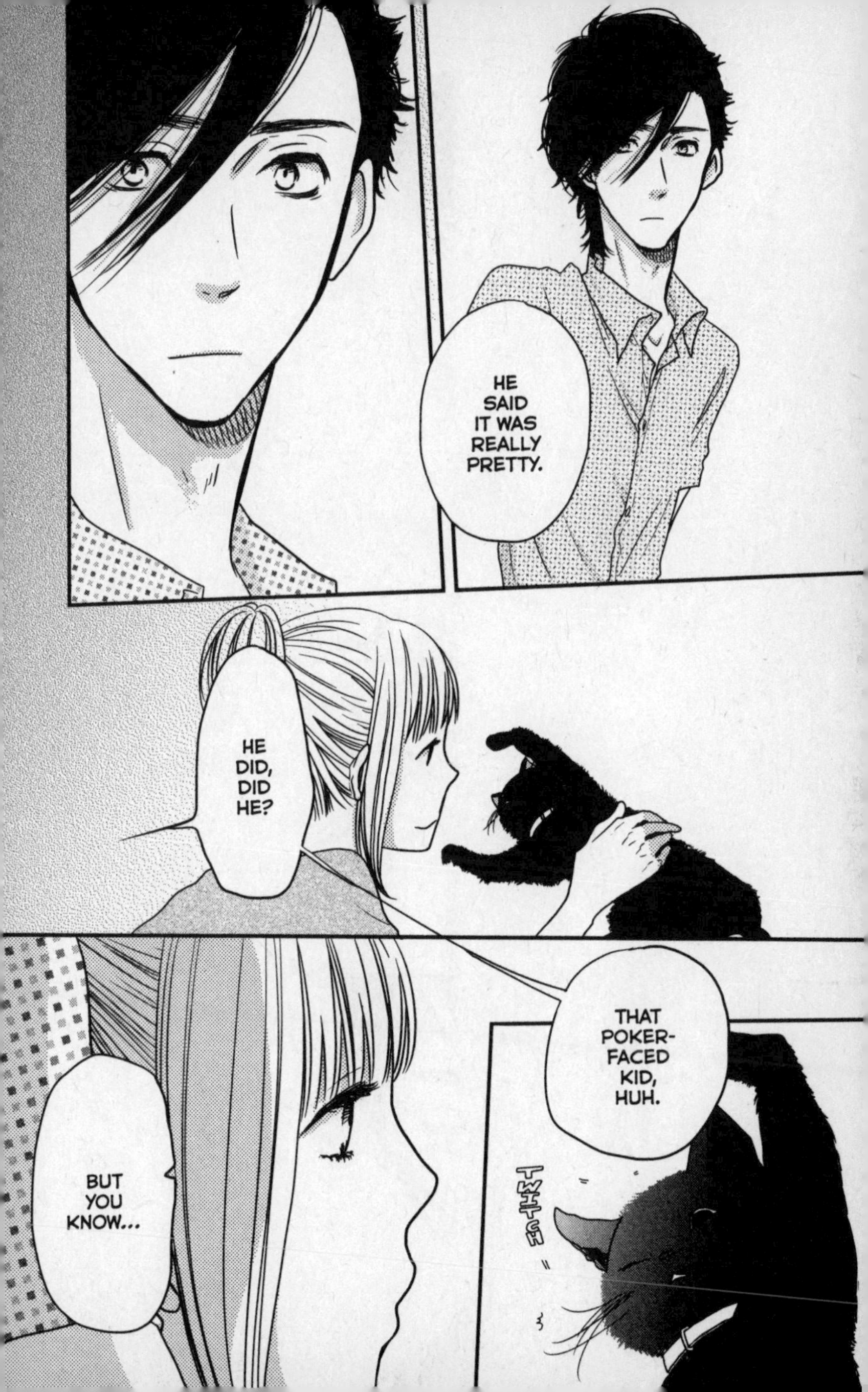
HE SAID IT WAS REALLY PRETTY.
HE DID, DID HE?
THAT POKER-FACED KID, HUH.
TWITCH
BUT YOU KNOW...

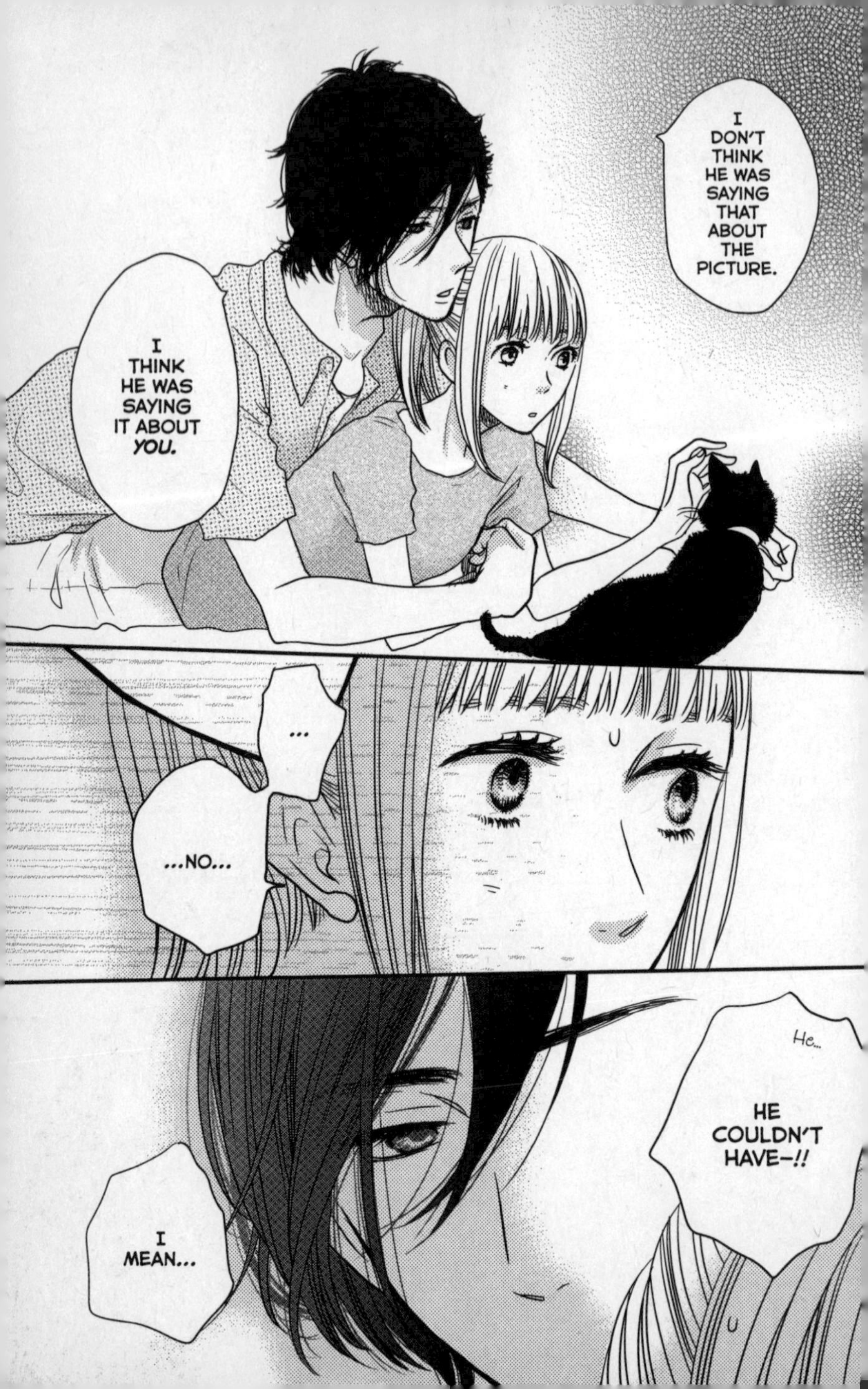
I DON'T THINK HE WAS SAYING THAT ABOUT THE PICTURE.
I THINK HE WAS SAYING IT ABOUT *YOU.*
...
...NO...
He...
HE COULDN'T HAVE–!!
I MEAN...

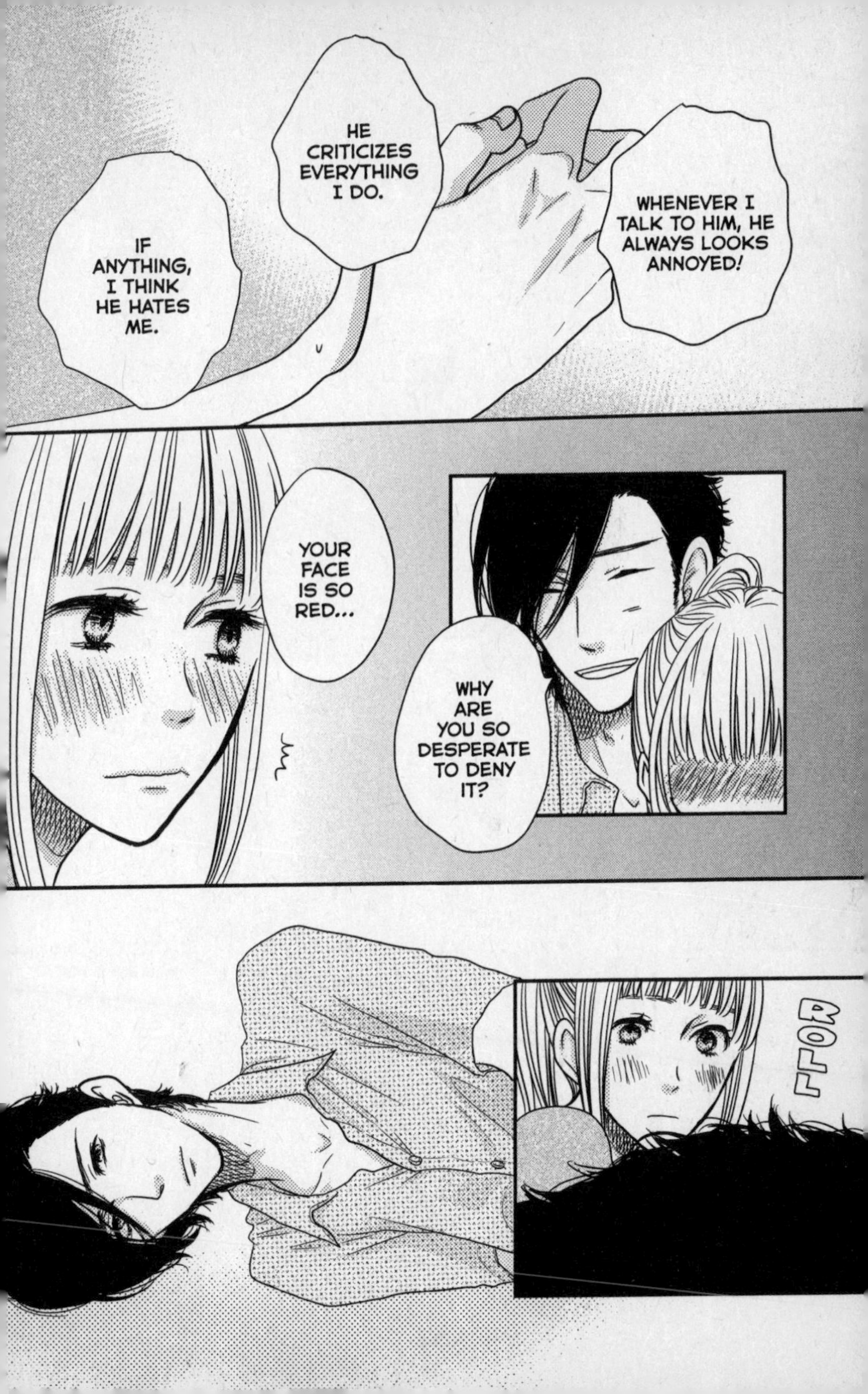
WHENEVER I TALK TO HIM, HE ALWAYS LOOKS ANNOYED!
HE CRITICIZES EVERYTHING I DO.
IF ANYTHING, I THINK HE HATES ME.
WHY ARE YOU SO DESPERATE TO DENY IT?
YOUR FACE IS SO RED...
ROLL

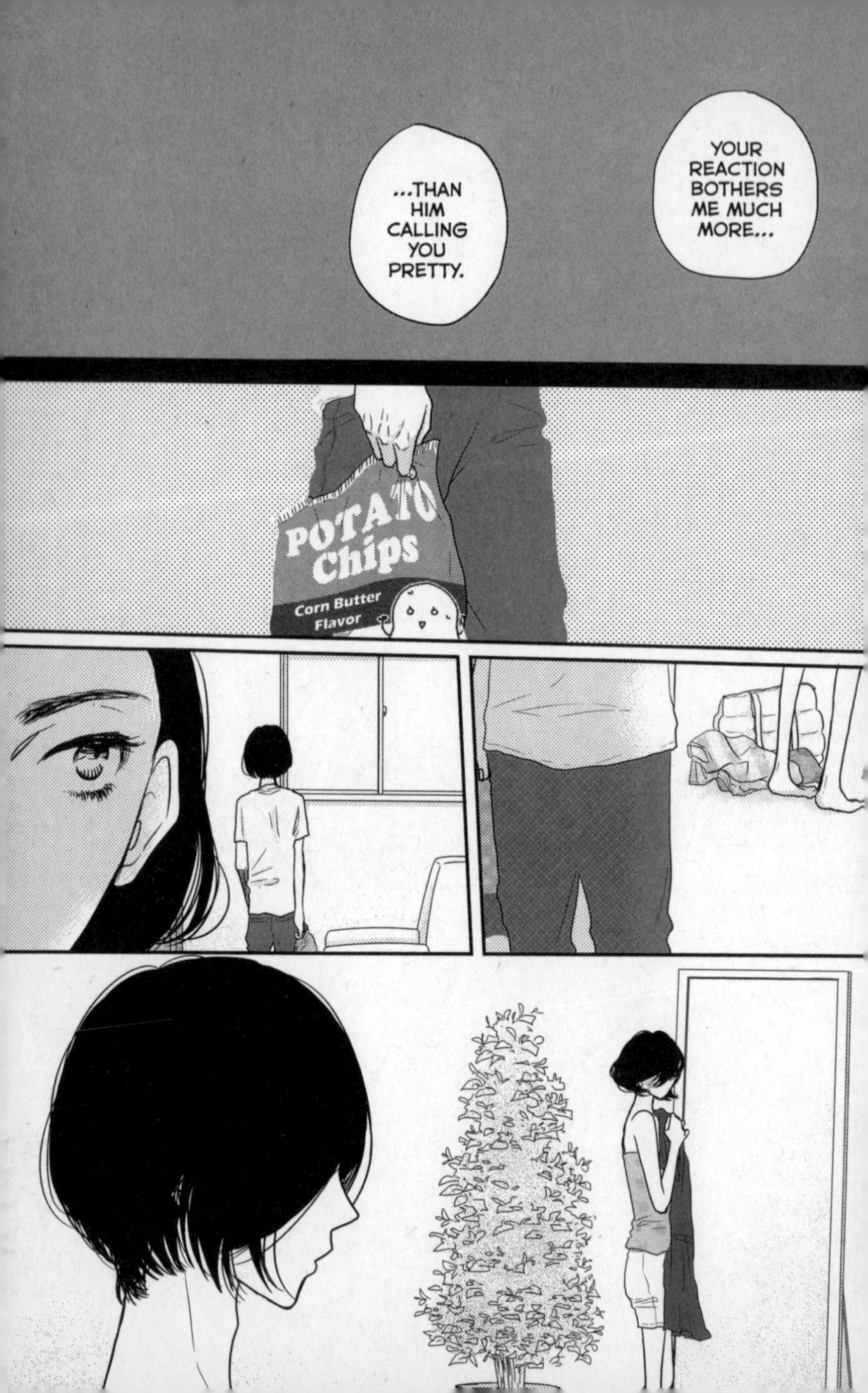
YOUR REACTION BOTHERS ME MUCH MORE...
...THAN HIM CALLING YOU PRETTY.
POTATO Chips
Corn Butter Flavor

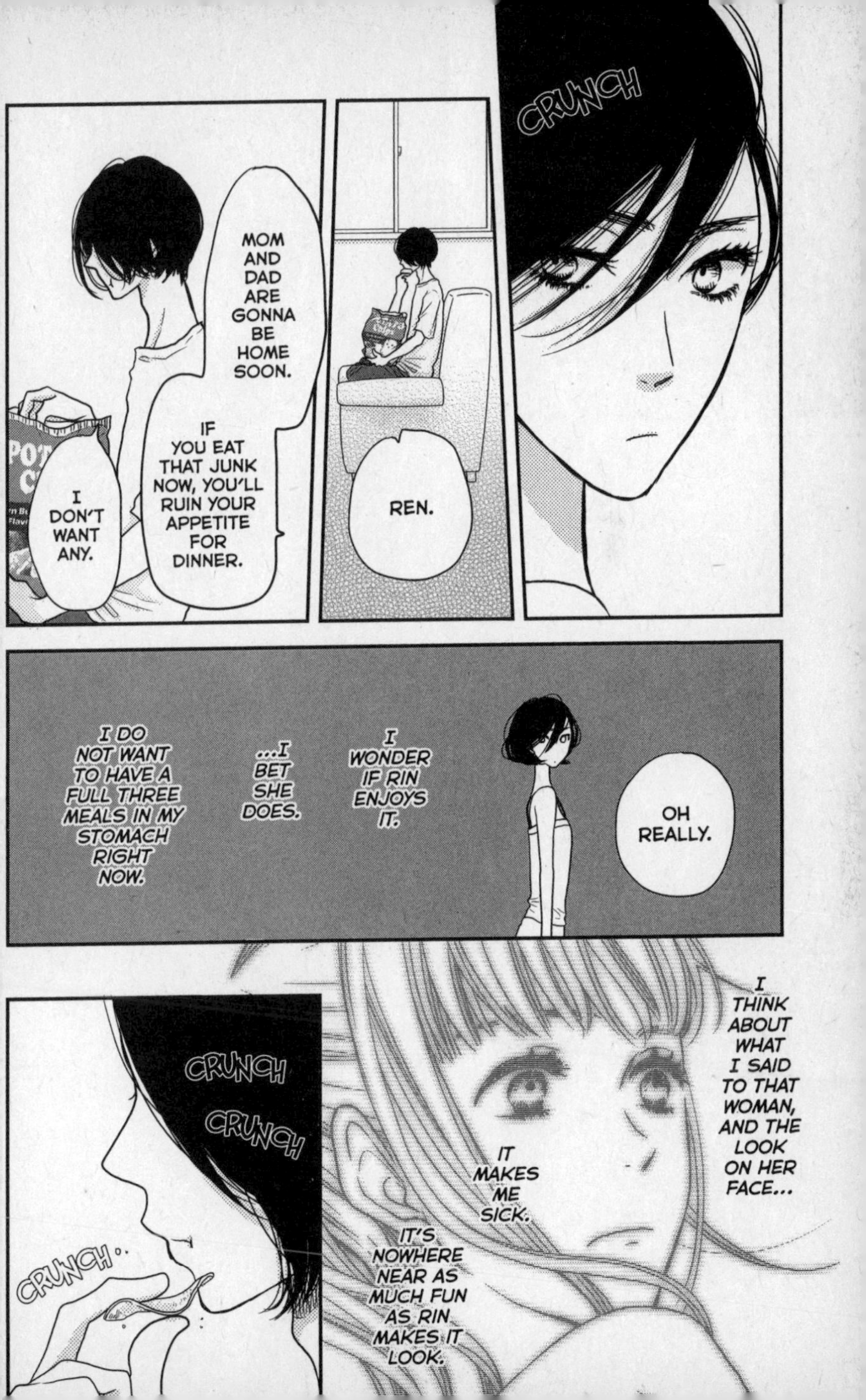
CRUNCH
REN.
MOM AND DAD ARE GONNA BE HOME SOON.
IF YOU EAT THAT JUNK NOW, YOU'LL RUIN YOUR APPETITE FOR DINNER.
I DON'T WANT ANY.
OH REALLY.
I WONDER IF RIN ENJOYS IT.
...I BET SHE DOES.
I DO NOT WANT TO HAVE A FULL THREE MEALS IN MY STOMACH RIGHT NOW.
I THINK ABOUT WHAT I SAID TO THAT WOMAN, AND THE LOOK ON HER FACE...
IT MAKES ME SICK.
IT'S NOWHERE NEAR AS MUCH FUN AS RIN MAKES IT LOOK.
CRUNCH
CRUNCH
CRUNCH

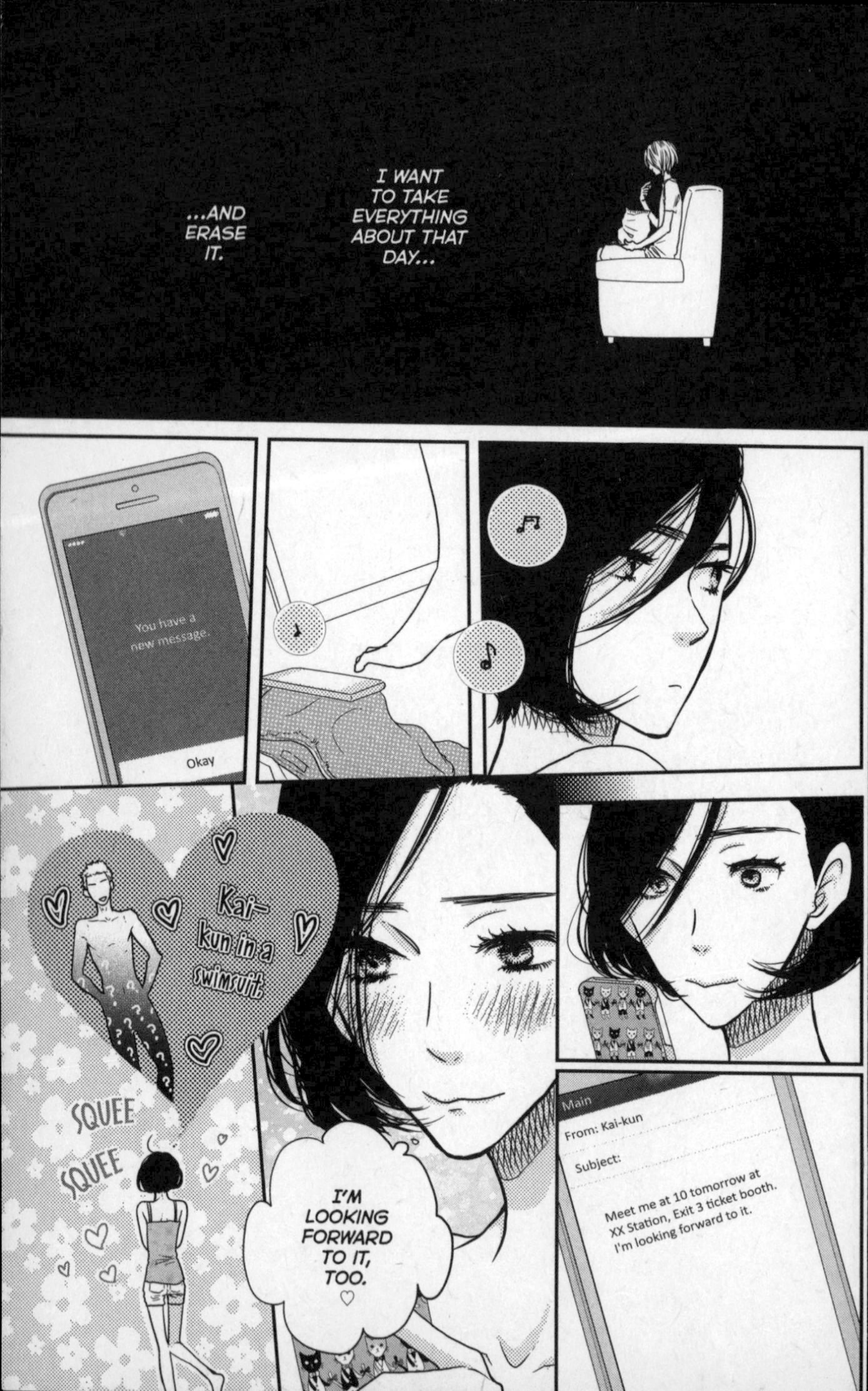
I WANT TO TAKE EVERYTHING ABOUT THAT DAY...
...AND ERASE IT.
You have a new message.
Okay
Main
From: Kai-kun
Subject:
Meet me at 10 tomorrow at XX Station, Exit 3 ticket booth. I'm looking forward to it.
I'M LOOKING FORWARD TO IT, TOO. ♡
Kai-kun in a swimsuit
SQUEE
SQUEE

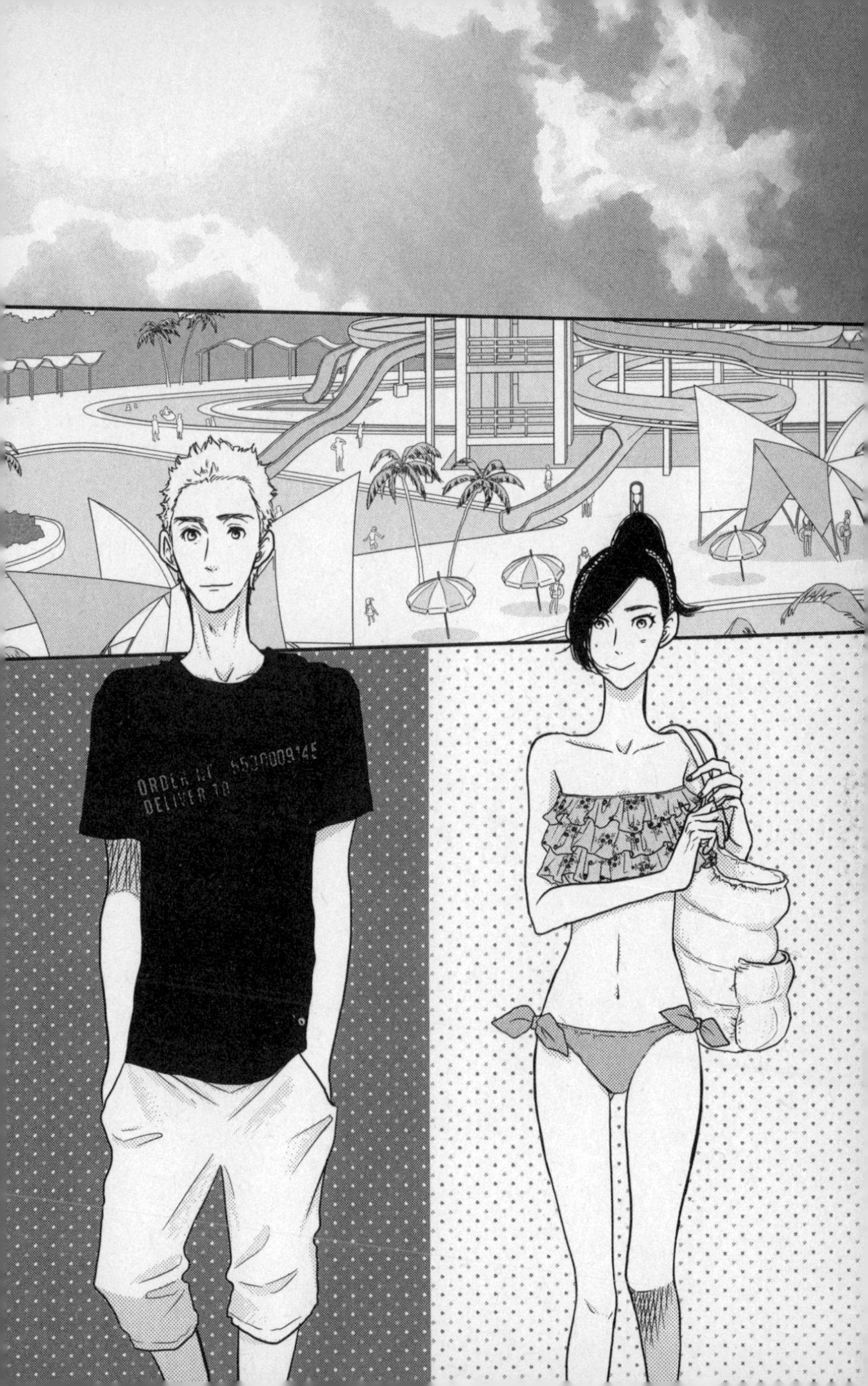
ORDER
DELIVER TO

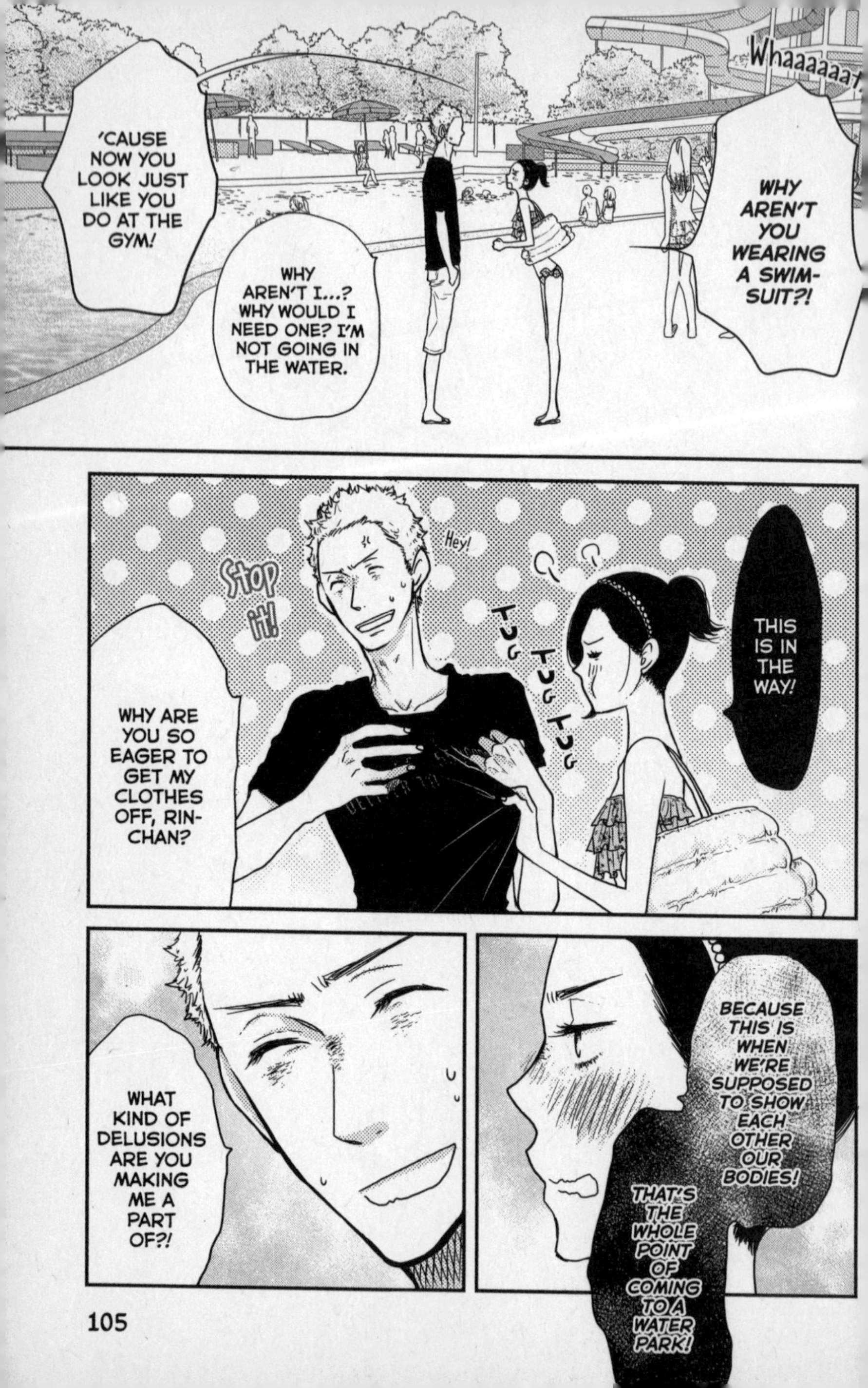
Whaaaaaat
WHY AREN'T YOU WEARING A SWIM-SUIT?!
WHY AREN'T I...? WHY WOULD I NEED ONE? I'M NOT GOING IN THE WATER.
'CAUSE NOW YOU LOOK JUST LIKE YOU DO AT THE GYM!
THIS IS IN THE WAY!
TUG TUG TUG TUG
Hey!
Stop it!
WHY ARE YOU SO EAGER TO GET MY CLOTHES OFF, RIN-CHAN?
BECAUSE THIS IS WHEN WE'RE SUPPOSED TO SHOW EACH OTHER OUR BODIES!
THAT'S THE WHOLE POINT OF COMING TO A WATER PARK!
WHAT KIND OF DELUSIONS ARE YOU MAKING ME A PART OF?!

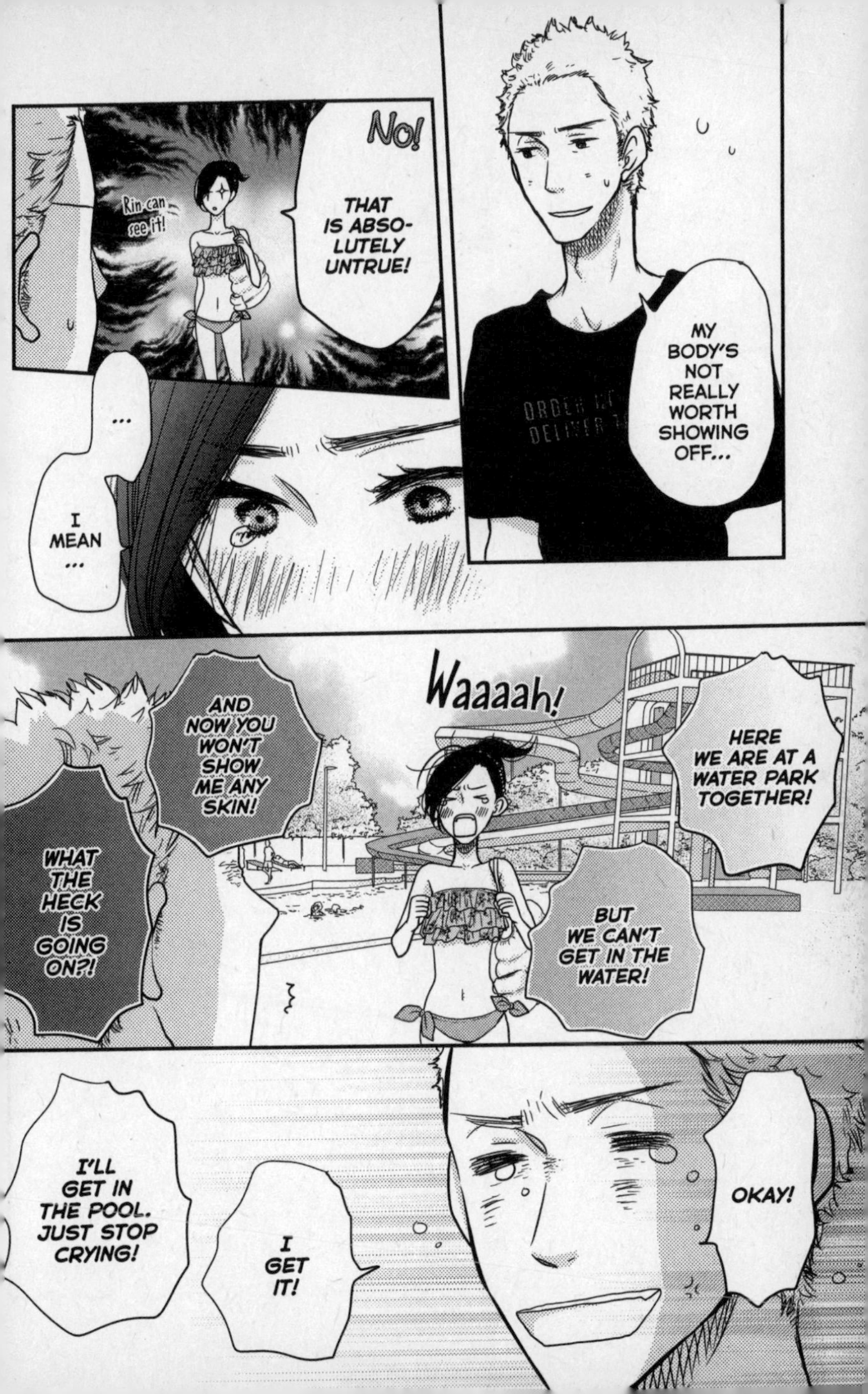
MY BODY'S NOT REALLY WORTH SHOWING OFF...
No!
THAT IS ABSOLUTELY UNTRUE!
Rin can see it!
...
I MEAN ...
HERE WE ARE AT A WATER PARK TOGETHER!
BUT WE CAN'T GET IN THE WATER!
Waaaah!
AND NOW YOU WON'T SHOW ME ANY SKIN!
WHAT THE HECK IS GOING ON?!
OKAY!
I GET IT!
I'LL GET IN THE POOL. JUST STOP CRYING!

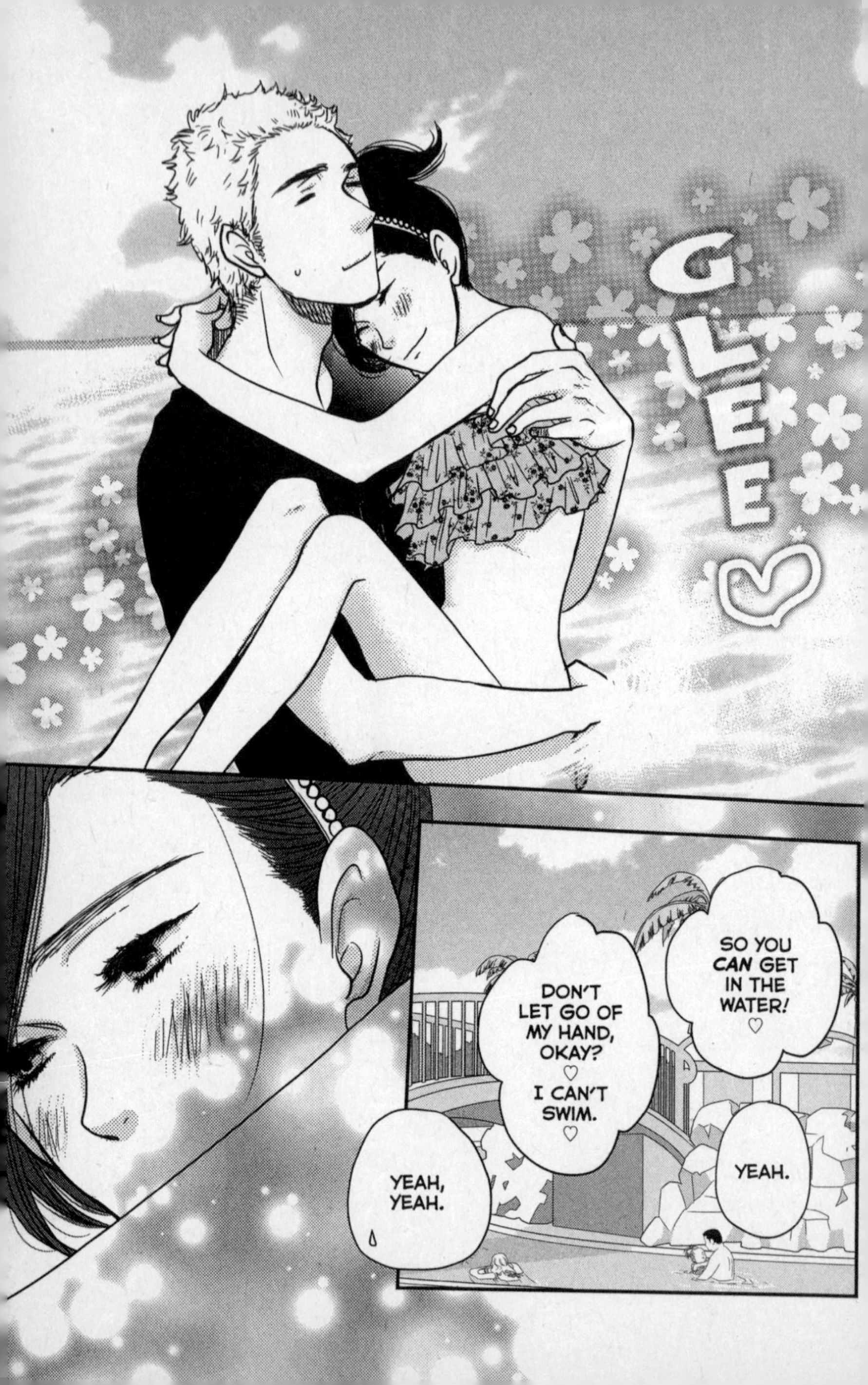
GLEE ♡
SO YOU CAN GET IN THE WATER! ♡
DON'T LET GO OF MY HAND, OKAY? ♡ I CAN'T SWIM. ♡
YEAH.
YEAH, YEAH.

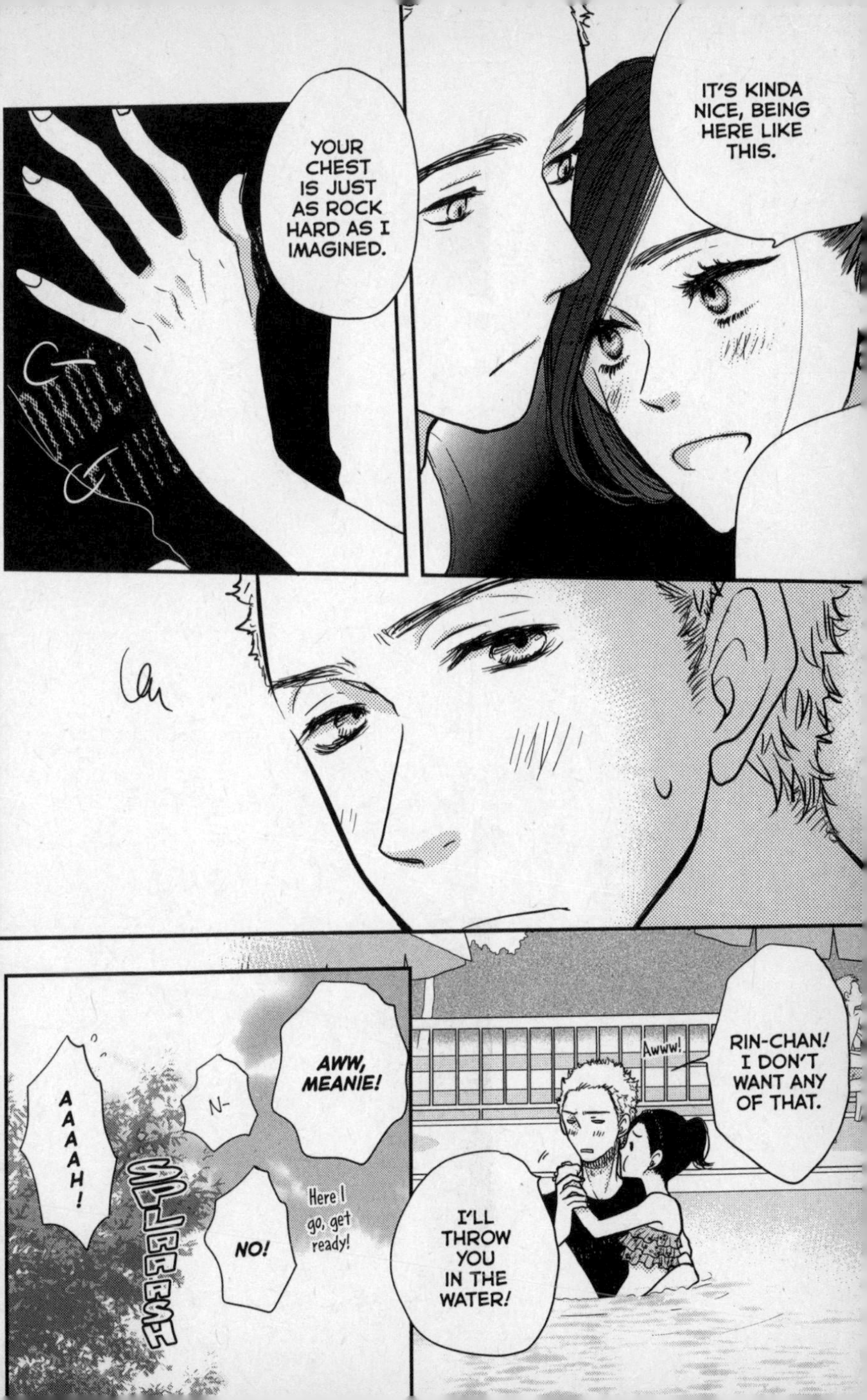
IT'S KINDA NICE, BEING HERE LIKE THIS.
YOUR CHEST IS JUST AS ROCK HARD AS I IMAGINED.
RIN-CHAN! I DON'T WANT ANY OF THAT.
Awww!
I'LL THROW YOU IN THE WATER!
AWW, MEANIE!
N-
Here I go, get ready!
NO!
AAAAH!

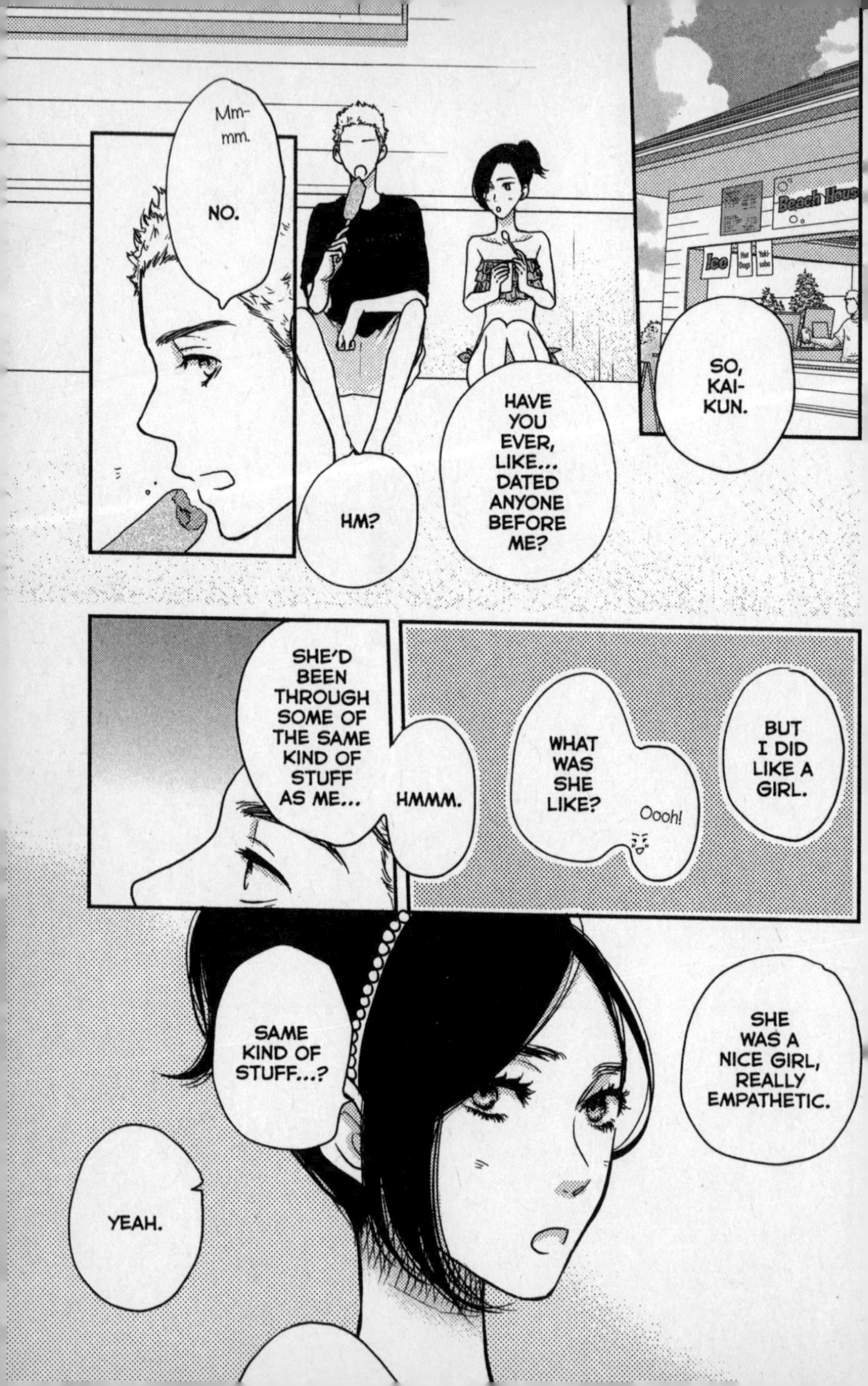
SO, KAI-KUN.
Ice
HAVE YOU EVER, LIKE... DATED ANYONE BEFORE ME?
HM?
Mm-mm.
NO.
BUT I DID LIKE A GIRL.
WHAT WAS SHE LIKE?
Oooh!
HMMM.
SHE'D BEEN THROUGH SOME OF THE SAME KIND OF STUFF AS ME...
SHE WAS A NICE GIRL, REALLY EMPATHETIC.
SAME KIND OF STUFF...?
YEAH.

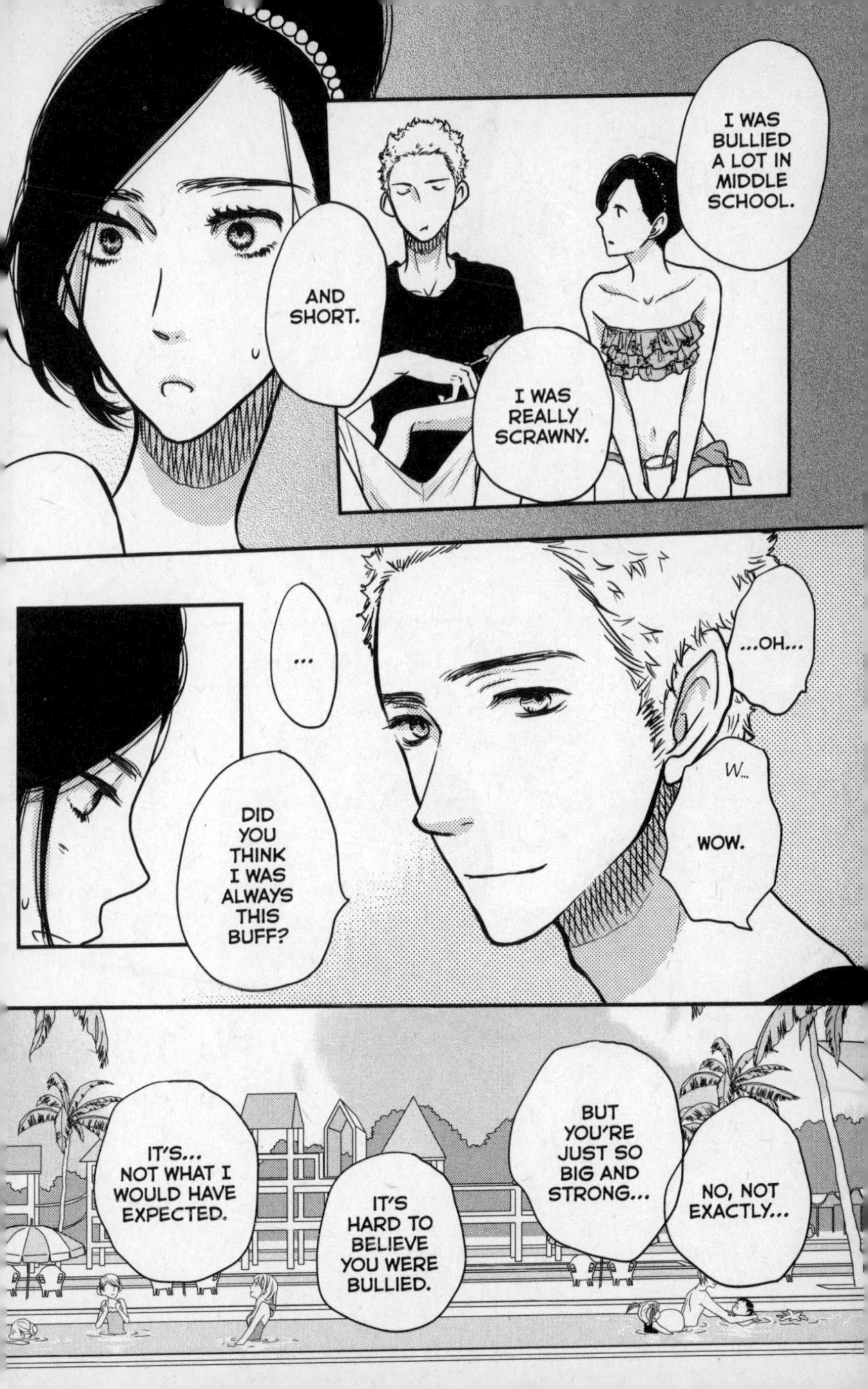
I WAS BULLIED A LOT IN MIDDLE SCHOOL.
I WAS REALLY SCRAWNY.
AND SHORT.
...OH...
W... WOW.
...
DID YOU THINK I WAS ALWAYS THIS BUFF?
NO, NOT EXACTLY...
BUT YOU'RE JUST SO BIG AND STRONG...
IT'S HARD TO BELIEVE YOU WERE BULLIED.
IT'S... NOT WHAT I WOULD HAVE EXPECTED.

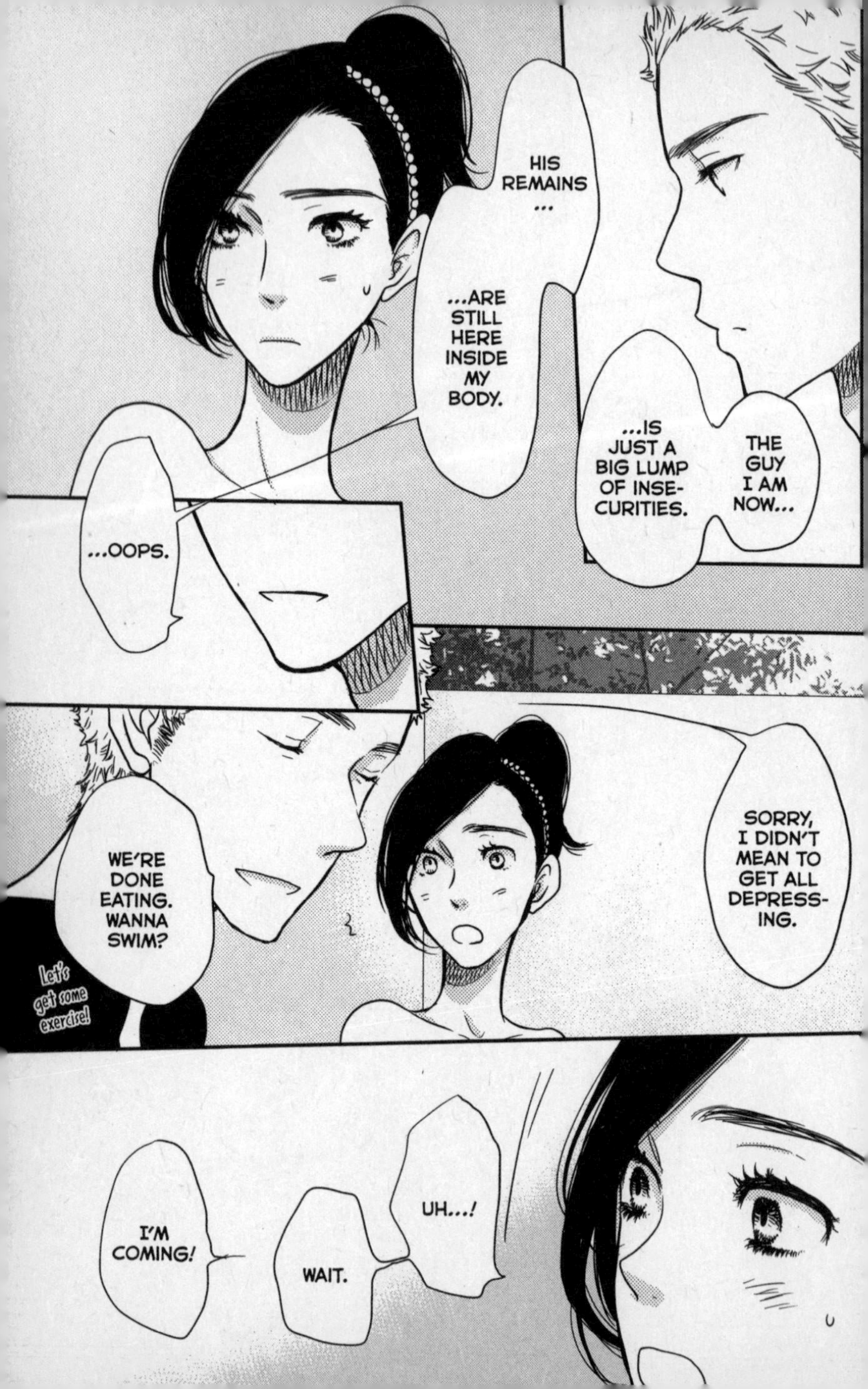
THE GUY I AM NOW...
...IS JUST A BIG LUMP OF INSE-CURITIES.
HIS REMAINS...
...ARE STILL HERE INSIDE MY BODY.
...OOPS.
SORRY, I DIDN'T MEAN TO GET ALL DEPRESS-ING.
WE'RE DONE EATING. WANNA SWIM?
Let's get some exercise!
UH...!
WAIT.
I'M COMING!

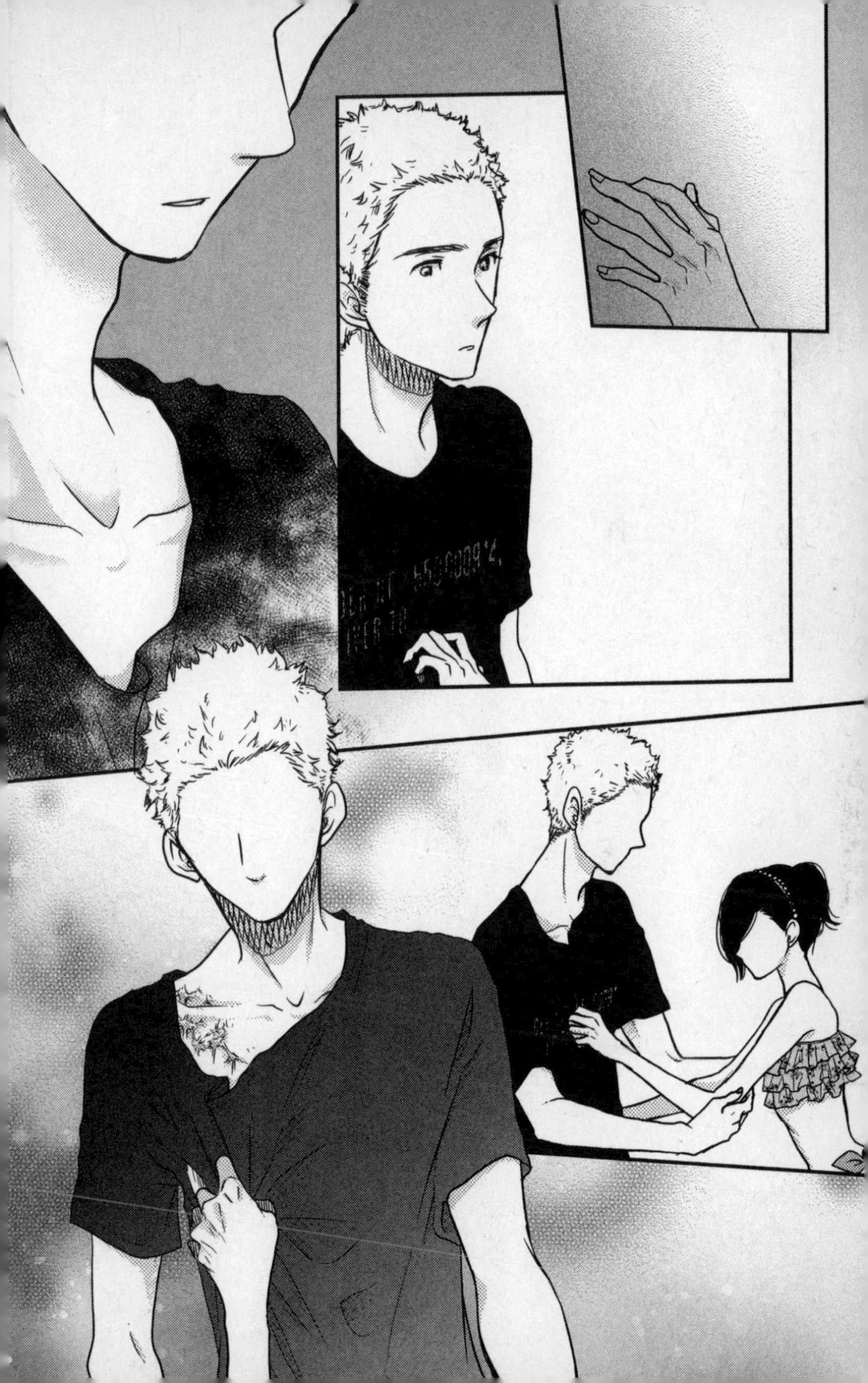

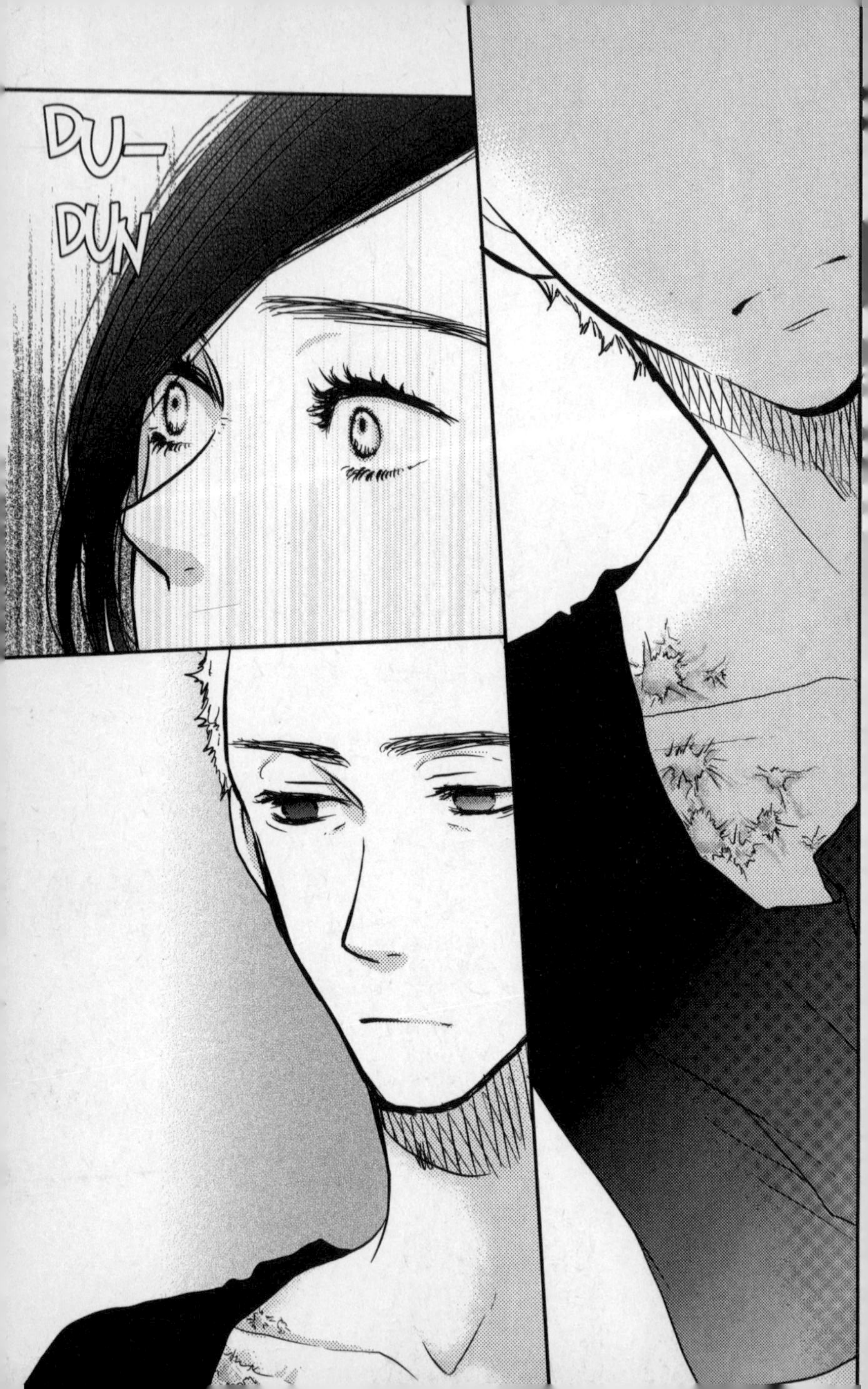
DU—DUN

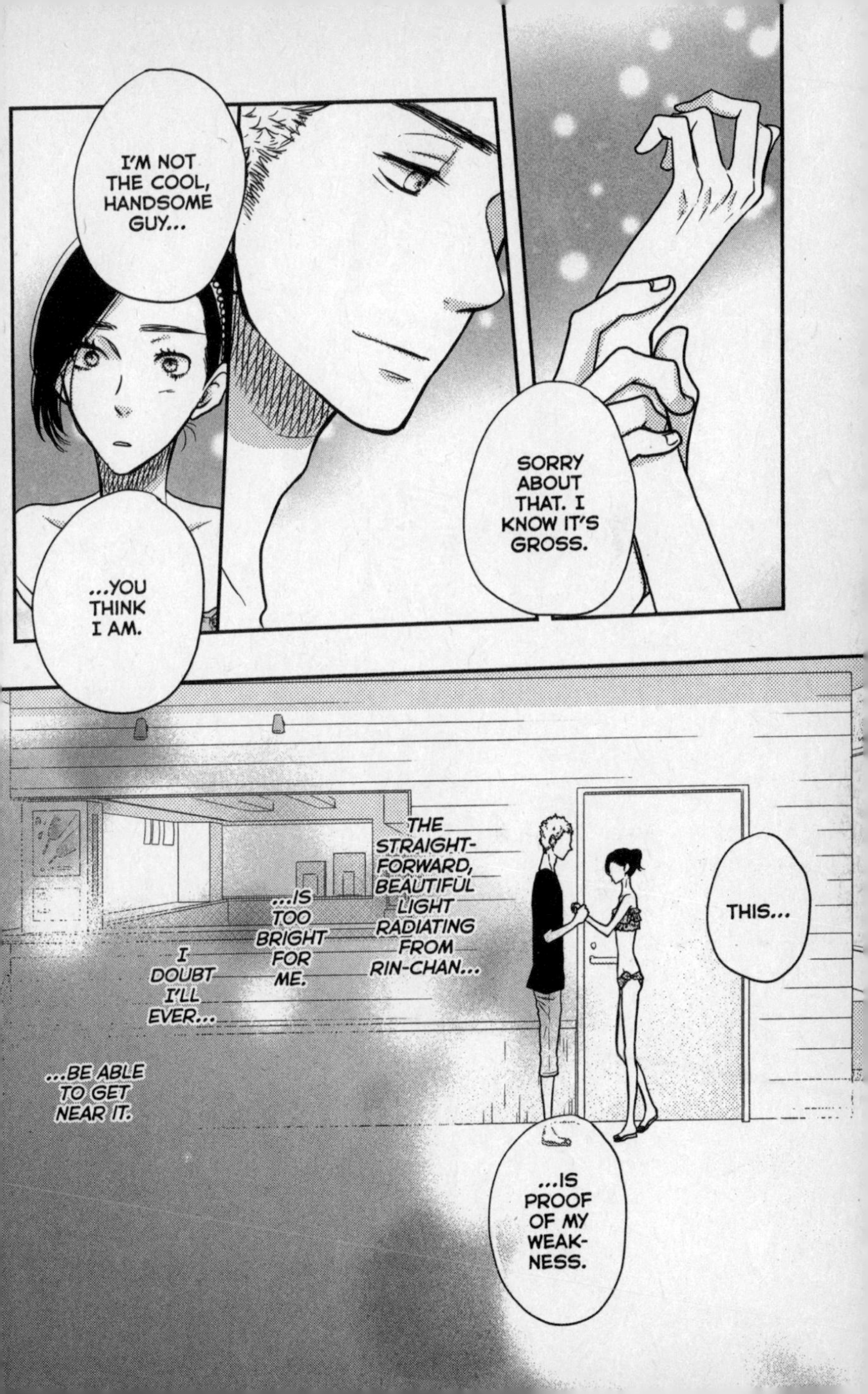
I'M NOT THE COOL, HANDSOME GUY...
...YOU THINK I AM.
SORRY ABOUT THAT. I KNOW IT'S GROSS.
THIS...
...IS PROOF OF MY WEAK-NESS.
THE STRAIGHT-FORWARD, BEAUTIFUL LIGHT RADIATING FROM RIN-CHAN...
...IS TOO BRIGHT FOR ME.
I DOUBT I'LL EVER...
...BE ABLE TO GET NEAR IT.

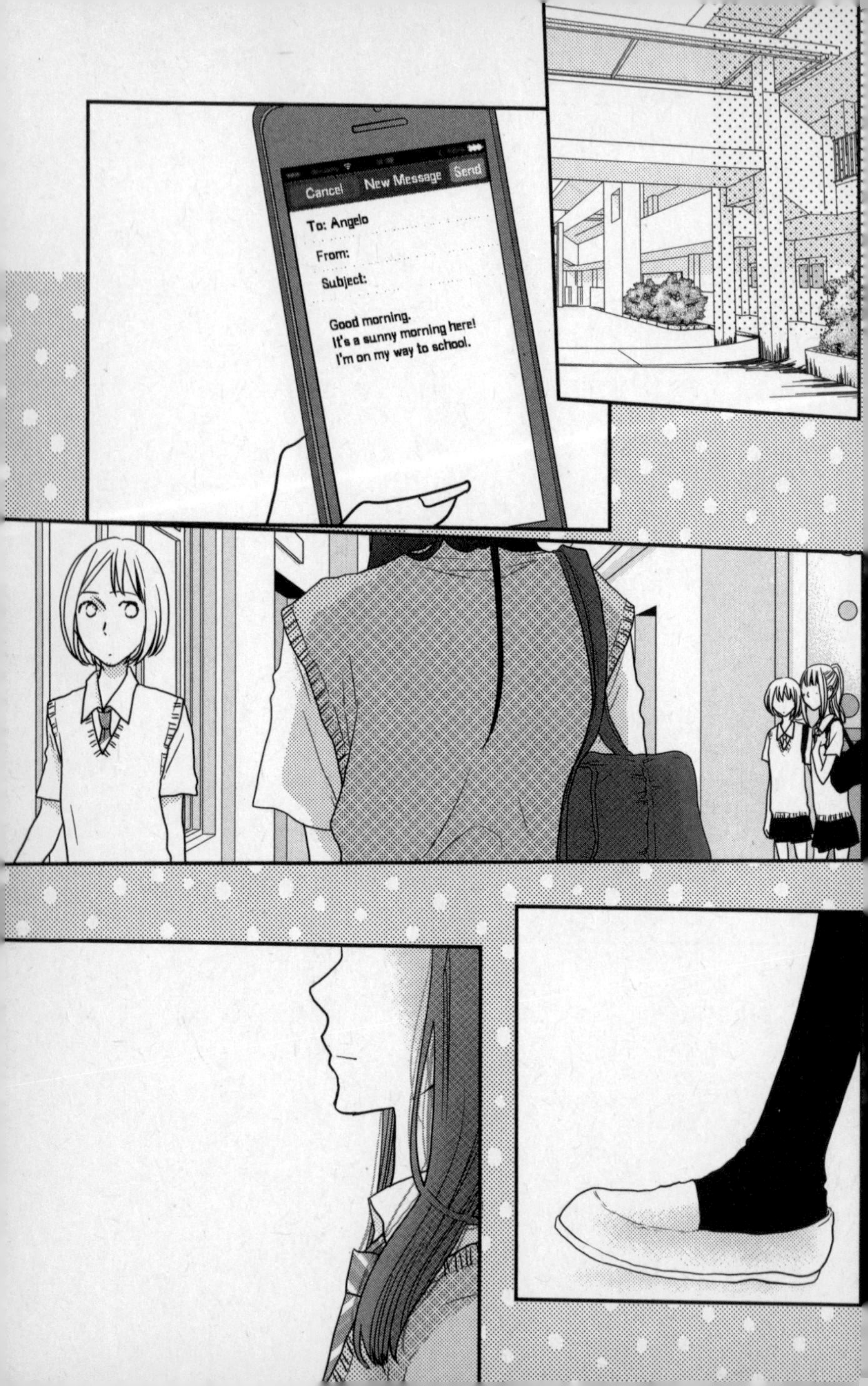
Cancel
New Message
Send
To: Angelo
From:
Subject:
Good morning.
It's a sunny morning here!
I'm on my way to school.

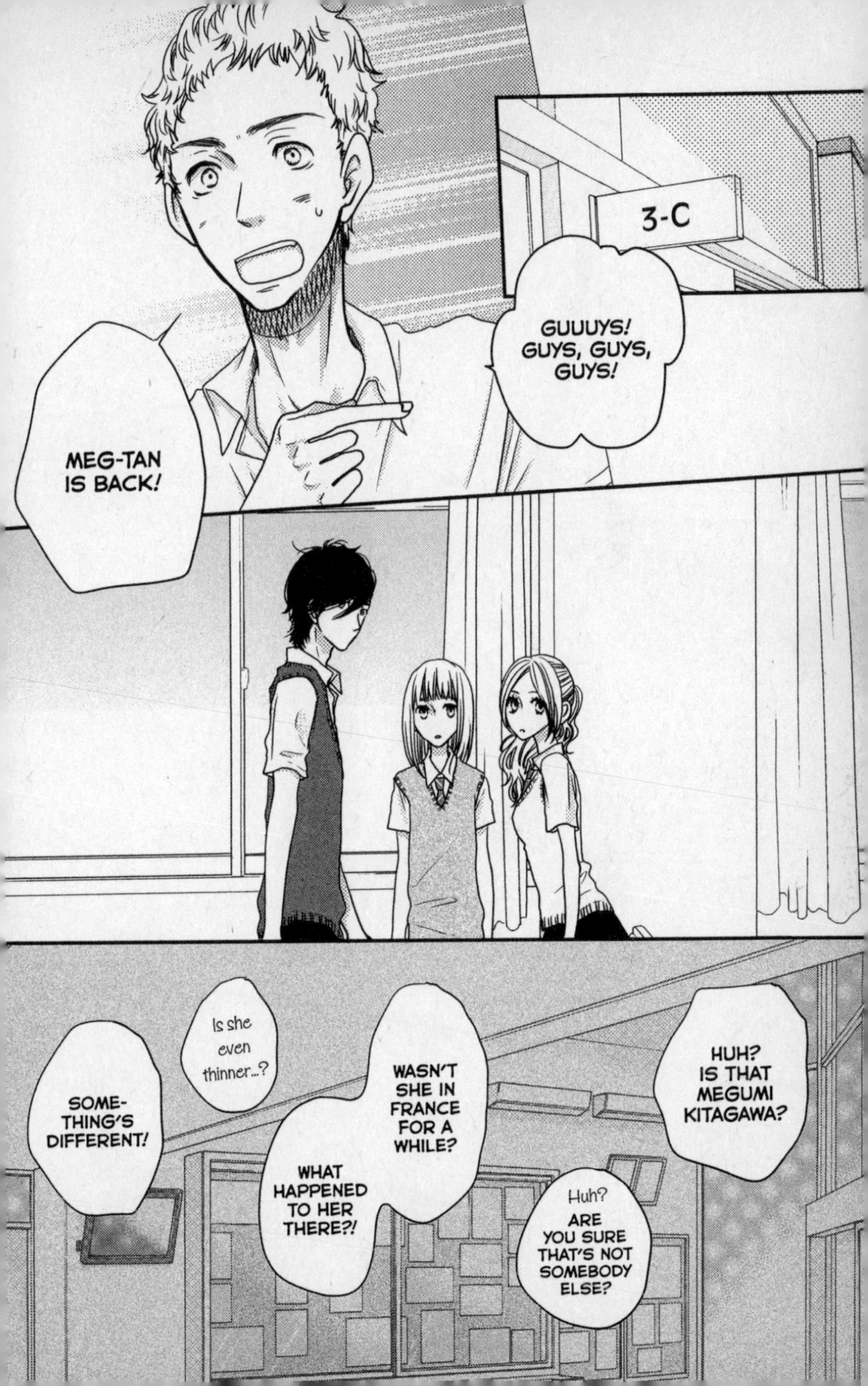
3-C
GUUUYS! GUYS, GUYS, GUYS!
MEG-TAN IS BACK!
HUH? IS THAT MEGUMI KITAGAWA?
Huh? ARE YOU SURE THAT'S NOT SOMEBODY ELSE?
WASN'T SHE IN FRANCE FOR A WHILE?
WHAT HAPPENED TO HER THERE?!
Is she even thinner...?
SOME-THING'S DIFFERENT!

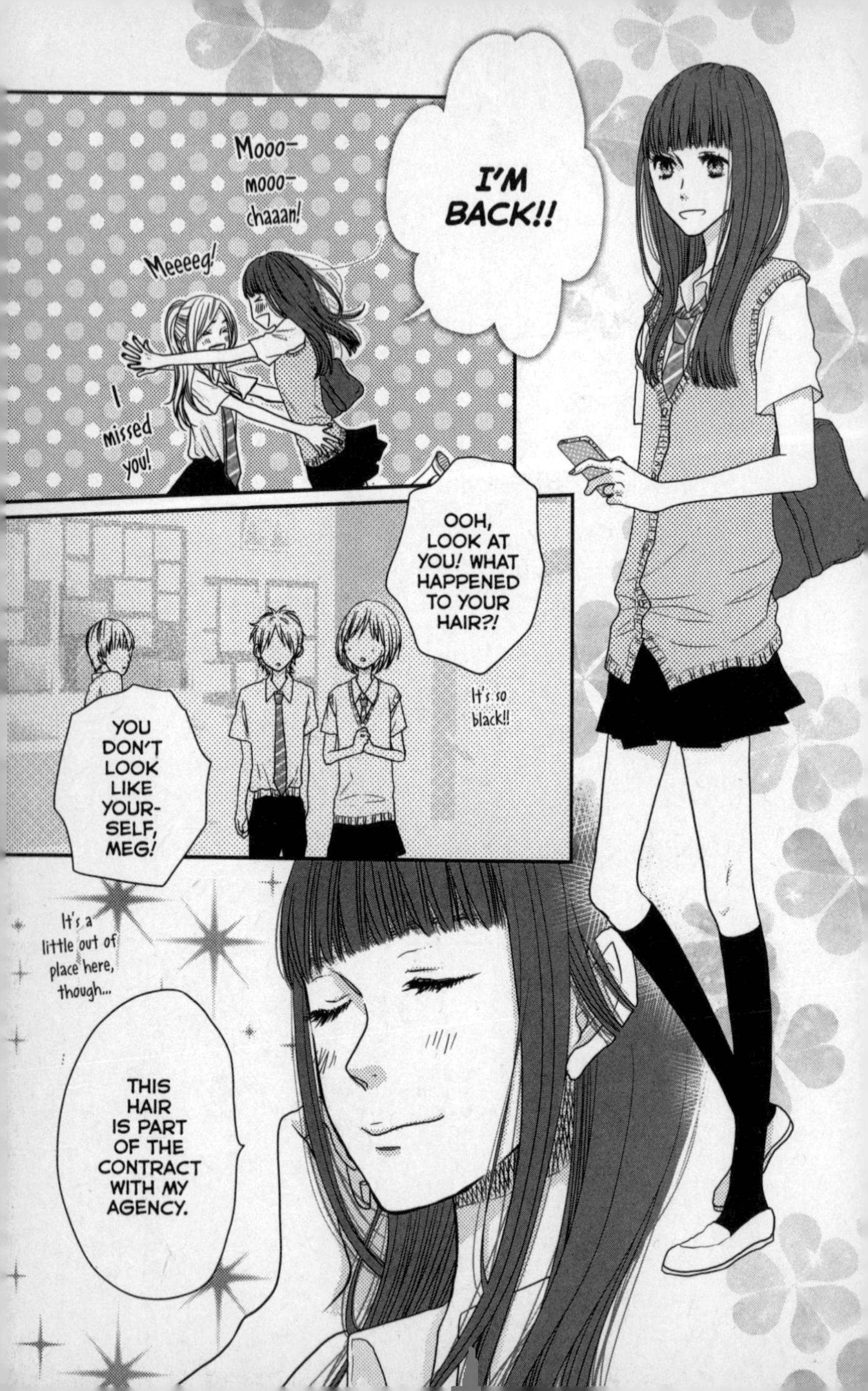
I'M BACK!!
Mooo-mooo-chaaan!
Meeeeg!
I missed you!
OOH, LOOK AT YOU! WHAT HAPPENED TO YOUR HAIR?!
It's so black!!
YOU DON'T LOOK LIKE YOURSELF, MEG!
It's a little out of place here, though...
THIS HAIR IS PART OF THE CONTRACT WITH MY AGENCY.

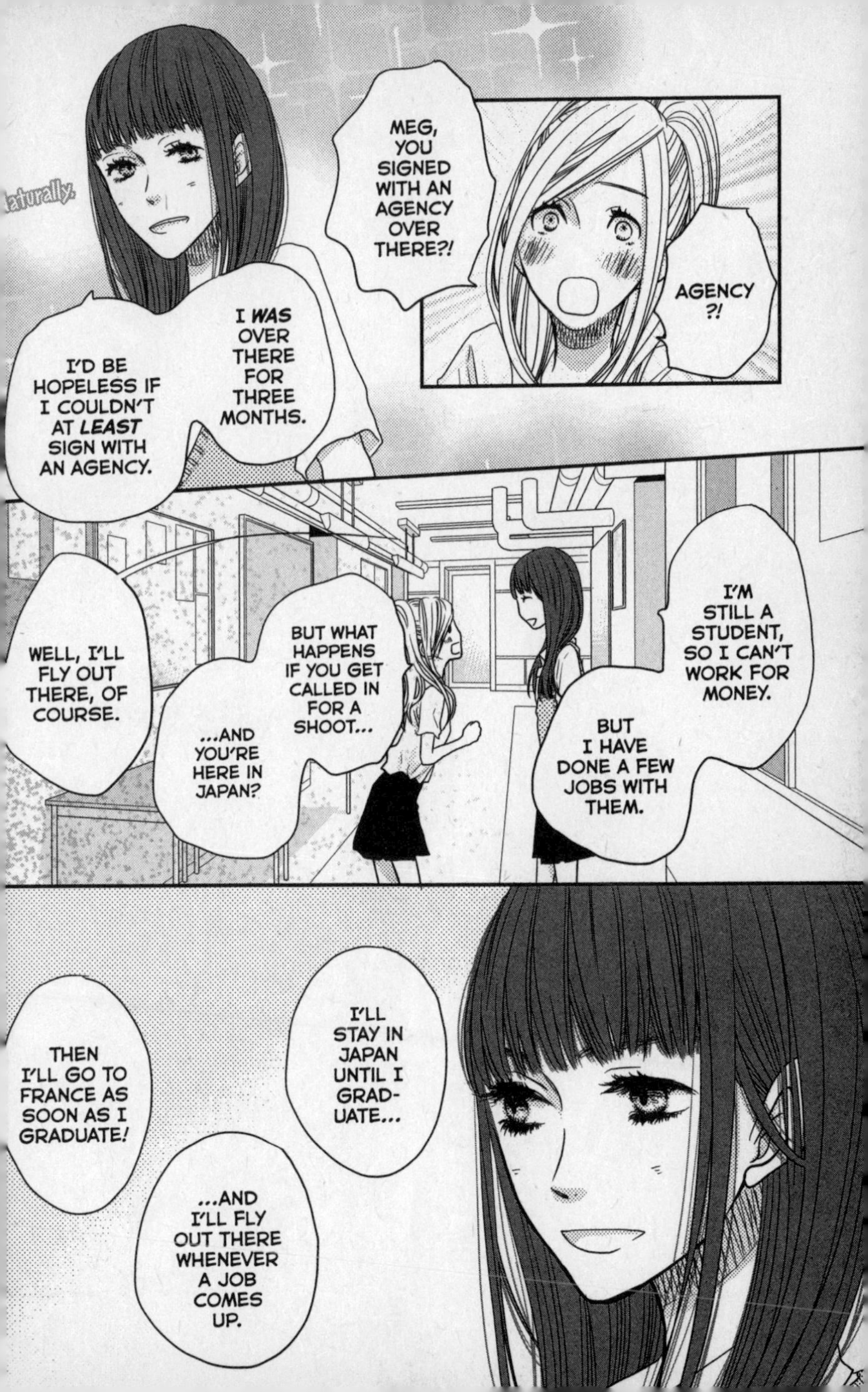
AGENCY?!
MEG, YOU SIGNED WITH AN AGENCY OVER THERE?!
aturally.
I *WAS* OVER THERE FOR THREE MONTHS.
I'D BE HOPELESS IF I COULDN'T AT *LEAST* SIGN WITH AN AGENCY.
I'M STILL A STUDENT, SO I CAN'T WORK FOR MONEY.
BUT I HAVE DONE A FEW JOBS WITH THEM.
BUT WHAT HAPPENS IF YOU GET CALLED IN FOR A SHOOT...
...AND YOU'RE HERE IN JAPAN?
WELL, I'LL FLY OUT THERE, OF COURSE.
I'LL STAY IN JAPAN UNTIL I GRAD-UATE...
...AND I'LL FLY OUT THERE WHENEVER A JOB COMES UP.
THEN I'LL GO TO FRANCE AS SOON AS I GRADUATE!

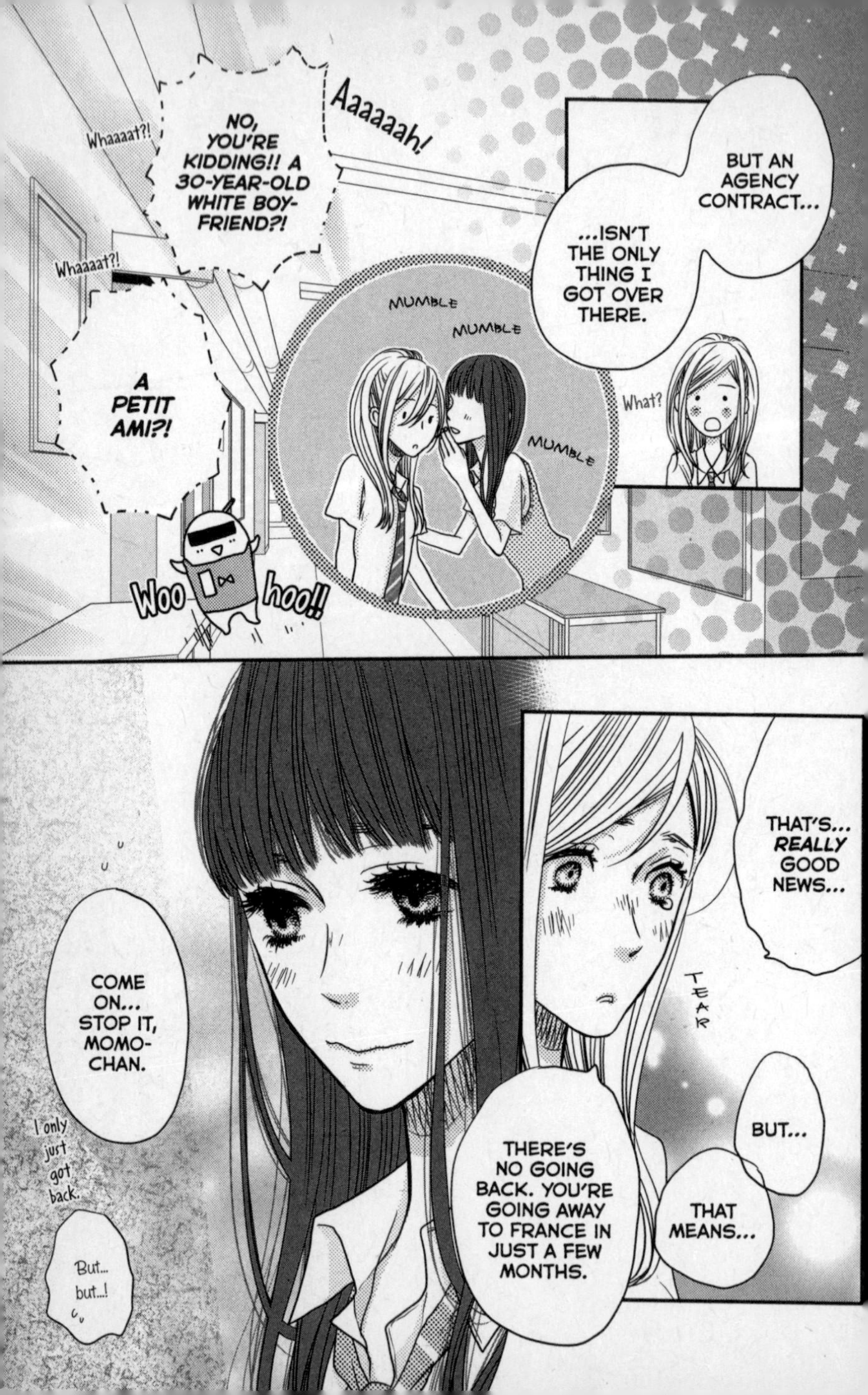
BUT AN AGENCY CONTRACT...
...ISN'T THE ONLY THING I GOT OVER THERE.
What?
Aaaaaah!
NO, YOU'RE KIDDING!! A 30-YEAR-OLD WHITE BOY-FRIEND?!
Whaaaat?!
Whaaaat?!
MUMBLE
MUMBLE
MUMBLE
A PETIT AMI?!
Woo hoo!!
THAT'S... *REALLY* GOOD NEWS...
TEAR
BUT...
THAT MEANS...
THERE'S NO GOING BACK. YOU'RE GOING AWAY TO FRANCE IN JUST A FEW MONTHS.
COME ON... STOP IT, MOMO-CHAN.
I only just got back.
But... but...!

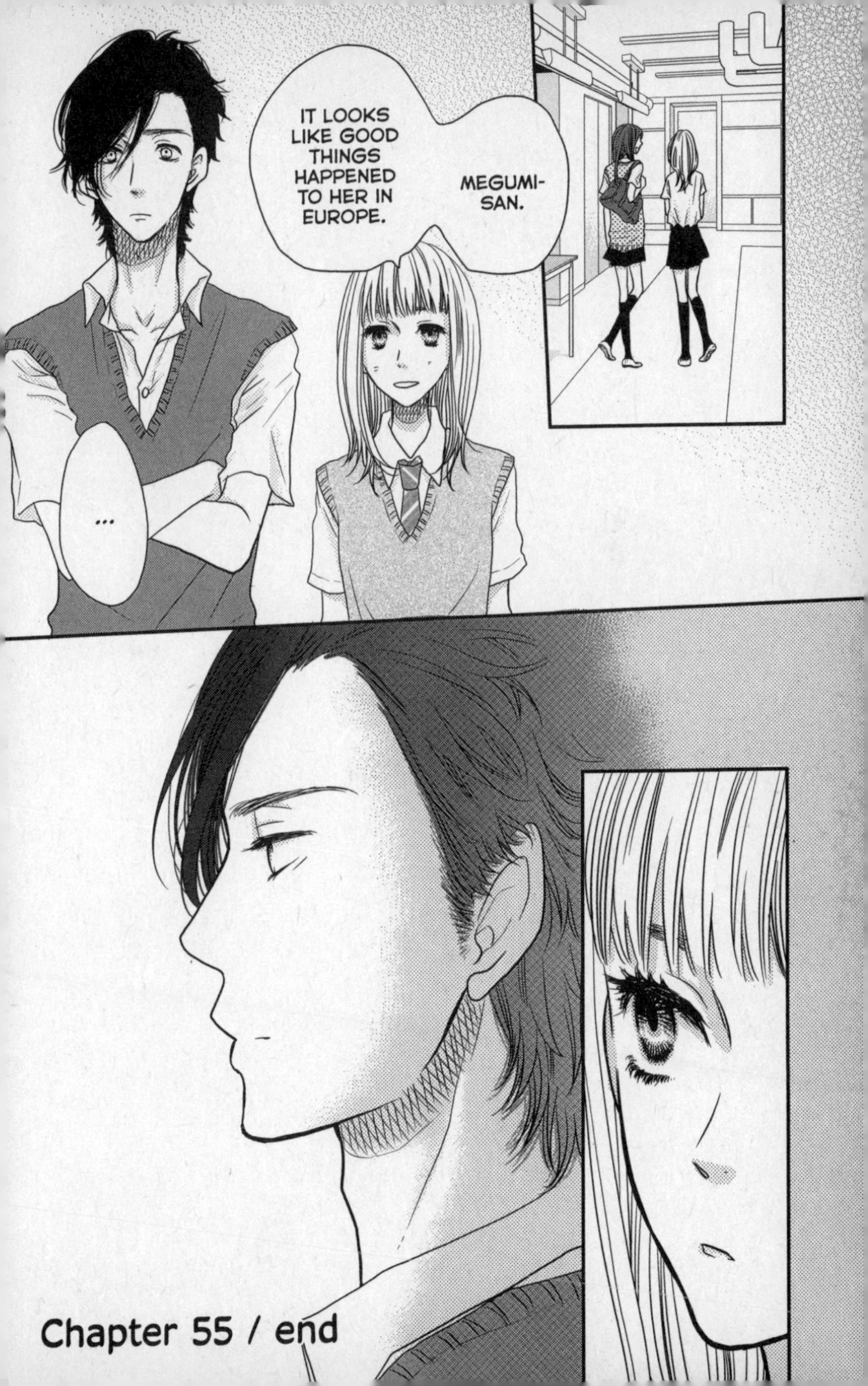
MEGUMI-SAN.
IT LOOKS LIKE GOOD THINGS HAPPENED TO HER IN EUROPE.
...

Chapter 55 / end

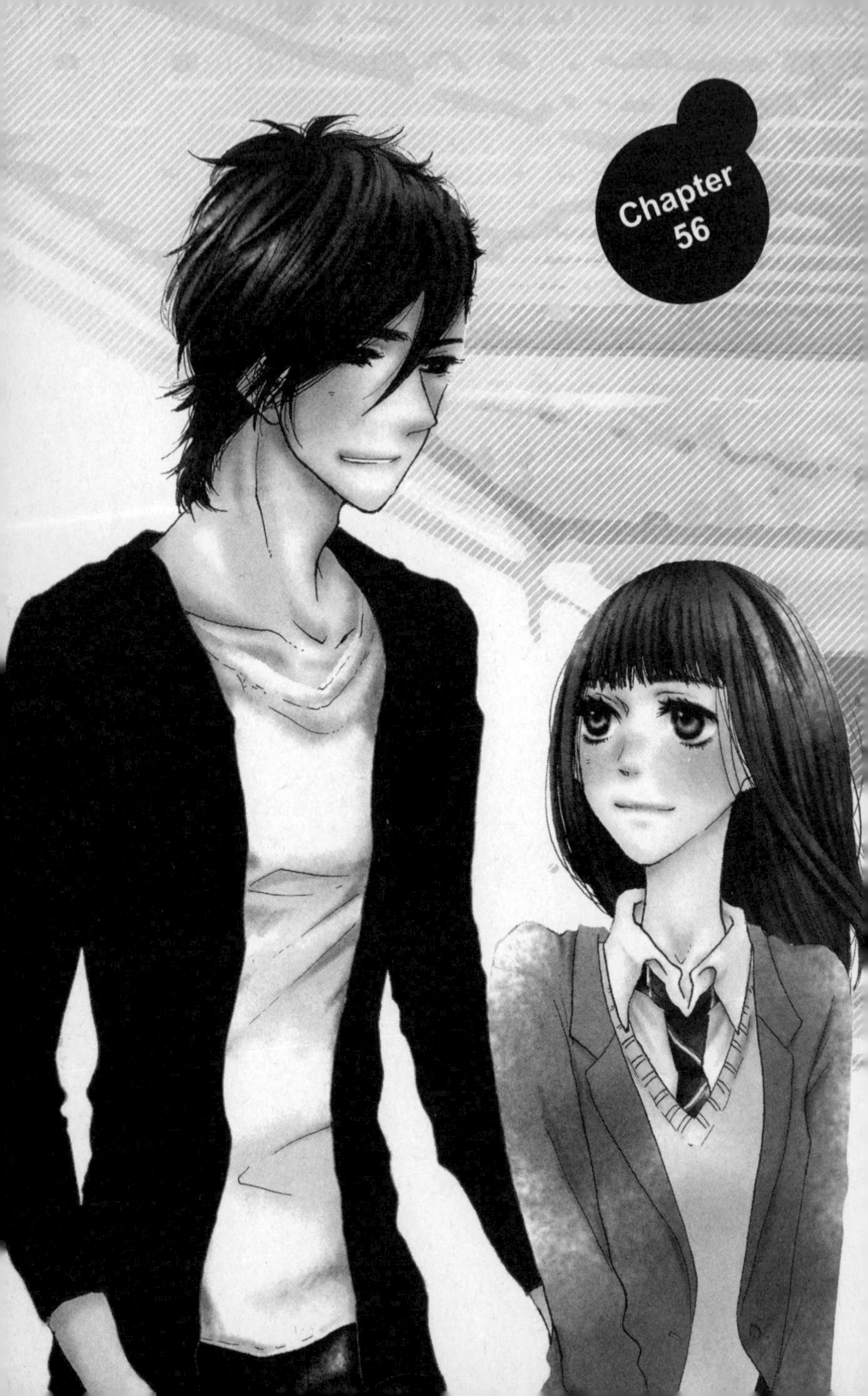
Chapter
56

Say "I love you".

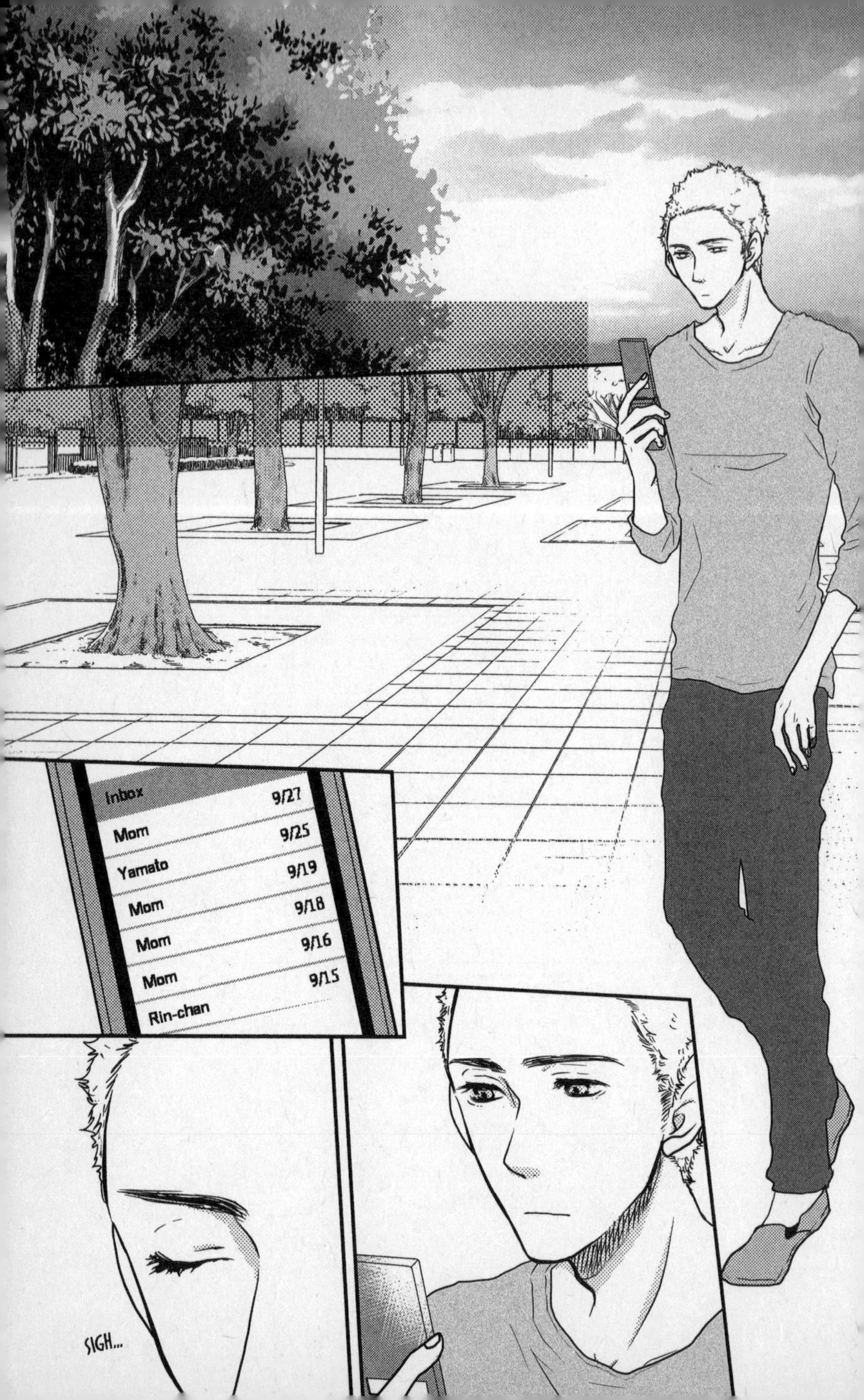
Inbox 9/27
Mom 9/25
Yamato 9/19
Mom 9/18
Mom 9/16
Mom 9/15
Rin-chan
SIGH...

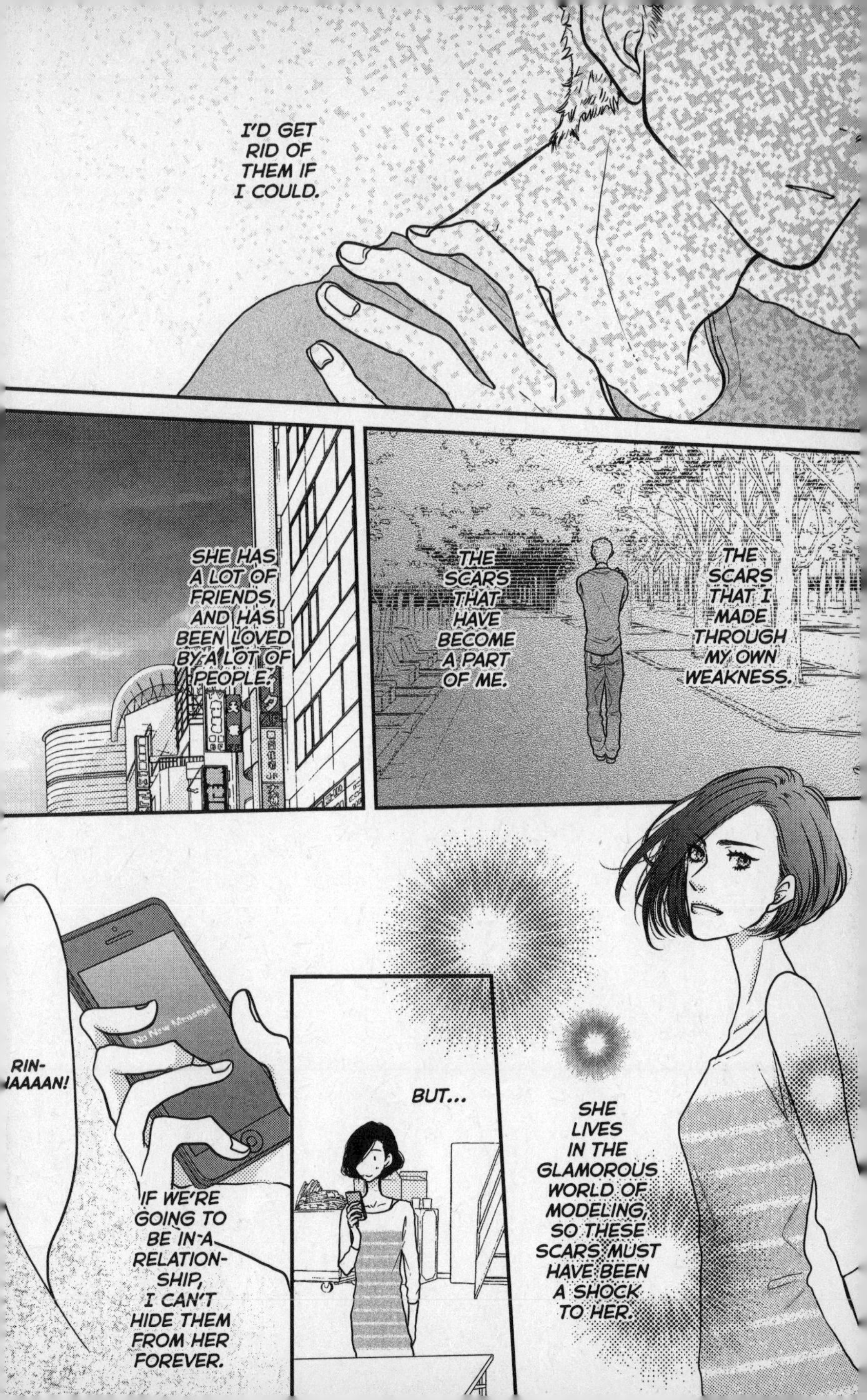
I'D GET RID OF THEM IF I COULD.
THE SCARS THAT I MADE THROUGH MY OWN WEAKNESS.
THE SCARS THAT HAVE BECOME A PART OF ME.
SHE HAS A LOT OF FRIENDS, AND HAS BEEN LOVED BY A LOT OF PEOPLE.
SHE LIVES IN THE GLAMOROUS WORLD OF MODELING, SO THESE SCARS MUST HAVE BEEN A SHOCK TO HER.
BUT...
No New Messages
RIN-AAAAN!
IF WE'RE GOING TO BE IN A RELATION-SHIP, I CAN'T HIDE THEM FROM HER FOREVER.

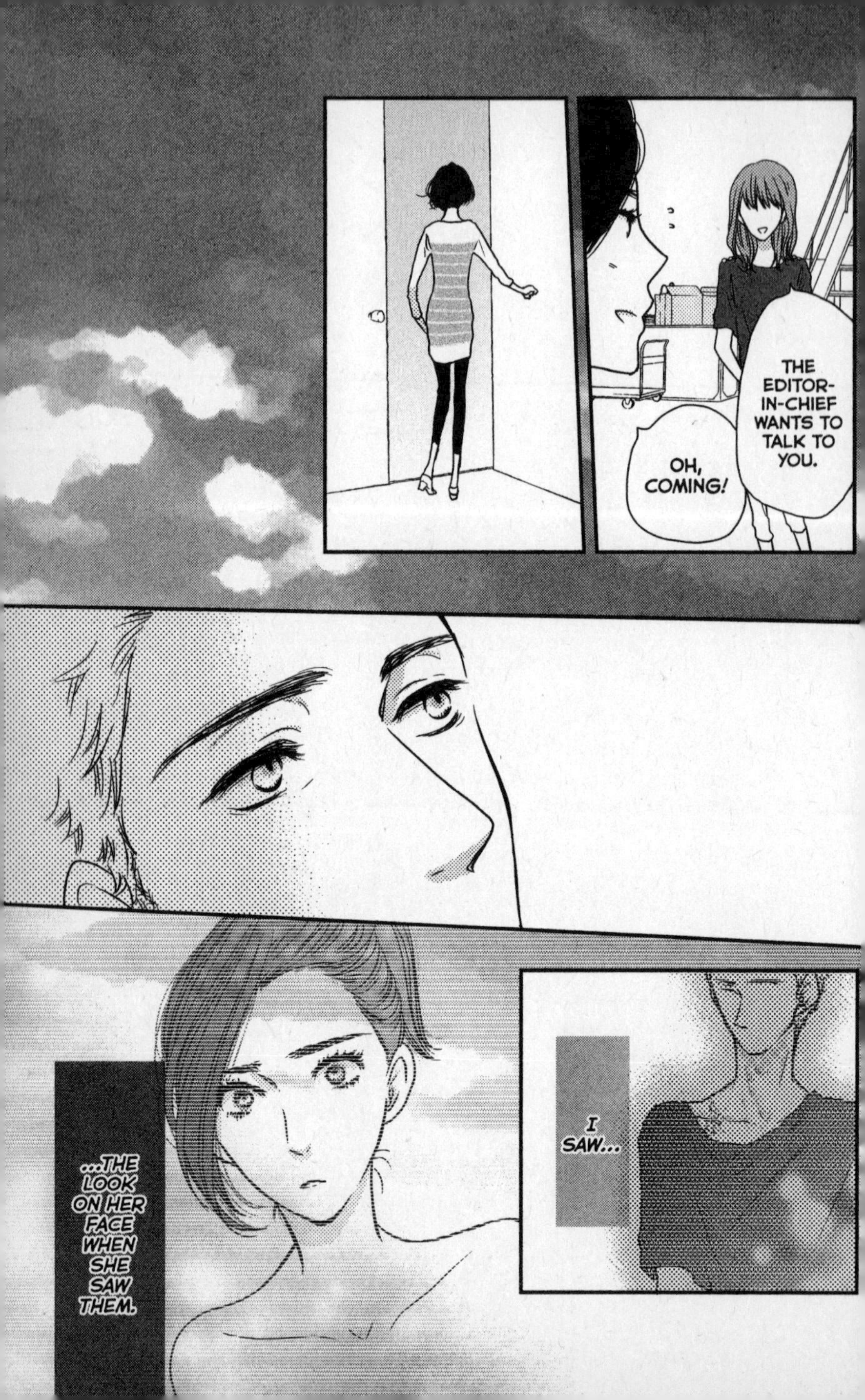
THE EDITOR-IN-CHIEF WANTS TO TALK TO YOU.
OH, COMING!
I SAW...
...THE LOOK ON HER FACE WHEN SHE SAW THEM.

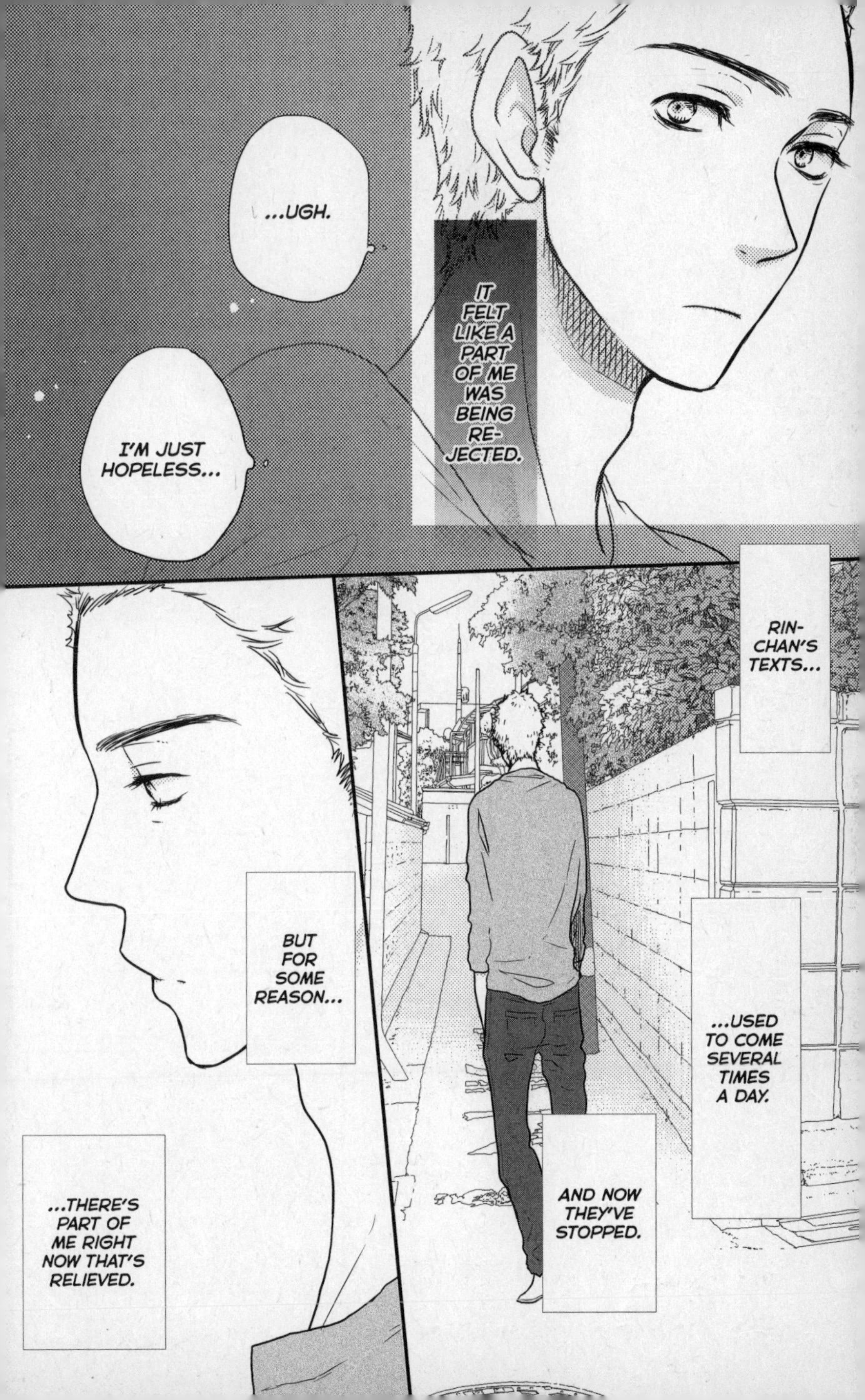
IT FELT LIKE A PART OF ME WAS BEING RE-JECTED.
...UGH.
I'M JUST HOPELESS...
RIN-CHAN'S TEXTS...
...USED TO COME SEVERAL TIMES A DAY.
AND NOW THEY'VE STOPPED.
BUT FOR SOME REASON...
...THERE'S PART OF ME RIGHT NOW THAT'S RELIEVED.

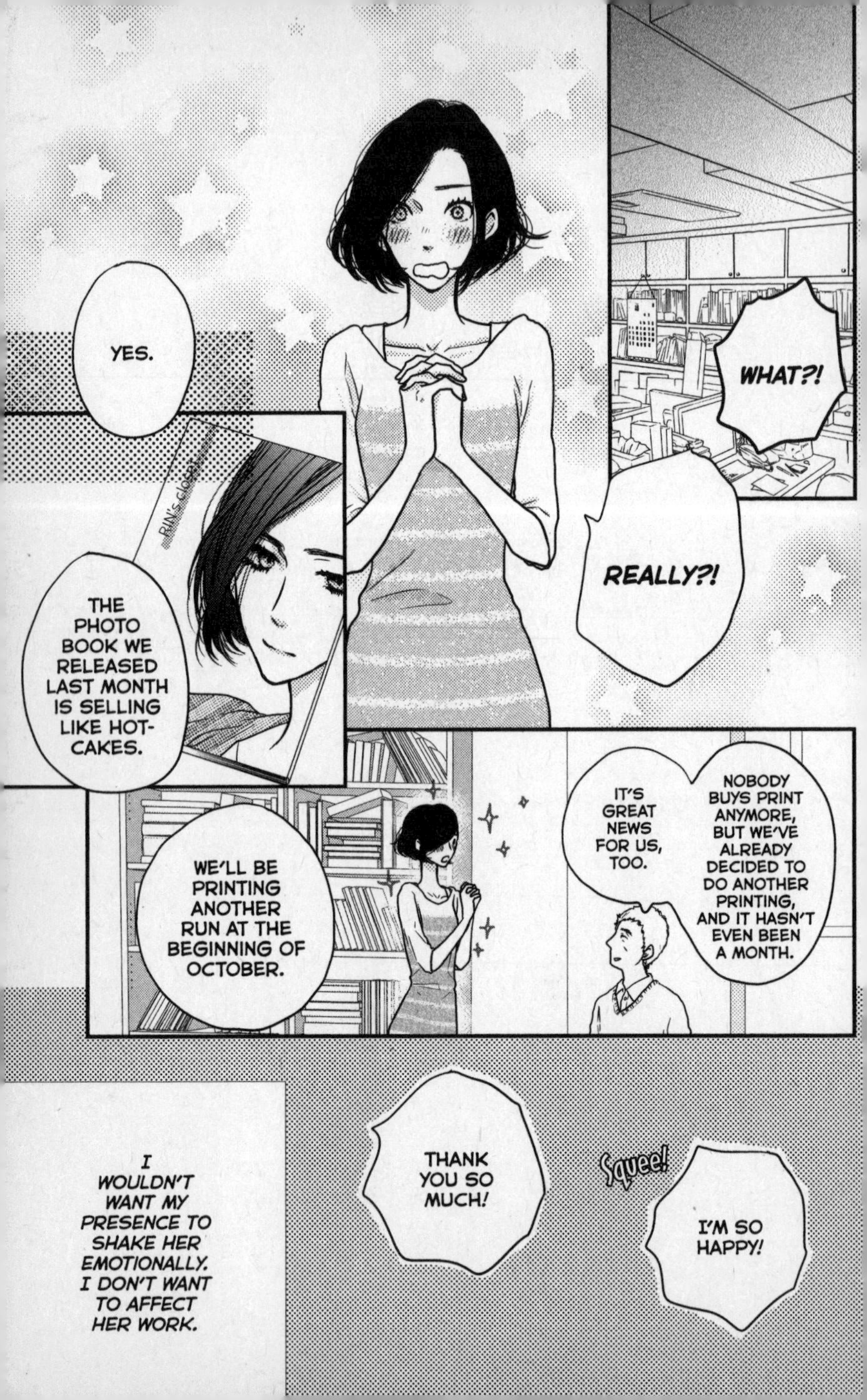

WHAT?!
REALLY?!
YES.
THE PHOTO BOOK WE RELEASED LAST MONTH IS SELLING LIKE HOT-CAKES.
NOBODY BUYS PRINT ANYMORE, BUT WE'VE ALREADY DECIDED TO DO ANOTHER PRINTING, AND IT HASN'T EVEN BEEN A MONTH.
IT'S GREAT NEWS FOR US, TOO.
WE'LL BE PRINTING ANOTHER RUN AT THE BEGINNING OF OCTOBER.
I'M SO HAPPY!
Squee!
THANK YOU SO MUCH!
I WOULDN'T WANT MY PRESENCE TO SHAKE HER EMOTIONALLY. I DON'T WANT TO AFFECT HER WORK.

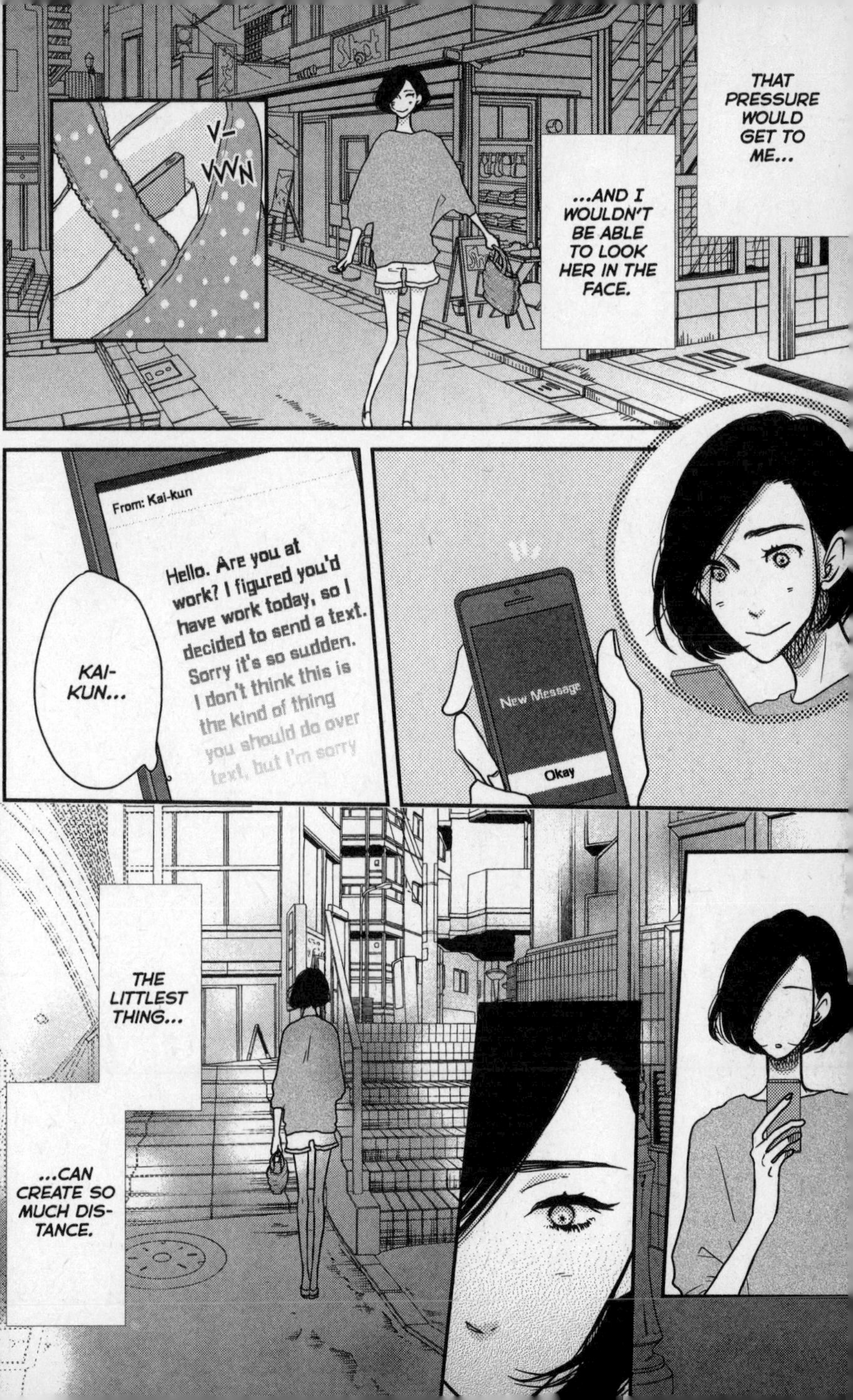
THAT PRESSURE WOULD GET TO ME...
...AND I WOULDN'T BE ABLE TO LOOK HER IN THE FACE.
V-VVVN
New Message
Okay
From: Kai-kun
Hello. Are you at work? I figured you'd have work today, so I decided to send a text. Sorry it's so sudden. I don't think this is the kind of thing you should do over text, but I'm sorry
KAI-KUN...
THE LITTLEST THING...
...CAN CREATE SO MUCH DISTANCE.

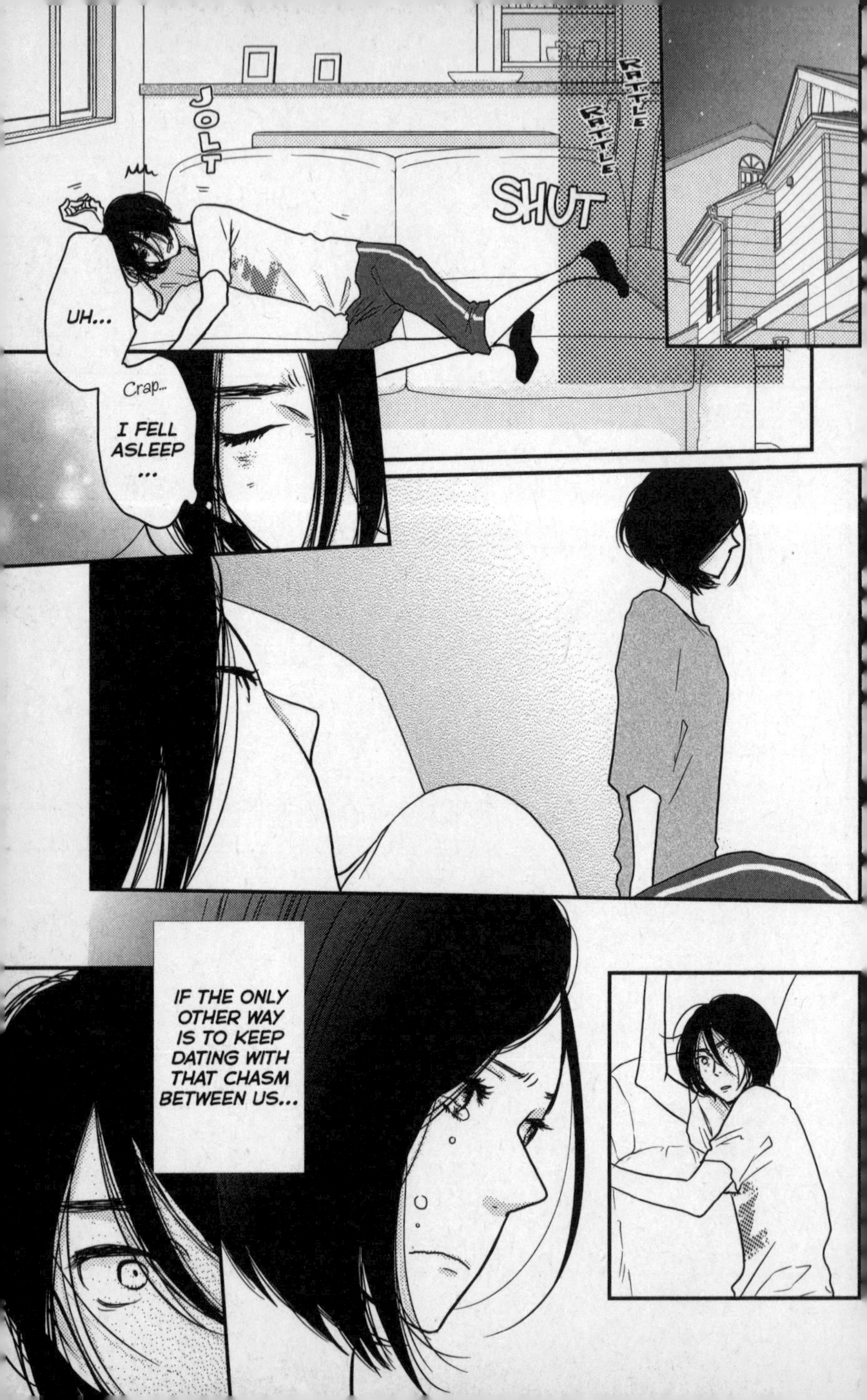
RATTLE
RATTLE
SHUT
JOLT
UH...
Crap...
I FELL ASLEEP ...
IF THE ONLY OTHER WAY IS TO KEEP DATING WITH THAT CHASM BETWEEN US...

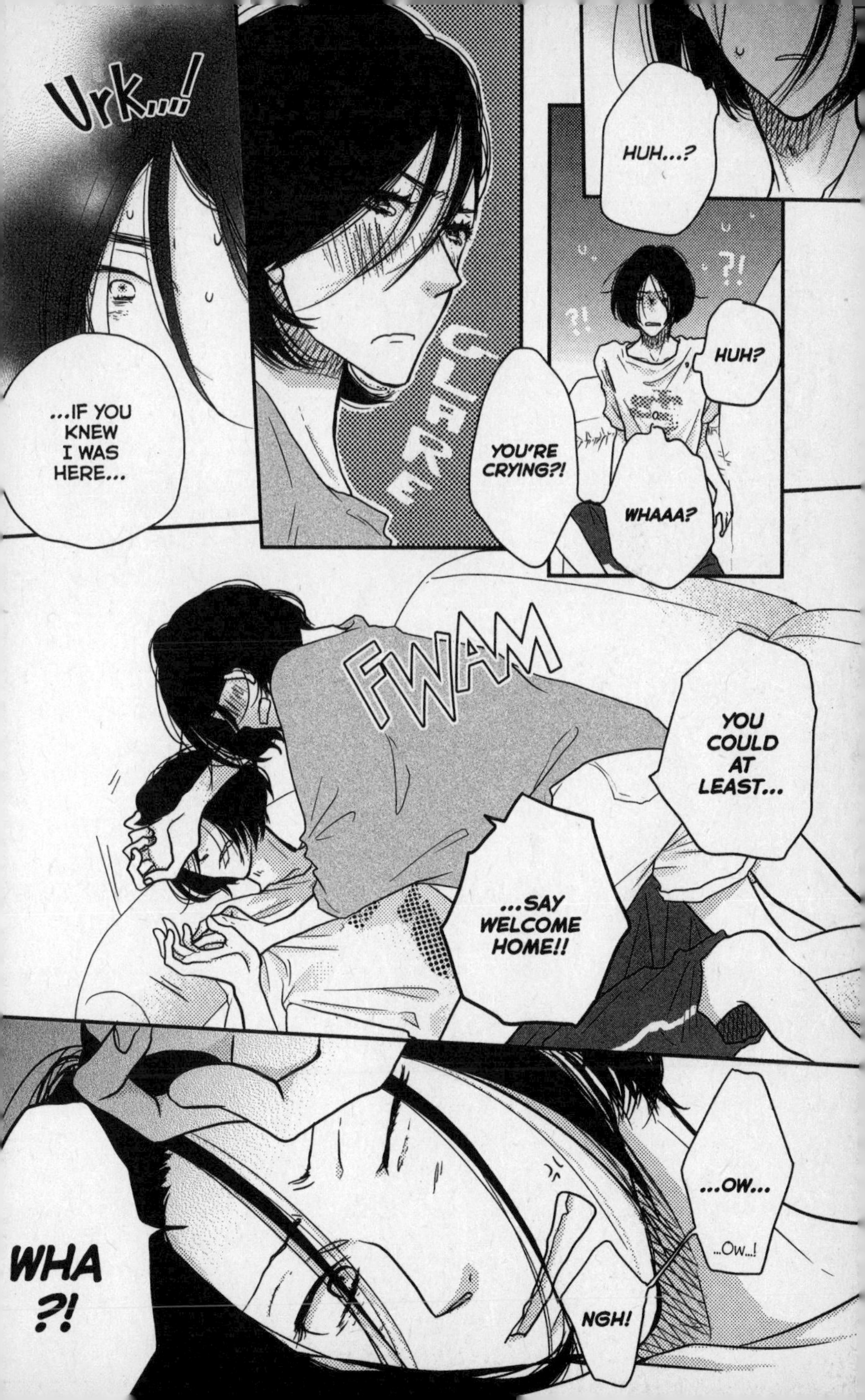
HUH...?
?!
HUH?
?!
YOU'RE CRYING?!
WHAAA?
GLARE
Urk...!
...IF YOU KNEW I WAS HERE...
YOU COULD AT LEAST...
...SAY WELCOME HOME!!
FWAM
...OW...
...Ow...!
NGH!
WHA ?!

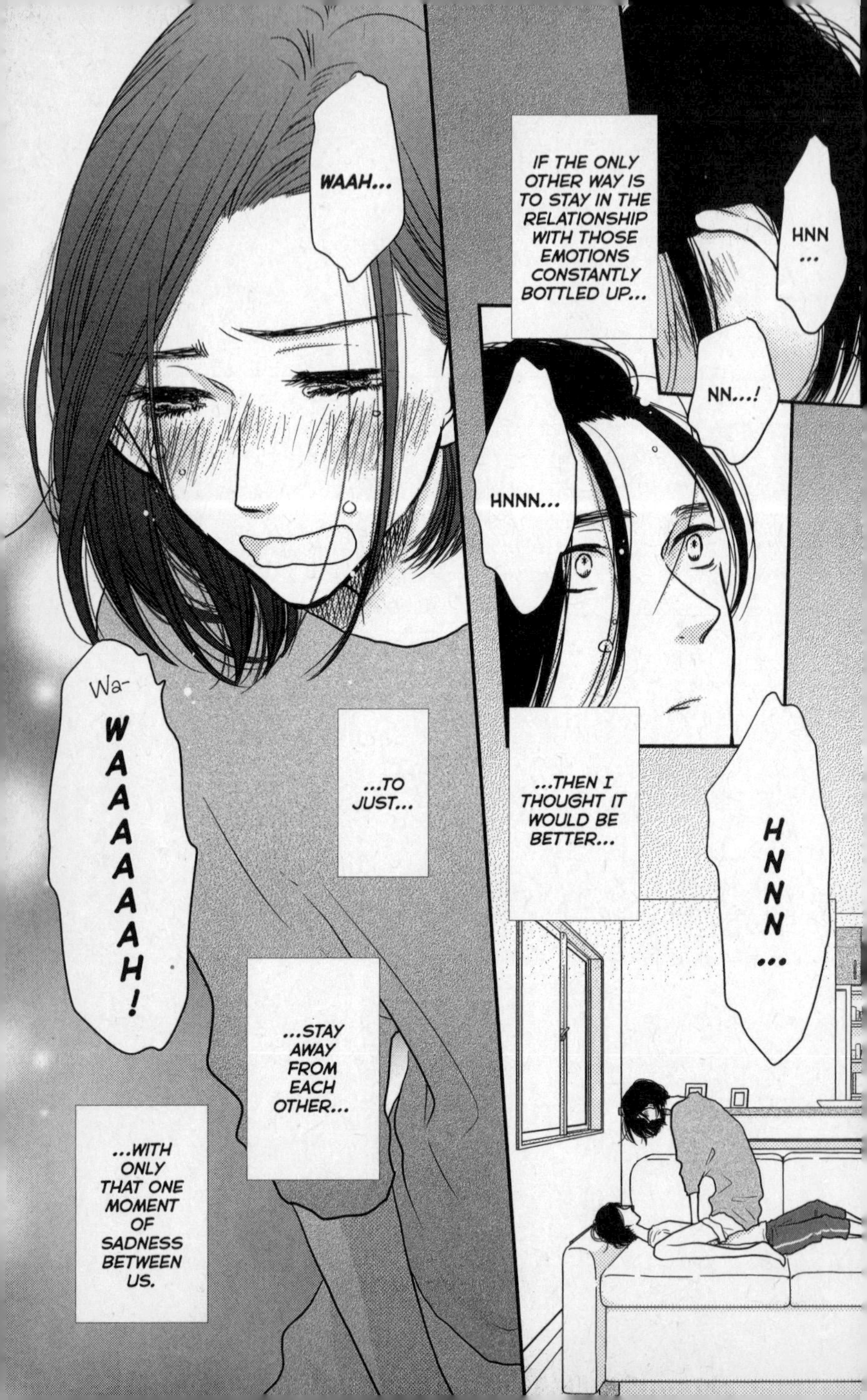
IF THE ONLY OTHER WAY IS TO STAY IN THE RELATIONSHIP WITH THOSE EMOTIONS CONSTANTLY BOTTLED UP...
HNN...
NN...!
HNNN...
...THEN I THOUGHT IT WOULD BE BETTER...
HNNN...
WAAH...
Wa- WAAAAAAAH!
...TO JUST...
...STAY AWAY FROM EACH OTHER...
...WITH ONLY THAT ONE MOMENT OF SADNESS BETWEEN US.

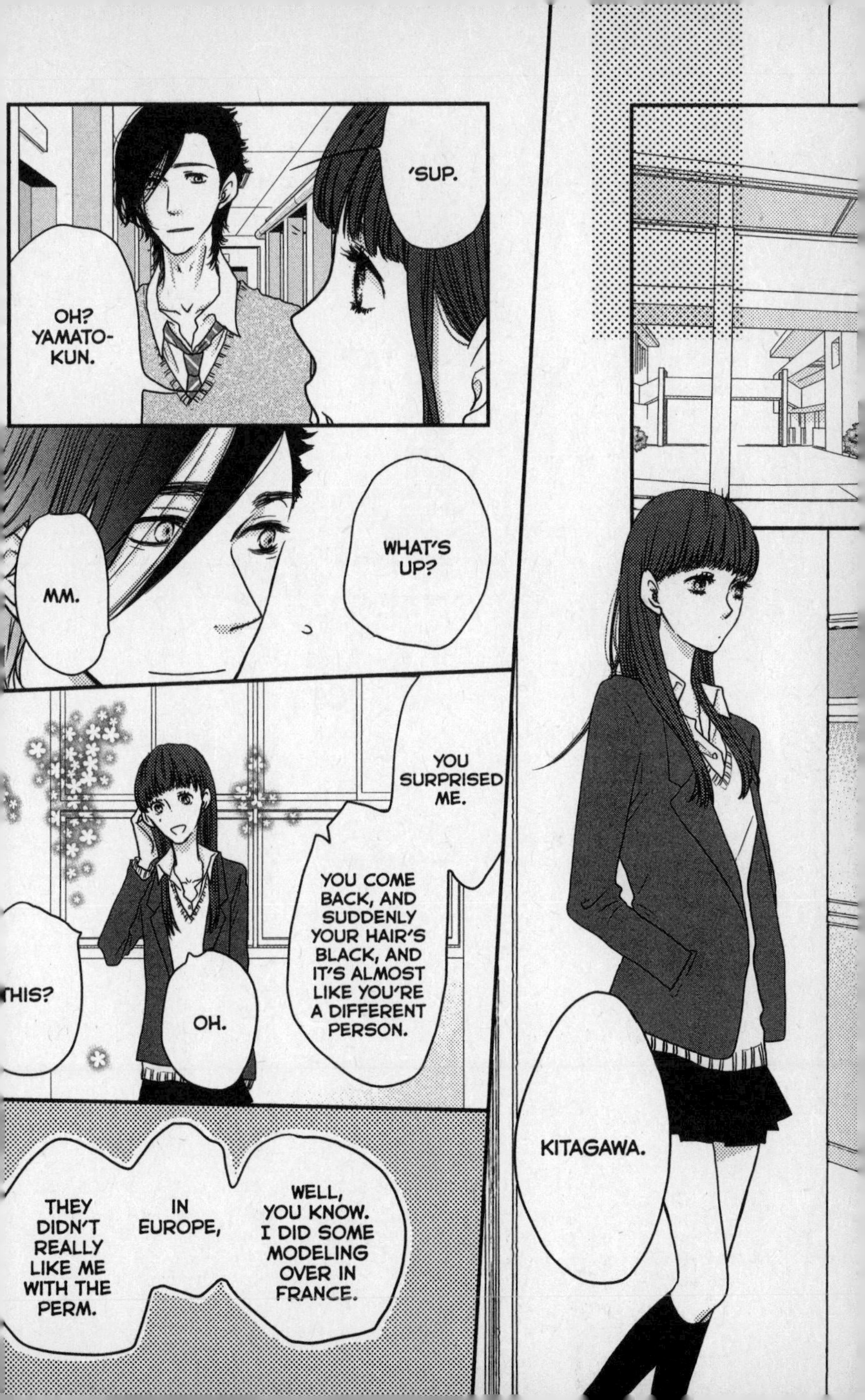
KITAGAWA.
'SUP.
OH? YAMATO-KUN.
WHAT'S UP?
MM.
YOU SURPRISED ME.
YOU COME BACK, AND SUDDENLY YOUR HAIR'S BLACK, AND IT'S ALMOST LIKE YOU'RE A DIFFERENT PERSON.
OH.
THIS?
WELL, YOU KNOW. I DID SOME MODELING OVER IN FRANCE.
IN EUROPE,
THEY DIDN'T REALLY LIKE ME WITH THE PERM.

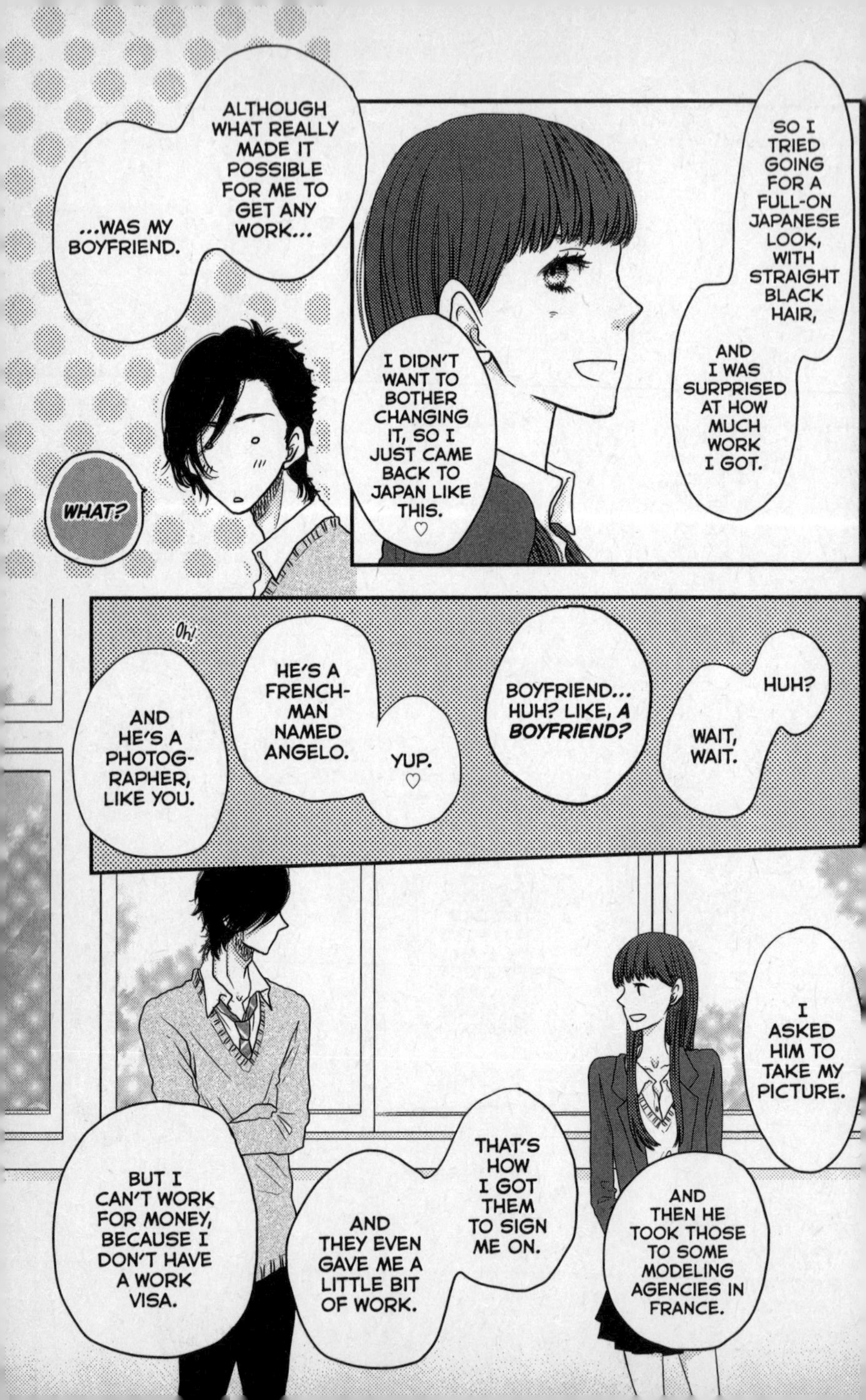
SO I TRIED GOING FOR A FULL-ON JAPANESE LOOK, WITH STRAIGHT BLACK HAIR,
AND I WAS SURPRISED AT HOW MUCH WORK I GOT.
I DIDN'T WANT TO BOTHER CHANGING IT, SO I JUST CAME BACK TO JAPAN LIKE THIS. ♡
ALTHOUGH WHAT REALLY MADE IT POSSIBLE FOR ME TO GET ANY WORK...
...WAS MY BOYFRIEND.
WHAT?
HUH?
WAIT, WAIT.
BOYFRIEND... HUH? LIKE, A BOYFRIEND?
YUP. ♡
HE'S A FRENCH-MAN NAMED ANGELO.
Oh!
AND HE'S A PHOTOG-RAPHER, LIKE YOU.
I ASKED HIM TO TAKE MY PICTURE.
AND THEN HE TOOK THOSE TO SOME MODELING AGENCIES IN FRANCE.
THAT'S HOW I GOT THEM TO SIGN ME ON.
AND THEY EVEN GAVE ME A LITTLE BIT OF WORK.
BUT I CAN'T WORK FOR MONEY, BECAUSE I DON'T HAVE A WORK VISA.

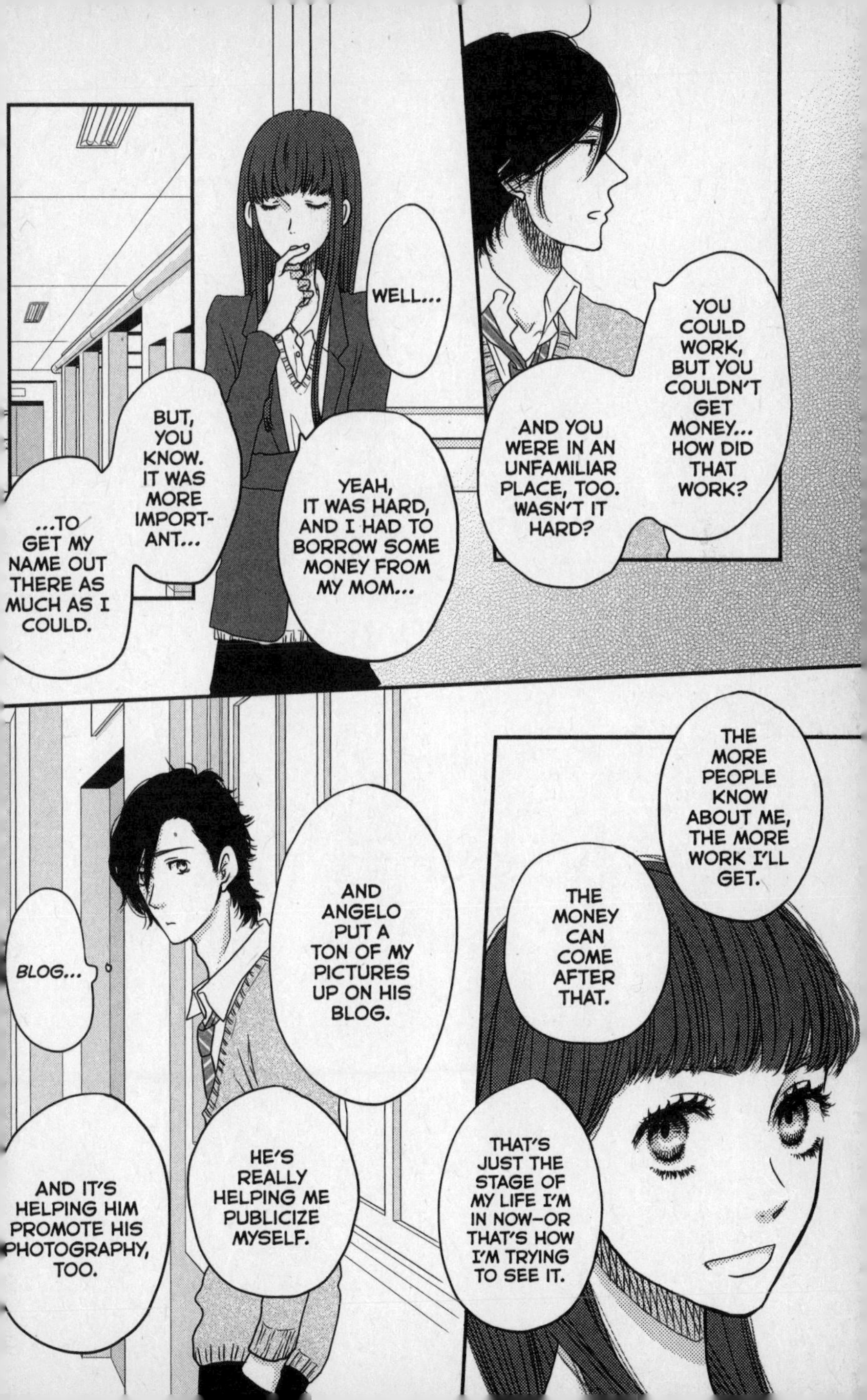
YOU COULD WORK, BUT YOU COULDN'T GET MONEY... HOW DID THAT WORK?
AND YOU WERE IN AN UNFAMILIAR PLACE, TOO. WASN'T IT HARD?
WELL...
YEAH, IT WAS HARD, AND I HAD TO BORROW SOME MONEY FROM MY MOM...
BUT, YOU KNOW. IT WAS MORE IMPORT-ANT...
...TO GET MY NAME OUT THERE AS MUCH AS I COULD.
THE MORE PEOPLE KNOW ABOUT ME, THE MORE WORK I'LL GET.
THE MONEY CAN COME AFTER THAT.
THAT'S JUST THE STAGE OF MY LIFE I'M IN NOW—OR THAT'S HOW I'M TRYING TO SEE IT.
AND ANGELO PUT A TON OF MY PICTURES UP ON HIS BLOG.
BLOG...
HE'S REALLY HELPING ME PUBLICIZE MYSELF.
AND IT'S HELPING HIM PROMOTE HIS PHOTOGRAPHY, TOO.

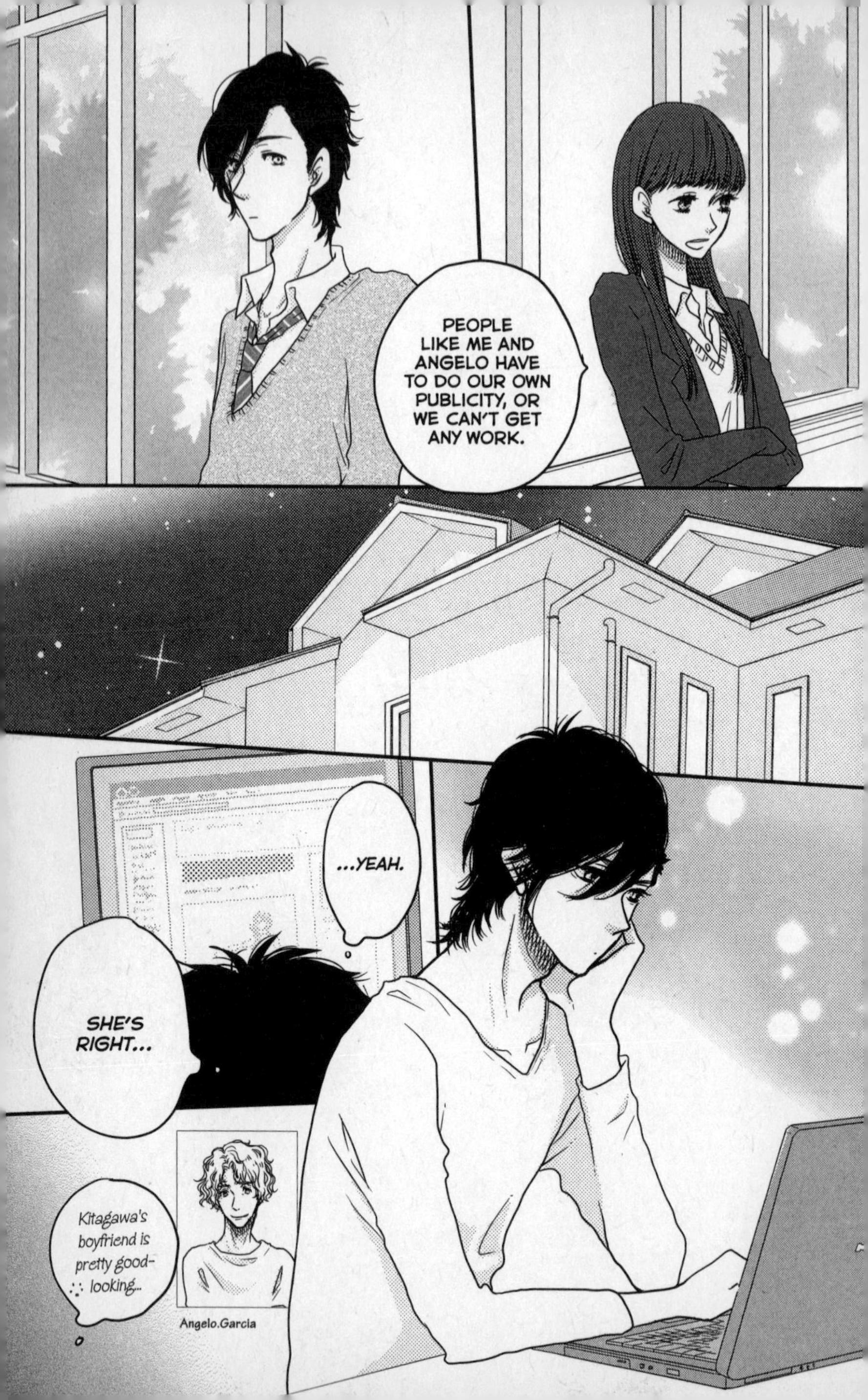
PEOPLE LIKE ME AND ANGELO HAVE TO DO OUR OWN PUBLICITY, OR WE CAN'T GET ANY WORK.
...YEAH.
SHE'S RIGHT...
Angelo.Garcia
Kitagawa's boyfriend is pretty good-looking...

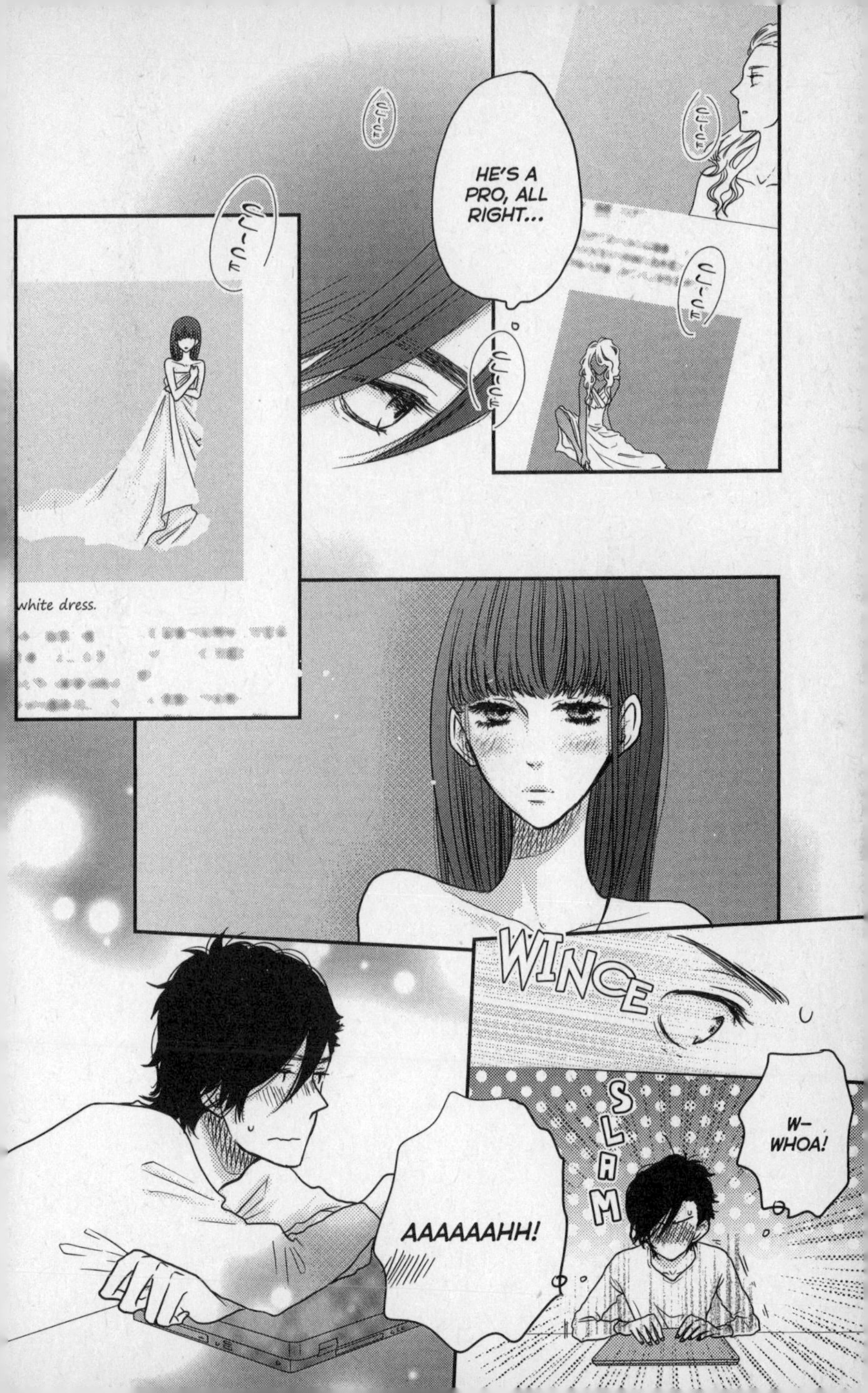
CLICK
CLICK
CLICK
HE'S A PRO, ALL RIGHT...
CLICK
CLICK
white dress.
WINCE
W— WHOA!
SLAM
AAAAAAHH!

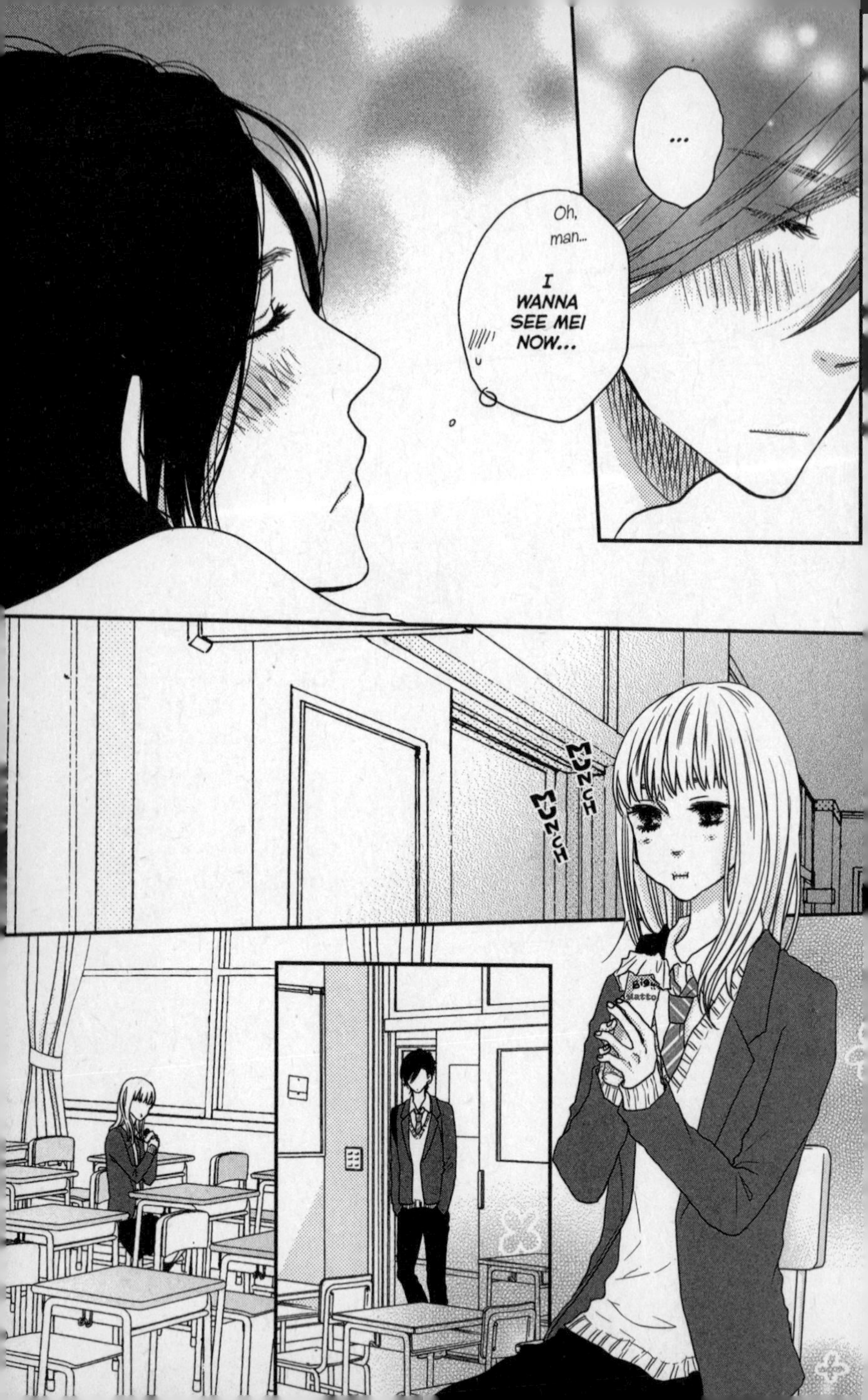
...
Oh, man...
I WANNA SEE MEI NOW...
MUNCH MUNCH
Big Matto

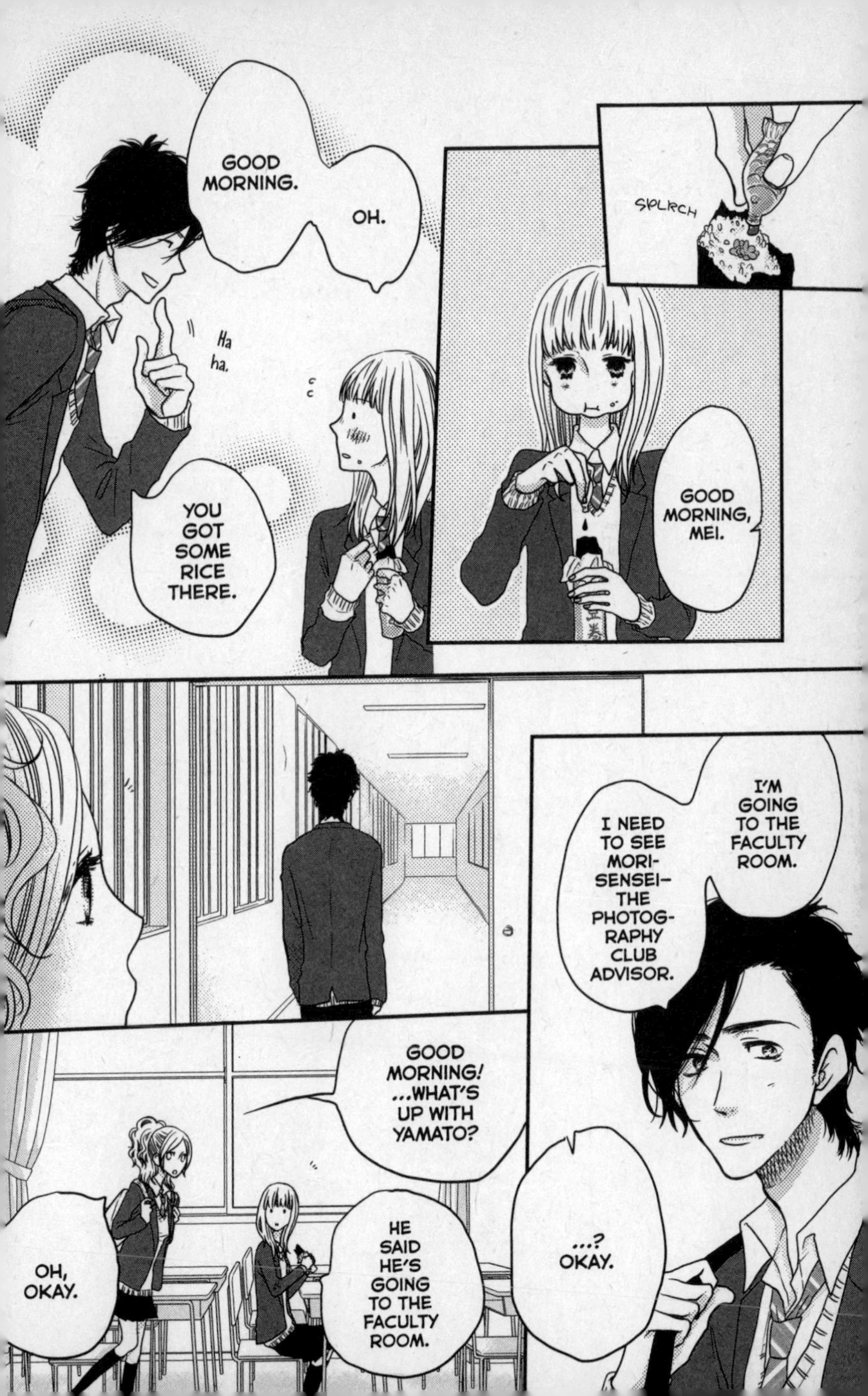
SPLRCH
GOOD MORNING, MEI.
GOOD MORNING.
OH.
Ha ha.
YOU GOT SOME RICE THERE.
I'M GOING TO THE FACULTY ROOM.
I NEED TO SEE MORI-SENSEI—THE PHOTOGRAPHY CLUB ADVISOR.
...? OKAY.
GOOD MORNING! ...WHAT'S UP WITH YAMATO?
HE SAID HE'S GOING TO THE FACULTY ROOM.
OH, OKAY.

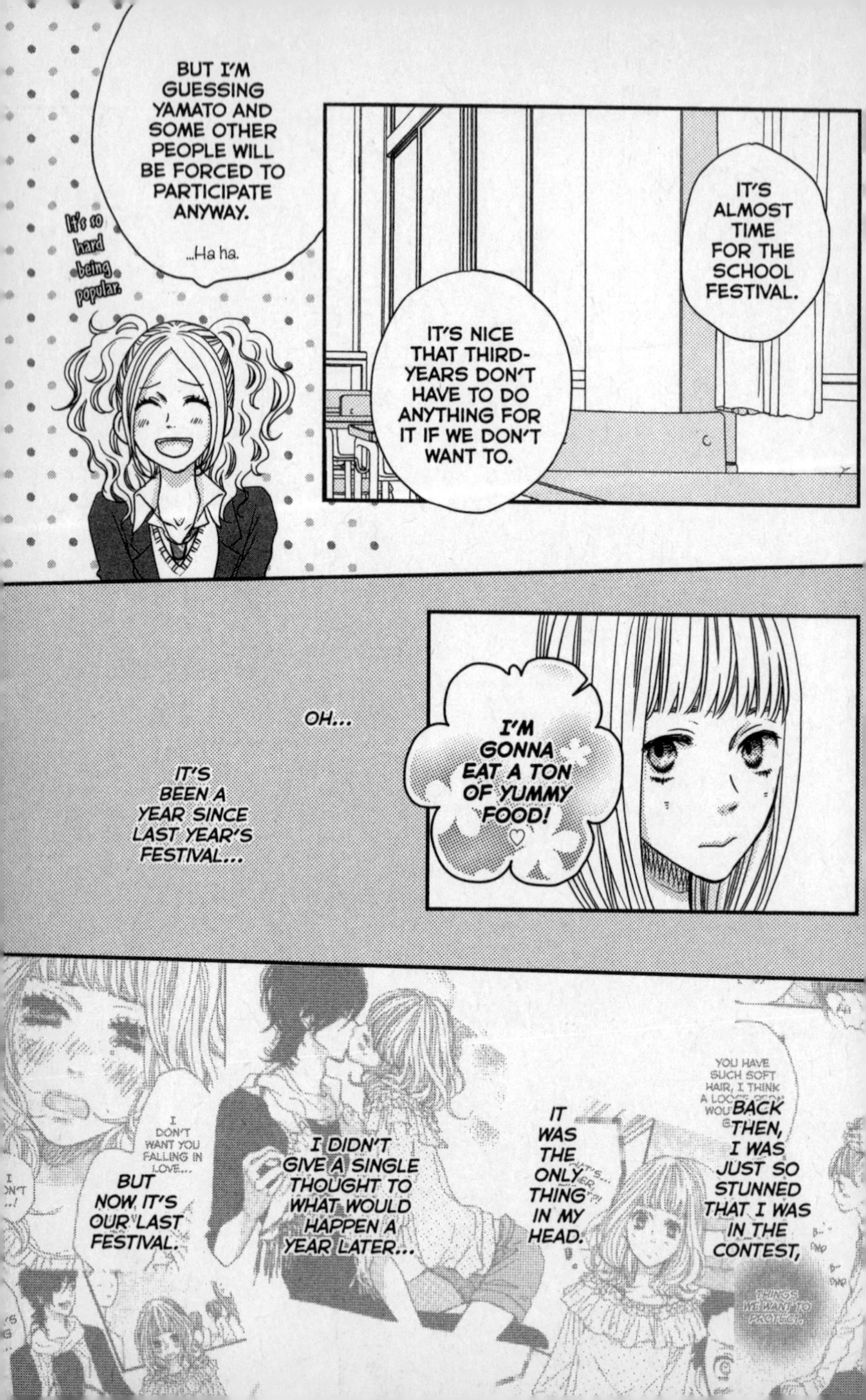
IT'S ALMOST TIME FOR THE SCHOOL FESTIVAL.
IT'S NICE THAT THIRD-YEARS DON'T HAVE TO DO ANYTHING FOR IT IF WE DON'T WANT TO.
BUT I'M GUESSING YAMATO AND SOME OTHER PEOPLE WILL BE FORCED TO PARTICIPATE ANYWAY.
...Ha ha.
It's so hard being popular.
I'M GONNA EAT A TON OF YUMMY FOOD! ♡
OH...
IT'S BEEN A YEAR SINCE LAST YEAR'S FESTIVAL...
BACK THEN, I WAS JUST SO STUNNED THAT I WAS IN THE CONTEST,
THINGS WE WANT TO PROTECT
IT WAS THE ONLY THING IN MY HEAD.
I DIDN'T GIVE A SINGLE THOUGHT TO WHAT WOULD HAPPEN A YEAR LATER...
I DON'T WANT YOU FALLING IN LOVE...
BUT NOW IT'S OUR LAST FESTIVAL.

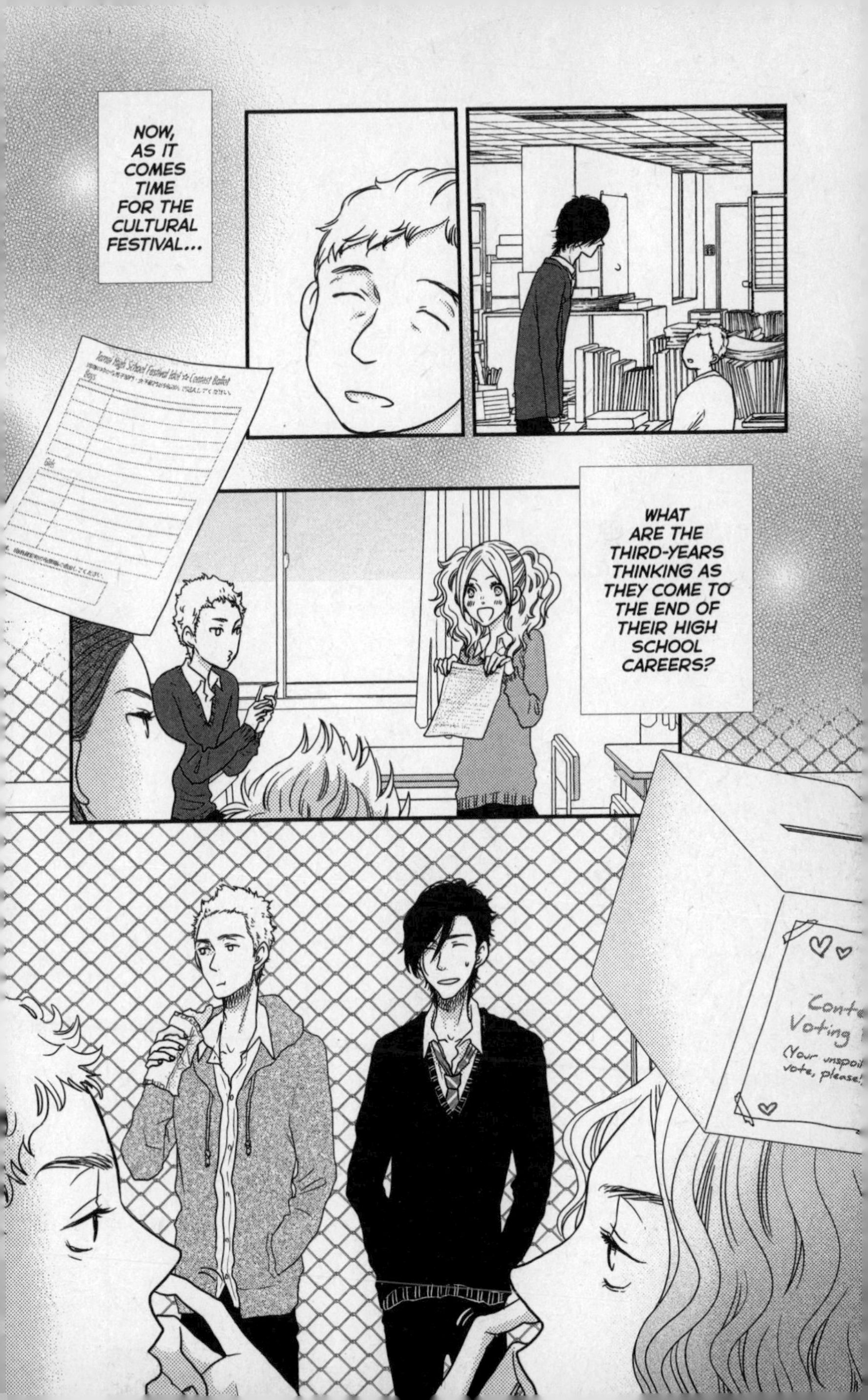
NOW, AS IT COMES TIME FOR THE CULTURAL FESTIVAL...
WHAT ARE THE THIRD-YEARS THINKING AS THEY COME TO THE END OF THEIR HIGH SCHOOL CAREERS?
Tamai High School Festival Idol ☆ Contest Ballot
Boys
Girls
Conte
Voting
(Your unspoi
vote, please!

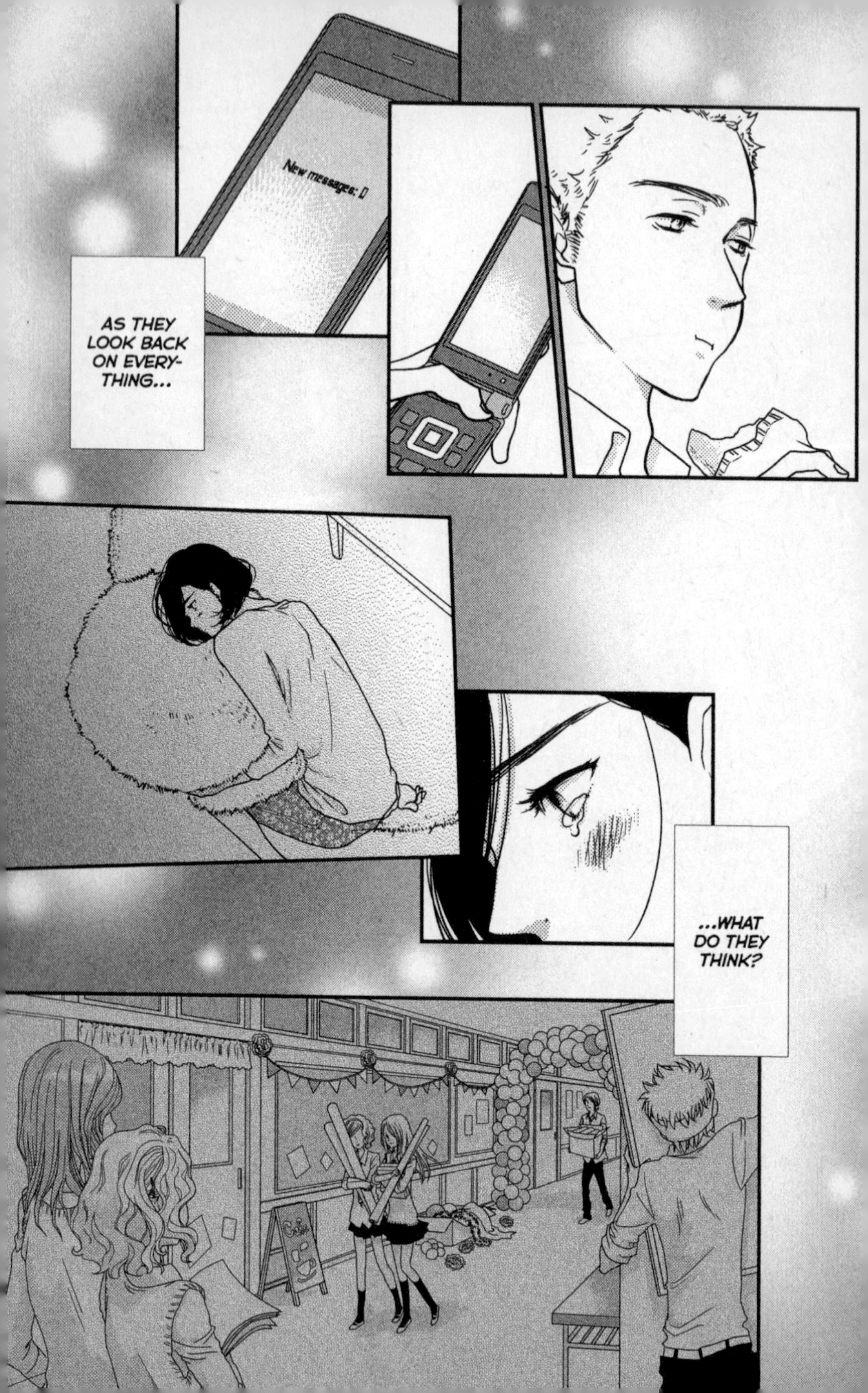
New messages: 0
AS THEY LOOK BACK ON EVERY-THING...
...WHAT DO THEY THINK?

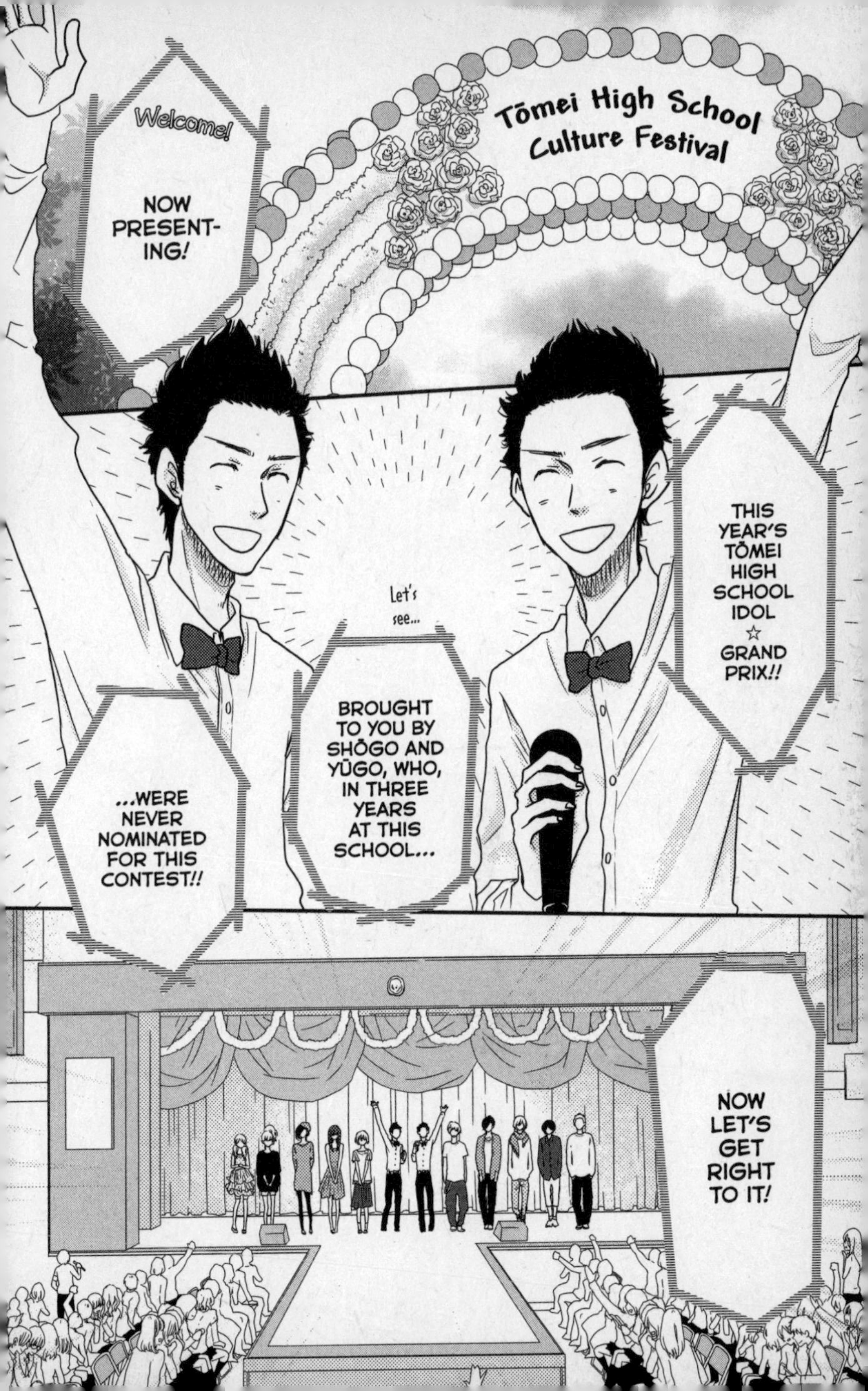
Tōmei High School Culture Festival
Welcome!
NOW PRESENTING!
THIS YEAR'S TŌMEI HIGH SCHOOL IDOL ☆ GRAND PRIX!!
Let's see...
BROUGHT TO YOU BY SHŌGO AND YŪGO, WHO, IN THREE YEARS AT THIS SCHOOL...
...WERE NEVER NOMINATED FOR THIS CONTEST!!
NOW LET'S GET RIGHT TO IT!

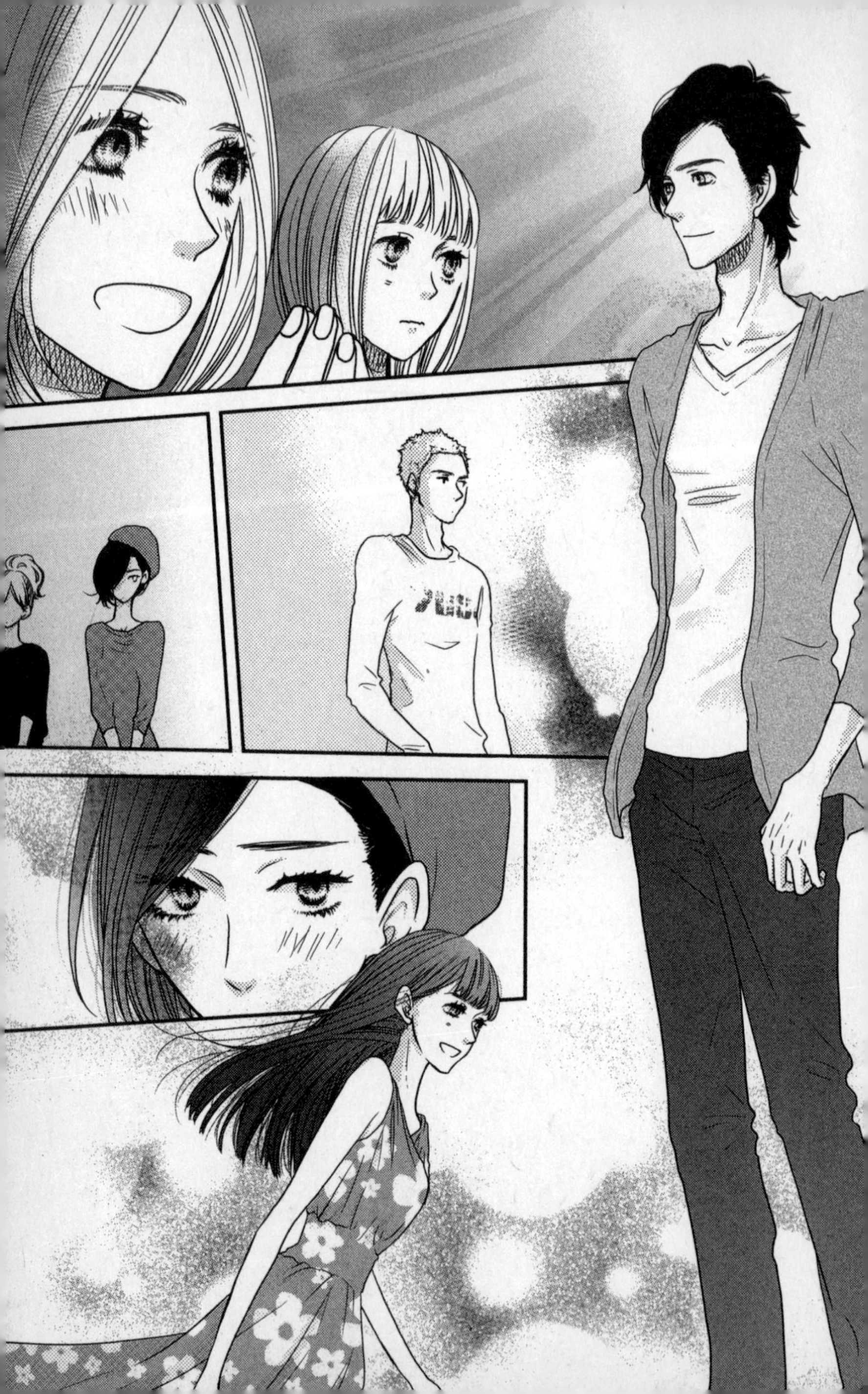

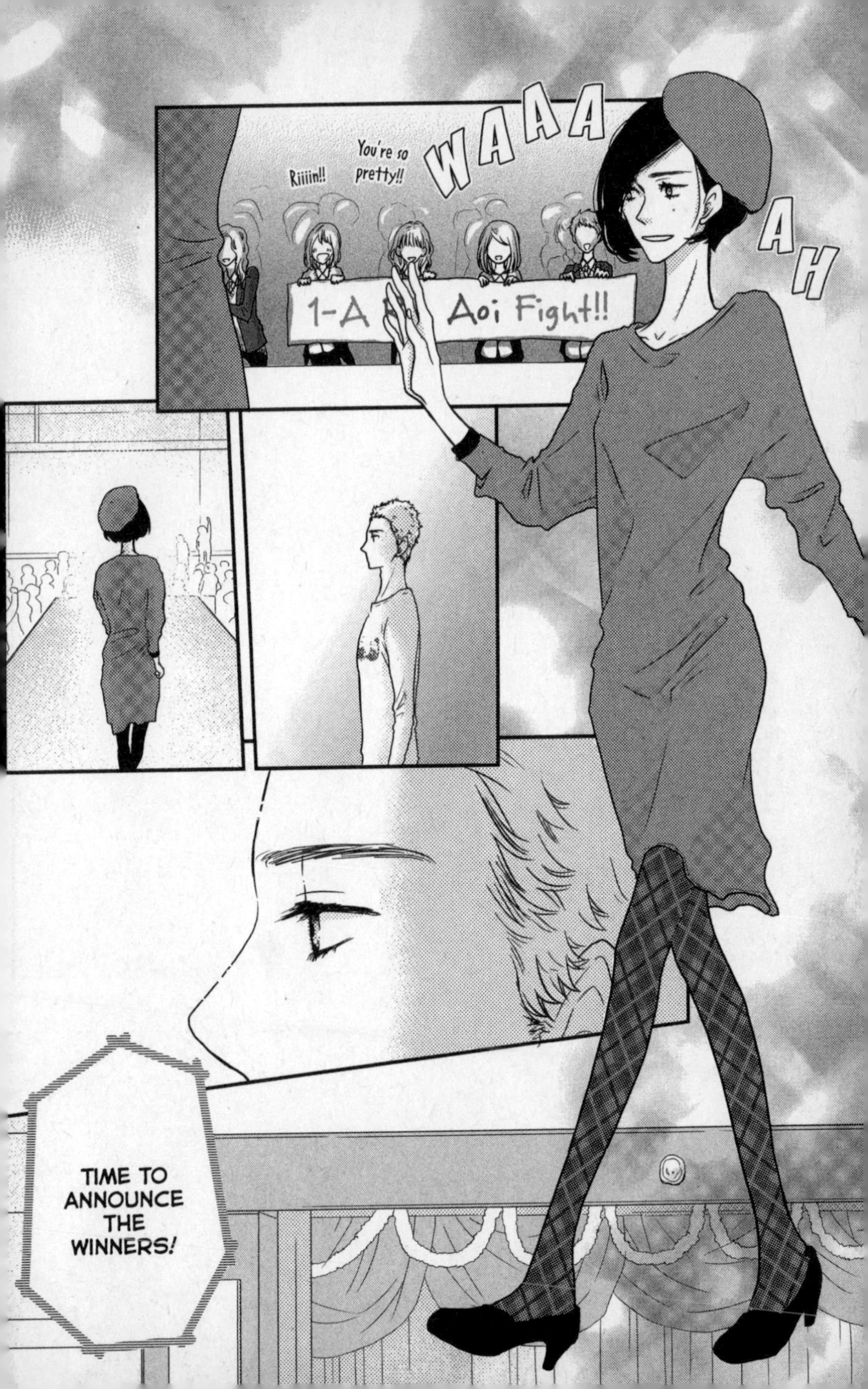
WAAAAAH
You're so pretty!!
Riiiin!!
1-A
Aoi Fight!!
TIME TO ANNOUNCE THE WINNERS!

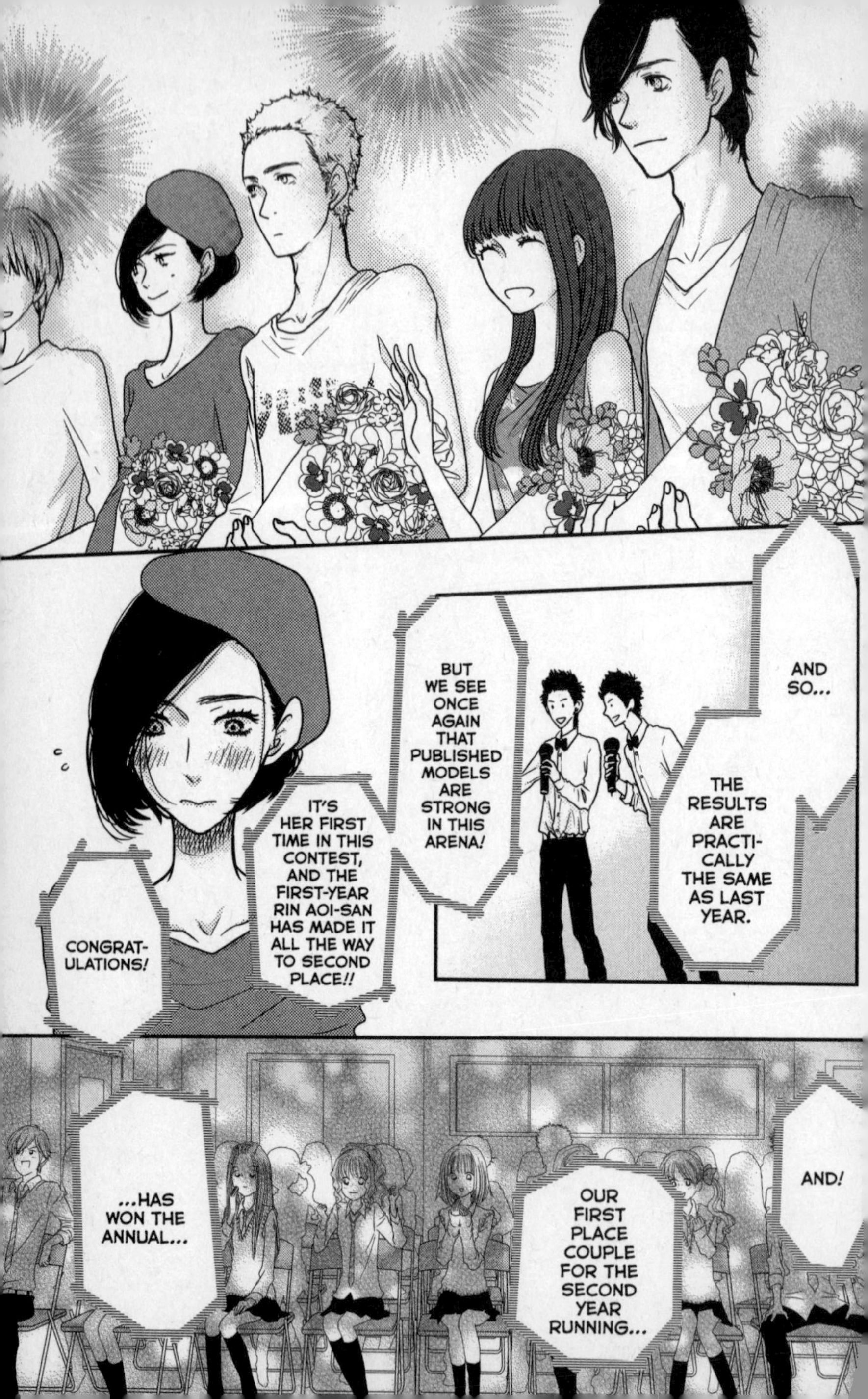
AND SO...
THE RESULTS ARE PRACTICALLY THE SAME AS LAST YEAR.
BUT WE SEE ONCE AGAIN THAT PUBLISHED MODELS ARE STRONG IN THIS ARENA!
IT'S HER FIRST TIME IN THIS CONTEST, AND THE FIRST-YEAR RIN AOI-SAN HAS MADE IT ALL THE WAY TO SECOND PLACE!!
CONGRATULATIONS!
AND!
OUR FIRST PLACE COUPLE FOR THE SECOND YEAR RUNNING...
...HAS WON THE ANNUAL...

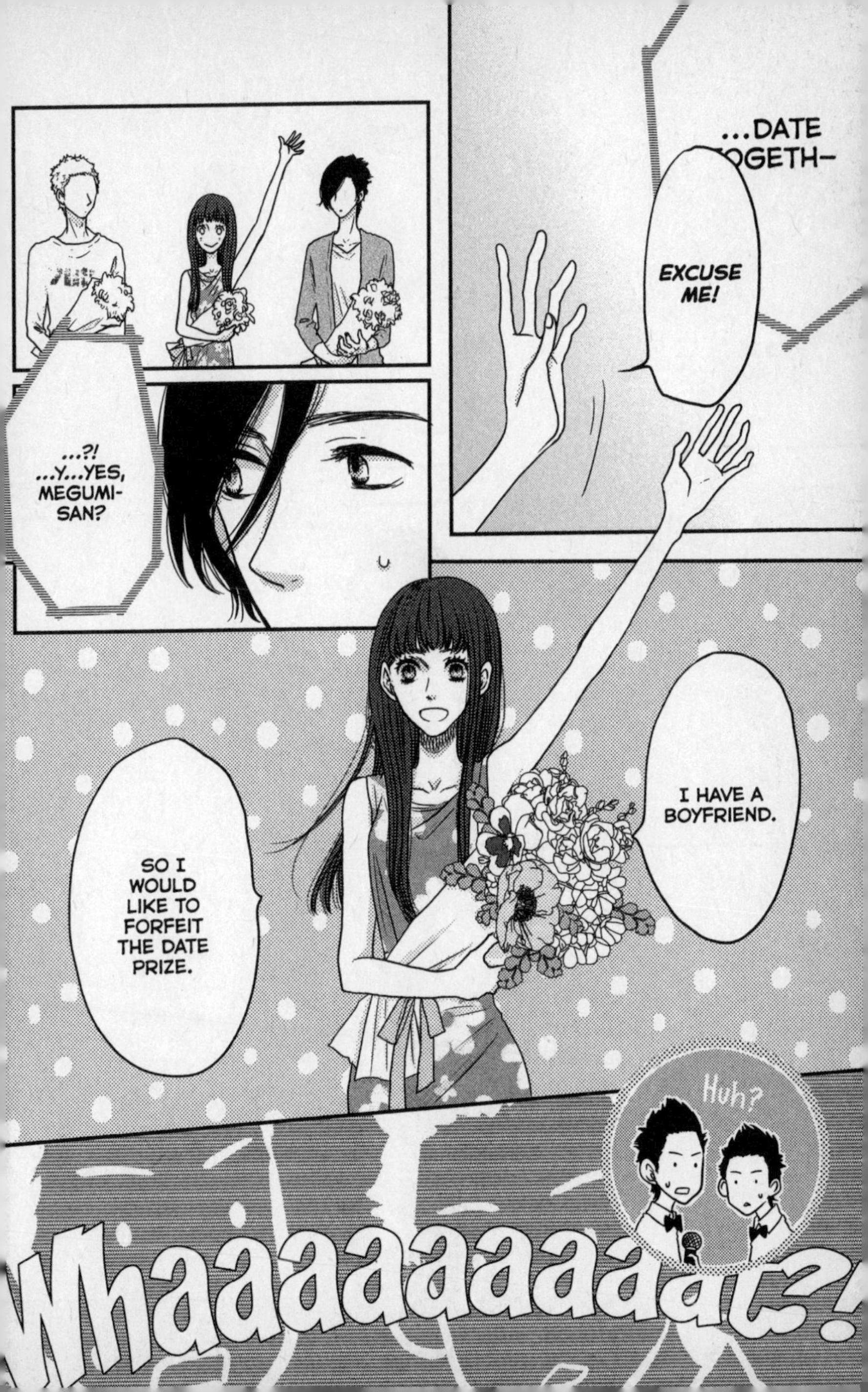
...DATE OGETH—
EXCUSE ME!
...?! ...Y...YES, MEGUMI-SAN?
I HAVE A BOYFRIEND.
SO I WOULD LIKE TO FORFEIT THE DATE PRIZE.
Huh?
Whaaaaaaaaat?!

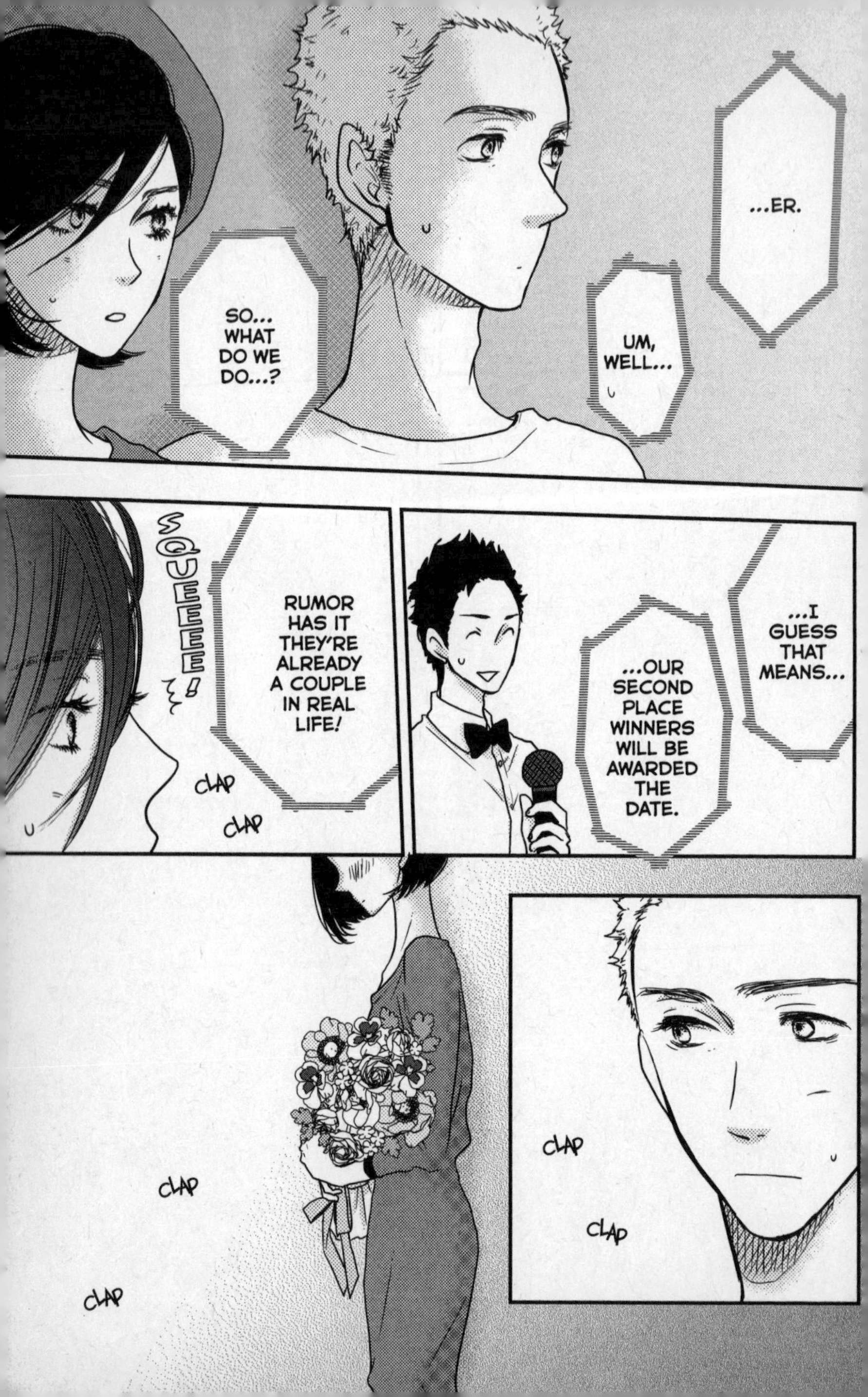
...ER.
UM, WELL...
SO... WHAT DO WE DO...?
...I GUESS THAT MEANS...
...OUR SECOND PLACE WINNERS WILL BE AWARDED THE DATE.
RUMOR HAS IT THEY'RE ALREADY A COUPLE IN REAL LIFE!
SQUEEEE!
CLAP
CLAP
CLAP
CLAP
CLAP
CLAP

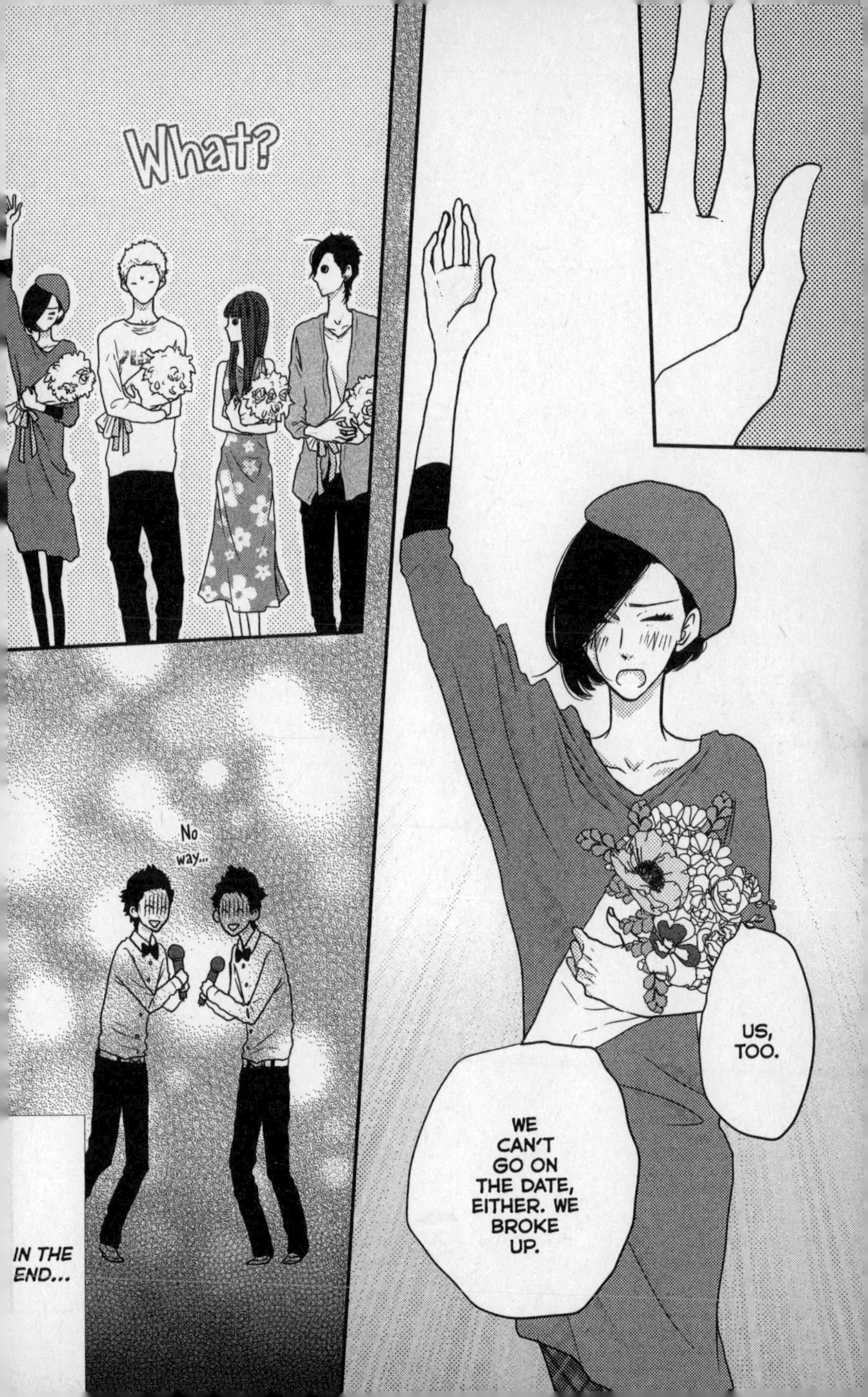
US, TOO.
WE CAN'T GO ON THE DATE, EITHER. WE BROKE UP.
What?
No way...
IN THE END...

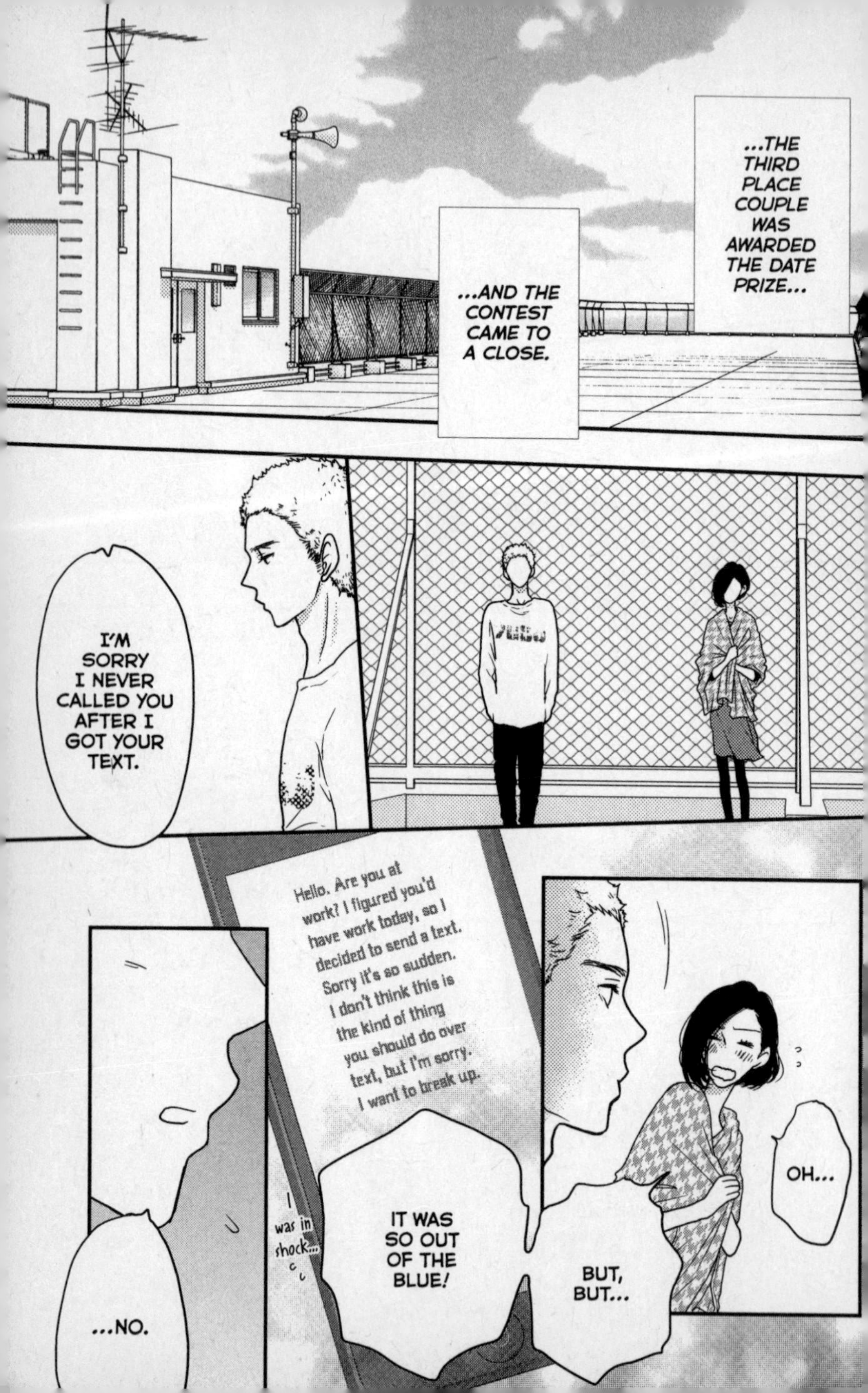
...THE THIRD PLACE COUPLE WAS AWARDED THE DATE PRIZE...
...AND THE CONTEST CAME TO A CLOSE.
I'M SORRY I NEVER CALLED YOU AFTER I GOT YOUR TEXT.
OH...
BUT, BUT...
Hello. Are you at work? I figured you'd have work today, so I decided to send a text. Sorry it's so sudden. I don't think this is the kind of thing you should do over text, but I'm sorry. I want to break up.
IT WAS SO OUT OF THE BLUE!
I was in shock...
...NO.

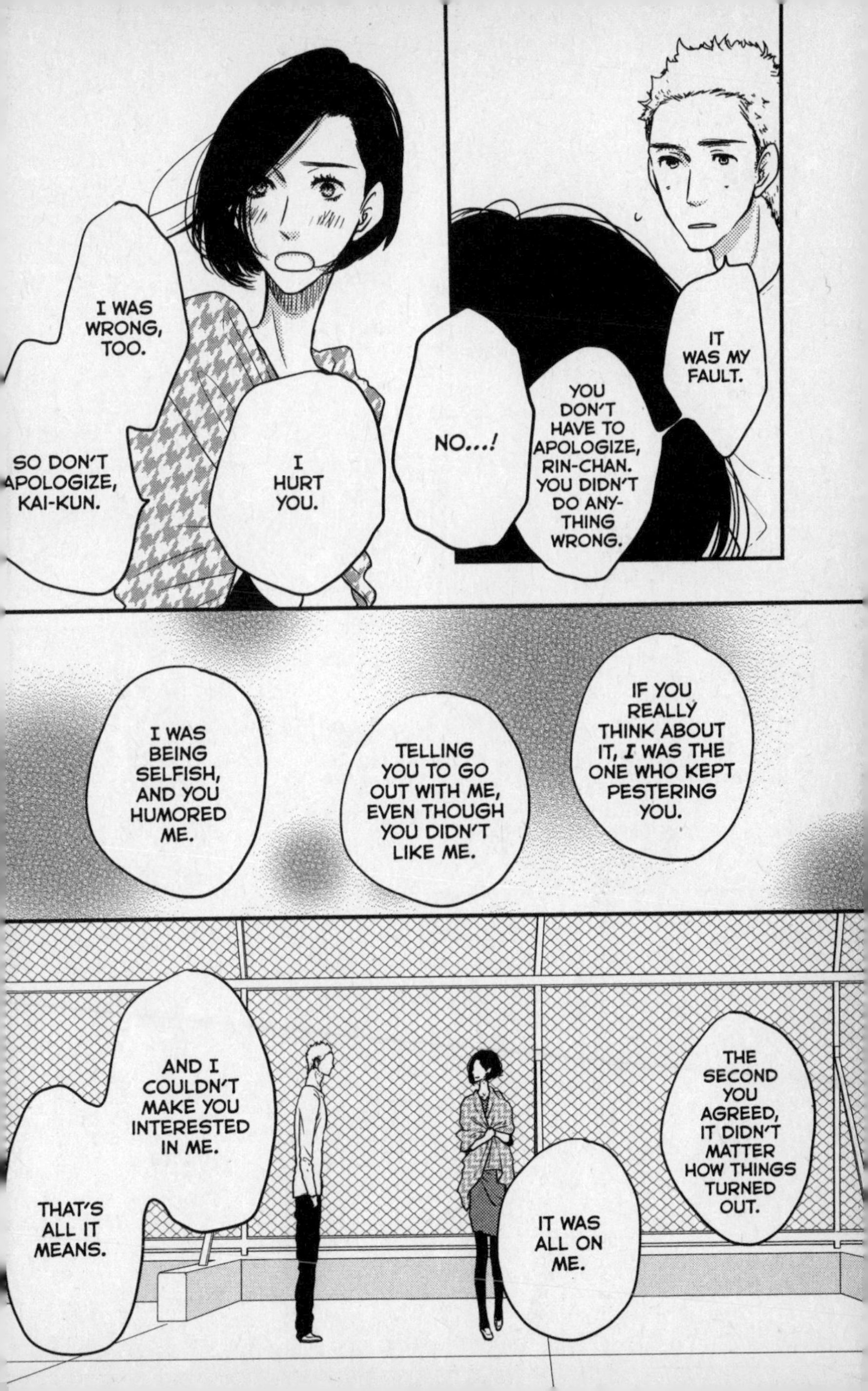
IT WAS MY FAULT.
YOU DON'T HAVE TO APOLOGIZE, RIN-CHAN. YOU DIDN'T DO ANY-THING WRONG.
NO...!
I HURT YOU.
I WAS WRONG, TOO.
SO DON'T APOLOGIZE, KAI-KUN.
IF YOU REALLY THINK ABOUT IT, *I* WAS THE ONE WHO KEPT PESTERING YOU.
TELLING YOU TO GO OUT WITH ME, EVEN THOUGH YOU DIDN'T LIKE ME.
I WAS BEING SELFISH, AND YOU HUMORED ME.
THE SECOND YOU AGREED, IT DIDN'T MATTER HOW THINGS TURNED OUT.
IT WAS ALL ON ME.
AND I COULDN'T MAKE YOU INTERESTED IN ME.
THAT'S ALL IT MEANS.

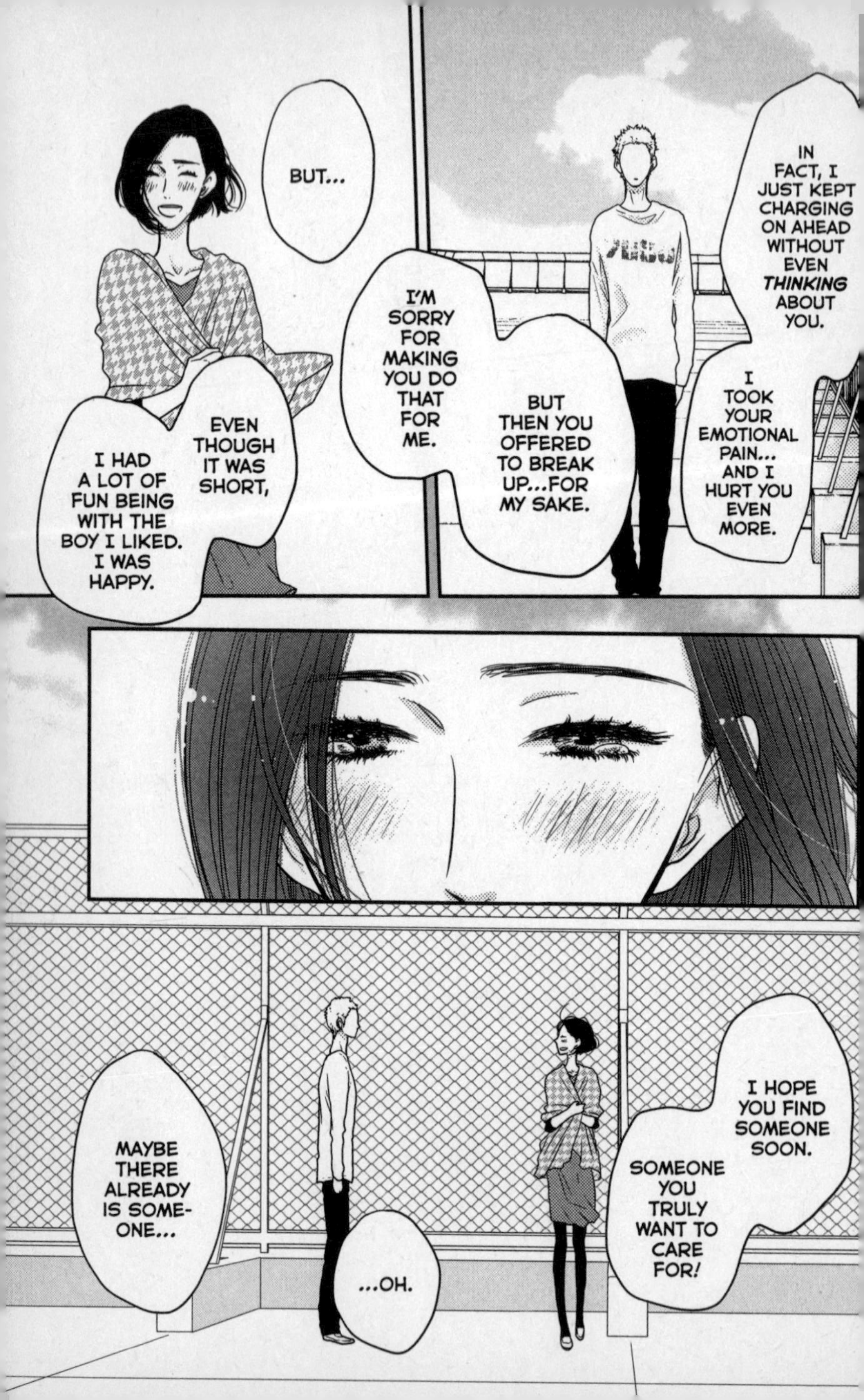
IN FACT, I JUST KEPT CHARGING ON AHEAD WITHOUT EVEN *THINKING* ABOUT YOU.
I TOOK YOUR EMOTIONAL PAIN... AND I HURT YOU EVEN MORE.
BUT THEN YOU OFFERED TO BREAK UP...FOR MY SAKE.
I'M SORRY FOR MAKING YOU DO THAT FOR ME.
BUT...
EVEN THOUGH IT WAS SHORT,
I HAD A LOT OF FUN BEING WITH THE BOY I LIKED. I WAS HAPPY.
I HOPE YOU FIND SOMEONE SOON.
SOMEONE YOU TRULY WANT TO CARE FOR!
...OH.
MAYBE THERE ALREADY IS SOME-ONE...

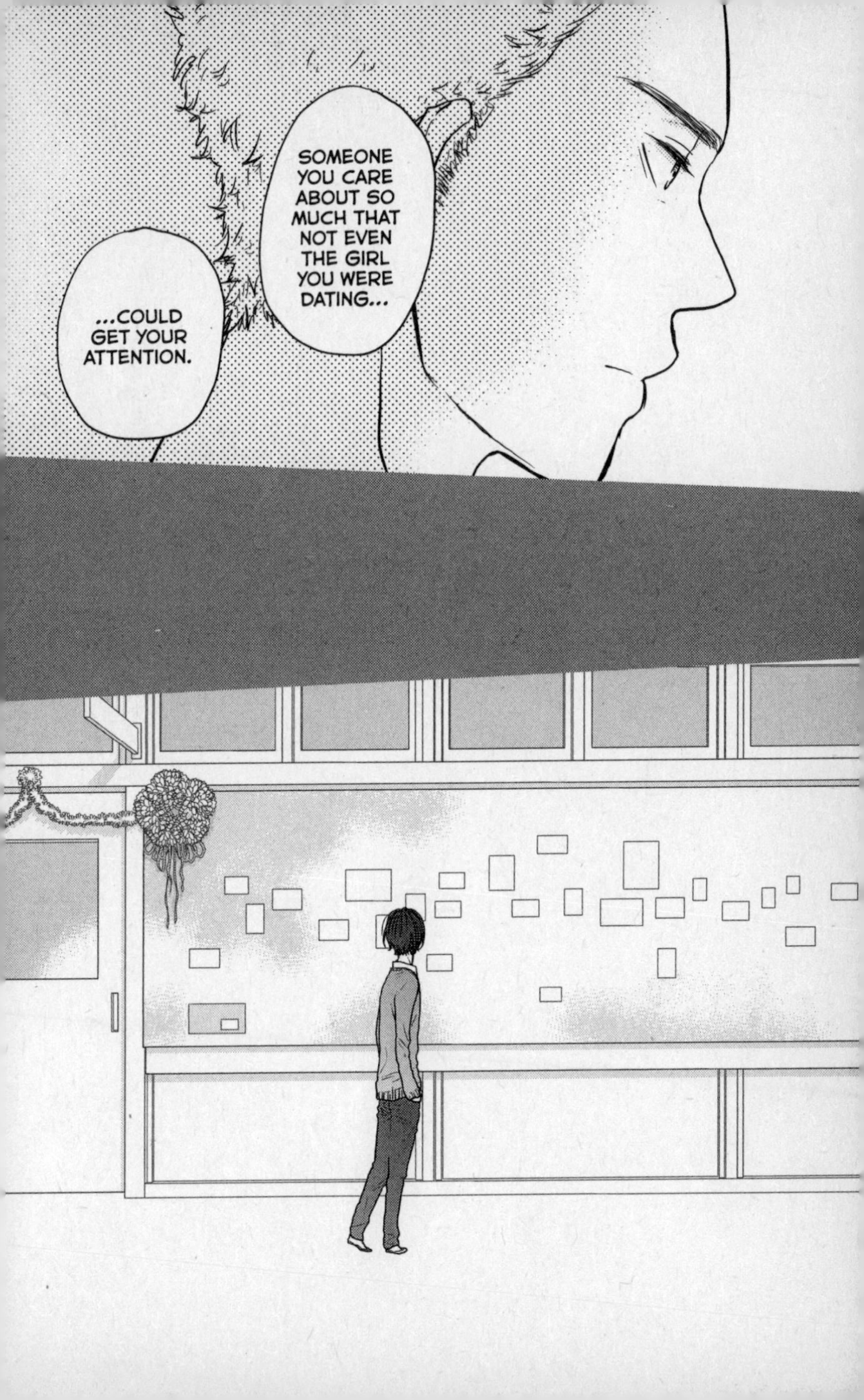
SOMEONE YOU CARE ABOUT SO MUCH THAT NOT EVEN THE GIRL YOU WERE DATING...
...COULD GET YOUR ATTENTION.

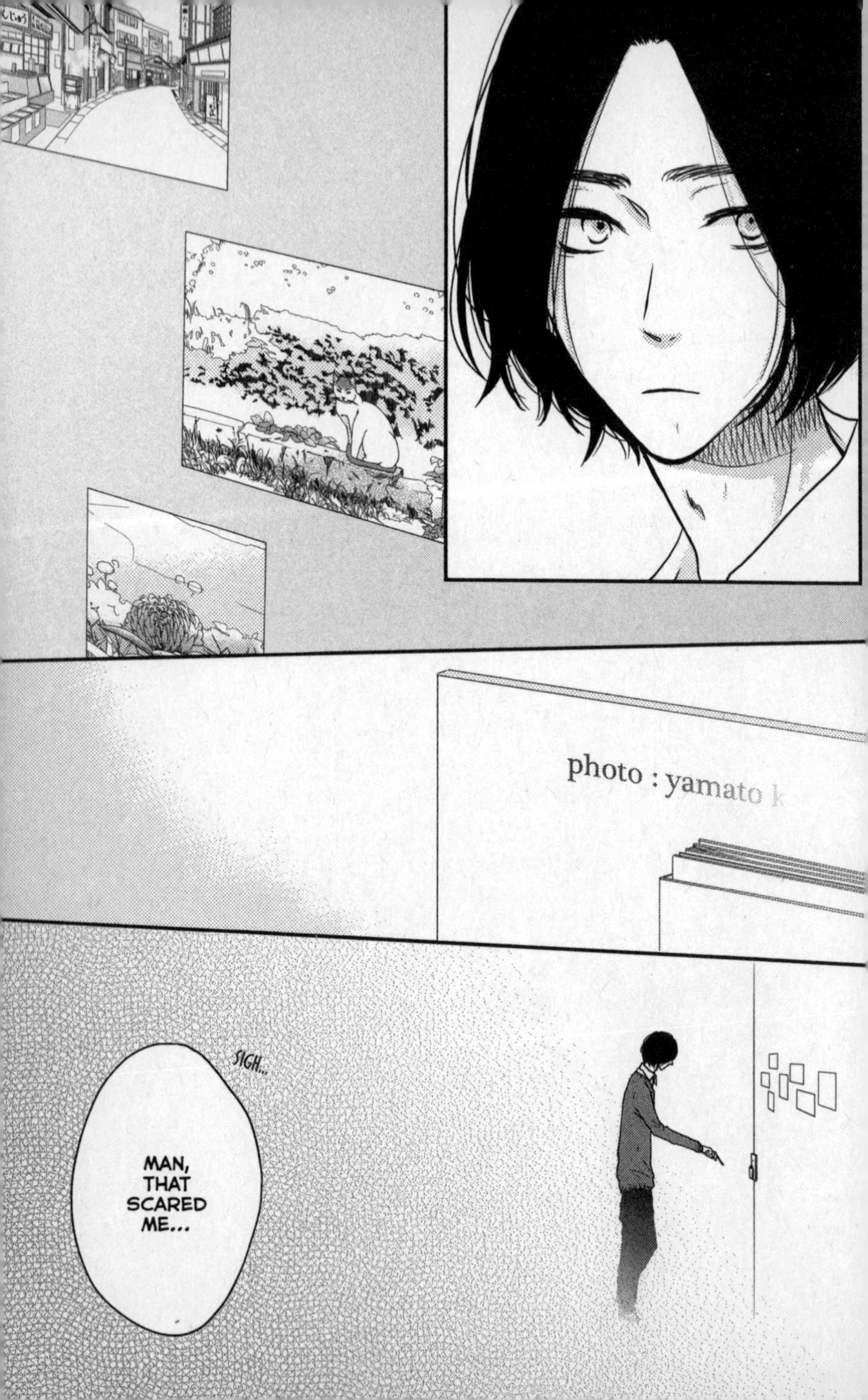
photo : yamato k
SIGH...
MAN, THAT SCARED ME...

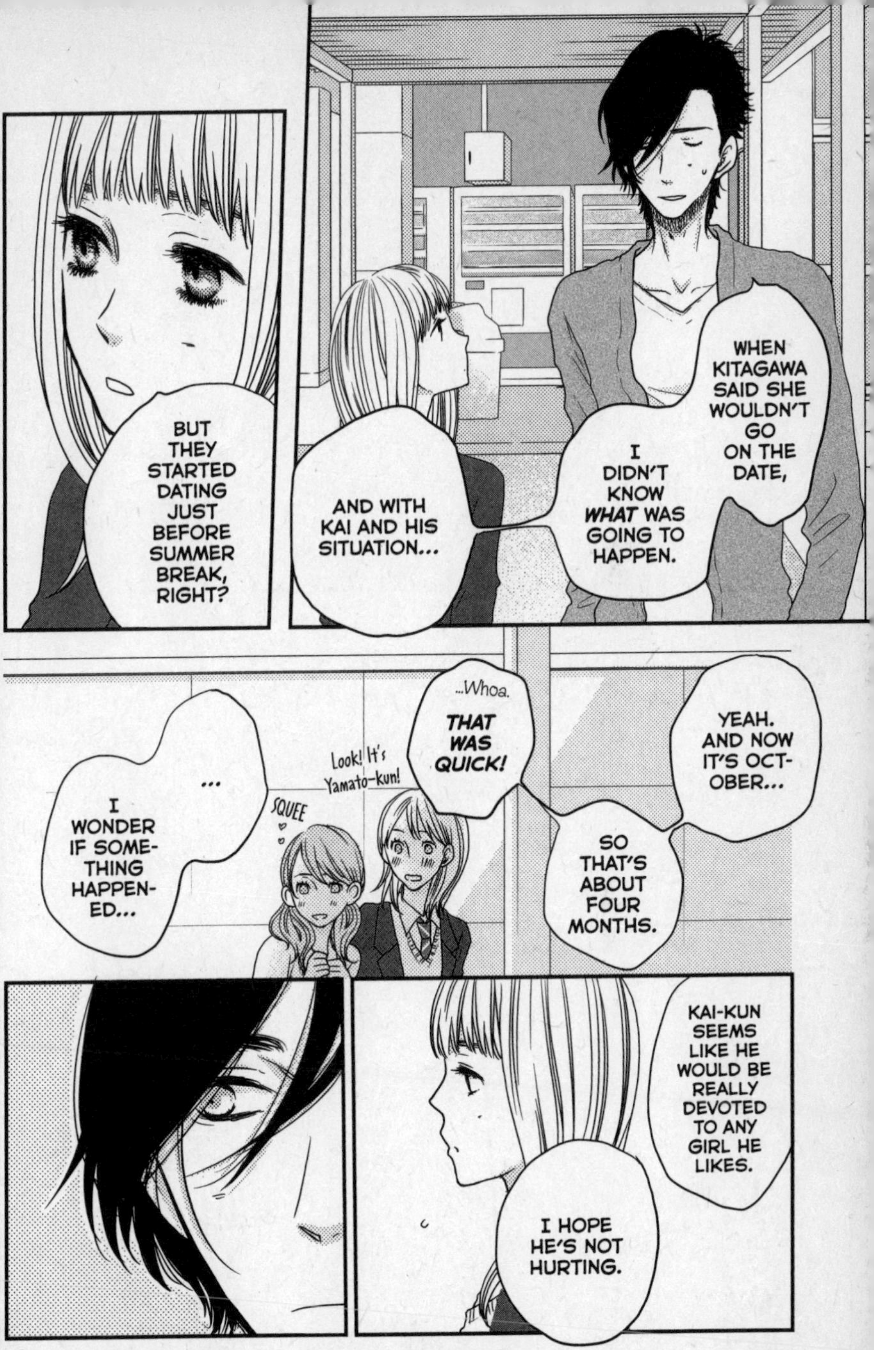
WHEN KITAGAWA SAID SHE WOULDN'T GO ON THE DATE,
I DIDN'T KNOW *WHAT* WAS GOING TO HAPPEN.
AND WITH KAI AND HIS SITUATION...
BUT THEY STARTED DATING JUST BEFORE SUMMER BREAK, RIGHT?
YEAH. AND NOW IT'S OCT-OBER...
SO THAT'S ABOUT FOUR MONTHS.
...Whoa.
THAT WAS QUICK!
Look! It's Yamato-kun!
SQUEE
...
I WONDER IF SOME-THING HAPPEN-ED...
KAI-KUN SEEMS LIKE HE WOULD BE REALLY DEVOTED TO ANY GIRL HE LIKES.
I HOPE HE'S NOT HURTING.

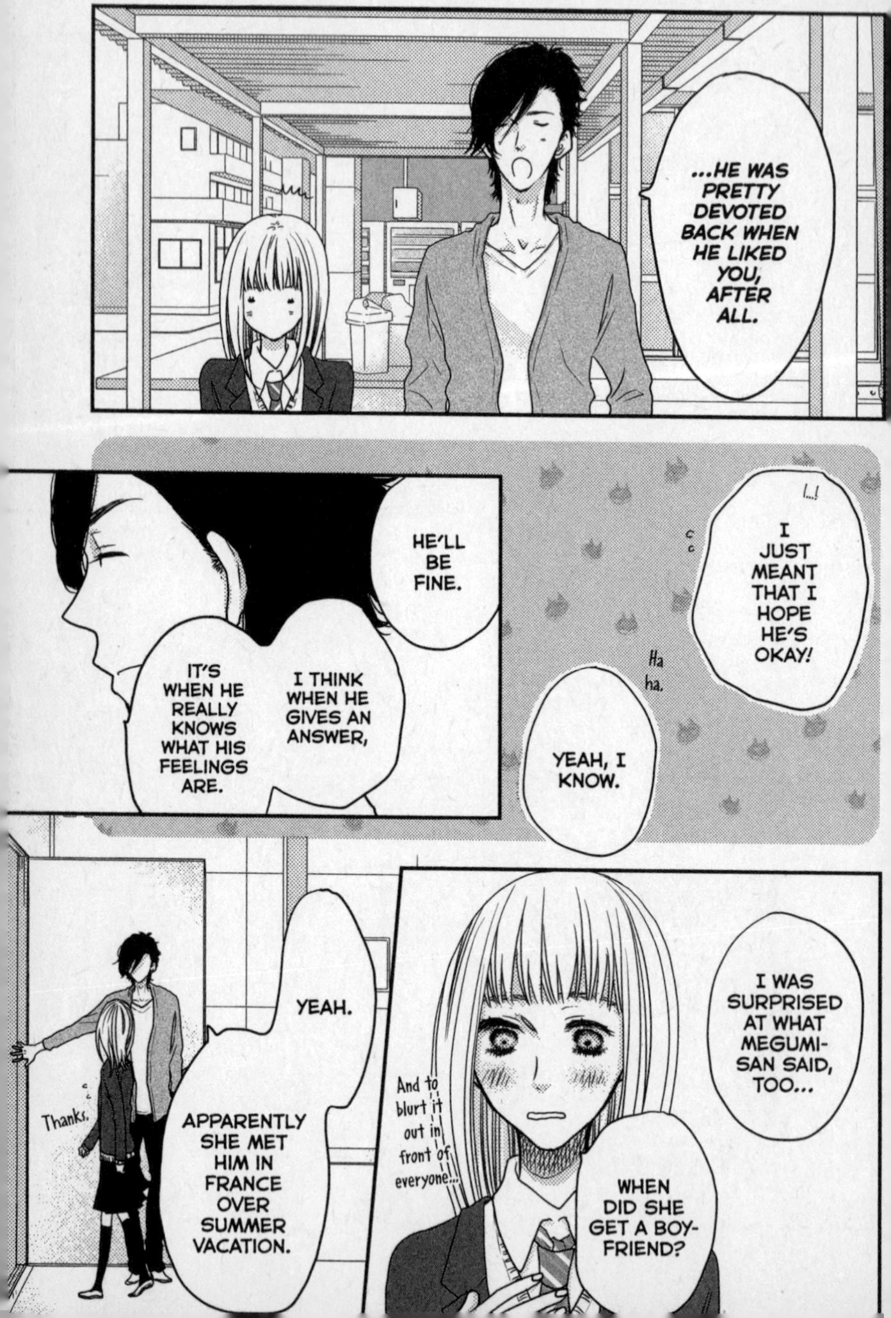
...HE WAS PRETTY DEVOTED BACK WHEN HE LIKED YOU, AFTER ALL.
!...!
I JUST MEANT THAT I HOPE HE'S OKAY!
Ha ha.
YEAH, I KNOW.
HE'LL BE FINE.
I THINK WHEN HE GIVES AN ANSWER,
IT'S WHEN HE REALLY KNOWS WHAT HIS FEELINGS ARE.
I WAS SURPRISED AT WHAT MEGUMI-SAN SAID, TOO...
And to blurt it out in front of everyone...
WHEN DID SHE GET A BOY-FRIEND?
YEAH.
APPARENTLY SHE MET HIM IN FRANCE OVER SUMMER VACATION.
Thanks.

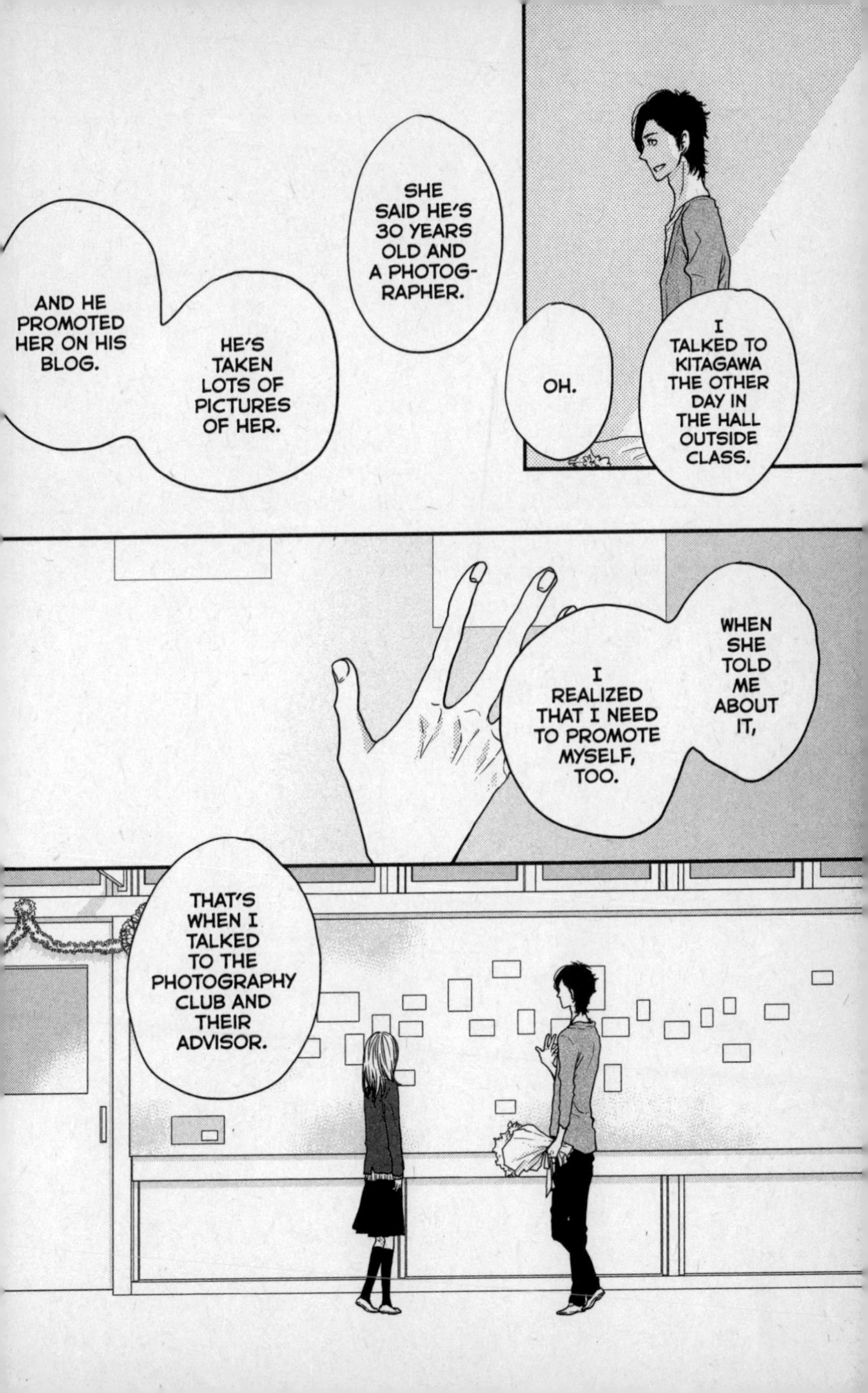
I TALKED TO KITAGAWA THE OTHER DAY IN THE HALL OUTSIDE CLASS.
OH.
SHE SAID HE'S 30 YEARS OLD AND A PHOTOG-RAPHER.
HE'S TAKEN LOTS OF PICTURES OF HER.
AND HE PROMOTED HER ON HIS BLOG.
WHEN SHE TOLD ME ABOUT IT,
I REALIZED THAT I NEED TO PROMOTE MYSELF, TOO.
THAT'S WHEN I TALKED TO THE PHOTOGRAPHY CLUB AND THEIR ADVISOR.

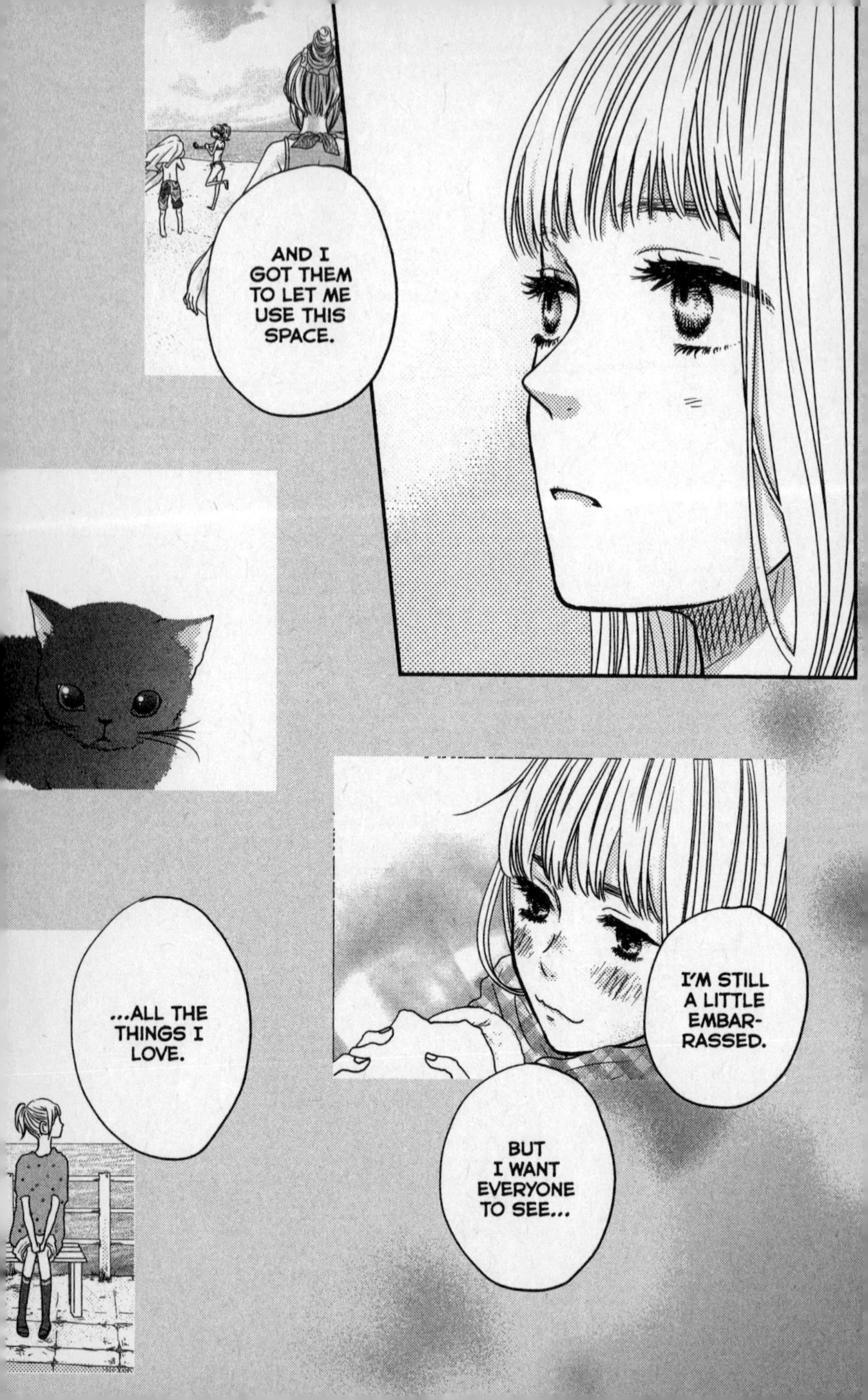
AND I GOT THEM TO LET ME USE THIS SPACE.
I'M STILL A LITTLE EMBAR-RASSED.
BUT I WANT EVERYONE TO SEE...
...ALL THE THINGS I LOVE.

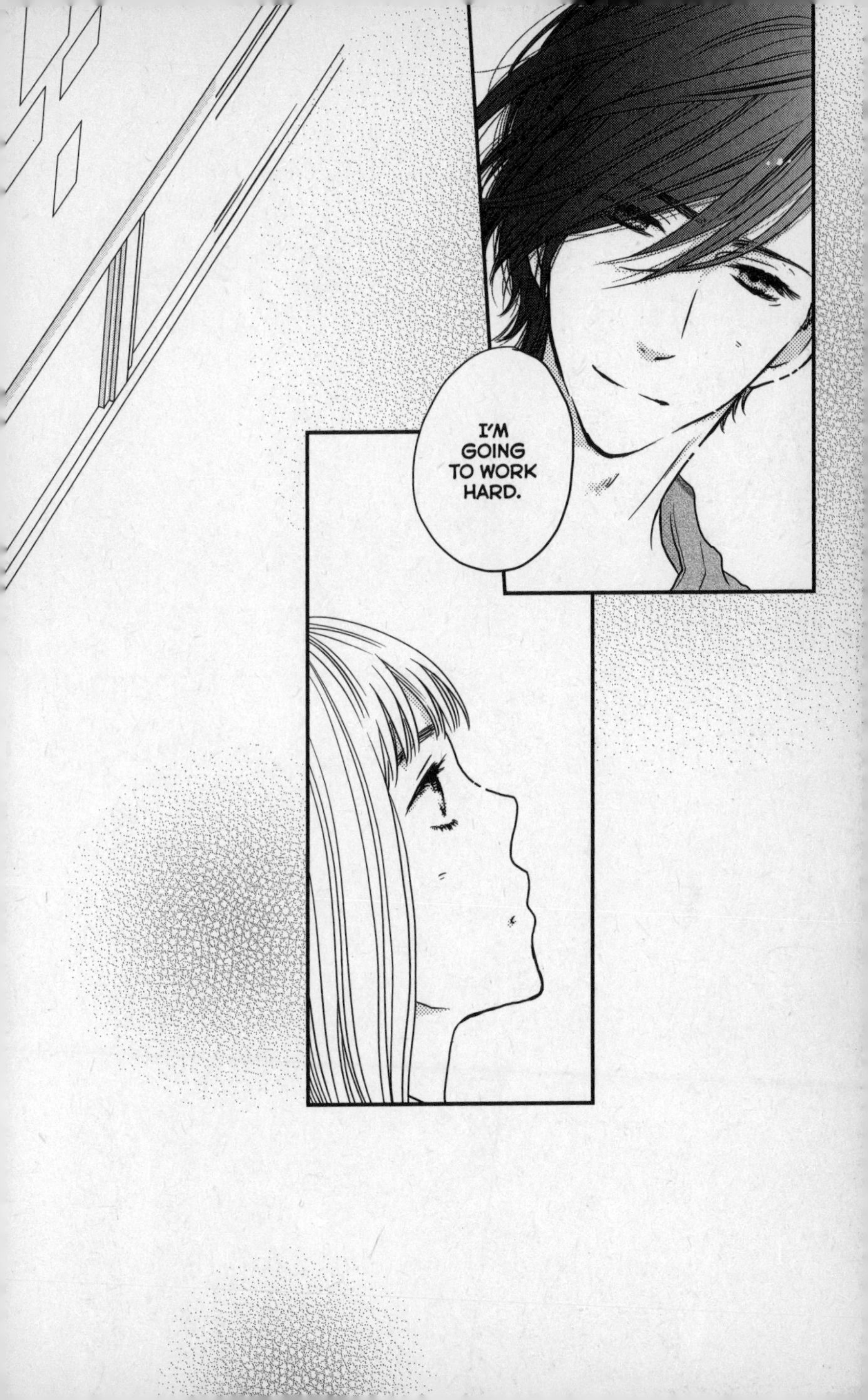
I'M GOING TO WORK HARD.

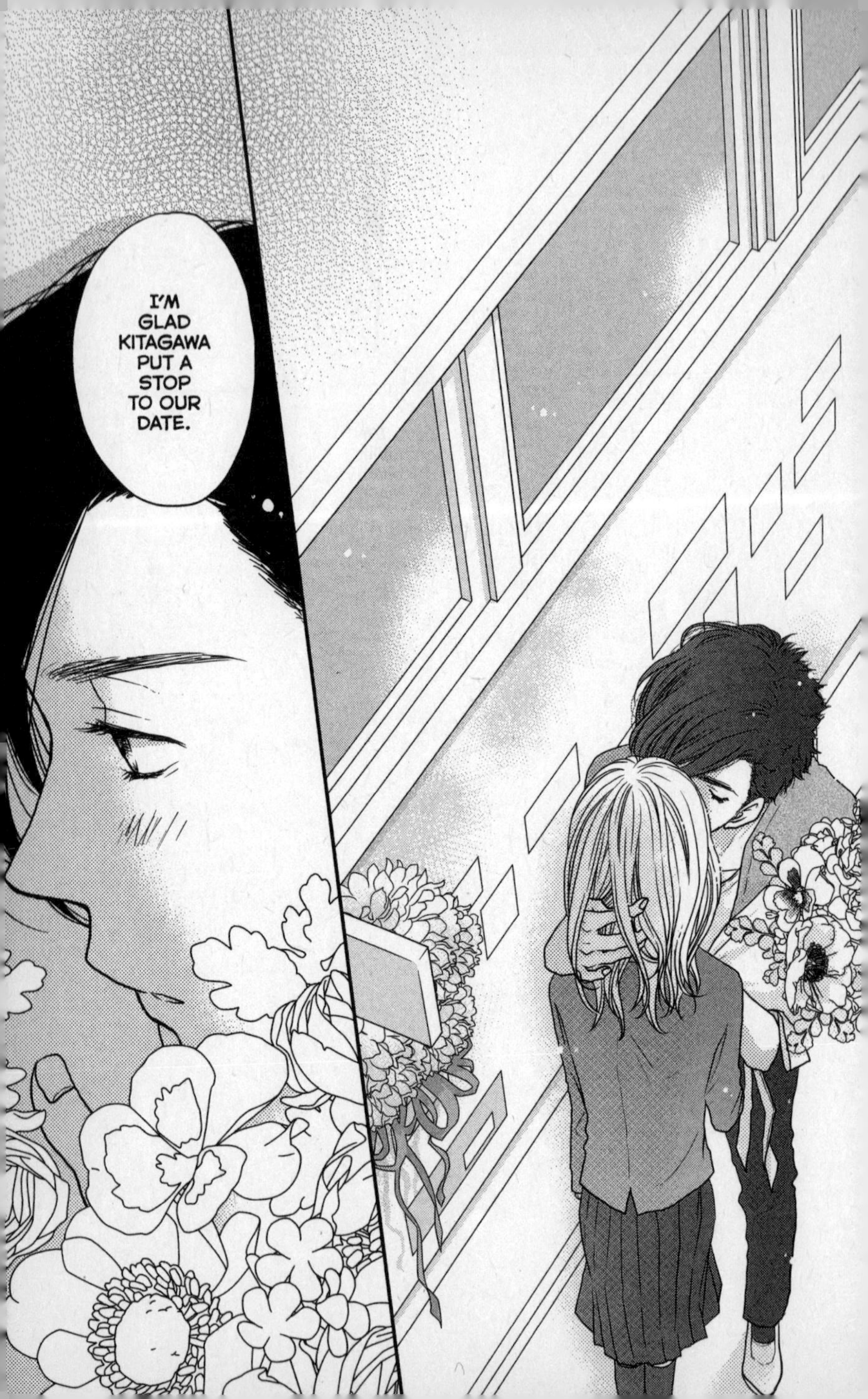
I'M GLAD KITAGAWA PUT A STOP TO OUR DATE.

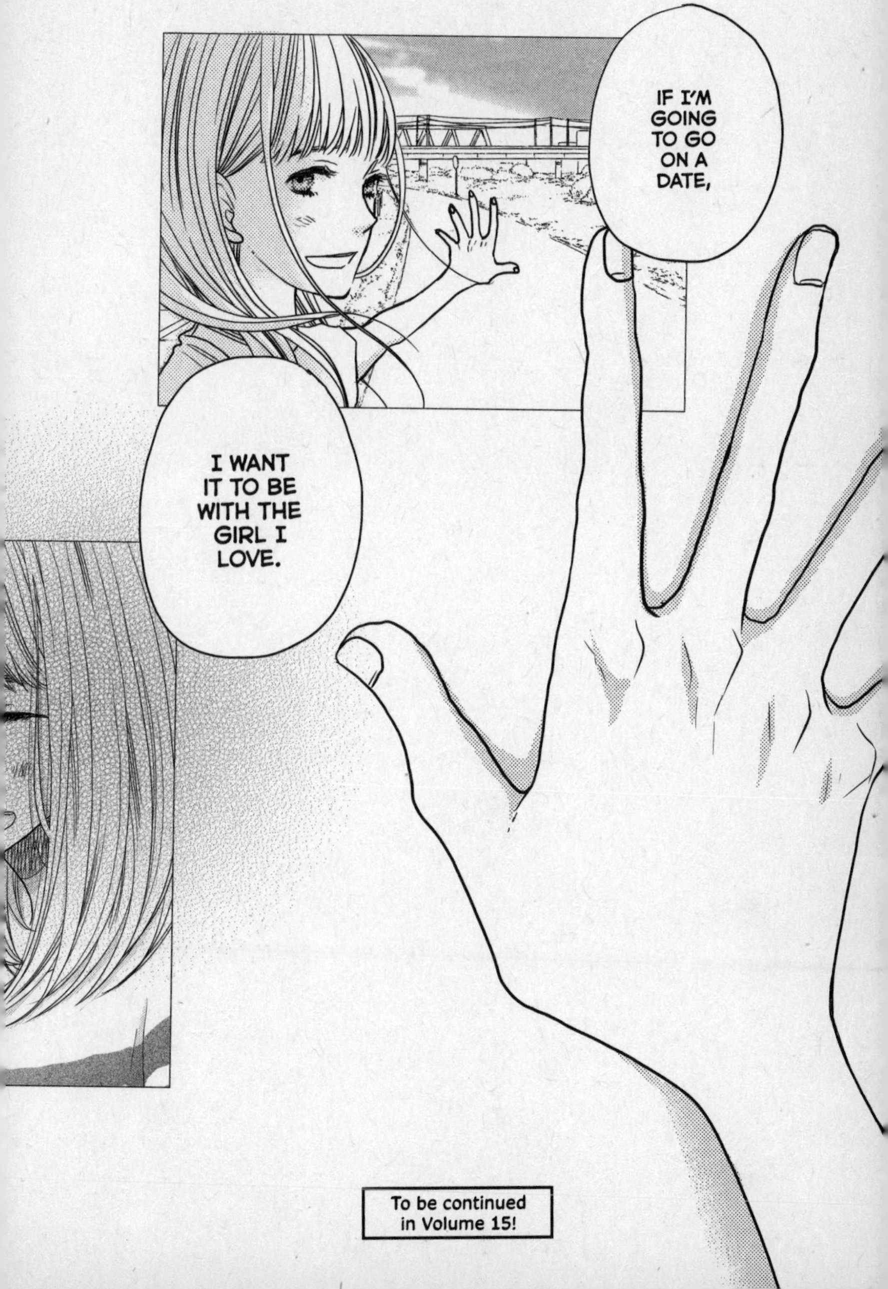
IF I'M GOING TO GO ON A DATE,
I WANT IT TO BE WITH THE GIRL I LOVE.

To be continued in Volume 15!

Say "I love you".

Hello. I'm Kanae Hazuki. This is volume 14.

When 13 came out, it was right after the movie was released, or I feel like it was. What is this feeling? It's like time's gone by so fast... Looking back on it, a lot of happy things happened, and a lot of sad things happened... But in all things, the important thing is to learn.

Now for this volume. It was their last summer vacation of high school, and their last high school trip. Did anything seem different from when they went on their trip the year before, I wonder? (Ha ha)

I like to draw Mei and Aiko talking to each other, so I had fun this time. And Kai, Megumi, Rin, and Ren all had their love stories start moving all at once... It's fun to draw it, but it's rea...really hard. (ha ha)

Most of all, before this series, I'd never drawn a manga that had that many love stories going on all at once... Even I'm wondering what I'm going to do every time I draw a new chapter. This is another thing to learn from.

And, if nothing else, I have to talk about Megumi's transformation (ha ha). Her fluffy waves have gone completely straight. Megumi, who said she can't be bothered to care about what other people think of her. There might be a lot of people saying, "But her other hair style was so good!" or "That's weird!" But *the* Megumi is trying to show that she means business.

A while ago, I was able to interview someone at a modeling agency about overseas modeling work and the like, and it's true that Japanese people have different facial structures, heights, and builds than people from overseas, so apparently it really is difficult for a Japanese (Asian) model to get a lot of work outside of Japan, and only a handful of them can make a name for themselves overseas. It's a ruthless world...

Even so, there are a lot of pop stars and singers who are popular and do lots of work overseas, and I personally think that, while those people worry about how to present themselves to the public, they know the answer. How do they present their individuality, and turn their shortcomings into strengths? I was always checking what the agency told me against Megumi. I wrote about this before, but I think that whoever takes their idiosyncrasies and shortcomings and makes them their own is the one who wins. We tend to hate our own shortcomings, but in a sense, they're parts of us that no one else has, and if we can notice our shortcomings, that means we can fix them or do whatever we want with them. It means knowing what's hidden inside ourselves, and acknowledging it.

I think that's the first step in making them our own. "I'm hopeless," is something that we only think about ourselves. And if someone says, "That person's hopeless," then they only think that. That's what I think now, after going through my years as a student. I realize that, back then, I really let what others said control me.

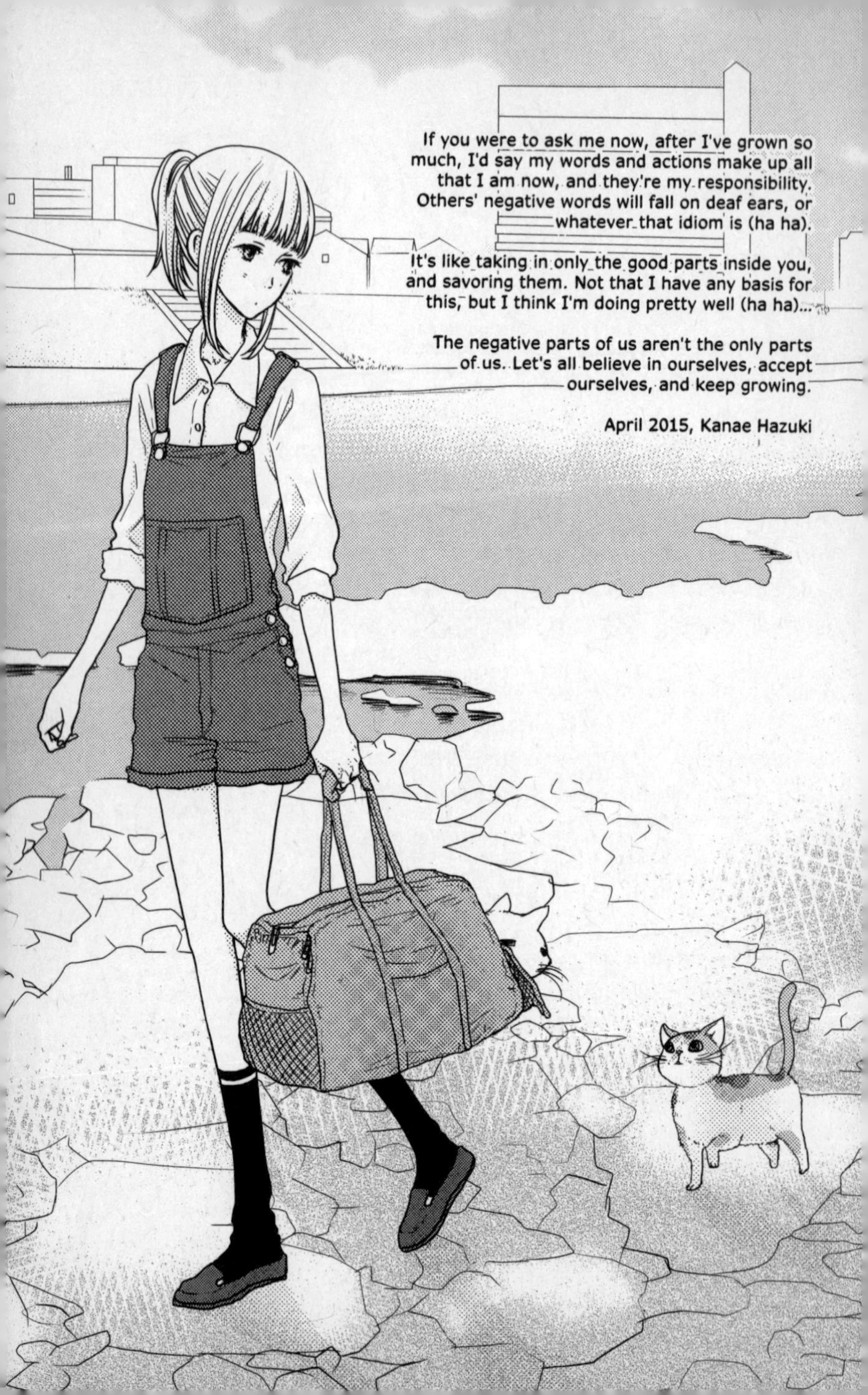
If you were to ask me now, after I've grown so much, I'd say my words and actions make up all that I am now, and they're my responsibility. Others' negative words will fall on deaf ears, or whatever that idiom is (ha ha).
It's like taking in only the good parts inside you, and savoring them. Not that I have any basis for this, but I think I'm doing pretty well (ha ha)...
The negative parts of us aren't the only parts of us. Let's all believe in ourselves, accept ourselves, and keep growing.
April 2015, Kanae Hazuki

TRANSLATION NOTES

Len's name change
The translators would like to apologize for misrepresenting Ren in previous volumes of this manga. In Japanese, there is no letter L or R, but there is one sound that is like a combination of the two. Usually this sound is expressed in English with an R, but because he uses the name "Len" as his online handle, they mistakenly assumed that he preferred to spell his name with an L. It has been brought to their attention that he only spells his name with an L on the internet, and IRL he spells it with an R, and so going forward, we will be using the correct spelling.

Some readers may wonder how on earth this makes his name any different than his sister's, because Ren and Rin would be pronounced almost exactly the same in certain American dialects, but in Japanese, the vowels are more distinct. Ren rhymes with "hen", and Rin rhymes more with "bean."

High school debut, page 52
The change from junior high to high school in Japan can be a very big one, because, instead of just going on to the local public high school, students can choose a high school from anywhere in the country—as long as they pass the required entrance exam. This makes it a good opportunity to make a new start, by changing your look, going to a school where know one knows you, etc. This is called a high school debut. Here, Ren is suggesting that something dramatic has changed about Rin since leaving middle school, and that has enabled her to get a boyfriend despite her lack of prospects.

Kabe-don, page 58

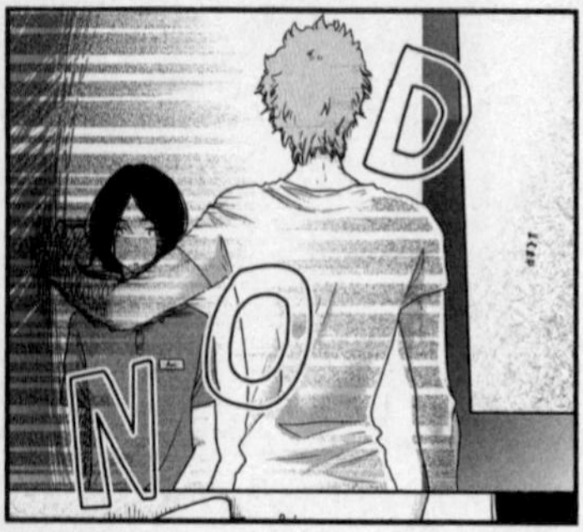
DON

Kabe-don is a manga and anime cliché that recently got a lot of attention on social media. Basically, it's what this man did to Ren. *Kabe* means "wall", and *don* is the sound of hitting a heavy object (such as a wall). Often tough guy characters will bar the way in front of the object of their affection, and slam the wall as a way to get their attention and look cool at the same time.

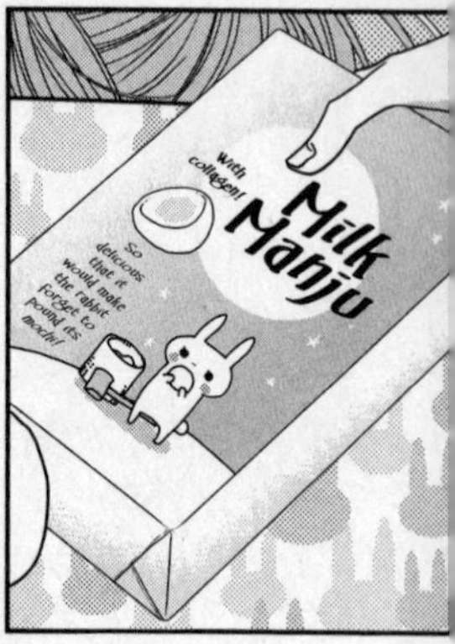
with collagen!
Milk Manju
So delicious that it would make the rabbit forget to pound its mochi!

Milk Manjū, page 77

A *manjū* is usually a bun with red bean paste (*anko*) filling. In this case, the filling is made with condensed milk so the *anko* flavor becomes more of a milky flavor. As for the rabbit forgetting to pound the *mochi, mochi* is a dessert made of sticky rice that is placed in a mortar and pounded with a mallet. Japanese folklore has it that there is a rabbit on the moon who spends all its time pounding *mochi.*

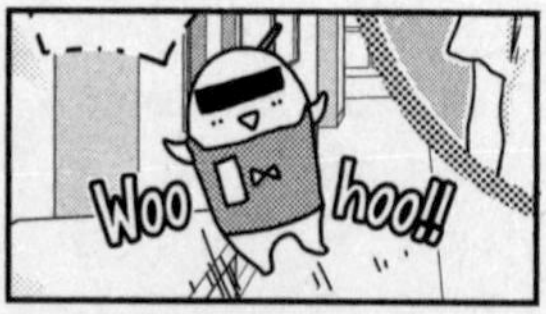
Woo hoo!!

Woohoo!!, page 119

The character next to the "woohoo" on this page is a call back to the extremely popular *yuru-kyara* (a type of promotional mascot), Funassyi. Funassyi is a pear-fairy who represents Funabashi in Chiba Prefecture, Japan. This city is known for its pears, which is why the character is a pear fairy and also why the name is Funassyi (Funabashi + *nashi* (JP: pear)). Funassyi has a very particular, high-pitched yell that does well to describe the amount of excitement in this scene.

My Little Monster

OPPOSITES ATTRACT...MAYBE?

Haru Yoshida is feared as an unstable and violent "monster."
Mizutani Shizuku is a grade-obsessed student with no friends.
Fate brings these two together to form the most unlikely pair. Haru
firmly believes he's in love with Mizutani and she firmly believes
he's insane.

KC
KODANSHA
COMICS